The Ministers Manual for 1983

FIFTY-EIGHTH ANNUAL ISSUE

MINISTERS MANUAL

(Doran's)

1983 EDITION

Edited by
CHARLES L. WALLIS

1817

HARPER & ROW, PUBLISHERS, SAN FRANCISCO

Cambridge, Hagerstown, New York, Philadelphia
London, Mexico City, São Paulo, Sydney

Editors of THE MINISTERS MANUAL

G.B.F. Hallock, D.D., 1926–1958
M.K.W. Heicher, Ph.D., 1943–1968
Charles L. Wallis, M.A., M.Div., 1969–1983

THE MINISTERS MANUAL FOR 1983
Copyright © 1982 by Betty W. Wallis. All rights reserved.
Printed in the United States of America. For information
address Harper & Row, Publishers, Inc., 10 East 53rd Street,
New York, N.Y. 10022. Published simultaneously in Canada
by Fitzhenry & Whiteside Limited, Toronto.

FIRST EDITION

The Library of Congress has cataloged the first printing of
this serial as follows:

The ministers manual: a study and pulpit guide. 1926– . New
York, Harper.

V. 21–23 cm. annual.
Title varies: 1926–46, Doran's ministers manual (cover
title, 1947: The Doran's ministers manual)
Editor: 1926– G. B. F. Hallock (with M. K. W. Heicher,
1942–)

1. Sermons—Outlines. 2. Homiletical illustrations. I. Hallock, Gerard Benjamin Fleet, 1856– ,ed.
BV4223.M5   251.058   25–21658 rev*
[r48n2]

ISBN 0-06-069027-5

82 83 84 85 86 10 9 8 7 6 5 4 3 2 1

CONTENTS

CONTENTS

SECTION I. General Aids and Resources

Civil Year Calendars

1984

JANUARY

S	M	T	W	T	F	S
1	2	3	4	5	6	7
8	9	10	11	12	13	14
15	16	17	18	19	20	21
22	23	24	25	26	27	28
29	30	31				

FEBRUARY

S	M	T	W	T	F	S
			1	2	3	4
5	6	7	8	9	10	11
12	13	14	15	16	17	18
19	20	21	22	23	24	25
26	27	28	29			

MARCH

S	M	T	W	T	F	S
				1	2	3
4	5	6	7	8	9	10
11	12	13	14	15	16	27
18	19	20	21	22	23	24
25	26	27	28	29	30	31

APRIL

S	M	T	W	T	F	S
1	2	3	4	5	6	7
8	9	10	11	12	13	14
15	16	17	18	19	20	21
22	23	24	25	26	27	28
29	30					

MAY

S	M	T	W	T	F	S
		1	2	3	4	5
6	7	8	9	10	11	12
13	14	15	16	17	18	19
20	21	22	23	24	25	26
27	28	29	30	31		

JUNE

S	M	T	W	T	F	S
					1	2
3	4	5	6	7	8	9
10	11	12	13	14	15	16
17	18	19	20	21	22	23
24	25	26	27	28	29	30

JULY

S	M	T	W	T	F	S
1	2	3	4	5	6	7
8	9	10	11	12	13	14
15	16	17	18	19	20	21
22	23	24	25	26	27	28
29	30	31				

AUGUST

S	M	T	W	T	F	S
			1	2	3	4
5	6	7	8	9	10	11
12	13	14	15	16	17	18
19	20	21	22	23	24	25
26	27	28	29	30	31	

SEPTEMBER

S	M	T	W	T	F	S
						1
2	3	4	5	6	7	8
9	10	11	12	13	14	15
16	17	18	19	20	21	22
23	24	25	26	27	28	29
30						

OCTOBER

S	M	T	W	T	F	S
	1	2	3	4	5	6
7	8	9	10	11	12	13
14	15	16	17	18	19	20
21	22	23	24	25	26	27
28	29	30	31			

NOVEMBER

S	M	T	W	T	F	S
				1	2	3
4	5	6	7	8	9	10
11	12	13	14	15	16	17
18	19	20	21	22	23	24
25	26	27	28	29	30	

DECEMBER

S	M	T	W	T	F	S
						1
2	3	4	5	6	7	8
9	10	11	12	13	14	15
16	17	18	19	20	21	22
23	24	25	26	27	28	29
30	31					

1983

JANUARY

S	M	T	W	T	F	S
						1
2	3	4	5	6	7	8
9	10	11	12	13	14	15
16	17	18	19	20	21	22
23	24	25	26	27	28	29
30	31					

FEBRUARY

S	M	T	W	T	F	S
		1	2	3	4	5
6	7	8	9	10	11	12
13	14	15	16	17	18	19
20	21	22	23	24	25	26
27	28					

MARCH

S	M	T	W	T	F	S
		1	2	3	4	5
6	7	8	9	10	11	12
13	14	15	16	17	18	19
20	21	22	23	24	25	26
27	28	29	30	31		

APRIL

S	M	T	W	T	F	S
					1	2
3	4	5	6	7	8	9
10	11	12	13	14	15	16
17	18	19	20	21	22	23
24	25	26	27	28	29	30

MAY

S	M	T	W	T	F	S
1	2	3	4	5	6	7
8	9	10	11	12	13	14
15	16	17	18	19	20	21
22	23	24	25	26	27	28
29	30	31				

JUNE

S	M	T	W	T	F	S
			1	2	3	4
5	6	7	8	9	10	11
12	13	14	15	16	17	18
19	20	21	22	23	24	25
26	27	28	29	30		

JULY

S	M	T	W	T	F	S
					1	2
3	4	5	6	7	8	9
10	11	12	13	14	15	16
17	18	19	20	21	22	23
24	25	26	27	28	29	30
31						

AUGUST

S	M	T	W	T	F	S
	1	2	3	4	5	6
7	8	9	10	11	12	13
14	15	16	17	18	19	20
21	22	23	24	25	26	27
28	29	30	31			

SEPTEMBER

S	M	T	W	T	F	S
				1	2	3
4	5	6	7	8	9	10
11	12	13	14	15	16	17
18	19	20	21	22	23	24
25	26	27	28	29	30	

OCTOBER

S	M	T	W	T	F	S
						1
2	3	4	5	6	7	8
9	10	11	12	13	14	15
16	17	18	19	20	21	22
23	24	25	26	27	28	29
30	31					

NOVEMBER

S	M	T	W	T	F	S
		1	2	3	4	5
6	7	8	9	10	11	12
13	14	15	16	17	18	19
20	21	22	23	24	25	26
27	28	29	30			

DECEMBER

S	M	T	W	T	F	S
				1	2	3
4	5	6	7	8	9	10
11	12	13	14	15	16	17
18	19	20	21	22	23	24
25	26	27	28	29	30	31

Church and Civic Calendar for 1983

JANUARY

1 New Year's Day
  The Name of Jesus
  Solemnity of Mary
5 Twelfth Night
6 Epiphany
9 The Baptism of Jesus
15 Martin Luther King, Jr.'s Birthday
16 Christian Unity Sunday
18 Confession of St. Peter
18–25 Week of Prayer for Christian Unity
19 Robert E. Lee's Birthday
25 Conversion of St. Paul

FEBRUARY

1 National Freedom Day
2 Groundhog Day
  Presentation of Jesus in the Temple
3 Four Chaplains Memorial Day
12 Lincoln's Birthday
13–20 Brotherhood Week
14 St. Valentine's Day
15 Shrove Tuesday
  Susan B. Anthony Day
16 Ash Wednesday
20 First Sunday in Lent
21 Presidents' Day
22 Washington's Birthday
27 Purim
  Second Sunday in Lent

MARCH

4 World Day of Prayer
6 Third Sunday in Lent
13 Fourth Sunday in Lent
17 St. Patrick's Day
19 Joseph, Husband of Mary
20 Fifth Sunday in Lent
  Passion Sunday
22 National Maritime Day
25 The Annunciation
27–4/2 Holy Week
27 Palm Sunday
  Passion Sunday (alternate)
29 First day of Passover
31 Maundy Thursday

APRIL

1 Good Friday
3 Easter
10 Holocaust Day
  Low Sunday
14 Pan American Day
22 Arbor Day
25 St. Mark, Evangelist

MAY

1 Law Day
  Loyalty Day
  May Day
  St. Philip and St. James, Apostles
1–8 National Family Week
8 Easter (Orthodox)
  Festival of the Christian Home
  May Fellowship Day
  Mother's Day
  Rural Life Sunday
12 Ascension Day
18 First day of Shavuot
21 Armed Forces Day
22 Pentecost (Whitsunday)
23 Victoria Day (Canada)
29 Trinity Sunday
30 Memorial Day
31 Visitation of the Virgin Mary

JUNE

5 Religious Liberty Sunday
10 Sacred Heart of Jesus
12 Children's Day
14 Flag Day
19 Father's Day
20 Corpus Christi
24 Nativity of St. John the Baptist
29 St. Peter and St. Paul, Apostles

JULY

1 Dominion Day (Canada)
4 Independence Day
22 St. Mary Magdalene
25 St. James the Elder

AUGUST

1 Civic Holiday (Canada)
6 The Transfiguration

15 Mary, the Mother of Jesus
19 National Aviation Day
24 St. Bartholomew, Apostle

SEPTEMBER

4 Labor Sunday
5 Labor Day
8 Birth of the Virgin Mary
  First day of Rosh Hashanah
11 Grandparents' Day
  Rally Day
14 Holy Cross Day
17 Citizenship Day
  General von Steuben Memorial Day
  Yom Kippur
21 St. Matthew, Apostle and Evangelist
22 First day of Sukkot
23 American Indian Day
  Francis Willard Day
24 Senior Citizens' Day
25 Christian Education Sunday
29 Shemini Atzerer
  St. Michael and All Angels
30 Simhat Torah

OCTOBER

2 World Communion Sunday
3 Child Health Day
9 Laity Sunday
10 Columbus Day
  Thanksgiving Day (Canada)
15 World Poetry Day
18 St. Luke, Evangelist
24 United Nations Day
29 St. Simon and St. Jude, Apostles
30 Reformation Sunday
31 Halloween
  National UNICEF Day
  Reformation Day

NOVEMBER

1 All Saints' Day
3 Election Day
4 World Community Day
10 500th Anniversary of the Birth of Martin Luther
11 Armistice Day
  Remembrance Day (Canada)
  Veterans Day
12 Elizabeth Cady Stanton Day
  Sadie Hawkins Day
13 Stewardship Day
20 Bible Sunday
  Christ the King
  Thanksgiving Sunday
21 Presentation of the Virgin Mary in the Temple
24 Thanksgiving Day
27 First Sunday in Advent
30 St. Andrew, Apostle

DECEMBER

1 First day of Hanukkah
4 Second Sunday in Advent
8 Immaculate Conception of the Virgin Mary
11 Third Sunday in Advent
15 Bill of Rights Day
17 Wright Brothers Day
18 Fourth Sunday in Advent
21 Forefathers' Day
  St. Thomas, Apostle
24 Christmas Eve
25 Christmas
26 Boxing Day (Canada)
  St. Stephen, Deacon and Martyr
27 St. John, Apostle and Evangelist
28 The Holy Innocents, Martyrs
31 New Year's Eve
  Watch Night

Lectionary for 1983

The following scripture lessons, with occasional alterations according to denominational preferences, are commended for use in public worship by various Protestant churches and the Roman Catholic Church and include first, second, and gospel readings according to Cycle C from January 1 to November 24 and according to Cycle A from November 27 to December 25.

CHRISTMASTIDE

January 1 (New Year's Day): Isa. 49:1–10; Eph. 3:1–10; Luke 14:16–24.

EPIPHANY

January 6 (Epiphany): Isa. 60:1–6; Eph. 3:1–6; Matt. 2:1–12.

January 9: Gen. 1:1–5; Eph. 2:11–18; Luke 3:15–17, 21–22.

January 16: Isa. 62:2–5; I Cor. 12:4–11; John 2:1–12.

January 18–25 (Week of Prayer for Christian Unity): Isa. 55:1–5; Rev. 5:11–14; John 17:1–11.

January 23: Neh. 8:1–3, 5–6, 8–10; I Cor. 12:12–30; Luke 4:14–21.

January 30: Jer. 1:4–10; I Cor. 13:1–13; Luke 4:22–30.

February 6: Isa. 6:1–8; I Cor. 15:1–11; Luke 5:1–11.

February 13: Jer. 17:5–8; I Cor. 15:12–20; Luke 6:17–26.

LENT

February 16 (Ash Wednesday): Zech. 7: 4–10; I Cor. 9:19–27; Luke 5:29–35.

February 20: Deut. 26:5–11; Rom. 10:8– 13; Luke 4:1–13.

February 27: Gen. 15:5–12, 17–18; Phil. 3:17–4:1; Luke 9:28–36.

March 6: Exod. 3:1–8, 13–15; I Cor. 10: 1–12; Luke 13:1–9.

March 13: Josh. 5:9–12; II Cor. 5:16–21; Luke 15:11–32.

March 20: Isa. 43:16–21; Phil 3:8–14; Luke 22:14–30.

HOLY WEEK

March 27 (Palm Sunday): Isa. 59:14–20; I Tim. 1:12–17; Luke 19:28–40.

March 28 (Monday): Isa. 50:4–10; Heb. 9:11–15; Luke 19:41–48.

March 29 (Tuesday): Isa. 42:1–9; I Tim. 6:11–16; John 12:37–50.

March 30 (Wednesday): Isa. 52:13–53:12; Rom. 5:6–11; Luke 22:1–16.

March 31 (Maundy Thursday): Num. 9:1– 3, 11–12; I Cor. 5:6–8; Mark 14:12–26.

April 1 (Good Friday): Hos. 6:1–6; Rev. 5:6–14; Matt. 27:31–50.

EASTERTIDE

April 3: Exod. 15:1–11; I Cor. 15:20–26; Luke 24:13–35.

April 10: Acts 5:12–16; Rev. 1:9–13, 17– 19; John 21:1–14.

April 17: Acts 5:27–32; Rev. 5:11–14; John 21:15–19.

April 24: Acts 13:44–52; Rev. 7:9–17; John 10:22–30.

May 1: Acts 14:19–28; Rev. 21:1–5; John 13:31–35.

May 8: Acts 15:1–2, 22–29; Rev. 21:10– 14, 22–23; John 14:23–29.

May 12 (Ascension Day): Acts 1:1–11; Eph. 1:16–23; Luke 24:44–53.

May 15: Acts 7:55–60; Rev. 22:12–14, 16–17, 20; John 17:20–26.

PENTECOST

May 22 (Pentecost): Isa. 65:17–25; Acts 2:1–13; John 14:25–31.

May 29 (Trinity Sunday): Prov. 8:22–31; I Pet. 1:1–9; John 20:19–23.

June 5: I Kings 8:41–43; Gal. 1:1–10; Luke 7:1–10.

June 12: I Kings 17:17–24; Gal. 1:11–19; Luke 7:11–17.

June 19: II Sam. 12:1–7; Gal. 2:15–21; Luke 7:36–50.

June 26: Zech. 12:7–10; Gal. 3:23–29; Luke 9:18–24.

July 3: I Kings 19:15–21; Gal. 5:1, 13–18; Luke 9:51–62.

July 4 (Independence Day): Dan. 9:3–10; I Pet. 2:11–17; Luke 20:21–26.

July 10: Isa. 66:10–14; Gal. 6:11–18; Luke 10:1–9.

July 17: Deut. 30:9–14; Col. 1:15–20; Luke 10:25–37.

July 24: Gen. 18:1–11; Col. 1:24–28; Luke 10:38–42.

July 31: Gen. 18:20–33; Col. 2:8–15; Luke 11:1–13.

August 7: Eccl. 2:18–23; Col. 3:1–11; Luke 12:13–21.

August 14: II Kings 17:33–40; Heb. 11: 1–3, 8–12; Luke 12:35–40.

August 21: Jer. 38:1–13; Heb. 12:1–6; Luke 12:49–53.

August 28: Isa. 66:18–23; Heb. 12:7–13; Luke 13:22–30.

September 4: Prov. 22:1–9; Heb. 12:18– 24; Luke 14:1, 7–14.

September 11: Prov. 9:8–12; Philem. 1: 8–17; Luke 14:25–33.

September 18: Exod. 32:7–14; I Tim. 1: 12–17; Luke 15:1–32.

September 25: Amos 8:4–8; I Tim. 2:1–8; Luke 16:1–13.

October 2: Amos 6:1, 4–7; I Tim. 6:11–16; Luke 16:19–31; (World Communion Sunday) I Chron. 16:23–34; Acts 2:42–47; Matt. 8:5–13.

October 9: Hab. 1:1–3, 2:1–4; II Tim. 1:3–12; Luke 17:5–10.

October 16: II Kings 5:9–17; II Tim. 2:8–13; Luke 17:11–19.

October 23: Exod. 17:8–13; II Tim. 3:14–4:2; Luke 18:1–8.

October 30: Deut. 10:16–22; II Tim. 4:6–8, 16–18; Luke 18:9–14; (Reformation Sunday) Exod. 33:12–17; Heb. 11:1–10; Luke 18:9–14.

November 6: Exod. 34:5–9; II Thess. 1:11–2:2; Luke 19:1–10.

November 13: I Chron. 29:10–13; II Thess. 2:16–3:5; Luke 20:27–38.

November 20: Mal. 3:16–4:2; II Thess. 3:6–13; Luke 21:5–19.

November 24 (Thanksgiving Day): Deut. 8:6–17; II Cor. 9:6–15; John 6:24–35.

ADVENT

November 27: Isa. 2:1–5; Rom. 13:11–14; Matt. 24:36–44.

December 4: Isa. 11:1–10; Rom. 15:4–9; Matt. 3:1–12.

December 11: Isa. 35:1–6, 10; Jam. 5:7–10; Matt. 11:2–11.

December 18: Isa. 7:10–15; Rom. 1:1–7; Matt. 1:18–25.

December 24 (Christmas Eve): Isa. 62:1–4; Col. 1:15–20; Luke 2:1–14.

CHRISTMASTIDE

December 25: Isa. 9:2, 6–7; Titus 2:11–15; Luke 2:1–14.

Four-Year Church Calendar

	1983	1984	1985	1986
Ash Wednesday	February 16	March 7	February 20	February 12
Palm Sunday	March 27	April 15	March 31	March 23
Good Friday	April 3	April 20	April 5	March 28
Easter	May 12	April 22	April 7	March 30
Ascension Day	May 22	May 31	May 16	May 8
Pentecost	May 29	June 10	May 26	May 18
Trinity Sunday	June 5	June 17	June 2	May 25
Thanksgiving	November 24	November 23	November 22	November 27
Advent Sunday	November 27	December 2	December 1	November 30

Forty-Year Easter Calendar

1983 April 3	1993 April 11	2003 April 20	2013 March 31
1984 April 22	1994 April 3	2004 April 11	2014 April 20
1985 April 7	1995 April 16	2005 March 27	2015 April 5
1986 March 30	1996 April 7	2006 April 16	2016 March 27
1987 April 19	1997 March 30	2007 April 8	2017 April 16
1988 April 3	1998 April 12	2008 March 23	2018 April 1
1989 March 26	1999 April 4	2009 April 12	2019 April 21
1990 April 15	2000 April 23	2010 April 4	2020 April 12
1991 March 31	2001 April 14	2011 April 24	2021 April 4
1992 April 19	2002 March 31	2012 April 8	2022 April 17

Traditional Wedding Anniversary Identifications

1 Paper	7 Wool	13 Lace	35 Coral
2 Cotton	8 Bronze	14 Ivory	40 Ruby
3 Leather	9 Pottery	15 Crystal	45 Sapphire
4 Linen	10 Tin	20 China	50 Gold
5 Wood	11 Steel	25 Silver	55 Emerald
6 Iron	12 Silk	30 Pearl	60 Diamond

Colors Appropriate for Days and Seasons

White. Symbolizes purity, perfection, and joy and identifies festivals marking events, except Good Friday, in the life of Jesus: Christmas, Easter, Eastertide,

Ascension Day, Trinity Sunday, All Saints' Day, weddings, funerals.
Red. Symbolizes the Holy Spirit, martyrdom, and the love of God: Pentecost and Sundays following.
Violet. Symbolizes penitence: Advent, Lent.
Green. Symbolizes mission to the world, hope, regeneration, nurture, and growth: Epiphany season, Kingdomtide, Rural Life Sunday, Labor Sunday, Thanksgiving Sunday.
Black. Symbolizes mourning: Good Friday.

Flowers in Season Appropriate for Church Use

January. Carnation or snowdrop.
February. Violet or primrose.
March. Jonquil or daffodil.
April. Lily, sweet pea, or daisy.
May. Lily of the valley or hawthorn.
June. Rose or honeysuckle.
July. Larkspur or water lily.

August. Gladiolus or poppy.
September. Aster or morning glory.
October. Calendula or cosmos.
November. Chrysanthemum.
December. Narcissus, holly, or poinsettia.

Historical, Cultural, and Religious Anniversaries in 1983

10 years (1973). *January 22:* Supreme Court repeals laws limiting abortions. *January 27:* end of the military draft. *February 22:* China and the United States agree to permanent liaison offices. *March 29:* last United States troops leave Vietnam. *October 6–24:* fourth Arab-Israeli war. *November 1:* Leon Jaworski named special Watergate prosecutor. *November 7:* Congress passes war powers bill.

20 years (1963). *May 15–16:* Gordon Cooper orbits earth twenty-two times. *June 3:* Pope John XXIII dies. *June 17:* Supreme Court declares recitation of the Lord's Prayer and Bible verses in public schools unconstitutional. *August 5:* Limited nuclear test ban signed. *August 28:* 200,000 attend civil rights rally in Washington, D.C., and hear "I have a dream" speech by Martin Luther King, Jr. *October 1:* Nigeria becomes a republic. *November 22:* John F. Kennedy assassinated.

25 years (1958). *January 1:* European Common Market established. *January 31:* Explorer I first United States earth satellite in orbit. *December 10:* first domestic jet airline passenger service. *December 21:* de Gaulle elected president of France.

50 years (1933). *January 13:* Philippines granted independence. *March 4:* Franklin D. Roosevelt inaugurated. *March 23:* Hitler becomes dictator of Germany. *March 28:* Nazis begin systematic boycott of Jewish businessmen and professionals. *June 16:* NRA first of New Deal legislation. *September 5:* church opposition begins in Germany. *November 17:* United States recognizes Soviet Russia. *December 5:* prohibition amendment repealed.

100 years (1883). *May 24:* Brooklyn Bridge opens. Frances E. Willard founds the WCTU. Robert Louis Stevenson writes *Treasure Island.* Nietzsche publishes *Zarathustra.*

150 years (1833). *August 23:* Britain abolishes slavery in British colonies. Oxford Movement begun. Gauss and Weber invent telegraph. Carlyle writes *Sartor Resartus.*

200 years (1783). *September 3:* Treaty of Versailles signed. *December 3:* General Washington bids farewell to his officers. Massachusetts outlaws slavery. Noah Webster publishes *American Spelling Book.* First aerial voyages in hot-air and hydrogen balloons invented by the Montgolfier brothers and S.A.C. Charles.

250 years (1733). Oglethorpe founds Savannah, Georgia. Bach composes *B-Minor Mass.*

300 years (1683). William Penn signs treaty with Delaware Indians and writes *General Description of Pennsylvania.*

350 years (1633). *June 22:* Galileo

forced by the Inquisition to renounce views of Copernicus.

500 years (1483). *November 10:* Martin Luther born.

750 years (1233). The Inquisition begins.

900 years (1083). Construction of Ely Cathedral undertaken.

Anniversaries of Hymns, Hymn Writers, and Composers in 1983

25 years (1958). Death of George Bennard (b. 1873), author and composer of "The old rugged cross"; Harold W. Friedell (b. 1905), composer of hymn-tunes HASTINGS-ON-HUDSON ("It is good to sing thy praises"), FINLAY ("O be joyful in the Lord"), RIDGEFIELD ("Into the woods my Master went"), and UNION SEMINARY ("Draw us in the Spirit's tether"); Robert Guy McCutchan (b. 1877), composer of hymn-tune ALL THE WORLD ("Let all the world in every corner sing"); and Ralph Vaughan Williams (b. 1872), composer of hymn-tunes DOWN AMPNEY ("Come down, O love divine"), KING'S WESTON ("At the name of Jesus"), RANDOLPH ("God be with you till we meet again"), and SINE NOMINE ("All praise to thee" and "For all the saints, who from their labors rest").

50 years (1933). Birth of Lawrence P. Schreiber, composer of hymn-tunes NATIONAL CITY ("All praise to thee") and THOMAS CIRCLE ("O thou whose favor hallows all occasions"). Death of Joseph S. Cook (b. 1859), author of "Gentle Mary laid her child"; Adam Geibel (b. 1855), composer of hymn-tune GEIBEL ("Stand up, stand up for Jesus"); James Mountain (b. 1843), composer of "I am his and he is mine," "Like a river glorious," and "Jesus, I am resting"; James Rowe (b. 1865), author of "Love lifted me"; Charles A. Tindley (b. 1856), author and composer of "When the storms of life are raging"; and Henry van Dyke (b. 1852), author of "Jesus, thou divine companion," "Joyful, joyful, we adore thee," and "They who tread the path of labor."

75 years (1908). Writing of "Forward through the ages" by Frederick L. Hosmer; "In Christ there is no east or west" by John Oxenham; "I thank thee, Lord, for strength of arm" by Robert Davis; "Let there be light, Lord God of hosts" by William Merrill Vories; and "Lord, wilt thou in this temple reign" by E. Leigh Mudge. Death of Edward Husband (b. 1843), com-

poser of hymn-tune ST. HILDA ("O Jesus, thou art standing"); Phoebe P. Knapp (b. 1839), composer of "Blessed assurance, Jesus is mine"; Lewis H. Redner (b. 1831), composer of hymn-tune ST. LOUIS ("O little town of Bethlehem"); Ira D. Sankey (b. 1840), composer of "Faith is the victory," "Grace! 'tis a charming sound," "Hiding in thee," "A shelter in the time of storm," "Trusting Jesus," and "Under his wings"; Walter Chalmers Smith (b. 1824), author of "Immortal, invisible, God only wise"; and Winfield S. Weeden (b. 1847), composer of "I Surrender All" and "Somebody did a golden deed."

100 years (1883). Writing of "O perfect love, all human thought transcending" by Dorothy Frances Gurney. Birth of George K. A. Bell (d. 1958), author of "Christ is the king"; George Henry Day, composer of hymn-tune GENEVA ("God almighty, God eternal"); C. Harold Lowden, composer of "God who touchest earth with beauty" and "Living for Jesus"; G. A. Studdert-Kennedy (d. 1929), author of "Awake, awake to love and work" and "When through the whirl of wheels"; and Sarah E. Taylor (d. 1954), author of "O God of light, thy word, a lamp unfailing." Death of William J. Irons (b. 1812), author of "Sing with all the sons of glory."

150 years (1833). Composing of hymn-tune CANONBURY ("Lord, speak to me" and "O grant us light") by Robert Schumann; RUSSIAN HYMN ("God the omnipotent") by Alexis F. Lvov. Writing of "Lead, kindly light" by John Henry Newman; "O happy home, where thou art loved" by Karl J. P. Spitta. Birth of James W. Elliott (d. 1915), composer of the hymn-tune DAY OF REST ("In heavenly love abiding"); Benjamin R. Hanby (d. 1867), writer and composer of "Who is he in yonder stall?"; and William G. Tomer (d. 1896), composer of the hymn-tune FAREWELL ("God be with you till we meet again"). Death of Edward Cooper (b. 1770), author of "Father of

heaven, whose love profound"; Louis J. F. Herold (b. 1791), composer of hymn-tune MESSIAH ("Take my life, and let it be").

200 years (1783). Birth of Gottfried W. Fink (d. 1846), composer of hymn-tune BETHLEHEM ("All nature's works his praise declare" and "Thy word is like a garden, Lord"); Nicolai F. S. Grundtvig (d. 1872), author of "Built on the rock the church doth stand" and "Most wondrous is of all on earth"; and Reginald Heber (d. 1826), author of "Bread of the world," "Brightest and best," "God, that madest earth and heaven," "Holy, holy, holy! Lord God almighty," "The Son of God goes forth to war," among others. Death of James Nares (b. 1715), composer of hymn-tune AMSTERDAM ("Praise the Lord who reigns above" and "Rise, my soul, and stretch thy wings"); William Tans'ur (b. 1706), composer of hymn-tunes BANGOR ("Alone thou goest forth, O Lord") and ST. MARTIN'S ("Come, let us use the grace divine").

250 years (1733). Birth of Thomas Haweis (d. 1820), composer of hymn-tune RICHMOND ("City of God, how broad and far").

350 years (1633). Death of George Herbert (b. 1593), author of "Let all the world in every corner sing."

400 years (1583). Birth of Orlando Gibbons (d. 1625), composer of hymn-tunes CANTERBURY ("Christ, from whom all blessings flow," "Holy Spirit, truth divine," "Jesus, with thy church abide," and "Never further than thy cross") and SONG ("Christ in his heavenly garden," "I dared not hope that thou wouldst deign to come," "Peace, perfect peace," and "Strong Son of God, immortal love").

500 years (1483). Birth of Martin Luther (d. 1546), author of "Christ Jesus lay in death's strong bands," "Come, Holy Spirit, God and Lord," "From heaven above to earth I come," "God of all power and truth and grace," and "Jesus Christ, our blessed Savior"; author and composer of "A mighty fortress is our God" and "Out of the depths I cry to thee."

Quotable Quotations

1. Time is too slow for those who wait, too swift for those who fear, too long for those who grieve, too short for those who rejoice, well spent for those who live.—Jeffrey Mitchell.

2. All the flowers of the tomorrows are in the seeds of today.—Chinese proverb.

3. The greatest sin is to stop traveling. Response to God always sets us in motion. —Ben Oliphint.

4. We are not the architects of destiny. We are not the creators or redeemers of the world. We are God's raw materials.—James S. Stewart.

5. All growth in the spiritual life is connected with the clearer insight into what Jesus is to us.—Andrew Murray.

6. Christians are united by virtue of the fact that they are Christians, not because as Christians they accept some plan which will unite them.—James O. Baird.

7. Christian brotherhood is not an ideal which we must realize; it is rather a reality created by God in Christ in which we may participate.—Dietrich Bonhoeffer.

8. The true way to be humble is not to stoop until you are smaller than yourself but to stand at your real height against some higher nature that will show you what the real smallness of your greatness is.—Phillips Brooks.

9. You don't live in a world all your own. Your brothers are here too.—Albert Schweitzer.

10. The man who has learned to pray is no longer alone in the universe; he is living in his Father's house.—William Adams Brown.

11. A Christian ought to make a difference. Wherever Paul went there was either a revival or a riot.—Wilson Franklym.

12. Love is an undeviating determination to act in a spirit of good will toward God, his creatures, and the world.—Earl L. Douglass.

13. The best life of Christ is his living biography written out in the words and action of his people.—Charles H. Spurgeon.

14. A church should be a power-house where sluggish spirits can be recharged and reanimated.—Samuel E. Eliot.

15. The Christian religion means one thing and one thing only: eternal life in the

midst of time by the strength and under the eyes of God.—Adolph Harnack.

16. No man can bring another man closer to Christ than he is himself.—Dwight L. Moody.

17. The man who shuts the door of opportunity upon his brother will have to answer to his Father in heaven.—Roy L. Smith.

18. When I think of God, my heart is so filled with joy that the notes fly off as from a spindle.—Joseph Haydn.

19. Prejudice is a great labor-saving device. It enables you to form an opinion without having to dig up the facts.—Laurence J. Peter.

20. On the basis of the eternal will of God we have to think of every human being, even the oddest, most villainous or miserable, as one to whom Jesus Christ is brother and God is Father; and we have to deal with him on that assumption.—Karl Barth.

21. Christianity is what one thinks, what one feels, and what one does about Jesus Christ.

22. The spinal cord of redemption is the nerve to submit all my images of the self to Christ and his people for correction.—Carlyle Marney.

23. We are Christ's advertisers as well as his advertisements.

24. He became what we are that he might make us what he is.—Athanasius.

25. Duty makes us do things well, but love makes us do them beautifully.—Phillips Brooks.

26. They are the true disciples of Christ, not who know most, but who love most.—Frederich Spanheim the Elder.

27. If you believe in no future life, I would not give you a mushroom for your God.—Martin Luther.

28. Love is a fruit in season at all times and within reach of every hand. Anyone may gather it and no limit is set.—Mother Teresa.

29. Most people are willing to take the sermon on the mount as a flag to sail under, but few will use it as a rudder by which to steer.—Oliver Wendell Holmes.

30. The promises of God are certain, but they do not all mature in ninety days.—A. J. Gordon.

31. God does not ask of a person any-thing that is false or beyond his power. Rather, God invites what is most human in every person to become aware of itself.—Louis M. Savary.

32. The character of worship is always decided by the worshiper's conception of God and his relation to God.—Evelyn Underhill.

33. Our hope and help are centered in God's everlasting and steadfast love.—W. Ralph Ward.

34. Without faith we are as stained glass windows in the dark.

35. I have made a ceaseless effort not to ridicule, not to bewail, nor to scorn human actions but to understand them.—Spinoza.

36. Religion is the vision of something which stands beyond, behind, and within the flux of immediate things.—Alfred North Whitehead.

37. Prayer enlarges the heart until it is capable of containing God's gift of himself.—Mother Teresa.

38. Wasting money is as much an act of violence against the poor as refusing to feed the hungry.—George Sweeting.

39. Religion gives you courage to make the decisions you must make in a crisis and then the confidence to leave the result to a higher power. Only by trust in God can a man carrying responsibility find repose.—Dwight D. Eisenhower.

40. The proof of Christianity really consists in following.—Søren Kierkegaard.

41. Our Lord does not care so much for the importance of our works as for the love with which they are done.—Teresa of Avila.

42. No man knows what he is living for until he knows what he'll die for.—Peter Bertocci.

43. So much has been given to me, I have no time to ponder over that which has been denied.—Helen Keller.

44. The Sabbath is the most precious present mankind has received from the treasure house of God.—Abraham Joshua Heschel.

45. Joy rather than happiness is the goal of life, for joy is the emotion that accompanies the fulfillment of our natures as human beings.—Rollo May.

46. Faith is the daring of the soul to go

farther than it can see.—William Newton Clark.

47. In laughing wholeheartedly a man must attain a certain freedom from selfishness, a certain purity; and the greatest saints are the merriest-hearted people.—Mary Webb.

48. It is doubtful whether God can bless a man greatly until he has hurt him deeply.—A. W. Tozer.

49. The Bible is the story of man's complete ruin in sin and God's perfect remedy in Christ.—C. H. MacIntosh.

50. The higher our spiritual level, the fuller is our view of life.—Richard W. Ricker.

51. There is no limit to the usefulness of one who, putting self aside, makes room for the working of the Holy Spirit upon his heart and lives a life wholly consecrated to God.—Ellen G. White.

52. The cross reveals to men that their goodness has not been good enough.—Johann Schroeder.

53. If there were such a thing as a perfect church, none of us could get into it.—Clovis Chappell.

54. This country will not be a good place for any of us to live in unless we make it a good place for all of us to live in.—Theodore Roosevelt.

55. Ask all the questions you want about religion, but ask the questions of faith and not the questions of skepticism.—Earl Layden.

56. We must claim absoluteness and finality for Christ and his finished work, but that claim forbids us to claim absoluteness and finality for our understanding of it.—Lesslie Newbigin.

57. Real blasphemy comes not chiefly by profaning the holy; it comes far more by deifying the essentially trivial.—Elton Trueblood.

58. I find that doing the will of God leaves me no time for disputing his plans.—George Macdonald.

59. When I go to church I don't want to be told where my duty lies. I know that. I want to hear whence cometh my help.—T. R. Glover.

60. It is easy to do the right thing; what's hard is to know the right thing to do.—Lyndon B. Johnson.

61. No Christian escapes a taste of the wilderness on the way to the promised land.—Evelyn Underhill.

62. The contagion of good values from one person to another has an immense impact on society. An exemplary act can affect millions of lives.—John Gardner.

63. Fear not that thy life shall come to an end but rather fear that it shall never have a beginning.—John Henry Newman.

64. When you have nothing left but God, then for the first time you become aware that God is enough.—Maude Royden.

65. The kingdom of God is the kingdom of right relationships.—Bruce Larson.

66. Christians are like the spokes of a wheel with Christ as the hub. The closer we are to Christ, the closer we are to one another.—*Christian Observer.*

67. Religion is knowing profoundly what you know already.—Blaise Pascal.

68. We do not get at the nature of words by asking what they contain but by asking what they effect, what they set going, what future they disclose.—Gerhard Ebeling.

69. Character is the sum total of the choices we have made.—*Missionary Tidings.*

70. True humility makes way for Christ and throws the soul at his feet.—John Milton.

71. God can do wonders with a broken heart if you give him all the pieces.—Victor Alfsen.

72. Our deeds are like stones cast into the pool of time. Though they themselves may disappear their ripples extend to eternity.—*Our Daily Bread.*

73. The modern world seems bent on producing a kind of man to whom the gospel cannot be preached.—Frederick Denison Maurice.

74. To build a brave new world, we need fewer architects and more bricklayers.—*St. Jude Notebook.*

75. I have lived to thank God that all my prayers have not been answered.—Jean Ingelow.

76. Despair has been called the unforgivable sin not presumably because God refuses to forgive it but because it despairs of the possibility of being forgiven.—Frederick Buechner.

77. To talk about changing human nature may seem idealistic, but to talk about changing human society and world

conditions without changing human nature is insanity.—Leslie D. Weatherhead.

78. You must count your work unsatisfactory unless you waken men's brains and stir their consciences.—Phillips Brooks.

79. Forgiveness of sins is a knot which needs God's help to untie.—Martin Luther.

80. Man cannot discover new oceans unless he has the courage to lose sight of the shore.—George L. Hunt.

81. Daily pressures can peeve, provoke, and perturb us; private prayers can strengthen, steady, and support us.—William A. Ward.

82. Everything that is done in the world is done by hope.—Martin Luther.

83. He who has God and many other things has no more than he who has God alone.—C. S. Lewis.

84. Study geography until for you there is no foreign land. Study humanity until there is for you no foreign person.—Edward McDowell.

85. No grace or blessing is truly ours until God has blessed someone else with it through us.—Phillips Brooks.

86. A man who trims himself to suit everybody will soon whittle himself away.—Charles Schwab.

87. The diamond cannot be polished without friction nor the man perfected without trials.—Chinese proverb.

88. None can believe how powerful prayer is and what it is able to effect but those who have learned it by experience.—Martin Luther.

89. If one understands creation as a system rather than as a hierarchy in which we rank the diversity of creation, then every-thing has creation-based value, and that's basically an equal value.—Elizabeth Dodson Gray.

90. The Bible is alive; it speaks to me; it has feet—it runs after me, it lays hold on me.—Martin Luther.

91. Grace is what our Lord Jesus Christ gives us to be more like him.—Michael Ramsey.

92. We need to learn to set our course by the stars and not by the lights of every passing ship.—Omar Bradley.

93. Give, you can never give enough. Give all: all is not too much.—Alfred Adler.

94. Real joy comes not from ease or riches or from the praise of men but from doing something worthwhile.—Wilfred T. Grenfell.

95. The man who has lived for himself has the privilege of being his own mourner.—Henry Ward Beecher.

96. To bestow the gift of the Christ child, God emptied the storehouse on high and depleted the resources of heaven.—Arnold V. Wallenkampf.

97. We can form no idea of the natural distance between God and man, but the infinite vacuum is filled up by the Messiah.—Christmas Evans.

98. The most brilliant light ever to shine in this world came from Bethlehem.—Malcolm Muggeridge.

99. What are the servants of God if not singers whose task is to lift up the hearts of men and urge them to spiritual joy?—Francis of Assisi.

100. What lies behind us and what lies before us are tiny matters compared to what lies within us.—Ralph Waldo Emerson.

Questions of Life and Religion

These questions may be useful to prime homiletic pumps, as discussion starters, or for study and youth groups.

1. How are we saved "through the grace of Jesus Christ" (Acts 15:11)?

2. What is the ministry of Gideons International?

3. What answers does the Bible give in answer to the question, "Who am I?"

4. Is the electronic church supportive of or in competition with the local church?

5. Why are the books of the Apocrypha not generally found in Protestant Bibles?

6. How can Christians protest huge expenditures for armaments?

7. Why is the cross an appropriate altar symbol?

8. If Jesus was sinless, why did he accept baptism at the hands of John?

9. Which of the prophets speak with greatest relevance to our needs?

10. Are there any generally accepted Christian guidelines regarding the social use of alcohol?

11. Did the twentieth-century church discover the liberation of women or has this been a part of the Christian heritage?

12. What influence does trouble offer in bringing faith to maturity?

13. How may I know that I have God's approval?

14. Is prayer self-centered?

15. Is there a built-in conflict between my civil responsibilities and my Christian obligations?

16. By what hopes have humans survived?

17. What differences are there between biblical translations and paraphrases?

18. What impels people to participate in violent crimes?

19. How can a church determine the proportion of its budget that should go to home and foreign missions?

20. Are there better ways of celebrating such days as Christmas and Easter than by exorbitant displays of altar flowers?

21. What do I need in my Christian life which the church cannot provide?

22. Should Christians try to determine levels of acceptable TV programing?

23. How does Christian faith help grieving persons?

24. What are the benefits of music in worship services?

25. How has Christian home life changed in recent years?

26. What particular emphases do the individual gospels contribute to our understanding of Jesus?

27. Does Christ need me, or is it I who need Christ?

28. Do you ever feel unworthy of God's love?

29. Does faith healing make medicine unnecessary?

30. How can I escape from the feeling that life is basically meaningless?

31. Why did Jesus so often teach in parables?

32. What are the signs of Christ's second coming?

33. How can a half-dead church become fully alive?

34. How can I come to terms with tragedy?

35. Where would you begin if you wanted to undertake a serious study of theology?

36. Should we always strive to win?

37. Is the resurrection more important than the crucifixion?

38. What is the function of the sermon in worship services?

39. How can I know God cares?

40. How can I improve my disposition?

41. Is it harder to believe in God today than it was in former generations?

42. Does religion influence the decisions which our national leaders must make?

43. Why are so many people lonely?

44. How can I be led by the Holy Spirit?

45. What are life's ultimate questions?

46. How can religion reconcile separated married couples?

47. How often should I take Holy Communion?

48. How is military preparedness a deterrent to war?

49. What do you do when you're tempted?

50. Why do people find particular churches attractive?

51. Are there biblical teachings that relate to the problem of gambling?

52. How can I be born from above?

53. What is the sword of the Spirit?

54. Why don't other people see things my way?

55. How does God speak to us?

56. What do statistics not tell us about a church?

57. How is a Christian different from a non-Christian?

58. How can I avoid a sense of boredom?

59. Is the effort of Christians making an impact on world hunger?

60. Should I keep praying when no answers come?

61. Does church attendance affect an individual's mental and physical health?

62. What motivates Christian stewardship?

63. What particular meaning does the church attach to Christ's ascension?

64. How can I love people I don't like?

65. Is it desirable to have a complete separation of church and state?

66. Do all churches require baptism for church membership?

67. Is the belief that Christ's kingdom will come on earth as it is in heaven an impossible dream?

68. Why did Judas betray Jesus?

69. Will you relate Old Testament prophecy to the twentieth century?

70. How can God be both merciful and just?

71. Why do I persist in doing what I know I shouldn't?

72. What does it mean to be meek?

73. Is our society too competitive?

74. What did Luther mean when he said that a Christian should be a "little Christ"?

75. What should we expect at the final judgment?

76. Does the biblical story of the creation exclude scientific discovery?

77. What Christian teachings do Catholics and Protestants hold in common?

78. How can I free myself from anxiety about the future?

79. In what ways does nature manifest God?

80. What should the attitude of the church be toward homosexuals?

81. How does a person handle a conflict among basic loyalties?

82. How can I settle on my purpose in life?

83. How is success in Christian missions measured?

84. How does the laity witness for Christ?

85. What does the Bible tell us about heaven?

86. Why did St. Paul describe himself as the chief of sinners?

87. Have the churches made any progress in Christianizing race relations?

88. What are the primary purposes of the Sunday school?

89. Is the cross anticipated in the Old Testament?

90. What does the word "covenant" mean?

91. What suggestions can you offer for daily devotions?

92. Why attend church services?

93. Am I my brother's keeper?

94. In what respects are we a nation "under God"?

95. How can the church respond to the challenge of the drug culture?

96. Will we know one another in heaven?

97. What should be a pastor's response to families which ignore the church except for weddings and funerals?

98. Is the church merely holding its own in foreign missions?

99. How can the church become a redemptive community?

100. What does the incarnation tell us about God?

Biblical Benedictions and Blessings

The Lord watch between me and thee, when we are absent one from another.—Gen. 31:49.

The Lord bless thee, and keep thee; the Lord make his face shine upon thee, and be gracious unto thee; the Lord lift up his countenance upon thee, and give thee peace.—Num. 6:24–26.

The Lord our God be with us, as he was with our fathers: let him not leave us, nor forsake us: that he may incline our hearts unto him, to walk in all his ways, and to keep his commandments, and his statutes, and his judgments, which he commanded our fathers.—I Kings 8:57–58.

Let the words of my mouth, and the meditation of my heart, be acceptable in thy sight, O Lord, my strength, and my redeemer.—Ps. 19:14.

Now the God of patience and consolation grant you to be likeminded one toward another according to Christ Jesus: that ye may with one mind and one mouth glorify God, even the Father of our Lord Jesus Christ. Now the God of hope fill you with all joy and peace in believing, that ye may abound in hope, through the power of the Holy Ghost. Now the God of peace be with you all.—Rom. 15:5–6, 13, 33.

Now to him that is of power to establish you according to my gospel, and the preaching of Jesus Christ, according to the revelation of the mystery, which was kept secret since the world began, but now is manifest, and by the scriptures of the prophets, according to the commandment of the everlasting God, made known to all nations for the obedience of faith: to God only wise, be glory through Jesus Christ for ever.—Rom. 16:25–27.

Grace be unto you, and peace, from God our Father, and from the Lord Jesus Christ.—I Cor. 1:3.

The grace of the Lord Jesus Christ and the love of God, and the communion of the Holy Ghost, be with you all.—II Cor. 13:14.

Peace be to the brethren, and love with faith, from God the Father and the Lord Jesus Christ. Grace be with all them that love our Lord Jesus Christ in sincerity.—Eph. 6:23–24.

And the peace of God, which passeth all understanding, shall keep your hearts and minds through Christ Jesus. Finally, brethren, whatsoever things are true, whatsoever things are honest, whatsoever things are just, whatsoever things are pure, whatsoever things are lovely, whatsoever things are of good report; if there be any virtue, and if there be any praise, think on these things. Those things, which ye have both learned, and received, and heard, and seen in me, do: and the God of peace shall be with you.—Phil. 4:7–9.

Wherefore also we pray always for you, that our God would count you worthy of this calling, and fulfill all the good pleasure of his goodness, and the work of faith with power: that the name of our Lord Jesus Christ may be glorified in you, and ye in him, according to the grace of our God and the Lord Jesus Christ.—II Thess. 1:11–12.

Now the Lord of peace himself give you peace always by all means. The Lord be with you all. The grace of our Lord Jesus Christ be with you all.—II Thess. 3:16, 18.

Grace, mercy, and peace, from God our Father and Jesus Christ our Lord.—I Tim. 1:2.

Now the God of peace, that brought again from the dead our Lord Jesus, that great shepherd of the sheep, through the blood of the everlasting covenant, make you perfect in every good work to do his will, working in you that which is well-pleasing in his sight, through Jesus Christ, to whom be glory for ever and ever.—Heb. 13:20–21.

The God of all grace, who hath called us unto his eternal glory by Christ Jesus, after that ye have suffered a while, make you perfect, stablish, strengthen, settle you. To him be glory and dominion for ever and ever. Greet ye one another with a kiss of charity. Peace be with you all that are in Christ Jesus.—I Pet. 5:10–11, 14.

Grace be with you, mercy, and peace, from God the Father, and from the Lord Jesus Christ, the Son of the Father, in truth and love.—II John 3.

Now unto him that is able to keep you from falling, and to present you faultless before the presence of his glory with exceeding joy, to the only wise God our Savior, be glory and majesty, dominion and power, both now and ever.—Jude 2:24–25.

Grace be unto you, and peace, from him which was, and which is to come; and from the seven Spirits which are before his throne; and from Jesus Christ, who is the faithful witness, and the first begotten of the dead, and the prince of the kings of the earth. Unto him that loved us, and washed us from our sins in his own blood, and hath made us kings and priests unto God and his Father; to him be glory and dominion for ever and ever.—Rev. 1:4–6.

SECTION II. Vital Themes for Vital Preaching

January 2. Resolutions for 1983

TEXT: Phil. 3:13–14.

I. I will mind my own business and not gossip nor believe anything discouraging about any person until I know it to be absolutely true, and even then I will not repeat it to anybody unless I mean to help that person.

II. I will not wear my feelings on my sleeve nor be so sensitive as to look for personal offenses or slights or be envious and suspicious of anyone.

III. I will wear a smile. When I am gloomy, I will go away rather than inflict myself on others who have troubles enough of their own.

IV. I will be kind to others and severe toward myself and do nothing to either another or myself which may become a bitter memory in after years.

V. I will not be headstrong and will remember that other people with different ideas from mine may be right.

VI. I will play the game of life on the square, doing nothing to discourage an honest man, offend a good woman, or cause a child to weep or go astray.

VII. I will hold my temper and each night ask God to forgive me as I have forgiven my neighbors.

VIII. I will face the world each morning with confidence, determined to be as true, happy, clean, and brave as I can. Believing in myself, I will not make excuses. I will strive at all times to be progressive, positive, and practical.

IX. I will move out into some battle for a worthy cause. I will get under some load of human need and help life, realizing that my personality will break down and my soul shrivel up to dryness if I do not give of myself in some unselfish service.

X. I will not be too proud or pagan to pray. Realizing I cannot accomplish these resolutions in my own strength, I will make God a partner in everything I do.— Carl J. Sanders.

January 9. What It Means to Go to Church

SCRIPTURE: Luke 18:9–14.

I. *Identity.* To worship is to say: "This is who I am. I am a Christian, and this is where I belong." To come to church regularly and to participate in worship and the programs of the church is to give a witness by our example to the community that our faith has meaning. We are here because we find meaning. We declare whose side we're on. By being in worship we are announcing to the world, "I believe in Jesus the Christ."

II. *Recognition of our dependency on God.* I cannot say, as did the Pharisee: "God, I have it made. I have done all this, God. I am self-sufficient and self-reliant." I am here because I confess by my very presence that I am dependent upon God for life, for strength, for peace of mind, for courage, and for all of his gifts. We are in need of God's forgiveness. We pray, "God, be merciful to me, a sinner." We recognize we all are dependent on God.

III. *To praise God and express our thanksgiving.* We say in recognition that we are dependent upon God, "God, thank you for your good gifts." We began our service with affirmations of praise, with an invitation from the choir to praise the Lord, and then we responded with a hymn of praise, "Holy, holy, holy, Lord God Almighty." With an awareness of the majesty of God, we can then say, "Thank you, God, for your gifts."

IV. *To receive nurture, personal and spiritual growth, fellowship, and support of this community of faith.* I am not alone. I worship with friends, and together we mutually encourage each other. The program of the church is not limited to this hour. Opportunities to grow abound in the church school, in growth groups, in fellowship groups, and in Bible study groups. Encouragement, nurturing support, and fellowship permeate the entire life of the church.

V. *To be confronted with the gospel and to experience the presence of God.* When scriptures are read and the Word is proclaimed, we experience the presence of God in our midst. We come to church to be confronted with the gospel—the message of the love of God for us and the power of God's love to change our lives.

VI. *To receive our marching orders.* We have come to receive strength for living, and motivation for service and witness. We are urged not to remain cloistered within these walls but to go out into all the world and share the good news that God loves each one of us and all of his people throughout the whole earth. We enter to worship and depart to serve.—C. Earl Gibbs.

January 16. Ready for Anything
Texts: Ps. 10:6; 30:6; 16:8.

I. *Ps. 10:6.* Here is a man inflated with his own importance. God is not at all in his thoughts. He says in his heart: "I shall never be moved. I shall never be in adversity." He sneers at his enemies. He says to himself: "I never fail. I'll never be in trouble."

II. *Ps. 30:6.* Here is a man who believes in God. He is on the crest of a wave. Life is smiling down on him. In a genuine outburst of joy, he says: "I shall never be moved. I'll never doubt again. In my prosperity I said: This is forever, nothing can stop me now. He has made me steady as a mountain. I'm ready for anything."

III. *Ps. 16:8.* Here again is the note of confidence, "I shall never be moved," but with a difference. This man has learned to trust his God at all times. "I have set the Lord always before me. Because he is at my right hand, I shall not be moved." He is ready for anything because he knows that he does not meet life in his own strength. He is spiritually alert. He keeps his soul alive by disciplines of prayer and worship and by practicing the presence of God.—Graham W. Hardy in *The Expository Times.*

January 23. How to Go the Second Mile
Text: Matt. 5:38–41.

The natural inclination on the part of all of us is to pay back in kind. But along comes Jesus with this plan of turning the other cheek, returning good for evil, and doing more than is required. The mechanics of his utterance are familiar to everyone. A blow on the cheek was an insult. To sue in court was to protect one's rights. To go the first mile was to be obedient to the Roman authorities. It is our Lord's singular departure from the customary and legal way of handling injury which makes this seem a gospel of foolishness. How can we go the second mile? For a working definition let us put the question this way: How can we do more than is expected of us?

I. Across the years only those who have done more than anyone could force them to do have reaped the rewards of great living. Why do you do so many things to make your community better? Why do you volunteer your time and energy and money to support our free institutions? Because you have it in your heart to go the second mile and to do more than anyone can demand of you. We can go the second mile because down deep within us there is an inner compulsion which is not at peace until we have gone beyond where anyone can make us go.

II. We shall find it possible to live in this larger dimension only as we keep our faith in human possibilities.

(a) Often we are sorely tempted to give up our faith in people. We loan money and they don't pay it back; we do a kindness and get no thanks; we give our best and get only their worst in return. How easily we remember the kicks, and how quickly we forget the pats on the back.

(b) It may be that we haven't been investing largely enough to impress those whom we help with the importance of living up to the investment. To go the first mile, to do just what we are asked to do, seldom impresses anyone. But to do what no one asks or expects—what bells start ringing then!

III. We can go the second mile only as we keep alive our faith in God. (a) In the matter of vengeance it is well to remember these insights: "Vengeance is mine, I will repay, saith the Lord" and "Whatsoever a man soweth, that shall he also reap." Let God punish the evil-doer. Things finally balance up for the evil-doer, even as they do for the right-doer.

(b) There is this other side of the matter: God knows what good you do, and every time you turn the other cheek and go the second mile you grow just a little closer to God and a little more like his Son who practiced this religion which he preached.—Homer J. R. Elford.

January 30. The Ancient Covenant Speaks to Us

Scripture: Gen. 17:1–8.

I. God's covenant with Abraham reaches down through the centuries to us. The canopy of the covenant covers us and all nations. The outreach of God through Abraham extends to all.

II. The covenant brings to us the reassurance of God's electing and eternal love. The covenant means that God has taken the initiative toward us. We cannot escape what God has done for us through Abraham any more than we can escape what he has done for us in Christ.

III. The covenant places upon us responsibility. It sharpens our relationship with God. We cannot act responsibly before God and act as though God had not made the covenant with Abraham.

IV. The covenant calls for faith. Abraham believed God and it was counted as righteousness before God. Faith is the true response to God and his covenant.

V. The covenant calls for obedience to God's claim upon our lives. Abraham obeyed and went out not knowing where he was headed.

VI. The covenant should evoke gratitude on our part. Gratitude flows from the heart that believes. The journey of faith is a journey of gratitude for the presence of God.—W. Aubrey Alsobrook.

February 6. Why Pray?

Text: Luke 18:1.

I. We ought always to pray because practice is necessary. (a) Some people try prayer in a hesitant, uncertain manner and then abandon it as an unsuccessful experiment. Because it never became a daily habit, they achieved no naturalness in performance and no satisfaction in results.

(b) Jesus told us to speak to God as to a father. There is something tragically wrong if conversation within a family is not a normal, daily affair. Prayer should be a constant practice, a regular, nourishing habit.

II. We ought always to pray because persistence is required. (a) After making this declaration about prayer, Jesus told of a widow who pleaded her case persistently before a judge. This, said Jesus, is the way to pray—insistently and consistently. It is not a once-in-a-while exercise.

(b) Prayer should be dominant desire, constant longing, and fervent pleading. It is through diligent, continuing prayer that God is able to work in us before he appears to work for us. By such means we become responsive to divine guidance and receptive to divine purpose.

III. We ought always to pray because power is needed. The only way we can get the help we need is to ask God for it. Through prayer we make vital connection with eternal and wonder-working power. Energy that appears inert or inaccessible is activated and made available by prayer. When we need power beyond human ability, prayer is the means of securing it.—Bramwell Tripp.

February 13. The Wrecking Crew (Brotherhood Week)

Text: I Cor. 13:12 (neb).

We live in a world full of fences. Daily we face barriers between rich and poor, between north and south, between people of color and people without color, between lay and clergy, between women and men. Part of our calling as Christians is that of a wrecking crew. Our God-given vocation sometimes calls us to be a demolition team, a battering ram. Christ actually sends us to tear down fences, to undermine walls, and to move high barriers.

I. Many of those fences are lovely antiques whose owners value them dearly. They have been handed down for generations in the family. Some walls are strongly built, heavily guarded, defended at great expense. We are told that if they fall the whole culture will fall with them. Some of these walls are decorated with our own achievements, titles, favorite objects.

II. We grow weary. We get tired of being the "prophetic ones," tired of seeing that glazed look come over faces as we stand to speak, tired of hearing the whispered wisecrack, "I know what she's going to say" or "Here he goes again." There are days when we get fed up with taking walls down brick by brick.

III. Christ began the demolition. With his own body he pierced the walls dividing rich and poor, Jew and Gentile, male and female. Somehow, in the mystery of it all, God asks us to use our bodies in the same way. As we tear down, we are also filling in those ditches. The bricks we pull down go to build highways. One day all people will flow freely among one another. One day there will not be a wall to hinder or a hole to stumble in. One day none will be overfed and none underfed. Do not weary of doing good. That kingdom which has no fences is coming.—Charles Summers.

February 20. A List for Lent
Text: II Tim. 1:6.
I. Do one thing you really enjoy. (See Matt. 25:23, 29.)
II. Stop doing one thing you dislike in yourself. (See John 8:11.)
III. Pray each day for yourself, for those you care about, and for those who need your prayers whom you may have a hard time caring for at all. (See Matt. 7:7.)
IV. Attend the Lenten prayer service every day you can, and come to church each Sunday. (See Matt. 18:20.)

V. Bring someone to church with you. People are waiting to be invited. (See Mark 1:17.)
VI. Live without TV one day each week and use this live prime time to—. (See Mark 13:32–33.)
VII. Rebuild a relationship in your life that is tattered, torn, or broken. (See John 15:14, 17.)
VIII. Read one chapter of a gospel each day. (See Luke 9:18, 20.)
IX. Give away one hour a week to a person or program that needs your love. (See Luke 6:38–39.)
X. Practice seeing your parents or children as God sees them. (See John 3:3.)
XI. Stop buying something—dessert, cigarettes, some nonessential—and give away the money. (See Matt. 6:19–21.)
XII. Take one problem or worry each day and live with the power of knowing that nothing can happen today that God and you can't handle. (See Matt: 28:20.)—John D. Elliott.

February 27. What Is the Church?
Text: Eph. 5:25.
What is the church? More specifically, what is the church to you? There have been many definitions, some biblical, others descriptive.

I. The church has been termed biblically the "Called Out People of God." This means that those who are reborn are called by God to separate themselves from worldly ways. However, they are then prepared by the spirit of God to go back into the world to lead the world to God. Thus the name "The Redeemed of God Redeeming."

II. One of the most biblical names for the church is "The Body of Christ." This mystical symbolism refers to the fact that Christ is the head of the church, and all who are truly members have many functions, each different but each of equal importance to the health of the entire body. This title also speaks of the oneness of all Christians and of the local congregation in particular. Where there is dissension, or criticism, or an indifferent or unwilling spirit on the part of one or several members, the health of the body has been impaired.

III. Another name for the church is "Fellowship of Believers." This implies that those who have become members of this organization hold to common beliefs about God, his revelation of himself and his will, and his giving of his Son for the redemption and reconciliation of mankind.

IV. Whatever name you prefer, you must realize that each implies that the church, both universal and local, is brought into being by the will of God and for the purposes of God. That is to say, the church has a mission.—Robert E. Markham.

March 6. Testing Our Faith (Lent)
TEXT: Jas. 1:22.

The pastoral concern of James is evident in his marvelous epistle. One thing he is exhorting all of us to do is to increase our faith. Emerging from the book are some tests for our faith.

I. A primary test of faith is our attitude toward God's Word. "Be ye doers of the word, and not hearers only." A person might look at his face in a mirror and see that his face is dirty but do nothing about it.

II. A second test concerns our attitude toward God's people. Apparently in those days there was a tendency to focus more attention upon the wealthy than the poor. James says we are to have the same respect to all. Every person is an immortal soul and his life is sacred to God.

III. Another test focuses upon our work. "Faith without works is dead." We are saved by grace, but we express our gratitude by willingly working for our Lord.

IV. A most sensitive test is in the manner of our speech. James talks about the power of the tongue. The same mouth ought not curse God and then try to praise God. "Let your yea be yea; and your nay, nay."

V. One other test is surfaced in the believer's attitude toward the world. Friendship with the world is enmity against God. We cannot love God and mammon. One is supreme. Paul expresses it with anguish when he writes, "Demas hath forsaken me, having loved the things of the present world."—Tom Madden.

March 13. Committed Christians (Lent)
TEXT: Matt. 16:24.

I. In order to be a committed Christian, a person must die to self or deny self. A basic foundation of godliness is self-denial. To deny signifies to put aside, to put off, to annihilate one's self. (See Gal. 2:20.) A minister made a statement, "To take care of self is the first law of nature." "Yes, sir," said an older minister in reply, "but to deny self is the first law of grace."

II. Christian commitment calls for an identification with Christ in his sufferings. "Take up his cross," it has been said. "Every high mission means the cross." Each committed Christian has a cross allotted him. It is a mistake to call all our suffering a cross. Even the wicked have sorrows, but they have no crosses. Our cross is that suffering which results from our faithful identification with Christ.

III. A committed Christian must follow Jesus. When a person receives Christ and commits his life to him, he begins a journey which leads to heaven. Christ leads the way, and the committed Christian follows him.—F. Murray Mathias.

March 20. No Greater Love (Passion Sunday)
TEXT: John 15:13.

Christians have always believed that there is help for the man who seeks it. That help is mediated to ordinary human beings through Christ our Lord. He did not just go about preaching love; he demonstrated what it means to love and that it is possible to love all sorts and conditions of men.

I. He loved the man who was a leper and reached out his hand to touch him.

II. He loved Simon Peter, even when Peter betrayed him on the night of his arrest and trial.

III. He loved the streetwalker who had sold her body to strangers.

IV. He even loved the scribes and Pharisees, going with them to their homes, talking with them, and disagreeing with them but always trying to understand them and to help them understand him.

V. He loved the soldiers who carried out Pilate's order to crucify him, praying, "Father forgive them, for they know not what they do."

VI. I think he loved Pilate.—Clarence J. Forsberg.

March 27. How to Look at the Cross (Good Friday)

Text: Luke 23:33.

I. Take time to view the cross. This means looking at him and, incidentally, looking too at the two criminals, one on each side of him. Stand back for a few moments and take in the details. There are certain things about the scene that are fairly well established in the Bible and, painful though it may be, we should let our eyes wander over the horrible scene that is pictured for us.

II. Think about what the dreadful scene you are viewing says about humankind. Jesus died by human hands. Everything about the scene on Good Friday is evidence of the depravity of humankind. Jesus was innocent. The ruler who pronounced the death sentence in his case admitted that there was nothing guilty of death in the man. And the sentence he passed stands as a lasting evidence of the unreliability of our systems of justice.

III. Believe that hanging there on Calvary's cross is the person who was and is the Son of God. This is the great testimony of the scriptures, a testimony that reaches a near fever pitch on the pages of the New Testament.

IV. Understand that through the crucifixion of Jesus Christ sin was paid once for all, Satan's grip upon the universe was broken, and the way was open into heaven for all those who believe in the Lord Jesus Christ. What you see when you view the Lord Jesus Christ on the cross is not merely an event that occurred in the life of a certain son of David, but you see a transaction carried out that resulted in making right everything that had gone wrong in God's great creation.

V. See that belief in Jesus and receiving forgiveness through his blood means that we ourselves must now live as his followers. Love, self-denial, and self-sacrifice are part of what it means to follow Christ. Whether or not one truly believes in Jesus is revealed in whether or not one is willing in the power of his Spirit to live the Christian way.

VI. As we observe the crucifixion, we are at the crossroads of our lives. Will the scene before us leave us basically untouched, or will we be moved in the depths of our persons by what we now experience?—Joel Nederhood.

April 3. Come to the Feast (Easter)

Text: Matt. 28:5–6.

"This is the day which the Lord has made, the Feast of Feasts." With these words the church for centuries has announced the celebration of Easter. The early church father Athanasius claimed, "The resurrected Christ makes of life a continual feast."

I. Easter is a feast and gives to the life derived from it a festive nature. Here we sense again the great wisdom of the biblican pattern of fast and feast. Life is not to be captive to things, which is expressed in the description of fasting, but neither is it to deny the gift of creation.

II. Let there be an extravagance in your trusting. The Easter message may not satisfy our questioning about what happens when we die, but it answers a more important question—in whom can I trust to the end? The joy and the confidence has evaporated for many of us because we have been preoccupied with more trivial questions. The real question has to do with trust.

III. Let there be an extravagance in your receiving. (a) We think of extravagant living as gross expenditures. The feast calls you to taste the gift of life and to be a glutton of the grace poured out for you. Francois Mauriac said, "We are forbidden to be dead persons."

(b) The power of the resurrection is the power of God to pick up our lives—no matter how much we have neglected them or smothered them or rejected them—and offer them back to us as a gift. The real sin that many of us need to confess is our subtle decision to die, to not let anything new happen to us, and to just ride out our days instead of awaiting the new birthing God has for us.

IV. Let this Easter be a feast for you. It is not a celebration of spring or of some life principle but of the victory of Christ over mistrust, fears, and death. It is a celebration because we can trust Christ with our life and our death. The stone has been removed, and we are forbidden to be dead persons.—Robert B. Wallace.

April 10. The Good News Joyously Proclaimed

TEXT: John 15:11 (TEV).

The early Christians, after the crucifixion, were faced with the fact of failure. Then came the resurrection. Those joyously enthusiastic Christians fanned out over the Roman Empire proclaiming their resurrection faith. Such a faith has to be joyous because it proclaims God's victory over death. What made those Christians so joyous?

I. *They depended on an inner stability and not on an outer security.* They had Jesus! They had seen him resurrected. They could face up to any persecution, confront any opposition, even accept death by violence—and continue to proclaim in their exuberance their joy in Christ.

II. Their joy came because *their well-being was not at the mercy of outward conditions.* Their stability in the face of a stormy life can be understood only when we understand that it was so well-grounded in their faith in Christ. Come what might, they could joyously endure it.

III. The joy of the Christians was not at the mercy of outward circumstances but came as an *indirect result of their feeling of usefulness.* One does not have to be a hero to know their joy. The joy of the Christian comes from the knowledge that he can be used of God for good. Faith calls for a self-forgetting devotion to something beyond self. For the Christian that something is someone—the God of Jesus. We find a redemptive joy in serving Christ and sharing the good news of great joy.—Hoover Rupert.

April 17. Praying in Jesus' Name

SCRIPTURE: John 16:23–30.

I. Prayer in Jesus' name is humble prayer. When someone asserts, "As I see it—and, of course, there is always the possibility I may be wrong—this is what God is telling me to do," then I have a better

reason to listen. Such a person is aware of his or her own nature, which can misread God. Such a person is likely to be more desirous of hearing the still small voice of God. What he or she says may be an authentic word from God.

II. Prayer in the name of Jesus should focus on our relationship to Jesus and our commitment to that relationship. When attention in prayer is primarily upon the answer we get to our prayers, we make God a partner to our own worldly orientation.

III. Prayer in the name of Jesus is prayer lived and prayed in awe of God. It is prayer in which we let God be God and in which total self-commitment is the center of our lives.

IV. Prayer in the name of Jesus is prayer in which the motive is love rather than satisfaction, pleasure, or personal gain.

V. Prayer in the name of Jesus is prayer in which we admit to our sins and selfishness. Confessing our faults, we rest in God's love, and upon his grace we depend to provide power for the amendment of our lives.

VI. Prayer in the name of Jesus does not succumb to the philosophy that no harm comes to the Christian. Prayer in the name of Jesus affirms the presence of God in suffering which may be intense. It affirms hope when all around us seems hopeless.

VII. Prayer in the name of Jesus brings us as human beings into a committed relationship with God where love prevails and life is lived in tune with the infinite and the divine.

VIII. Our prayer as Christians centers in Jesus Christ. He is the key to what we seek and what we receive. When we pray in his name, we are moving into a beautiful relationship with God which Jesus Christ enjoyed.—Marbury Anderson.

April 24. From Dream to Reality

SCRIPTURE: Gen. 28:10–19; Acts 16:6–13.

I. Dreams are a universal experience. Generally, there are two kinds of dreams—those which are an escape from reality and those which are steps toward reality.

II. Dreams can actually become the stuff out of which reality can be fashioned.

III. Most of the finest achievements of people, whether in science, art, industry, education, and religion, were perceived as pictures of the mind in human imagination—the essence of which dreams are made.

IV. Proper motivation is surely indispensable, if you would proceed from dream to reality. Genuine love is the primary incentive to concrete action—love of God and love of persons.—Emil Kontz.

May 1. The Church in Your House (National Family Week)

TEXT: Philem. 1:2.

I. Consider how many times Jesus was present when meals were shared. (a) There was a meal he enjoyed in the publican's home which he used as an opportunity for salvation.

(b) Two of the disciples on the road to Emmaus discovered the risen Lord when they invited a stranger to stop with them and have supper.

(c) Many of Jesus' most important lessons were taught while he was a guest at banquets.

(d) He chose to spend the last evening of his life having a meal with his disciples.

(e) Later he came back to visit his disciples who had gone fishing. In the mists of dawn they recognized Jesus. By the time they beached their fishing boats, Jesus had a fire going and breakfast cooking. It was not until they had shared the breakfast meal that Jesus gave them the great message that he had for them.

II. The early Christian church was a fellowship of neighbors who gathered in each other's homes.

(a) Paul's letters refer to such occasions. He speaks about "the church in your house." We cannot remove friendly hospitality from the first three centuries of Christianity's growth.

(b) Kenneth Scott Latourette observed that Christians succeeded against all odds in the Roman Empire because "a Christian holding membership in a local unit of the church would be among friends in whatever city or town he found others of his communion." Simple hospitality made the Christian churches the most inclusive and strongest of the various organizations in the Roman Empire.

(c) How did the movement acquire this characteristic of friendly hospitality? It was faith in Jesus and his resurrection which gave birth to the Christian fellowship.

III. Perhaps the most effective tool with which to fashion a new and better world will be what Christianity has always made use of so effectively.

(a) We can offer to God the hospitality of our homes and the warmth of our genuine personal interest in gatherings such as this one.

(b) This tool overwhelmed the Roman Empire. It sent the Reformation movement on its way. It certainly was essential to the Wesleyan revival in England. It cradled the frontier church.

(c) The hunger for God today indicates that your home and your heart contain a resource sorely needed by God as he tries to feed his sheep. We believe in the feast of God's love.—A. Allison Childs.

May 8. Hannah's Blessing (Mother's Day)

SCRIPTURE: I Sam. 1:9–18.

The delightful story of Hannah illustrates the triumph of grace in the life of a woman who was prepared to pay the price of blessing.

I. *The heartache of a barren life.* "And Hannah . . . said . . . I am a woman of a sorrowful spirit" (v. 15). The reason for Hannah's sorrow was threefold.

(a) She was fruitless. "The Lord had shut up her womb" (v. 5). Like all normal women, she longed for children, and it vexed her soul that this heritage was denied her.

(b) Hannah was fretful. "Her adversary also provoked her sore, for to make her fret, because the Lord had shut up her womb" (v. 6). The devil used Peninnah to provoke her concerning her state.

(c) Fretfulness led to frustration. "She wept, and did not eat" (v. 7). This is always Satan's method, but thank God, where grace reigns in the heart, even the sorrow of fruitlessness, fretfulness, and frustration can lead to victory.

II. *The heartcry of a broken life.* "And she was in bitterness of soul, and prayed unto the Lord, and wept sore" (v. 10).

(a) Whenever sorrow leads to genuine

prayerfulness before the Lord, there is certainty of triumph. Hannah's prayer was one of concentration. She prevailed in prayer until she had won through.

(b) Her prayer was one of dedication. She vowed that if God granted her a man child, she would give him back unto the Lord all the days of his life, and see that no razor would come upon his head (v. 11).

(c) Her prayer was full of expectancy. She believed God would answer the burden on her heart.

III. *The heart throb of a blessed life.* "And Hannah prayed, and said, My heart rejoiceth in the Lord, mine horn is exalted in the Lord; my mouth is enlarged over mine enemies; because I rejoice in thy salvation" (2:1). Because Hannah was prepared to pay the price in constant, committed, and confident praying and because her motives were pure, God brought her into the blessing of answered prayer, a radiant testimony, and consecrated living.—Stephen F. Olford.

May 15. Men That God Can Use

RESOURCE: Acts 3–4.

I. *Men of prayer.* These disciples were busy. Yet Acts 3:1 shows that in the midst of their busyness they maintained a disciplined prayer life.

II. *Men of philanthropy.* Peter responded to the lame beggar, "I have no silver and gold, but I give you what I have" (Acts 3:6, RSV). "Such as I have I give" is always the autobiography of a committed life.

III. *Men of perception.* After Peter healed the man, people gathered to see what had happened. Acts 3:12 says, "When Peter saw it." What did he see? He saw an opportunity to speak a word for Jesus. These men God used had unusual perception of opportunities for service.

IV. *Men of persistence.* Opposition raised its head, and the easiest pathway would have been to give it up. Yet hear their testimony (Acts 4:20). Success in God's work comes not through ability or charisma but through persistence to the task.—Brian L. Harbour.

May 22. Specimen Day (Pentecost)

SCRIPTURE: Acts 2:1–4.

"The day of Pentecost," wrote D. L. Moody, "was a specimen day." Indeed it was. It was the kind of day which for the Christian every day should be—a day for receiving the Comforter, a day for being filled with the Spirit of the living God.

I. The punctuality of Pentecost. "When the day of Pentecost was fully come."

II. The plurality of Pentecost. "They were all with one accord in one place."

III. The prodigality of Pentecost. "There came a sound from heaven as of a rushing mighty wind, and it filled all the house where they were sitting . . . and they were all filled."

IV. The personality of Pentecost. "With the Holy Ghost."

V. The peculiarity of Pentecost. "They . . . began to speak with other tongues, as the Spirit gave them utterance."—Ian Macpherson.

May 29. Who Am I? (Baccalaureate)

TEXT: Acts 17:28.

We want a meaning for our lives. We want to know who we are and how we can live effectively. Three fundamental desires must be satisfied if we are to experience the overriding desire for a meaningful life. They are the desire to be, the desire to belong, and the desire to do.

I. We want to be someone. Many people are searching for assurance that they really are people of worth and significance.

(a) One of the strange paradoxes of life is that there is an inverse ratio between the scientific advances and the sense of real worth experienced by individuals. Except in a few isolated instances, our relationships with other people have been reduced to case numbers or serial numbers. We are often counted as so many customers or so many votes.

(b) Impersonality has become the accepted criteria for estimating the worth of individuals in practically every relationship. Our lack of a sense of individual identity is real. We long to personally feel and to be known by others as individual persons of divine worth.

II. We find life meaningful when we fulfill the desire to belong. We need to belong to the larger social group which extends throughout the world.

(a) Our real identity comes when we admit we are children of God and akin to all mankind. Individual life is important because it is a creation of a loving heavenly Father who has created us to serve him and help him in his glorious goal of on-going creation. Even as we may take justifiable pride in belonging to a family which bears a common blood-stream and heritage, so we may take great satisfaction from our membership in the divine family of mankind. We can say, "I belong to that!"

(b) Belonging requires participation. Being a card-carrying member may be all right if one's only purpose is, for example, to be able to call the Triple A when he needs emergency automobile service. Simply having one's name on the church rolls does, indeed, entitle one to have that information published in his obituary.

(c) Really belonging to a church, like really belonging to a baseball team or anything else, requires involvement. When people are really working at their membership in anything from a ping-pong team to church membership, they seldom ask if life is worth living. They never wonder, "Who am I?" They know they truly belong to something which draws forth their best energy of body, mind, and spirit.

III. Doing supplements belonging. Belonging, even when it involves participation, becomes meaningful when we belong to something which accomplishes something significant.

(a) There are people who belong to clubs, teams, and organizations and get considerable satisfaction from those relationships. But at the close of a day, a month, a year, or a lifetime, what have they accomplished? What have they to show for it? Some trophies, perhaps, but have they really done anything which has made any real difference to the upbuilding of mankind?

(b) Those who find meaning in life really do something creative, lend the stubborn ounces of their strength to pushing away the clouds of darkness, light candles along the way, and put their shoulder to someone's load, making someone's burden lighter because they consider him to be their brother. When we apply our best energies in those directions, we seldom ask, "Who am I?"—Homer J. R. Elford.

June 5. Pulpit and Pew

SCRIPTURE: Matt. 13:18–23.

Jesus tells us not only of the importance of preaching the Word but also of hearing it. This is the truth he seeks to emphasize in the parable of the sower. Good seed was sown in each instance, but the results varied from place to place according to the nature of the soil into which the seed fell. Some withered, some was choked, some was carried away by the birds, and some brought forth abundantly. It all depended not only upon the sower and the seed but also upon the reception the seed got. So preaching the Word and hearing of it become one activity. Effective preaching is not alone my activity. It is yours also.

I. The pew must give the Word of God hospitality. As the minister prepares himself to preach the Word, so the layman must prepare himself to receive it. This means that the layman will go to church not merely because the Rev. John Doe is to preach. It means he is going there to find God and to know his will. The layman will not say, "I will now hear what the reverend has to say," but "I will now hear what the Lord my God will speak through the voice of the minister."

II. The pew must give the Word of God authority. It is one thing for the pulpit to proclaim life abundant in Christ; it is quite another thing to demonstrate this so convincingly that the preached Word has authority in the eyes and ears of the world. The man in the street must find in our pews the unbreakable Christ fellowship preached in the pulpit.

III. The pew must give the Word the widest possible application. The laity must take the Word into the homes, schools, factories, offices, stockyards, insurance establishments, chambers of commerce, government circles, and department stores. The layman must take the spirit of Christ and apply it to the world in all its aspects.—Ernest Edward Smith.

June 12. Family Heritage (Children's Day)

TEXT: Matt. 19:13.

I grew up in a large family. Some things we didn't have, but there were other things my mother had that I am eternally indebted to her for.

I. Mother had a Savior. Often she would tell us about her experience of trusting Jesus.

II. Mother had a church. The earliest recollection I have of any place, other than my own home, is the church. Mother loved her church and loved her pastor and taught us to love.

III. Mother had a Bible. My mother's Bible was always close by. Many of the passages were marked.

IV. Mother had a pathway to the throne of grace. She prayed often. The day was never too busy for her to have some time alone with God.

V. Mother had a hope. She had a hope for her own soul. She had hopes and dreams for her children.—Tom Madden.

June 19. My Father's Gifts (Father's Day)
TEXT: Gen. 33:11.

I. The first gift he offers us is a trusting heart. (a) His faith was not a complicated matter. So far as I can tell, it rested on three basic convictions: God, who created the world, loves us and cares for us, particularly in our time of need; God sent Jesus to remind us of this love, to forgive us, and to show us how to live our lives in obedience to his will; the Christian life is one of speaking truthfully, acting with integrity, forgiving those who wrong you, bearing the burdens of others.

(b) That certainty is an uncomplicated faith, but after years of study of Christianity I have found none more profound. And it was a faith that not only was articulated but, even more importantly, lived fully. My father's faith and his life were of the same cloth; they enriched each other.

II. My father's second gift is a lively hope. (a) Hope is no other, says Calvin in his *Institutes,* "than an expectation of those things which faith has believed to be truly promised by God. Faith is the foundation on which hope rests; hope nourishes and sustains faith." My father believed in the power of hope to sustain faith.

(b) Calvin said also that hope expects the manifestation of God's truth in due time. My father had a paraphrase for that

statement. He said simply, "God has his own good time." To trust in God is to believe that he will not deceive. To hope in God is to believe that in his time the truth will be revealed.

III. My father's final gift is the spirit of love. (a) The Communion service represented for him the high point of the Christian experience. My father treated Communion with great reverence. He dressed immaculately, arrived at the church very early to be certain everything was adequately prepared, and throughout the service carried himself in a manner that suggested both dignity and humility. Christ's loving act in our behalf came alive in his person and provided for him the centering he needed to live his life.

(b) This centering affected the way he approached other people, those he knew and those he did not know. His hand was always open and ready to grasp the other in friendship, and his face was alive with anticipation. One could almost feel the love flowing from his body.

(c) Emerson said that love is "our highest word." My father believed that, especially the love that "seeks not its own" but sacrificially and spontaneously seeks ever the neighbor's good. This love allows one to give oneself away without fear. It allows others to come into our life without reserve. It destroys the walls that separate us from each other.

(d) Love is the taproot from which all life flows. Though love may not solve all the world's problems, without it none will be solved. My father's gift of love is a precious gift in a world which hovers on the brink.—Paul Sherry in *A.D.*

June 26. What Is Worth More Than Gold?
SCRIPTURE: Acts 3:1–10.

The lame man looked up to Peter and John with the expectation of receiving something from them. Perhaps he held out his cup and looked for a coin from them. Peter said that he had no silver or gold, "But such as I have give I thee: in the name of Jesus Christ of Nazareth rise up and walk." What was it that Peter had to give to the lame man?

I. Peter gave his time. He stopped,

though he was on his way to the temple to pray. Peter did not pass by on the other side of the lame man.

II. Peter gave the lame man his strong hand and lifted him to his feet. Peter reached out to the man with caring and compassion.

III. Peter shared his faith in Jesus Christ with the lame man. In Peter's mind there was the lame man, but there was also in his mind what Jesus Christ could do for him.

IV. Peter gave the lame man Jesus Christ for he said to him, "In the name of Jesus Christ of Nazareth rise up and walk." The lame man was made strong. He stood up, walked, leaped, and praised God. Here we see Peter in the power of the Holy Spirit. He is no longer vacillating in his faith. He is sure and steadfast.—W. Aubrey Alsobrook.

July 3. Bases of Freedom (Independence Sunday)

Text: Jas. 2:12.

A government of the people, by the people, for the people depends on three things.

I. Each citizen must keep himself informed on the issues. This is not easy, but democracy is not a lazy man's form of government. You can't make a valid judgment on the basis of no information, misinformation, or half-information.

II. You've got to work at freedom to keep it. The educated, informed man who takes himself out of the system because he sees its imperfections is worse than the ignorant man. The machinery of participation is there, and it works if it's used. There are ways to make your voice heard, and if you sometimes get the feeling that yours is a voice crying in the wilderness, remember that no worthwhile cause began as a mass movement.

III. Your freedom and the success of the democratic process depend on your willingness to guarantee your neighbor's freedom. Any infringement on one man's liberty is an infringement on the liberty of us all. If my brother is treated unjustly today and I fail to cry out against it, who will speak for me when injustice is my lot? If my neighbor is discriminated against and I deny him redress, who will hear my complaint when I am injured?—Philip E. Collier in *The War Cry*.

July 10. A Healthy Faith

Text: Matt. 7:21.

I. Good religion begins with God, reaches out to others, and only then asks, "What's in this for me?" Self-centeredness and selfishness are dominant in many thriving churches, cults, and movements.

II. Good religion is not afraid of knowledge or discovery. It believes that God has given us a mind and expects us to use it. Rigid thought control is practiced by many groups. Or there is the unchallenged appeal of those in power to remain loyal to our tradition. A healthy faith has room for questions and seeks to grow.

III. Good religion does not depend on the will or fortune of persons who hold positions of authority. There is but one Lord. The seeds of tragedy are planted where people surrender their wills to others and put their ultimate trust in other human beings, whether charlatans or saints.

IV. Good religion produces good deeds. Those who like to cross every "t" of doctrine or try to build a cozy refuge in a suffering world may lack the chief qualities by which the gospel says we are to be judged—our love for God's world and our courage to carry the cross.—James L. Merrell in *The Disciple*.

July 17. When Christians Greet Christians

Text: Col. 1:1–2 (rsv).

I. When we meet someone, what is the quality of our greeting? How much interest in the other person does our greeting reveal? Do we exhibit attractive qualities about ourselves?

II. When the apostle Paul wrote letters to his Christian friends, his first word to them set a tone of authority, great personal interest, and mutuality. We would do well to present ourselves to others in such a manner.

(a) Paul establishes his authority. He presents himself. He is an apostle sent out by the will of God to be God's ambassador to them.

(b) He establishes personal interest in

them by addressing them in a complimentary manner: "To the saints and faithful brethren."

(c) He couches the greeting in a spirit of mutuality. Paul, Timothy, and the Colossians are in the same work as a part of the brotherhood in Christ.

III. How do we establish personal relationships? Do we so adequately present ourselves, place interest in the other person, and establish a mutuality? The authority of Christ is respected when we speak on his behalf and make others feel important.—John C. Wakefield.

July 24. God Behind the Traditions
Text: Jude 24–25.
The writer of Jude knew that the traditions of the faith handed down to us, valuable as they are, by themselves are not sufficient. They give direction. They serve as a foundation on which to build. But the life of the traditions is the God to whom they witness.

I. "He is able." This affirms God's power. God's power is not for display or to be kept in reserve. It is constantly being spent—healing, sustaining, summoning, guiding, and keeping.

II. "To keep you." This attests to God's providence. The benediction sweeps a vacillating congregation—and all of us who waver—into the providence of a God who more than matches human effort with divine power.

III. "From falling." This reveals God's purpose. It is not to let us fall but to pull us out of our stumble. Up to this point our writer has spoken of our need to be faithful; now he speaks of God's power which keeps us faithful. Human effort is never sufficient.—Paul B. Brown.

July 31. Attitudes That Enrich
Scripture: Ps. 51:1–10.
There are three key attitudes which we can develop that will enrich our lives and make us more effective for God.

I. First is an attitude of acceptance toward ourselves. Psychologists tell us that this is essential for mental health.

II. Second is an attitude of understanding toward others. In Eph. 4:2, Paul said, "Accept life with humility and patience, generously making allowances for each other because you love each other" (Phillips).

III. Third is an attitude of assurance toward God. Believe that he loves us, believe that he watches over us, and believe that his power is ours for the asking.—Jewell Abdallah.

August 7. When Life Seems Dull
Text: John 10:10.
I. Obviously the psalmist was discouraged when he wrote these lines, but he did not despair. Instead he took positive steps to recover his happiness.

(a) He reprimanded his soul, questioning its right to be downcast. He did this in light of the previous help that God, out of the goodness of his providence, had offered him.

(b) He exhorted himself to hope in God rather than to remain disquieted or dissatisfied.

(c) He determined that he would praise God again in spite of his depression.

II. We can learn several things from the psalmist's example. (a) We need to take charge of ourselves rather than allow our feelings to have charge of us.

(b) We need to remember the care God gives for us, and let that recognition energize us with hope.

(c) We need to act on the hope that is ours, and praise God even if we don't feel like it.

III. John Drakeford, a Christian psychologist and author, says: "It is easier to act yourself into a new way of feeling, than to feel yourself into a new way of acting." When discouragement threatens your happiness, sing, shout, worship, and rejoice your way out of it.—Hoover Rupert.

August 14. Take Charge of Your Feelings
Text: Ps. 42:5.
I. What happens to dull our lives? (a) There are times and seasons when our life situation seems to offer little meaning.

(b) Life becomes dull and boring when, for whatever reasons, we avoid the risk and adventure of life.

(c) A third element enters into a life

which has been made dull in its drama of living—emptiness.

(d) The dull life has no attachment to anything outside the circle of self-interest.

II. Options for a dull life. (a) We can stay empty and live out our days of boredom in bitterness and pessimism.

(b) A second choice is to accept some substitute form of experience which promises the kind of meaning and purpose that we covet for our lives.

(1) Some seek escape through the narcosis of drugs.

(2) Some seek escape from boredom through activity.

(3) Some seek escape from boredom through amusement.

(c) We can live life solely on the physical sense level with things our only value and materialism our only gospel.

(d) We can resolve to move outward from self and find something to live for and fasten to, which brings meaning and purpose and zest into the realm of everyday living.

III. What Christ can do for us. (a) The Christian faith holds that it is Jesus Christ alone who can fill the emptiness of life.

(b) Christ can come into our lives and fill our dull days with holy purpose.

(c) When Christ comes into our lives, he gives us courage and insight to take risks without which life loses its luster.

(d) No life is dull and empty which has accepted the innate spiritual yearning which God has put into every human mind and heart.—David Michel.

August 21. Seeking Permanence

Text: Isa. 40:8.

I. Hans Küng says the aim of his book *On Being a Christian* is "an attempt, in the midst of an epoch-making upheaval of the church's doctrine, morality, and discipline, to discover what is permanent." To discover what is permanent in the swift passage of our lives needs to be our universal endeavor. Willa Cather in *Death Comes for the Archbishop* wrote of "the universal yearning for something permanent, enduring, without shadow of change."

II. At the lowest level this desire gave birth to "the permanent"—a hairset that lasts four to forty days. The boom in exercise and diet grows from the wish to pro-

long life and improve its physical quality. We seek permanence in life itself. We want life to last longer than breathing. Some seek it through deeds worthy of remembrance. Others try to perpetuate themselves in offspring or protege. What is permanent? Whitman was warm: "Nothing endures but personal qualities."

III. What is eternal lives over and above time. Ps. 46 knows the earth will be removed and the mountains be cast into the sea. Jesus adds, "Heaven and earth will pass away, but my word will not pass away" (Matt. 24–35). God makes an everlasting covenant with his people. His promises will endure. Eternal life means "to know the only true God" (John 17:3).—Turner N. Clinard.

August 28. On Being Judged

Text: Gal. 6:1.

I. If one does right and is judged to be right, he will be neither angry nor hurt. He may, if he is humble, be pleased—is it not right to be glad that right is done?—but he will not be proud.

II. If one who is proud does wrong and is judged to be wrong, he will be both angry and hurt.

III. If one who is proud does right and is judged to be wrong, he also will be both angry and hurt.

IV. If one who is truly humble does wrong and is judged to be wrong, he will not resent it but will in gratitude and humility, no matter what it costs him, heed the judgment and repent.

V. If one who is truly humble does right and is judged to be wrong, he will not give the judgment a second thought. It is his Father's glory that matters to him, not his own. He will "rejoice and be exceeding glad," knowing for one thing that a great reward will be his, and, for another, that he thus enters in a measure into the suffering of Christ—"when he suffered he made no threats of revenge. He simply committed his cause to the one who judges fairly."—Elisabeth Elliot in *Christian Herald*.

September 4. Mountains That Moved Mankind

Texts: Ps. 121:1; Matt. 17:20.

I. The Old Testament recounts several dramatic incidents which have contributed immensely to our understanding of God's purposes for human life.

(a) *Moses on Mt. Sinai.* On this rugged mountain Moses received the ten commandments which have served for many centuries as the basis of our relations with God and our fellowman. (See Exod. 19: 20.)

(b) *Abraham on Mt. Moriah.* On this mountain the pioneer Hebrew patriarch learned the price of absolute loyalty to God. (See Gen. 22:1–2.)

(c) *Elijah on Mt. Carmel.* On this mountain was demonstrated the truth that the sincere worship of God prohibits any sort of ambivalent compromise. (See I Kings 18:20–21.)

II. At critical points in the life of Jesus, he had experiences which were crucial in his life and instructive for ours.

(a) *Jesus tempted on mountain.* Temptation is the acid test of sincerity and fidelity in the faith for everyone, even for the Son of God. (See Matt. 4:1–9.)

(b) *Jesus taught on mountain.* The sermon on the mount was delivered by Jesus on a high elevation among the hills of Galilee. (See Matt. 5:1–2.)

(c) *Jesus struggled on mountain.* The inner serenity with which Jesus moved toward Calvary came only after a terrible wrestling with alternatives which confronted him. Under the brooding trees in the Garden of Gethesemane of the Mount of Olives, Jesus confronted the issues of life and death. (See Matt. 26:36–39.)

(d) *Jesus crucified on mountain.* On a cross-topped hill Christ accomplished our redemption and in forgiving love reconciled us to God. (See John 19:16–18.)—Emil Kontz.

September 11. The Master Teacher and How He Taught

Text: Matt. 22:16.

I. Jesus taught by word and deed, by illustration and parable, even by question. He prepared, he presented, and he concluded.

II. Jesus taught in such a way that even the unlearned understood, for his figures of speech made the truth plain.

III. Jesus was the most wonderful storyteller that ever lived on this earth. His parables were simple, full of action, and had a point.

IV. Jesus asked questions that made his listeners think until they found the truth.

V. Jesus always kept his teachings on the plane of his hearers' experience.

VI. Jesus always brought his lessons to a definite conclusion, and he usually was able to make those who listened reach the conclusion themselves.

VII. Jesus taught by what he did as well as by what he said.—Katherine Bevis in *Church of God Evangel.*

September 18. Christian Giving

Text: Matt. 5:42.

Giving means more than bestowing material gifts and money.

I. It means giving cheer, kindness, joy.

II. It means instilling hope and courage by patience and love.

III. It means bringing sunshine and sweetness into sad lives.

IV. It means cheerfulness and fortitude in adversity, gentle answers to harsh words, overcoming dislike, pride, and prejudice, and inspiring more by practice than by professing.

V. Cheerful giving is cheerful living and is not always easy for it means subduing all selfishness.—Edna Dessar Wells.

September 25. Called to Be Sons of God

Text: Gal. 4:7.

I. As sons of God we are called to claim our inheritance. (a) This is a claim we have to file ourselves. God has given us the possibility of being his sons and daughters and of inheriting his kingdom, but God will not force himself upon us. It is our task to file the claim. It is our task to open the door and let him into our lives.

(b) We have inherited the right to be sons of God if we respond to the knock of Christ upon the doors of our lives. God will not force this inheritance upon us. We have to claim it ourselves. To receive our full inheritance as heirs of the kingdom, we have to file our claim to be sons of God.

II. As sons of God we are called to live as servant people. (a) One of the unusual characteristics of Jesus Christ is that he was a servant. Matt. 20:28 has Christ say, "The Son of man came not to be served, but to serve." Christ lived by serving those he came in contact with. He served the lepers by healing them. He served the blind by helping them to see. He served the crippled by stretching out his hand and commanding them to walk. He served you and me by going to the cross of Calvary so that we might be able to live life to its fullest as sons of God.

(b) If we are to claim our inheritance as sons of God, we are called to live as a servant people. We are called to be servants that help the troubled. We are called to be servants that suffer with the suffering. We are called to show care and concern because we are the sons of God. We are called to be a people who know how to listen to the needs of others, a people who know how to give of themselves, and a people who know how to love because we are loved.—Robert L. Allen.

October 2. God Makes Me Laugh

TEXT: II Cor. 5:6.

I. We can laugh because God takes the burden off our shoulders.

II. We can laugh because of his mercy and grace.

III. We can laugh because we are accepted in spite of our complicity in the situation.

IV. We can laugh because there are alternatives we had not previously seen.

V. We can laugh because love wins the day.

VI. We can laugh because the world had us fooled but the world was wrong.

VII. We can laugh because our fears had fooled us, our hatreds had fooled us, and our anxieties had fooled us, but now the truth is out. The fears and anxieties and hatreds and guilts were all wrong.—William H. Creevy.

October 9. Two Kinds of Wisdom

TEXT: Rom. 12:2.

Conventional wisdom and the wisdom born of the Spirit seldom run in the same direction. One is of this world. The other is not of this world. Each sounds like foolishness to the other. When we try to blend them, we become hopelessly double-minded.

I. Conventional wisdom says we must be our own authority. Spiritual wisdom invites us to completely trust another authority.

II. Conventional wisdom says, "What's mine is mine!" Spiritual wisdom says, "What's mine is God's and thus it is ours!"

III. Conventional wisdom often leads to loneliness under the guise of self-actualization. Spiritual wisdom leads to community because it is rooted in the very opposite of loneliness and insularity.

IV. Conventional wisdom pursues power and personal advantage. Spiritual wisdom understands servanthood and sacrificial living.

V. Conventional wisdom can ignore the quivering suffering of others because it knows the issues are too complex for any real solution. Spiritual wisdom knows that in anyone else's suffering part of one's own self is diminished, and it must be addressed.

VI. Conventional wisdom suggests that sin and guilt are psychological relics. Spiritual wisdom knows the power of evil and our need for forgiveness and cleansing at the deepest level.

VII. Conventional wisdom offers the illusion that we can save ourselves. Spiritual wisdom knows our need for a Savior.—Bernard E. Johnson.

October 16. Guidelines for Confrontation

TEXT: II Cor. 13:11.

I. Confront caringly. Only after experiencing real care for the others, confront primarily to express real concern for another.

II. Confront gently. Do not offer more than the relationship can bear. Do not draw out more than you have put into the friendship.

III. Confront constructively. Take into consideration any possible interpretations of blaming, shaming, and punishing. These are the negative side effects of most confrontation unless one's intentions are clearly expressed in credible ways.

IV. Confront acceptantly. Respect the other's intentions as always good. For the average person, motives are inevitably mixed, and the conscious intention is invariably good when rightly understood. Little is to be gained in impugning motives or evaluating another's hopes, wishes, and goals.

V. Confront clearly. Report what is fact (observation), what is feeling (emotion), and what is hypothesis (conclusion). Sharpen your skills of differentiating between facts and their interpretations. Do not confuse them. Do not state an interpretation as though it were fact.—David Augsburger.

October 23. Sleeping at a Time Like This
TEXT: Jonah 1:6 (LB).

Jonah recognized the tensions building within him related to his work load and decided he needed to get away from it all and relax. So he took a cruise, rested, and slept. During a raging storm the captain of the ship went to Jonah and asked, "What do you mean sleeping at a time like this?" As the Lord's church we might do well to pay attention to the question a heathen captain asked God's relaxed prophet.

I. What do you mean sleeping when danger is imminent? The ship was about to sink, lives were about to be lost, and the only man on board who knew the Lord was asleep. Few people would argue with the fact that we are sailing rough seas today. The winds of economic, political, and moral crises blow around us. In the midst of such danger we ought to hear the sounds of our marching song: "Rise up, O men of God! Have done with lesser things."

II. What do you mean sleeping when there is something you can do? What could Jonah do? The pagan sailor told the prophet. Pray! Jonah could call on his God, asking for help and acknowledging his wrong. He could act. He could get to the place where God wanted him to be in the first place.

III. What do you mean sleeping when the consequences are so great? If Jonah were to keep on sleeping, thousands would not hear of God's love, God's people would not get to see miracles, and the glory of God would not be seen real.—Jim Futral.

October 30. Every Minute Has Meaning
TEXT: Ps. 27:14.

Every minute which you spend in the sanctuary should have meaning. The building, the music, the movement of the service, and the symbols can bring you into a closer and deeper relationship with God.

I. *Adoration.* Aware that we have gathered together to worship God, we begin with words and songs of praise through which we his people celebrate the majesty, glory, and eternal love of God.

II. *Confession.* Having been brought into the holy presence of God through symbols, song, and word, we are naturally moved to an examination of our inner selves and the need for confession.

III. *Illumination.* Inner examination leads us to draw upon the resources of the Christian faith and scripture, prayer, and the contemporary spoken word of the message.

IV. *Dedication.* In response to God's invitation, we dedicate ourselves to a life of Christian witness and service.—Donald L. Germain.

November 6. The Way of Peace (World Community Day)
TEXT: John 16:33.

I. The Creator of the universe is the God of peace who makes wars to cease to the end of the earth. He has called us to peace and intends the peace of God to prevail in all places of his dominion.

II. He who has derived all the inhabitants of earth from a common origin is the Lord of history, making himself known through the prophets sent to the nations, prospering nations that serve his purpose of good, and plucking up and destroying nations that reject his will.

III. Jesus, wonderful counselor and prince of peace, came to guide our feet into the way of peace. He preached peace to those who are far off and to those who are near. By the blood of his cross he created one new humanity.

IV. The Spirit of God is the spirit of inquiry and understanding, leading us to seek for knowledge of other lands and cultures that we may break down every dividing wall of hostility.

V. Peace is God's gift to those of good will who provide forgiveness for the enemy, haven for the refugees, liberation for the oppressed, food for the hungry, and a just society with fair shares for all.

V. The church is appointed to bring good tidings to the nations. Peace and salvation are inseparable. Those who bear the name of Christ are bound to pursue what makes for peace and for mutual upbuilding and so to gather the harvest of righteousness sown by those who make peace.—J. Carter Swaim.

November 13. Levels of Giving (Stewardship Day)

Text: Mark 12:41–44.

I. *The Lord's interest in giving.* As the Master watched those who cast their money into the bronze chests, his interest was not so much what people gave but how they gave.

II. *The Lord's interpretation of giving.* The Master's interpretation of giving was from the standpoint of heaven's evaluation. As God sees it, the moral attitude is more important than the material amount (II Cor. 9:8).

III. *The Lord's incentive to giving.* As the omniscient One, Jesus not only sees all we give but also rewards when we give in the right spirit (Heb. 6:10). The Savior's commendation of this woman not only reached the ears of the twelve disciples but has also influenced an innumerable company of God's people throughout 2,000 years.—Stephen F. Olford.

November 20. The Psalmist's Thanksgiving (Thanksgiving Sunday)

Scripture: Ps. 103:1–5.

Thanksgiving is an expression of an emotion, a feeling from within. The psalmist knew this for he said, "Bless the Lord, O my soul; and all that is within me, bless his holy name." Almost indescribable are the feelings we experience when we realize how great is God's love to us. Like the psalmist, we want to praise God when we remember what he has done for us.

I. Thanksgiving is counting your blessings. (a) In Ps. 103 five great blessings are mentioned: who forgiveth, healeth, redeemeth, crowneth, and satisfieth.

(b) What else could one wish for in this life? Within those five words are adequate blessings to meet every need in one's life.

Count your blessings and you will want to praise God also.

II. Thanksgiving is dedication. The author of Ps. 103 was one who could not only praise God verbally but also could translate verbal praise into daily living. Isn't the way one lives the real expression of his praise and thanksgiving?—Robert J. Sanderson.

November 27. Living Hopefully (Advent)

Text: Rom. 15:14 (neb).

I. Hope encourages us to see beyond the obvious—to see a deeper reality. Hope does not gloss over disappointments but inspires us to rise above them. Spurgeon said, "Faith goes up the stairs that love has made and looks out of the windows which hope has opened."

II. Hope encourages us to see beyond the present. We need such hope, for there is really no today without a tomorrow. A man writing about his concentration camp experiences said that the prisoner who lost faith in the future—his future—was doomed. Without faith in the future he lost his interest in life and declined mentally and physically. Health requires hope —a faith in a tomorrow.

III. Hope encourages us to see beyond ourselves. We must see God. Human vision is blurred; human strength is limited. Seeing God, we interpret the full range of life through his love and power. "Be of good courage, and he shall strengthen your heart, all ye that hope in the Lord" (Ps. 31:24).—Bramwell Tripp.

December 4. John Prepares the Way (Advent)

Scripture: Matt. 3:1–12.

Matthew presented John the Baptist in his role of forerunner and herald of Christ, who boldly announced the presence of the king and the nearness of the kingdom of heaven. Concerning this remarkable preacher, who had such an effective ministry, three things are noteworthy.

I. *His preparation.* In addition to the instruction which John the Baptist received in the godly home in which he was born and reared, he studied the Old Testament. Then he went into the wilderness where he lived an ascetic life and underwent a discipline which fitted him for the task which he was to perform. God prepared John in the wilderness, far from politically decadent Rome and spiritually dead Jerusalem.

II. *His preaching.* This striking preacher was heavily burdened on account of the prevailing wickedness of the people. His preaching attracted the multitudes, so he fearlessly denounced sin and rebuked sinners. He challenged his hearers to change their minds with respect to sin, God, and self.

III. *His prediction.* The preaching of John the Baptist kindled afresh the messianic hope in many. It is not strange some began to wonder if the preacher himself were not the long-expected messiah. As soon as he learned what they were thinking, with characteristic humility he at once disabused their minds of that idea by asserting he was only the "voice of one crying in the wilderness."—H. C. Chiles.

December 11. He Shall Be Called Wonderful (Advent)

TEXT: Isa. 9:6.

I. He is wonderful in his conception. "That which is conceived in her is of the Holy Ghost" (Matt. 1:20).

II. He is wonderful in his development. "And Jesus increased in wisdom and in stature and in favor with God and man" (Luke 1:52).

III. He is wonderful in his self-consciousness. "I am the way, the truth, and the life" (John 14:6).

IV. He is wonderful in his self-restraint. There are many things he could have done that he did not do.

V. Wonderful was he in his mastery over the forces of nature. The winds and the waves obeyed his voice.

VI. Wonderful was our Lord in his doings. He remains the only man who could say at the close of his life, "Father, I have finished the work thou gavest me to do."

VII. He was wonderful in his blessings and influence and homage in the places he occupies.

VIII. He was wonderful not only in his teaching but in the finality of his teachings. He is the only teacher we know who makes no provisions for amendments to or abandonment of anything he says. "The grass withers, the flower fades, but the Word of God abideth forever."

IX. Last of all, wonder of wonders to me, is not that Christ was and is all that we claim for him but that this wonderful Christ is my personal Savior.—Tom Madden.

December 18. Anticipating Christ's Coming (Advent)

SCRIPTURE: Luke 21:25–28, 34–36.

The image of Jesus coming as an infant on Christmas morning with angels and shepherds and the wise men needs to be integrally tied up with the reality of the second coming. Jesus has come once a couple of thousand years ago, but now we must join that with the fact that he's coming again, and we should be excited that he is coming in our time.

I. The reality of the second coming should be strongly reawakened in our anticipation of Christmas.

(a) It's much easier to live in anticipation of one's death. This is healthy. But in many ways the anticipation of Jesus' second coming is more important. We are called as Christians to have a deep relationship with Jesus. Our own death can be a strong incentive for this. But our life in Jesus also calls for a more global vision. The world we live in is to be renewed and transformed. This is the goal of our actions as we wait for Jesus' second coming.

(b) Living the reality of Christmas in the context of the second coming is difficult. It takes a great deal of hope and faith. We are continually going upstream. The world is continually asking: "Since Jesus came in Bethlehem 2,000 years ago, has there been any real progress toward the coming of the kingdom that you are looking for? How do you account for so many evils and crimes?"

II. When Christmas is tied to the second coming as the gospel directs us, we can see the light at the end of the tunnel.

(a) We believe that the power of the Lord is greater than the discouragement of men's sins. In faith we believe that the Lord is radically changing the world and his coming will cap-off that coming. With the end in sight we can expend ourselves. With the expectant hope and faith in Jesus we believe a new world will emerge. We are called to work hard to be channels of the Lord.

(b) Our foolishness is similar to marathon runners. The whole course is twenty-six miles. They will run twenty-five and three-fourths miles in pain and thirst and anguish, and then when they come in for the home stretch, entering the stadium to the cheers of the crowd, they will start a kick and sprint for the last quarter mile like they didn't have any better sense. We must be like those racers. We can love and be patient and use energy we never thought we had as long as we know that the end is near.—Michael Manning in *Pastoral Life.*

December 25. Everybody's Baby

Text: Luke 2:11–12.

The coming to earth of the Son of God, like other mysteries of the Christian faith, involves both creation and what is beyond creation, both what is part of our earthly order of things and what is transcendent.

I. The birth of a child is naturally a happy event. In all its helplessness and ignorance, an infant is an object of wonder. To its mother it is the most beautiful baby in the world. The expression of its eyes and mouth and the movements of its little fingers and toes are all a delight to parents, to brothers and sisters, to relatives and close friends.

(a) Proud parents are the first to admit that the wonder of their child is more than they can claim credit for. We are made vividly aware that the value of the new life far transcends the small physical package in which it is embodied.

(b) All of this is no less true of the birth of Jesus Christ. We learn to love our Lord not first because of lofty theological concepts but because he came among us and lived and died as one of us, and this began with his incarnation, birth, and infancy.

(c) Most of us have loved babies in our own families or babies we have had close contact with, but everyone all over the world can love the Christ child. He came in a unique way to be everybody's baby, the newborn child for the entire human family.

II. What is the entire human family? How did we come to get such an idea?

(a) In large measure it is a Christian idea, coming out of the Judeo-Christian belief in one God who is the Creator of us all. The idea of a universal human family has gained poignancy and force from the faith that Jesus Christ came to be a brother to all other human beings.

(b) Jesus said and did many wonderful things. Yet the hearts of men, women, and children everywhere seem to be most stirred by the recollection of his humble birth and of his painful death, the two events prior to the resurrection singled out by the creeds. Jesus in the arms of his mother and Jesus stretching out his arms on the cross convey, as nothing else does, the message of Christianity.

(c) Babies are loved within families. Yet in another sense, it is babies who create families, who bring together men and women in communities of love, of caring, and of sacrifice. In this sense the infancy of Jesus Christ is at the heart of the gospel. In his blessed kingdom will be the very biggest family of all.—H. Boone Porter in *The Living Church.*

SECTION III. *Resources for Communion Services*

SERMON SUGGESTIONS

Topic: The Bread Christ Offers

Text: Matt. 4:3.

I. Jesus was not the first young man tempted to seek a shortcut to the good things of life. What is wrong with that ambition? Everyone must have bread. Perhaps it is wrong to expect it without the price of constructive effort. Maybe in fairness we should trade a part of our energy to match that of the worker who produced the bread. To feed without personal cost is to be a parasite.

II. If Jesus possessed the power to change stones into bread, he would have been accepting a shortcut to the good things of life not open to everyone. His power would have placed him above or beneath the necessity of struggle. No man can be a savior of others who does not share in their struggle. How could the father of starving children pray in the name of one who felt neither the pain of hunger nor the weariness of toil?

III. Jesus did give humanity the bread by which life was possible. It was the bread of his own broken body. He would not feed the world through any miracle except that of sacrifice. He knew that men must live; he knew that bread alone could not sustain all of life.—Roy L. Minich.

Topic: The New Covenant

Text: I Cor. 11:25.

In this, his darkest hour, when to the human eye his mission was about to end in utter failure, he ate his last meal with his disciples. During the course of the meal, as Mark tells the story, he took bread, broke it, and gave it to them, and said, " 'Take; this is my body.' And he took a cup, and when he had given thanks he gave it to them, and they all drank of it. And he said to them, 'This is my blood of the covenant, which is poured out for many.' " In the *RSV* margin and in Paul's account it is the new covenant, referring, it would seem, to the new covenant predicted by Jeremiah. What did Jesus mean to signify by these simple words and this simple transaction? Taking the account in the three synoptic gospels along with the earliest account preserved by Paul (I Cor. 11:23–26), there seem to have been at least six basic ideas.

I. *Commemoration.* "This do in remembrance of me." True, this injunction does not occur in the synoptic accounts, but in Paul's account, which is the oldest of all, it is repeated three times (I Cor. 11:24–25). "In remembrance of me"—not his death alone as an isolated event but to a life lived in perfect obedience to God's will and carried out to the bitter end (Heb. 10:1–10).

II. *Confession and remission of sins.* "For this is my blood of the covenant, which is poured out for many for the forgiveness of sin." Those of us who drink of the cup are imperfect men and women, flawed, falling short of our obligations, even as were those first disciples. None of us can center our thoughts on Jesus, his life and his death, without realizing that and seeking and finding forgiveness.

III. *Commitment, consecration.* The cup "is my blood of the covenant." It is in the sacrament we recommit our lives and renew our vows of obedience to carry on Jesus' mission. That mission, as is already seen in Jesus' own statement of his mission in Luke 4:16–21, and its elements, have been identified as proclamation, compassion, justice, reconciliation, partnership, and education.

IV. *Communion with Jesus and with one another* (I Cor. 10:16–17). From a communion with Jesus we draw our strength; in fellowship with our fellow members we double our strength.

V. *Celebration.* Eat, drink "until he comes" (I Cor. 11:26). "Until that day, when I drink it new in the Kingdom of God." In the sacrament we are intended to look not only backward in remembrance and not only to present covenant renewal but also forward to the future, to the glorious consummation of the Christian hope when with others whom we have loved long since and lost a while we shall eat and drink anew in the presence of our Lord.

VI. *Proclamation.* "As often as you eat this bread and drink this cup, you proclaim the Lord's death." The observance is public, and in the sacrament we witness for all to see what God has done for us and to whom we now again commit our hearts and lives.—Ernest Trice Thompson.

Topic: Seeing the Invisible

Text: Heb. 11:1–3 (neb).

Paul, writing to the people of Colossi, said, "Jesus is the image of the invisible God." The invisible God—the God whom no man has seen at any time—became visible for those who looked to Jesus as "the author and finisher of our faith."

I. Holy Communion is an opportunity for the followers of Jesus to relate themselves to this visible manifestation of the invisible God who is the ground of all our being.

II. We celebrate the fact that in Jesus the invisible nature of God, which is love, forgiveness, mercy, and compassion, became visible enough for everyone to really see what God is like.

III. The gospel of John heralds the conviction that at a given point in time the invisible God became a human being and lived among us that we might learn what God is like, hear what he wants us to know, and do among people what God wants done to help him redeem us all.

IV. This human manifestation of God in the person of Christ told people like ourselves that we could experience his quality of life now and throughout eternity only as we took up our crosses and followed him and only as we became living extensions of his life, teaching, and ministry. In the service of Holy Communion, when we consider most reverently this great invisible reality, we are invited to make fresh commitment to this divine calling to be instruments of God.—Homer J. R. Elford.

Topic: In Memoriam

Text: Luke 22:19.

I. How tremendously symbolical was the ritual of that ancient Jewish festival of the Passover.

(a) There was the piece of parsley or lettuce that was dipped in the bowl of salt water and eaten. Parsley represented the hyssop with which the lintel had been smeared in Egypt. The salt water stood for the tears of Egypt and for the waters of the Red Sea.

(b) There was a collection of bitter herbs to remind them of the bitterness of slavery in Egypt.

(c) There was the paste called charosheth to remind them of the clay from which bricks had been made in Egypt and sticks of cinnamon to remind them of the straw with which bricks had been made.

(d) There was, of course, the Passover lamb, which provided the blood, by which sign they had been saved from the angel of death.

II. And there was bread. On the table were three circles of unleavened bread. At one point in the feast, the bread was broken and a little of it was eaten. The bread reminded the Jews of the bread of affliction which they had eaten in Egypt. It was broken to remind them that slaves never had a whole loaf but only broken crusts to eat.

(a) Jesus took the bread of affliction, and, when he had given thanks, he broke it and gave it to them. The bread of affliction became the bread of redemption; the bread of oppression became the bread of salvation.

(b) "Whoever is hungry, let him come and eat." As we eat, we become douloi—bond slaves—not of Egypt but of Christ.

III. And there was wine—four cups of it. At different stages of the Passover feast these cups were drunk. They were to remind the Jews of the four promises in Exod. 6:6–7.

(a) Jesus took the cup. The promises had been fulfilled; they had come true. The blood of lambs had become the blood of the Lamb of God; the life of the vine had become the life of the true vine.

(b) The old covenant, entirely dependent on law, had become a new covenant, solely dependent on love.—David Irvine.

Meditation: Pilgrims of the Road
Text: Matt. 7:13–14.

We are pilgrims. That is common knowledge. In our pilgrimage we have a fellow traveler and companion along the way. That makes the big difference. Our traveling companion said, "I am the way." He encourages us to choose the hard road that leads to life. He himself chose that road. It led him to Jerusalem where his enemies mocked him and crucified him and buried him in a grave. But on Easter evening this same Jesus, whom God raised from the dead, met two lonely and discouraged pilgrims on the dusty road that went from Jerusalem to Emmaus. They welcomed him though they did not know him, and at their journey's end they invited him into their house where they broke bread together. It was then that they recognized him in the breaking of bread. After he left, they said to each other, "Did not our hearts burn within us as we talked with him on the way?"

In like manner we too come to break bread together at the communion table. May we recognize his presence, and may our hearts burn within us as we once again know him as "the way, the truth, and the life."

If we can do this, he will lead us away from the easy road where life has no more meaning than idle and fleeting pleasure. He will lead us away from what Thackeray called "the downhill journey." "As we go on the downhill journey," said Thackeray, "the milestones are gravestones, and on each more and more names are written."

We have a choice to make. The choice is which road we will travel. If we choose the low road, the easy road, then life becomes what Shakespeare called "a tale told by an idiot, full of sound and fury, signifying nothing." If we choose the high road, the hard road, we have the assurance of the risen Lord, "Lo, I am with you always, even to the end of the age."

Then at the end of the road we shall experience what Shakespeare also said, "Journeys end in lovers meeting." And that is a great thing. For we are all called lovers of God and lovers of our fellowmen, and that sometimes is a hard road. But finally we come to the end of the road. There we shall find our rest from the journey that was hard and difficult.—Harold W. Kaser.

INVITATIONS TO COMMUNION

The Lord's Supper summons us to look away from the dreary frustrations of wrecked vows and broken dreams and to a cross towering o'er the wrecks of time, to a love that has borne our own sins in its body on the tree, and to the living Lord who still comes back to his friends on the first day of the week and communes with them and is known in the breaking of bread. It is on Jesus, crucified and risen, that all our thoughts this day are focused. Beyond our futile striving shines his sufficiency and beyond our perplexities his peace. Come aside with us, and look away from self to the Savior.

When Jesus was on earth, he did not ask those who came to him, "Are you worthy to come?" He was glad that they came, and with his whole heart he wanted to help them. In the Lord's Supper is the representation of Christ in all the graciousness of his person. Such as went to him then can come to him now. For all who come humbly and sincerely, seeking help and light and guidance, there is the same loving welcome as Jesus Christ gave when he was on earth.

One aspect of the celebration of the Lord's Supper is looking back to "the night in which he was betrayed." On that night as Jesus instituted the Supper he gave the command, "This do in remembrance [as a memorial] to me" (I Cor. 11: 24). That statement is often misunderstood. Here we must never forget the biblical conception of memory. "To remember something in Hebrew fashion is not merely to entertain a pale and static idea of it; it is to make the past event present again and therefore to remember Christ and his death at the Supper is to make the living Lord present again in the power of his accepted sacrifice" (A. M. Hunter). The risen Lord is present with his people in keeping of the Supper.

Shortly after suffering a stroke, Reinhold Niebuhr said he would rather receive the gospel of God's eternal love through the Eucharist than hear some theologian or preacher theorize about it. There is, said he, a directness and a reality in the sacramental symbols of the Word that our own spoken words do not have. The sacraments are, so to speak, the enacted gospel when these symbols are received in faith and when the judgment and love of Christ are received through them in real inner repentance and trust, Christ is really present to us and present in the most direct and real manner possible. He is the Word of God's judgment on our sins and of God's mercy and love that will accept us. In the Eucharist Christ is made very real to us.

This is the Lord's Table. The marks of his ownership are upon it. The emblems of broken body and shed blood tell us once again it is his table. It is an old table. For more than nineteen hundred years it has been in existence. Time has not weakened it nor destroyed it. It remains. It is a long table. Today it reaches around the world. Men of all nations and races are seated about it as his guests. Here Jesus sits at the table in the midst of his people. It is a family table. Those at his table are members of his family. At his table the floor is level. He loves us all.

When the Lord's Supper is kept, it is very important that we understand what we are doing. A leading theologian says we are living in an age of the church in which we are threatened with "the death of the sacraments." Even if the sacraments are observed as often as ever, it may still be true "that they are becoming stranger and stranger and less and less meaningful to those who share in them." In the Bible the sacraments are built into the very structure of the church. So much so that the same theologian states that disappearance of the sacraments would mean the dissolution of the church. For many the sacraments have become mere ritual rather than reality. If the church is to be true to itself in our day we must come to understand what we do when we keep the Lord's Supper.

The Lord's Supper is often spoken of as a sacrament. It is not a word that is found in the Bible; it was taken by the church from the military life of Rome. The oath taken by a Roman soldier when he was inducted into the army was called a *sacramentum*—a sacred oath. The Roman soldier took an oath that he would be loyal to the emperor and serve the empire with his life. When we are baptized, we take an oath of allegiance to Jesus as Lord. When we worship at the Lord's table, we renew that oath of allegiance to Jesus as Lord and pledge ourselves to be good soldiers of the Lord Jesus Christ. Take seriously your pledge this day.

The Lord's Supper is the central act of Christian worship. Wherever the church takes root, there its life is quickened, nourished, and manifested in the celebration of the Lord's Supper. It is central in worship because it gathers up, expresses, and makes effective the whole meaning of the spiritual life. It proclaims the Christian gospel. In it God comes to us with his forgiveness and his strength. One by one as we partake we respond to him with gratitude and awe. "It is the richest, the most appealing, the most mysterious, the tenderest of all. It gathers into its fathomless depths the unsearchable riches of Christ." So may it be to you today.

What we celebrate at the Lord's table is not our worthiness but the worthiness of Jesus Christ. He welcomes all who come constrained by love and seeking to make their lives more worthy of him. The unworthiness that should forbid our coming to the table consists in having wrong motives. If we do not think what we are doing, if we have no intention of carrying out the promise we give, if we attend only to keep our name on the church roll, if we come for respectability's sake, and if we are consciously living in sin, it is clear we have no right to come. To all who want to be better than they are, Christ says "Come."

Is there any danger that you and I are not worthy to partake of the Lord's Supper? Often people refuse to participate because they think they are not good enough. We come because we are not good enough and want to be better. If you have sinned, ask for forgiveness. If you are perplexed, seek God's guidance. If you are in sorrow, accept God's peace and comfort. Only if you are insincere, have no appreciation of the cost of God's love, no reverence for the meaning of the Lord's Supper, and no intention of pleasing God, do you partake unworthily. "Let a man examine himself, and so eat of the bread and drink of the cup?"—Myron J. Taylor.

ILLUSTRATIONS

BREAD FROM HOME.   During the Spanish Civil War a severely wounded soldier was taken to the field hospital. There was a good chance for his recovery, except that he would not eat. The nurses and nuns tried everything, but he refused all food. One of his buddies realized that his pal was homesick, so he offered to go to the wounded man's home and bring his father. He reached his friend's home and explained the situation. His father got ready to go while his mother wrapped up a loaf of bread for her son. The patient was happy to see his father, but he still would not eat until his father said, "Son,

here is some bread your mother baked." The boy brightened: "Oh, bread made by my mother. Give me some." He was soon on the road to recovery.

You and I are in that story. We have been wounded in the battle of life by sin, by forgetfulness of God, and by the troubles and trials and pains of everyday life. We lose our taste for food that will strengthen our souls. Then we hear Jesus say: "My Father gives you the real heavenly bread. God's bread comes down from heaven and gives life to the world." Just as the father in our story said to his son, "Here is some bread your mother made," so Christ says to you, "Here is some Bread your heavenly Father made."—Arthur Tonne.

DIVINE IMPRINT.   We can create neither bread nor wine. Both begin with nature's gifts, but without our labor the wheat remains grain, the juice of the grape is captive and dead. Bread and wine come to birth when we lay aside our work in the dark and silent places where dough rises and wine comes into being. With our help but through power which we do not create, the grain and the fruit become bread and wine. No longer only earthy, they are signs of earth in human hands.

But those creative hands are themselves heirs of the image of the creative God, who is the author of all things. We, bearing the image of earth, grasp and grapple with it so that the imprint of the divine is united with it. For the eyes of faith, every loaf of bread, every glass of wine is a sign of the mystery we bear in ourselves, earthy and yet formed in God's likeness. We might well see ourselves in each loaf, each cup.—John L. Kater, Jr. in *The Living Church.*

BIRTHDAY PARTY.   A young father decided to allow his three-year-old son to go with him to Communion one Sunday. On the way home from church, he asked his little boy if he understood what they were doing at Communion. "Yes," the little boy replied, "we were having a birthday party."

In a three-year-old life the most supreme joy, the most exciting happening, the most important sign of love, generosity, and friendship is a birthday party. While Holy Communion means much more than a birthday party, at least the little boy was on the right track toward a growing understanding of the Lord's Supper.—William H. Willimon.

ONE BREAD.   For what is the bread? The body of Christ. What do they become who partake of it? The body of Christ—not many bodies but one body. Many grains are made into one bread so that the grains appear no more at all, though they are still there. In their joined state their diversity is no longer discernible. In the same way we are also bound up with one another and with Christ. You are not nourished from one body and the next man from a different body but all from one and the same body. For this reason Paul adds, "We have all partaken of one bread. If of one and the same bread, then we are all become the same thing."—John Chrysostom.

SECTION IV. *Resources for Funeral Services*

SERMON SUGGESTIONS

Topic: Help for the Brokenhearted
Text: Isa. 61:1.

I. Nothing is more characteristic of the human condition than the potential for a broken heart. In matters of the heart survival is at stake. The mind will grasp at any straw to avoid the inevitable pain of a broken heart, but when the conditions align, the facts accumulate, and the realization comes, shock sets in and the mind is numbed so that a broken heart throbs for comfort that does not exist. Destitute and forlorn are the brokenhearted, for once they had hopes and dreams but now only frustration and despair.

II. Perhaps the deepest validity of the religion of the Bible is that it speaks to the poor in spirit, the downtrodden, and the brokenhearted from a position of total empathy and identification. Who among the company of the brokenhearted does not recognize their peers in the predecessors and person of Jesus?

(a) Jesus walked the way of the brokenhearted. Rejected, abandoned, betrayed, and denied, it is Jesus' broken heart that cries from the cross, "My God, My God, why have you forsaken me?" He had plowed the depths of despair and in a moment of lucid hopelessness gave up his spirit.

(b) This life had broken all its promises of fulfilment. His youth, virility, charisma, wisdom, and insight measured nothing against his failure and broken heart. The apostle Paul speaks of being "so utterly unbearably crushed that we despaired of life itself." But that is not the final word. For as does the first word, so does the last word ever belong to God.

III. Words like resurrection or transformation are not merely words of consolation when spoken by God to our situation, but they are also lifelines to a new mode of existence beyond the helplessness and futility of despair and brokenheartedness. In the pit of despair it is difficult to seize the lifeline that is our hope, but we must, for it is our only way out.

(a) Then we can see the God who "calls into existence that which does not exist."

(b) Then we can see the God who raised Jesus from the dead.

(c) Then we will be able to say with the apostle Paul, "We felt that we had received the sentence of death; but that was to make us rely not on ourselves but on God who raises the dead."

(d) Then we will be able to say "Amen" to the resurrection mode of existence for that truly is the last word.—Randal Lee Cummings.

Topic: Be of Good Cheer
Text: John 16:33.

I. We can be cheerful in an hour of tribulation because Jesus overcame death on the cross and by his glorious resurrection. He stormed the citadel of death and opened the gates of eternal life for all believers. He turned the sunset of life into a sunrise, death into life, and sorrow into joy. This means that because he lives we live too.

II. We can be cheerful at a Christian funeral because of the condition of the dead in Christ.

(a) If the deceased has life, what kind of

life is it? Is it worth living? Is it more than the mere existence we sometimes have on earth? Jesus said, "I go to prepare a place for you that where I am there you may be also."

(b) What is heaven? It is being with Jesus. And what is it like to be with Jesus? From the scriptures we have learned that where Jesus is there is light, love, peace, and joy. Isn't that the real life? In heaven there is no night, for Christ is the ever-burning light. There is no hunger, for Christ is the bread of life. There is no sorrow, for God himself wipes away all tears from the saint's eyes.

(c) In heaven with Christ there is the fullness of life. Knowing this we can be happy for those who die in Christ. They have peace. They are happy. They are contented and have security and stability in God's love. At a funeral we may feel sorry for ourselves, but we can be happy for the deceased.

III. We can be cheerful at a Christian funeral because we know that it is only a temporary separation.

(a) Jesus said, "In a little while you shall not see me and in a little while you shall see me." That is what we can say to our loved ones who have died in Christ. When death comes we no longer see them, but in a little while we shall see them. Heaven is a communion of saints; it is the church triumphant. There is a fellowship in which we shall be known to each other and we will have fellowship with each other.

(b) Can't you imagine the scene of the reunion? On the other shore there will be a great mass of friends and family to meet you when you arrive. They will shout their welcome and they will hug and kiss you without limits. And it will be a reunion that will never have an end.

IV. In an hour like this we have mixed emotions. When we think of the tribulation of death, we are sorrowful and our eyes fill with tears because of our loss. When we think of the good news of our text that Jesus overcame the world of death for us, we want to rejoice. How can we put these two together? We have the tears, and they are normal and natural at a time like this. We have the joyous good news of eternal life. Why not put the two

together and smile through our tears?—John R. Brokhoff.

Meditation: Someone Came Back
TEXT: John 11:43.

In the fifteenth century rumors were circulating throughout Europe about an expanding world. In Spain, Portugal, and Italy there were tales of strange lands beyond the "Ocean Sea," by which they meant the vast waters beyond the Straits of Gibraltar. Two Venetians, Niccolo and Antonio Zeno, had made a successful voyage to the Faroes Islands far to the north. There they had heard of even stranger journeys by Norse mariners—tales of the mythical Estitoland and of sailors who boasted they had actually sailed to places called Iceland and Greenland and even farther west to a shore they simply named Newfoundland.

Most people in those years believed the earth was round, but still there was a lingering uncertainty. What if the scholars were wrong? And many old-timers, while they accepted the theory of a globe, believed that the Atlantic sloped west. If anyone ventured too far in that direction, it would be impossible to sail back home—uphill.

Christopher Columbus from Genoa and Martin Pinzon from Palos in Andalusia were determined to make such a voyage. Columbus talked with a mariner in Madeira who claimed he had been blown across the Atlantic in a fierce gale to lands inhabited by strange peoples. Then, after skirting that unknown coast, he had beaten his way back east. Columbus believed the story. And we know the result. Toward the close of the fifteenth century America was opened to the Europeans.

Someone had come back with first-hand information.

This is a parable of immortality. Through the centuries rumors, yearnings, instinct, and now and again a flash of divine revelation had opened men's hearts to the possibility of life after death.

At the Bethany home Jesus' close friend Lazarus had died. Our Lord spoke words of comfort to the family, especially to Martha. He said, "Your brother shall rise again." She replied in that same nebulous way so common among the people of her day: "I know that he will rise again in the resurrection at the last day."

Then Jesus made a declaration that brooked no compromise or concession: "I am the resurrection and the life! He who believes in me, though he die, yet shall he live. And whoever lives and believes in me shall never die."

There was no backing down from that lofty and positive statement. He went to Lazarus' grave, he prayed, and he commanded, "Take away the stone!" There was the expected objection. His friend had been dead for four days, and it was a hot country. Embalming as we know it was not practiced. "Take away the stone!" Then the divine fiat: "Lazarus, come forth!" And he who had been dead came out alive. Someone had come back.—Charles A. Platt.

Topic: Born to Eternal Life

TEXT: John 17:3.

I. Dying to the world, and being born into Christ.

II. Dying to self with its selfish self-centeredness, and being born to the unselfishness we find in Christ.

III. Dying to a life without meaning and purpose, and being born through Christ into a life of significance and purpose.

IV. Dying to the fear of death with its darkness and doom, and being born to the assurance that our life is eternal, today, tomorrow, and forever.

V. Dying to ignorance and superstition and fear, and being born to confident trust and the life-changing faith that our God gives life eternal.

VI. Dying to the pessimistic gloom of life with no tomorrow, and being born to the positive optimism of Christian hope which has faith in the future because it has faith in the God revealed in Jesus Christ. —Hoover Rupert.

Topic: His Cup and Ours

SCRIPTURE: Mark 14:32–42.

I. J. B. Phillips captures the Gethsemane drama in this paraphrase: "Jesus began to be horror-stricken and desperately depressed. 'My heart is breaking with a death-like grief,' he told them."

(a) Who thinks of Jesus as horror-stricken and desperately depressed? Yet how does anyone feel in the face of unexplained death? We have pictured Jesus as a passive vehicle through which God worked. In so doing we miss the greatest thing he ever did.

(b) Jesus was not above temptation. He had faced the tempter for forty days in the desert. He had overcome the temptation to perform miracles to show his power. But now he was facing the temptation to be something less than God intended for him to be.

(c) In the garden Jesus is almost dead with distress. Sorrow was so intense that death would seem to offer relief. Jesus was living through the greatest possible degree of infinite horror and suffering.

(1) He prays to God to escape the indescribably heavy trial ahead, his cup of trouble. But he is resolved at all costs to accept and do God's will, not his own.

(2) He prays to the Father that he might not die. "Take away this cup from me. Yet I want your will, not mine." His death made no sense. It was irrational, his mission was unfulfilled, and his disciples were asleep. Is it any wonder his heart was breaking?

II. God let it all happen, consenting to the path which led directly into suffering and not around it.

(a) God himself consented to endure genuine inner grief in the garden that night. It pained God to see Jesus suffer, but in that suffering Jesus entered more fully into the human situation than he ever had. Because he suffered, Jesus became brother and friend as well as savior and lord. Jesus plunged into the muck and mire of the human situation.

(b) God consents to our suffering too. It is our cross. He doesn't cause it, he may seem to turn his back on it, and we may seem forsaken. But it is the price of Jesus-like discipleship. Ultimately we must face it head on. When we do, we too fight for life. We pray in the imperative mood Jesus did, "Remove this cup from me." We expect it to happen but are ultimately willing for God to work his way.

III. When Jesus returned to the disciples the third time, his attitude was different. He was composed, and his soul was at ease.

(a) The great decision had been made. Jesus would offer his death as a part of his life to God. That was his comfort and his strength for the days ahead. Jesus would be liberated from the body to the realm of perfection with God. There would be no more questions of God. The events would unwind toward Calvary.

(b) When God denied Jesus' request for the cup to be removed, he gave him the strength to take it. He will do the same for us. That's when suffering becomes redemptive, when questions of existence and purpose and meaning are answered, when God will reveal his face to us, and when we stand with Jesus and say, "If possible, remove this cup of pain from my lips, nevertheless, not what I want, but what you will."—Michael C. Blackwell.

Topic: Death in Christian Perspective

Text: I Cor. 15:53.

I. Early Old Testament thought viewed death as the normal end to life.

(a) Human life at full maturity was plucked like a ripe stalk at harvest time. (See Job 5:26.) Death was spoken of as being gathered to one's people and as going the way of all earthly creatures. (See Gen. 15:15; 28:20–21; Job 30:23.) In some Old Testament passages little hope seems to have been attached to an afterlife. One person, pleading with David to be reconciled to his estranged son, proclaimed, "We all must die, we are like water spilt on the ground, which cannot be gathered up again" (II Sam. 14:14). The grave (Sheol) was a region where praise of God was impossible and the person lived a shadowed, undefined existence. Even the recollection of God was annihilated. (See Ps. 6:5; 28:1.)

(b) With the passing of the centuries, views of death changed. In Amos and in Psalms the power of Yahweh is extended to the grave. (See Amos 9:2; Ps. 139:7–10.) In Jeremiah, sleep that had been thought of as eternal was no longer so. In Daniel hope in a resurrection was expressed (12:2). In Isaiah there is even a reference to the disappearance of death: "He will swallow up death for ever, and the Lord God will wipe away tears from all faces, and the reproach of his people he will take away from all the earth; for the Lord has spoken" (25:8).

(c) In Old Testament thought there was a developing hope in a future life, but it was an undefined hope and not an understanding. Understanding had to wait for God's revelation through his Son Jesus.

II. Jesus revealed the nature of God and defined the issues of life and of death.

(a) Death is the most calamitous of human ills, yet it is here that God has most surely revealed his love. (See John 3:16.)

(b) Christ lived as one laying down his life not in one great act but from step to step throughout his ministry. To him death was more than a single action, and it was different from bodily death. To him there were two realms for man's soul. One was leading toward God and to life, and the other was leading away from God and to death. (See John 11:25–26.)

(c) Further understanding of death in Christian perspective comes with Paul and other New Testament writers. Death became an actuality for men because of disobedience in the beginning. God could have, with man's obedience, conferred immortality, but because of sin he would not. In a sense death can be called a consequence of sin. But sin and death did not have the final word: "As in Adam all die, so also in Christ shall all be made alive" (I Cor. 15:22).

III. This being made alive comes through faith in terms of personal commitment to God in Christ.

(a) Those who are unbelieving and unresponsive are, according to Paul, "dead in trespasses and sins" (Eph. 3:1).

(b) Christians too are dead in a sense. They die with Christ when they cling with faith to the truth that Christ died for them. Their death in this sense is a dying to sin, a renunciation of evil, and a watchfulness against every evil influence. This is to be constant. Paul explained, "I die daily."

(c) True Christianity results in death to the old self. Union with Christ produces a moral and spiritual change that is analogous to the resurrection. What death is depends upon what life is.

(d) Paul's realization that he would inevitably depart this life, even with the strong possibility of his death being an early and violent one, gave him renewed energy, increased hope, and calm fortitude. It can do the same for us.

(e) Living for Christ can and should prepare us for our own physical deaths and the deaths of those whom we love. Those who have heard the voice of Christ in life should have no apprehension about hearing it in the moment of death. When we are taken away from our familiar surroundings, let us think of it as a natural sequence in the plan of God.—H. Lawrence Martin.

Topic: Christian Death

TEXT: Rev. 14:13.

I. Our present life implies something beyond it. (a) The very fact that you can think implies something that you do not often recognize. The fact that I can think about myself and my own end is something that lifts me above the level of transient creatures. It lifts me into a realm above and beyond the purely transient. The fact that I can look down, as it were, upon my own human condition and with my memory go back into the past and with my imagination leap forward into the future sets me apart from the passage of time and its devastating destruction. It leads me to believe that there is something beyond and other than that which comes and goes.

(b) All of you have had some experience of being lifted up above the realm where time and space were transcended. This is one ground on which Christians dare to look for the life of the world to come.

II. The other ground is the life Christians live in Christ which begins not when they die but when they are baptized or whenever it is that they are really incorporated into the body of Christ.

(a) This may not happen when they are babies; it may come later on. But whenever it is that they are really incorporated into the body of Christ, something in them dies. This is their real death, as something else begins to live.

(b) That new life has hard going from time to time, and sometimes they think it will not survive the rough and tumble of everyday existence. But they are aware of it, nevertheless, and they know that they are living in something in which death has no real place. The life they live in him is not interrupted by death; it continues and grows.

(c) Think of a musician becoming a member of the Boston Symphony. When he does that something dies in him, for he has to sacrifice a great deal of his own personal freedom to come and go as he will, to play as he will. When he surrenders himself to the body into which he will then be incorporated, he both dies and is born. He lives in that body and that body communicates its life to him; its glory is his glory; its reputation is his reputation. And even when he retires or withdraws or dies he is still part of that living body. That is the way a great many people feel about their life in Christ.—Theodore P. Ferris.

ILLUSTRATIONS

NEAR TO GOD.   Wherever and whatever heaven is, it is not far away. If being in heaven means being near to God, then it surely stands to reason that we who are left on earth, whenever we are near to God are wonderfully near also to those whom we have loved and lost awhile and who are nearer to God than we are.—Leonard Small.

FOREVER DAY.   How long is a day? That depends on where you live. In New York it is said that the longest day lasts about fifteen hours; at Montreal, Canada, it is sixteen hours; at Hamburg, Germany, it is seventeen hours; at Stockholm, Sweden, it is eighteen and one-half hours. At Faroe, Finland, there have been days when the inhabitants enjoyed twenty-two hours of sunlight. Even farther north in Warzburg, Norway, the days have been known to last from two to three and one-half months. These are long periods of sunlight indeed, yet they are short and insignificant in comparison to the day predicted in Rev. 22:5. God tells us that in the capital city of the New Jerusalem day will last forever, for "there is no night there."—Nixon R. Knight.

BEYOND TIME.   When Sir William Russell, the English patriot, went to the scaffold in 1683, he took his watch out of his pocket and handed it to the physician who attended him in his death. "Would you kindly take my timepiece?" he asked. "I have no use for it. I am now dealing with eternity."

IF DEATH ENDS ALL.   To talk about the fatherhood of God, who begets children, only to annihilate them, is absurd. The goodness of God is plainly at stake when one discusses immortality, for if death ends all, the Creator is building men like sand houses on the shore, caring not a whit that the fateful waves will quite obliterate them all. If death ends all, the struggle and aspiration of humanity have meant no more to him than the mist that rests in the morning on the Alps and at noon is gone. If death ends all, there is no God on whom goodness, in any connotation imaginable to man, can be predicted.—Harry Emerson Fosdick.

HARMONY AND LIFE.   Beethoven had a friend, a baroness, who lost her only child and was desolate from the loss. Beethoven was so close to this family that he personally felt the loss and shared it as his own. When he visited his friend after the memorial service, he could find no word of comfort to speak for he had no word of comfort to say. He went to the piano and started to play a melody we now know as "The Moonlight Sonata." Even in the darkest night, he was trying to express the thought that there is harmony and life if we are sensitive enough to appreciate and hear. Afterward the baroness said, "He told me everything I needed to know."—Frank A. Court.

BIBLE GUIDANCE.   A layman was asked to conduct a funeral. He went to the New Testament to see how Jesus conducted funerals. From his search he realized that Jesus did not conduct funerals. He conducted resurrections.—E. Stanley Jones.

SECTION V. *Resources for Lenten and Easter Preaching*

Topic: By the Light of the Cross

TEXT: I Cor. 1:23–24.

I. The cross is to be interpreted "by its own light." We begin with the experience of the redeeming efficacy of the cross and seek to understand its implications. Doctrine should not be shaped by forcing faith into certain molds but should be the outcome of faith thinking in terms of history and experience. This is why we can never feel that any theory of the cross is completely adequate. For the cross unfolds more and more of its meaning as we grow in the Christian life.

II. The cross is concerned with the relation of persons. Theories of the cross are not helpful except as they show how through the death of Christ men may be brought into a right relation with God and enter into the fellowship of sons. "Christ also suffered for sins once . . . that he might bring us to God" (1 Pet. 3:18).

III. The cross reveals God's attitude to sin, both in his resistance of it and in his condemnation of it. It is impossible for anyone who views sin in the light of the cross to treat it with levity. The sense of sin, as sin against God, has been born at the cross as nowhere else, as men have realized what sin did to the eternal Son of God and what God in Christ did and endured in order to express his condemnation of sin and to overcome it.

IV. The act of reconciliation in the cross was the act of God. "God so loved the world, that he gave his only begotten Son" (John 3:16). Nor does the power of the cross lie in the fact that it shows us human nature at its highest in Jesus Christ, offering its best to God—though incidentally it does that. But the cross derives its saving power from the fact that it was a sacrificial act of God in Christ on behalf of man.

V. The supreme motive of the cross was the love of God. The divine love active in the cross had as its object not merely individuals but the whole race. Jesus Christ in the power which he exercises through the cross has become the head of a new humanity. It was not for nothing that the early Christians were called by their contemporaries "the third race." They had become a new race, different from Greeks and Barbarians and from Jews and Gentiles—"new creations," "an elect race, a royal priesthood, a holy nation, a people for God's own possession," to "show forth the excellencies of him who called you out of darkness into his marvellous light" (1 Pet. 2:9). The cross is the means of the creation of a new humanity, obedient to new laws, governed by new forces and manifesting a new collective righteousness.—H. Maldwyn Hughes.

Topic: Hope and Hostility

SCRIPTURE: Luke 19:37–40.

I. Holy week is not an enjoyable week. It began so beautifully and ended so brutally. It starts out on such a high note of hope. The hostility that accompanied it created a painful combination of experiences. How often hope and hostility are partners!

II. Out of the grating together of hope and hostility comes the new life that is offered us by God. God can take the hope and hostility that is present in the world and in each of us and create new life. That is why it is necessary to walk through each day of Holy Week in order to come to Easter. That is why there are both palm branches and a crown of thorns to symbolize this week.

III. Palm Sunday calls us to accountability. How are we contributing to hostility in our homes, our schools, our places of work? It is so easy to go to a parade and wave palm branches, so easy to attend church on Sunday. What do we intend to do when the parade is over, when the benediction is pronounced? Holy Week requires more than talk. It calls us out of our complacency to action.

IV. The good news happened but not automatically. It begins when we can honestly face the hostility within ourselves. Out of that hostility, we claim the hope of the gospel.—Carole Cotton-Winn in *The Circuit Rider.*

Topic: From the Empty Tomb

Text: Mark 16:4.

I. From that empty tomb has come the most powerful spiritual force the world has ever known.

(a) From that empty tomb came the courage of the Christian martyrs, the faith of St. Paul.

(b) From that empty tomb came the spirit of Hugh Latimer, burned at the stake at Oxford because he refused to forsake the truth, yet before he died crying out to Nicholas Ridley, "Be of good comfort, Master Ridley, and play the man: we shall this day light a candle by God's grace in England as I trust shall never be put out."

(c) From the empty tomb came the resoluteness of Father Damien discovering that he had at last contracted leprosy and could finally be at one with his beloved lepers.

(d) From the empty tomb came the faith of Martin Luther King the night before his murder, joyfully declaring to the Memphis garbage collectors that he had arrived at the mountaintop.

(e) From the empty tomb comes the compassion of Mother Teresa serving among the starving masses of India.

II. From the empty tomb springs the strength of Christians everywhere to stand up for their faith and the courage to be different, to be a fool for Christ's sake.

III. From the empty tomb comes the faith that can heal the wounds of a broken relationship, comfort the grieved, and awaken the depressed.

IV. From a symbol of death comes the fulness of life. Such a strange irony, is it not? From its emptiness springs our fulness, from its musty sense of death springs our glorious sense of new life, from its stark loneliness and silence springs our community of love and concern for all people.—Craig Biddle III.

ILLUSTRATIONS

BURNT TO BLOSSOM. Carefully the Indians set fire to the forests in Michigan's Upper Peninsula. It wasn't in vengeance, destructiveness, anger, or pagan ritual. It was their custom to burn away parts of the underbrush and trees in order to encourage the growth of berries. They had learned how to use the fire so it would not kill the roots of the berry vines. The fire enabled the rebirth and lush growth of the berries. Freed from the underbrush, the berry vines grew more quickly to a fullness of life. Their fruit could also be more easily harvested. When the underbrush again began to over-grow the vines, the process was repeated. The fiery purge was frequently necessary if the vines were to bear fruit.

Lent comes as a time to burn away all which wants to over-grow the fruit of our faith. Lent encourages a new growth in the spirit. It's a time to get back to basics, to burn away that which would choke off our spiritual development and the practical evidence of our Christian faith.—Russell H. Mueller in *The Clergy Journal.*

RISEN AND CRUCIFIED. I heard someone say that we must not worship a crucified Christ who is risen but a risen Christ who was crucified. That's a nice turn of phrase which certainly says it as it is. How to implement that phrase in our worship and our preaching becomes a more difficult question. About the best I can do is to remind myself that it is a continuing question every Sunday. Even on Easter we should see the shadow of the cross, but on Good Friday we should certainly hear the distant trumpets of resurrection.—Howard C. Hageman.

OMISSION.   In John Galsworthy's novel *The Forsyte Saga* there is a scene where the whole family has gathered to bury the much-beloved dog, Balthasar. A young boy is there, puzzled about death and wondering about the God of whom he has heard very little in his family circle. "Do you believe in God?" he asks his father. "Of course," the father replies, "if by God one means the power which is behind everything that exists, or if by God one means the sum of human goodness." "That leaves out Christ, doesn't it?" the son perceptively replies.

TOUCH OF LOVE.   The cross is the most profound condescension of God to man and to what man—especially in difficult and painful moments—looks on as his unhappy destiny. The cross is like a touch of external love upon the most painful wounds of man's earthly existence.—Pope John Paul II.

SACRIFICE.   In Charles Dickens' *A Tale of Two Cities,* Darnay has been sentenced to death by the guillotine. The night before the execution is to take place Sidney Carton, an English lawyer who has largely wasted his talents and his life, steals into the dungeon in which the condemned man is confined and changes clothes with him. Darnay, the man marked for death, escapes from the dungeon and is free. The next morning the generous Carton, with his hands tied behind his back, climbs the scaffold to stand where Darnay should be standing and sacrifices himself for his friend. What strange and stirring thoughts must well up within a man when he sees another die in his stead! What deep regrets and high resolutions must crowd his

heart! What a refining experience it must be!—Armin C. Oldsen.

SIGN OF CHRIST.   I witnessed a baptism in a small church in a Latin American village. The community of faith had gathered, they had recalled God's gracious acts, they had proclaimed the gospel, and now they were about to make a response. The congregation began the mournful sounds of a funeral hymn as a solemn procession moved down the aisle. A father carried a child's coffin he had made from wood, a mother carried a bucket of water from the family well, and a priest carried their sleeping infant wrapped only in a native blanket. As they reached the chancel, the father placed the coffin on the altar, the mother poured the water in the coffin, and the priest covered the wakening baby's skin with embalming oil. The singing softened to a whisper. The priest slowly lowered the infant into the coffin and immersed the child's head in the water. As he did so, he exclaimed, "I kill you in the name of the Father and of the Son and of the Holy Spirit."

"Amen!" shouted the parents and the congregation.

Then quickly lifting the child into the air for all to see, the priest declared, "And I resurrect you that you might love and serve the Lord."

Immediately the congregation broke into a joyous Easter hymn. But it was not yet over. The priest covered the child with the oils of birth; he dressed the child in a beautiful homemade white robe. Once again the singing quieted as the priest, anointing the child, made the sign of the cross on the child's forehead and said, "I brand you with the sign of Christ so that you and the world will always know who you are and to whom you belong." As the singing continued, the people came forward to share the kiss of peace with the newest member of their family.—John H. Westerhoff III.

CHECKMATE.   Chess, often called the royal game, originated about the seventh century in India. Its name is believed to have come from the Persian word for king —*shah.* The Persian words *shah mat,* later to be spoken "checkmate," mean, "The king is dead."

Even those who are unfamiliar with the game know that nothing is spared in defending the king. Queen and castle, bishop and knight, and surely all the pawns are gladly sacrificed to save the king. That's the way it is in our world. Kings are to be saved, not wasted.

That is not the way of the sovereignty of God. The crown is made of thorns, and Christ the King is lifted high on a cross to die. The crowd mocked, "He saved others; he cannot save himself."—John K. Bergland in *Circuit Rider*.

IN GOD'S HEART. In Paris there is a famous picture by Zwiller called "The First Night Outside Paradise." Adam and Eve have been driven out of the Garden of Eden. In the distance is the angel with the flaming sword, but the eyes of the exiles are not fixed upon him. They are gazing far above his head in wondering awe at a cross. That picture enshrines an enormous truth. With human sin came divine suffering of the Lamb that hath been slain from the foundation of the world. A cross was planted in the heart of God even before sin darkened human history.—Henry Cariepy.

THE PASQUEFLOWER. Have you ever heard of the Pasqueflower? It's precocious beauty accounts for its name: a flower of the Pasque, or Easter. Earliest among the rites of the western spring is the blossoming of this lovely flower.

Its annual renewal is a symbol—the first spirited flowering against the blasts of winter. It dares to bloom when the winter of which we have wearied is not yet gone. It comes on the heel of winter without peer. The Pasqueflower survives the winter and stores energy in its roots. A hollow stem allows bending before the wind and lets the floral head face the spring sun.

The flower gives us the first glimpse of paradise in the Persian walled garden from which this term derives. The flowers hint of Eden. Life persists, with grace, through storms. As the rainbow is a sign that life would not be destroyed, so too is the Pasqueflower a reminder of life's survival, a prospering with hope of paradise. The sacred character of life is seen in its struggling beauty.

The flower has been associated with Easter and the Passover, recalling in Christianity and Judaism alike the passing out of bondage, the passing by of death, and a release into freedom and newness of life.—Claude A. Frazier in *The Living Church*.

WERE YOU THERE? They were all there that day on top of the hill—the friends of Jesus and his enemies. The church people, they were there, as well as the people who never went to church, the people who were always talking about the church and always talking about the Lord, the pious people on whose lips there were always glib quotations from the scriptures—they were there. The unbelievers were standing beside them. When we consider who were there and when we are honest with ourselves, we know that we were there and that we helped to put Christ there. Every human being was represented on Calvary. Every sin was in a nail or the point of a spear or the thorns. Calvary still stands. And you and I erect the cross again and again and again every time we sin. The hammer blows are still echoing somewhere in the caverns of your heart and mind—every time we deny him and every time we sin against him or fail to do what he commanded. He is being crucified again and again and again. Were you there when they crucified my Lord? I was. Were you?—Peter Marshall.

AT THE CROSS. Walking through an art gallery one day, I noticed a painting of the crucifixion. Looking at the giant painting, I couldn't help but observe the scene taking place beneath the cross of Jesus. The crowd that had gathered was made up of three groups of people. Each group left a distinct impression on me. First there was a small group that seemed to be looking down, caring little of what was taking place above. They were interested only in Jesus' garments and their own greed. The second group was much larger. They were looking around and didn't seem to care about the event taking place. Their interest was on persons in the crowd. The third group was smaller. They were looking up with their eyes fixed on the cross of Jesus. Their faces expressed sorrow, pain, grief, and wonder. All of us stand beneath the cross today. The question is, in what group are we standing?—W. J. Mosny.

GOD'S LOVE AND MAN'S SIN. Someone has said that the cross is both revelational and transactional. It is revelational in the sense that it reveals the unlimited extent to which God's love will go to redeem men. In this sense the cross does not change anything; it reveals something that is eternally true—the boundless love of God. But the cross is also transactional. In the cross we see the picture of a just God dealing with human sin. God cannot by his very nature shrug off sin as trivial. A sinner is a standing assertion that there is no God. That is essentially why many of us go on sinning; deep down inside we doubt whether there is a God anywhere who will take note of our sinning or any action concerning it. But the cross reminds us that in this universe there is a just and holy God whose love requires him to deal with the sin of every man.—Ivan B. Bell.

SECTION VI. *Resources for Advent and Christmas Preaching*

SERMON SUGGESTIONS

Topic: A Word for Advent

Text: Luke 1:46.

I. "Magnify" is Mary's word used in the Magnificat, a very good word but it seems to have fallen into desuetude. When we read the Psalter, we hear it: "O magnify the Lord with me, and let us exalt his name together" (34:3). Or read the words of Paul, "Christ shall be magnified in my body" (Phil. 1:20).

II. The only times we hear it in ordinary conversation concern amplification of sound or enlargement of picture. We need to restore the meaning and use of magnify of the psalmist, Mary, and Paul. The psalmist invites us to praise God commensurately with his worth. Mary praises and rejoices in God's choosing her to bear his Son. Paul is determined in life or death so to live as to reflect praise and honor upon God.

III. All times are good to make God favorably known, but this season is superlative. We do not have to enlarge or inflate the significance of Christ's coming. But we can do him honor in our daily words and actions, even in the great joy in our faces. Our lives can be a walking praise to Christ our Savior.—Turner N. Clinard.

Topic: What Christmas Does to Us

Text: John 3:16.

At Christmas we reach our peak as human beings. Whatever kindness we have expressed during the year, at Christmas we exceed that. Regardless of how much concern for other people we have shown at any other time of the year, at Christmas we surpass that. No other season of the year reaches so deep into the soul and draws out so much goodness that lies dormant therein. How can we account for the mysterious majesty of the Christmas season? What is there about Christmas that makes us reach so high?

I. We are inspired to such heights of benevolence at Christmas because then, as at no other time of the year, we understand that God loves us.

(a) Is not Christmas all about the birth of a person? And is not that person Jesus Christ, the Son of God? And does not the golden text of the Bible tell us that he is God's gift of love to us? "For God so loved the world, that he gave his only begotten Son, that whosoever believeth in him should not perish, but have everlasting life" (John 3:16).

(b) Jesus is the ultimate expression of the love of God for man and of his good intentions toward men. In him we get a glimpse of God that we can get in no other way. At Christmas we respond to this supreme display of God's love and "the best comes out in us."

II. We reach our peak as human beings during the yuletide season because then we understand, as at no other time, that God believes in us.

(a) In what other way can we explain the gift of his Son? If he did not see that we have the potential to be much more than what we are, why would he have made such a sacrifice?

(b) In the gospel there is a story about a woman who was caught in the act of adultery. Her accusers obviously wanted to see her stoned, but Jesus forgave her: "Go, and sin no more." It was his way of saying, "I believe in you." He looked beyond her past and her failure and encouraged her to be what she could be. He challenged her to a higher level of living. It must have made her want to stretch herself to be all that she was capable of being.

(c) At Christmas we are reminded that the Lord of glory believes in us and it elevates us to a higher plane of living.—Homer G. Rhea, Jr.

Topic: Advent in 1800 b.c.

TEXT: Gen. 49:10.

I. One of Jacob's sons, Judah, was promised that the rulership (scepter) of the nation would not depart from his family until it came into the hands of the descendant to whom it belonged. That promise must have forced Judah to begin looking ahead, to ask what was in store, and in particular to ask who could possibly be the one to whom the rulership belonged.

(a) Just what specifics occurred to Judah's imagination, we'll never know. He might have wondered why the rulership should have come to his family rather than to his oldest brother's (Reuben's) family. He might have inflated with arrogance, remembering the time when he interceded on behalf of Joseph's life, concluding now that he deserved rulership on that account. Or he might have turned a bit sour inside with envy, eaten with the growing awareness that his own rulership was not the premier one, that he was only to pass it along the family line until it came to the deserving descendant.

(b) We know that the incarnation fulfilled that promise to Judah. Jesus was the one to whom the rulership belonged, and he was born as a son of the tribe of Judah some 1,800 years after the promise. He deserved the rulership all along, he was greeted—at least by some—as the king of kings when he arrived, and his rulership will be consummated in some great day to come.

II. Judah didn't know that Christmas Day was coming, at least not in any concrete sense.

(a) It is most unlikely that his anticipation of the one "to whom (rulership) belongs" included even a glimpse of the suffering Savior who would one day be born in a stable in Bethlehem.

(1) Judah and his family were aliens in Egypt at the time, having escaped a famine which drove them from their own land. When his descendants would return to their land under Moses and the judges, they'd have to take it by force from other occupants. Judah knew that his blessing was greater than that of his brothers and that his family would realize great things in years to come.

(2) He had no idea how long he and his descendants would have to wait, nor what they should look for. He simply had to trust the promise and begin looking ahead for the fulfillment of the blessing.

(b) We have it so much easier. Perhaps that tempts us to take Advent casually. We've been through it before. We know what's coming. The great longing builds, if at all, for a mere four weeks, not for centuries. We lack the sense of mystery. The obscure expression, "until he comes to whom it belongs," doesn't puzzle us.

(c) We might do well to learn from Judah's advent. He had only this one, so far as we know, only the promise he received as his father lay near death. He and his children had to hold to that promise for a very long time and through severely daunting circumstances. Some of Judah's children clung to that promise better than others. Many lost sight of the coming ruler altogether.

(d) We could lose sight of the coming ruler too. The shortness of our Advent season could destroy its significance just as the length of Judah's eroded it—and eventually destroyed it—for many in his family. Our familiarity with the story could reduce its power just as the obscurity of the promise could have reduced its power for Judah. Lest that happen this Advent, recall the perseverance to which God called Judah in the promise of 1800 b.c.

Rejoice in the clarity with which that promise was fulfilled in Jesus Christ. Live in the significance and power of the season.—John Stapert in *The Church Herald*.

Topic: Repentance and Christmas

TEXT: Matt. 3:3.

I. The Advent is bigger than infancy stories. Without the whole picture, no star blazed over Bethlehem and no magi knelt in adoration. John, the trailblazer, fulfilled Isa. 40:3 in the style of Elijah (II Kings 1:8) as he opened the human wilderness to the gift of Christ. John's message was the same initially proclaimed by Jesus (Matt. 4:17).

(a) Repentance is not a fearful bid for exemption from judgment. It is a turnaround, with fruit bright in contrasted living. With judgment comes the kingdom of heaven, to Gentile ears kingdom of God (Mark 4:26).

(b) The "fire" baptism was that of judgment, but the "Holy Spirit" baptism opened the doors of the kingdom. Water baptism for repentance was not abandoned, but the gift of the Spirit was added when at Pentecost the church emerged as the kingdom John had forecast (Acts 2:38).

II. Where does John the Baptist fit in Christmas? Redemption, the fruit of repentance, is the indispensable ingredient of Christmas. Lacking it, the holy season is simply a noisy respite in our jumbled calendar.

(a) In the kingdom of forgiveness and change, joy knows no season. Christmas celebration is in tune with the whole year. Those who know only the Christ child know not Christ at all, for the child without the child's history is simply the rising of a splendid curtain upon an empty stage.

(b) Judgment and fire seem to play hob with Christmas carols. We sense untuned harps, melted tinsel, and Santa's white beard singed by other than chimney ashes. But without judgment, without the axe at the root of the tree, where is bright grace, where are sweet fruits of repentance? When in repentance we learn the forgiveness of God, "Joy to the World" is any Sunday's song.—Roger N. Carstensen in *The Disciple*.

Topic: Christmas Questions

TEXT: Matt. 2:2.

I. Has God appeared in Jesus Christ? Christ is the only claimant to incarnation. Other world religions have deities of various sorts and some of them have many deities, but only in Christianity is it claimed that "the word was made flesh" (John 1:14). Jesus has no competition so far as what he claimed is concerned.

II. If God has not appeared, how do we explain Christ? How do we explain his amazing life and influence? How explain the persistence in history of his influence and teaching and the persistence of the faith of his followers? How else explain the historical church except to remember Christ's words, "The gates of hell shall not prevail against it" (Matt. 16:18)?

III. If God has not revealed himself, then why not? Why would God remain in the shadows without speaking, without giving some assurance to the many hearts that cry out for his being and his love? Why would God leave all the questions about himself eternally unanswered? Why would he leave us to live in confusion as to purpose, identity, and destiny?

IV. If you will not receive God in Christ, then in what manner of revelation would you receive him? What better personal revelation could he give you than Jesus? What better image of God could you possibly imagine than that he be just like Jesus? That is, insofar as human outline can reveal God. If you would not receive him in this form, how can he reach your free soul? How could you be led to believe?

V. If Bethlehem's story is not true, then why can't history dispose of it or blur it and like myths change with time?—Frank Owen in *Western Recorder*.

Topic: What Happens at Christmas?

SCRIPTURE: Matt. 2:1–15.

It is amazing the various reactions and happenings that take place at Christmas. It has always been this way. At the first Christmas we find the same range of emotions, the same joys, hardships, and conflicts. Observe the reactions of Herod and the wise men and see in their attitude toward Christmas some of the things that do happen to people during this season of the year.

I. We may miss the spirit of Christmas (Matt. 2:2–3). Herod and the people of Jerusalem missed the spirit of Christmas because the Bible says they were troubled. Many are troubled today because, like Herod, they are not following Christ.

II. We may miss the point of Christmas. Herod missed the point. Instead of rejoicing because the messiah had come, he was suspicious. He ordered the slaughter of little babies and caused grief to the people. Many today will have heavy hearts because somebody missed the point.

III. We may find the joy of giving. This was true of the wise men, the first Christian givers. In the way these first Christian givers brought their gifts is a lesson for all of us today. These wise men prepared their offering, protected their offering, presented their offering to Christ, and provided for the need of the Christ child with their offering.

IV. We may find Christ this Christmas. The wise men did. We do not know how many days, weeks, or months they spent searching for Christ. At the end of their journcy thcy found the Savior.—John E. Barnes.

Topic: Two Views of Christmas

TEXT: Luke 1:28.

There are two views of Christmas in the New Testament.

I. One is the close-up view of Christmas. In the center of the picture is a stable, and in the stable a man, a woman, and a child are the focus of our attention. Standing by them are the shepherds, above them are the night skies, and the hills of Bethlehem are clustered round them in a kind of sheltering embrace.

II. The other view is as though a man went up high into the sky and photographed what he saw from there.

(a) Bethlehem would then be only a point in the center of the picture, and the centuries would roll before and after it. Instead of the hills of Bethlehem would stand the eternal purposes of God.

(b) What happens to the close-up view? Do we lose all the stars and the stable and the baby and the mother? Not at all. They are simply gathered together and caught up into the mystery of eternity. The love of Mary becomes the channel of God into the life of every mother, baby becomes the incarnate act by which God makes himself known in every age to every generation, and the village in Bethlehem becomes every village street.—*Forward.*

ILLUSTRATIONS

FOCUS.   During Advent we focus not simply on what is happening in our world. We focus on what has happened to our world through the coming of Jesus Christ almost twenty centuries ago. We focus on what will happen when Jesus comes at the end of time. Advent constrains us to quit complaining about what the world has come to and to rejoice because of what has come to our world.—Robert M. Shelton.

INESCAPABLE IMPACT.   A man was taking a civil service examination for a job as postman. One of the questions on the exam was, "How far away from the earth is the sun?" The postman answered, "It is so far away that it will not make any difference to my delivering mail on Main Street." This was partially true but not altogether. He will feel the force of the sun. He will find it making a difference on Main Street.

And so with the event in Bethlehem. However removed the place and however garlanded with tradition, its impact is inescapable. It was an event in eternity that will never be obliterated. It was a cradle that rocked the world.—Robert M. Blackburn.

SANTA AND THE CHILD.   Santa Claus certainly symbolizes the spirit of Christmas. It's a time of good cheer, friendliness, love, and generosity. Yes, Christmas is certainly all of these, but does Santa Claus truly symbolize the spirit and meaning of the Christ Mass?

Christmas as the Christ Mass reminds Christians that God came into our world;

that he came into our world poor, unwanted, unexpected, unrecognized; came into our world as a child—born as all of us are born; came into our world to give to us God's free gift of himself; came as God's free gift to the bad as well as to the good; came as a Savior of sinners, and not as a reward for the righteous. But what about Santa Claus?

Santa is not depicted as poor, but as wealthy and affluent, not as hungry but as extremely well fed, not as unwanted but as longed for, not as unexpected but as eagerly awaited, not as unknown but as well known, not as one born but as one who has always lived, not as the giver of free gifts but as the giver of earned gifts. Santa Claus is not the giver of gifts to sinners but the distributor of rewards to the righteous. Santa Claus is not the giver of unexpected gifts but anticipated gifts.

Santa Claus does not come as the Christ child for whom there was no room and no welcome but into homes long and lavishly prepared and made ready. The Christ Child came as a fact of history, but Santa Claus comes again and again only in legend and make-believe.—Norman H. V. Elliott in *The Living Church.*

AND HE SHALL COME AGAIN. To grasp the meaning of the Advent season, we need to give heed to the message of two angels. The first is the angel who appeared to the startled shepherds out in the fields saying, "Fear not: for behold, I bring you glad tidings of great joy, which shall be to all people. For unto you is born this day in the city of David a Savior, which is Christ the Lord."

We need to give heed to the message of that other angel who appeared to the eleven disciples on the Mount of Olives, The end of Jesus' earthly ministry has come. During the forty days since his resurrection he has been instructing the disciples concerning the kingdom of God. Now he climbs that little elevation just east of Jerusalem, and after saying a few parting words, he is caught up from them into heaven and returns to the Father and to the place of honor at his right hand. And the angel of the Lord says to the disciples: "Men of Galilee, why do you stand looking into heaven? This Jesus, who was taken up from you into heaven, will come again the same way as you saw him go into heaven."

The message of Advent involves looking backward in time 2000 years to our Savior's first coming and a looking forward to the end of the age when he shall come in power and great glory to set up his eternal kingdom. You and I live between his first and his second comings.—Everett L. Fullam.

SECTION VII. *Evangelism and World Missions*

SERMON SUGGESTIONS

Topic: World Mission

Text: John 20:21.

I. *Our mission.* Jesus did not saunter around the synagogue. He went out into the world where the people were. As God sent Jesus into the world, so we are to go into the world.

II. *Our motivation.* Compare Luke 5:10, Mark 5:19, Mark 16:15, Matt. 28:19–20, and Acts 1:8 with our text. In each verse the Lord is speaking, and he commands us to go. The primary motivation for evangelism is obedience to the command of the Lord.

III. *Our message.* What are we to say? Jesus told the disciples that they were to go into the world, as he did, with the message of God's redeeming love.

IV. *Our method.* How are we to implement this mission? As Jesus did, on a person-to-person basis. This does not rule out mass evangelism or media outreach. It does mean that the primary method for evangelism is for one person to confront another person with the good news of God (II Tim. 2:2).—Brian L. Harbour.

Topic: The Messenger Is the Message

Scripture: Luke 10:1–20.

I. The seventy returned, not shouting about those who responded to the gospel, but saying, "The demons obeyed us." They became enamored with their own power over the forces of life and lost sight of the people. Jesus, seeing that, said to them, "Don't be glad because the evil spirits obey you; rather be glad because your names are written in heaven."

II. The message and the messenger cannot be separated. Jesus didn't say to his disciples, "Whoever rejects your message rejects me." He said, "Whoever listens to you listens to me; whoever rejects you rejects me." The rejection is of the messenger.

III. The message of the kingdom of God is not only in what is said but also in who says it and how it is said.

(a) Jesus told the seventy to go to the towns, to be with people in their homes, to eat meals with the people, to sleep on the divan in the people's livingrooms, to heal the sick among the people, and to say to the people, "The kingdom of God has come near you."

(b) This is an important sequence. The first step in being a church is caring for one another, getting to one another, and showing compassion to one another. After we enter into these relationships of sharing, then we can think in terms of speaking the message to people.

IV. The giving of the gospel begins with the messenger of the gospel. The messenger is the message. Equally important is the urgency with which the seventy went from town to town, believing that without their message the people in the towns faced death. We should be concerned that the people in our towns and villages get the message we are commissioned to take to them.

V. The story of the seventy is about people going out two by two with an important message, about people impelled to share that message, and about a message that cannot be separated from the manner, method, and attitude of the messenger who is a part of the message. Convinced that the messengers are really interested in their welfare and lives, people will hear the message of the kingdom. But only through forming relationships and by sharing life on all levels can people hear more than words and see more than images.—Edward R. Snider, Sr.

Topic: Turning to God

Text: Matt. 18:3.

I. "Turning to God" is a literal translation of the word which frequently appears in the Bible as "convert."

(a) Beginning with John Wycliffe's translation in the middle of the fourteenth century and continuing through the 1946 rsv, the seven major translations of this text use the word "turn" in place of "convert." More recent translations use "turn around," "turn back," and "change." Some read "change your whole outlook," "unless your hearts be changed," or "become again."

(b) If we are to experience godlikeness, we must turn our mind and heart and life in God's direction.

II. What is involved in the terms "salvation" and "saved"? (a) Fundamentally the term "salvation" means "being right with God." It is the opposite of the religious meaning of the term "sin," which refers literally to being "apart from God." "Salvation" means having turned to God, while "sin" means "turning away from God."

(1) Sin is contrary to the right, the true, the honest, and the good as we know it. It is choosing the lesser, lower values and not the Christlike values.

(2) "Salvation" is the sincere way of life, "sincere" meaning the clear, pure, reliable, and responsible.

(b) The "saved" person has turned toward God so completely that he is in harmony with God's will, his laws, his purposes, and the perfect example of how God wants us to live as we find that example in Jesus Christ. It is an experience which requires discipline, continual self-examination, and perseverance.

III. Turning toward God involves repentance. The Greek word "convert" is often used interchangeably with the Greek word "repent," for it also means to "turn about" or to "change one's mind."

(a) The principal difference is that to repent involves being sorry for one's misdeeds, sorry enough to ask forgiveness and to set a new course. This is the key to becoming a new person or, as the scriptures speak of it, to being born again. It means having a new spirit, a new attitude toward God and one's fellowmen, a new relationship with God and man.

(b) While repentance means we regret what we have done amiss, it is also positive. True repentance finds the mind, the emotions, and the whole life turning toward God and living according to the way, the truth, and the life God has set before us in Christ. Once one has made this turn toward God, he finds that he has passed from darkness to light and from death to life.—Homer J. R. Elford.

Meditation: Missionary Motive

Text: John 13:3–4.

The whole inspiring motive of the missionary movement can be summed up in the story of Fred Pyke and Frances, his wife, both of whom were born of missionary parents and both of whom spent forty years as missionaries in China.

At the outbreak of World War II they were in Peking. When the Japanese came within a few miles of the city, the Methodist Board of Missions ordered all missionaries home on the *Gripsholm*, which was sailing in two weeks, but Fred and Frances refused to leave.

When they would not go at the order of the board, their Chinese bishop came to see them and to order their return to America.

"Those are my orders! You must leave China!" said Bishop Wong.

"But we are not going to leave, bishop!"

"You must leave! I am your bishop, and I tell you that you must leave! You will be thrown into an internment camp if you stay and you may be killed!"

"Frances and I have thought it through, we have prayed about it, and we are not going to leave!"

"Why won't you leave?" the bishop asked.

"Because our people, the Chinese, need us now more than they ever needed us. They will need the prestige that American missionaries can give them when the Japanese take Peking. We have invested forty years in these people, and we do not intend to lose that investment by deserting them now in their hour of need."

"Is that your final word, Fred?"

"It is, bishop!"

Then a strange and beautiful thing happened. That stoical Chinese bishop, normally a rigidly disciplined man, as are all Chinese, stood there, gripping Fred Pyke's hands as he said: "That's what I wanted you to say, Fred! That's what I wanted you to say! But it was my duty as your bishop to order you to leave!"

And Fred and Frances Pyke stayed. So did hundreds of missionaries and in so doing bound those peoples of foreign lands to the church of God with bands stronger than steel. They stayed because they had a tender care that nothing of spiritual value be lost.

Fred and Frances Pyke were thrown into an internment camp at once and remained there for two years. Fred's task assigned by the Japanese generals was to clean out the latrines for two thousand English and American prisoners, the intention being to make Fred Pyke, a man of great power among the Chinese, lose face, as they calculated that lowly, menial task would cause him to do.

But the Japanese miscalculated in that as they did in so many other things. For, instead of making Fred lose face, that heroic, self-sacrificing service made him gain face with the Chinese.

The Japanese miscalculated because they did not know that Fred and Frances Pyke, and all other missionaries, were followers of a lowly Christ who long years ago dressed himself in the garments of a slave, got down on his knees, and washed his disciples' feet. And in that drama of service he taught the world that he who is greatest among humankind is he who serves—he who has a tender care that nothing be lost.—William L. Stidger.

ILLUSTRATIONS

PROCLAMATION. We carry the message of Christ to all people everywhere because we believe not only that the grace of God revealed in Jesus Christ holds the promise of improving the quality of one's life but also through Christ God gives deliverance from both the power and the penalty of sin. Our evangelism is an invitation to a new life in which justice and righteousness prevail. Authentic Christian evangelism is the proclamation of the latest edition of God's good news.—Roy C. Nichols.

THE SAME ROAD. On one occasion I was talking with one of the great missionary pioneers of Guatemala, who, then in his sixties, was getting ready to make one of his customary walking trips of several weeks out through the mountains in order to visit Indian congregations in the small villages. I asked him why he did not drive his car in view of his increasingly poor health and the new road which had just gone through that region, for he could have driven to many of the places he proposed to visit. His reply was simply, "Oh, I never drive, for the people that I want to reach are not used to someone driving up in a car. What is more, I have never found a man I could not speak to about Jesus Christ, if only we were walking down the same road together."—Eugene A. Nida.

A NEW NAME. Years ago in Scotland a fisherman called Old John was bound by strong drink. He took the money earned from his catch and spent it on liquor while his wife and children suffered. They lived in a hovel at the end of the fishing village and eked out an existence in extreme poverty. But Old John came to know the Lord Jesus Christ as his personal Savior. After that he brought all his money home and gave it to his wife. He worked steadily, and soon there were new clothes, plenty of food, and coal for the fire. After a few weeks of this transformed existence, the wife said, "John, if you are going to keep on like this, we should move into a better house." "Right," said John, "I shall go and see the landlord at once." He made his way through the town to the landlord and asked to rent a certain house. The landlord said, "I would never rent a good house to you, Old John." "Why do you say that?" asked John. "You don't know me at all!" "Of course I know you," said the landlord. "You are drunken Old John, the fisherman." "You are mistaken," said John. "You have never seen me before. Old John is dead. I am New John, a new creature in Christ Jesus." And he poured out a handful of coins before the astonished landlord. Soon New John was living in a new house.—William R. Taylor.

THE SKEPTICAL PATIENT. One of our medical missionaries set down in a book his experience with people who could not understand the Christian desire to serve. "Who is this Jesus?" they asked. "Surely all of these missionaries cannot be related to him. Yet they all talk about serving him."

A skeptical man came to the hospital full of questions which had to be answered before he could be treated. As an important man in his own village, he wanted priority attention but soon found that everybody was equal in the eyes of the doctor. He asked for the most expensive medicine because surely this would be best, but the patient doctor told him that for some ailments the cheapest remedies were better. In his particular case, said the doctor, medicines would not help; his goiter must be cut out. "With a big knife?" howled the terrified man. "No, with a small knife," replied the doctor. "Then you will be hacking away at me for hours!" groaned the fault-finder.

He insisted on gathering evidence from the other patients. He had heard some foolishness in his village about a Jesus who died for others. Why did the Westerners make such a bad impression on gullible Chinese with their nonsensical lies? What were these Christians in this hospital up to? One man told how the nurses had stayed by his bed night after night. Another reported that a precious drug costing much money had been brought by airplane for a very poor woman. Finally the skeptical Mr. Mau underwent the operation, and the goiter was successfully removed. As he was discharged, the doctor said: "Now you have seen what we have done. Do you still think that story about Jesus was only a lie?" "It seems impossible," said the serious man, "but even that could have happened too."—Stewart W. Herman.

MOODY'S GRAMMAR. A fault-finding minister said to Bishop J. C. Ryle as they sat in one of D. L. Moody's meetings in England, "Do you hear that young Yankee smashing the Queen's English?" Ryle replied, "Yes, but do you see him breaking sinner's hearts in the gallery?"

THE FINDING GOD. Among other desires of God-in-Christ, he beyond question wills that persons be found—that is, be reconciled to himself. Most cordially admitting that God has other purposes, we should remember that we serve a God who finds persons. He has an overriding concern that men should be redeemed. However we understand the word, biblical witness is clear that men are lost. The finding God wants them found—that is, brought into a redemptive relationship to Jesus Christ, where, baptized in his name, they become a part of his household. He is not pleased when many findable sheep remain straggling on the mountain, shivering in the bitter wind. The more found, the better pleased is God.—Donald McGavran.

RETURN TO THE EAST. An American agricultural missionary in Burma spoke to a missionary conference in Florida. He said: "You got your Florida mangoes from Burma. But you've improved them here, and I'm taking them back with me. You got your Florida oranges from the East, but you've improved them from sour little things to sweet, juicy Valencias. And I'm taking those improved oranges back to my Burma people. You got your chickens from the East too, but you've taken that spindly Chinese chicken and put meat on its breast and made it tasty. And I'm taking that Plymouth Rock hen to my Burma farmers so they won't have to grow opium for a living. You got your pigs from the East too, but you took that scrawny Eastern pig, broadened its back, stretched out its intestines, and put big fat hams on it.

I'm taking that improved pig back where you got it. And you have Christ here. You got him from the East too. You haven't improved him, but he has improved you, and I'm taking him back to the East where you got him.''

COMFORTING WORDS.　Dr. Wilfred T. Grenfell's first line of ministry was as a medical missionary, but at all times he ministered as well to all the needs of his people. One of the Labrador stories was of a call he received one day from a fishing boat off the coast. Answering their distress signal, he went out and found on that fishing boat an eighteen-year-old girl who had shipped aboard as a cook. Quite unknown to the rest of the crew, she had given premature birth to a baby, and, unattended, had fallen into a critical condition. By the time Grenfell reached her, the best he could do was too little to save her. After doing everything he possibly could medically, he began speaking to her tenderly of one who said, "Come unto me, all ye that labor and are heavy laden, and I will give you rest." And, said the doctor, "She found that peace which passeth understanding. Then," he added, "we laid her tenderly away on a headland jutting out into the Atlantic. And from its summit you could see across the restless waters. On the grave I planted a rude wooden cross on which we carved these compassionate words of Jesus, 'Neither do I condemn thee.' ''

EACH ONE TEACH ONE.　Frank Laubach felt a special vocation to fight illiteracy. His work among the Moros (Muslims) in Lanao (Philippines) began despite great suspicion. One day at a meeting called to ask for volunteers to train as teachers, fifty-one young men offered themselves. Sadly Laubach admitted that there was insufficient money to pay them. After a long silence the chief of southern Lanao declared: "This campaign shall not stop for lack of money. It is Lanao's only hope. Everyone who learns has got to teach. If he doesn't, I'll kill him!" Laubach felt that the world's most wonderful idea had dawned upon him. "Each one, teach one" became the theme of a campaign nothing could stop.

ON HIS KNEES.　"Praying" John Hyde, missionary to India at the turn of the century, was greatly used by God in bringing many to a saving knowledge of Christ. He took no credit for this himself but attributed the success of his mission to answered prayer. John Hyde's friends spoke often of his many hours spent in prayer. He spent so much time on his knees in prayer that his knees looked and felt like elephant hide. Imagine, calluses on his knees! What a high price to pay for those he led to Christ.—Shirley Murphey.

COMPASSION.　When the Indian Christian, Samuel Rahator, started to preach the gospel in the villages around the city of Naski, two towns rejected his message. He was stoned, and later an angry crowd nearly killed him. Months later Rahator heard that plague was raging in that town. Immediately he filled his medicine case and set off through the hills. He ministered to the sick from house to house and prayed with the dying. His compassion won the hearts of his former enemies.

BY JOHN R. BROKHOFF

Topic: Happy 500th Birthday to Luther
Scripture: Eph. 4:11–16.

I. Five hundred years ago, on November 10, 1483, a baby boy was born to poor peasants in a little German town, Eisleben.

(a) When he became a man, he did more than anyone else to initiate and establish the Protestant faith. He launched the most gigantic revolution in the history of the Christian church. He is one of the very few men of whom it can be said that the history of the world was profoundly altered by his work.

(b) No one can deny his preeminent place in the history of the church. Roland H. Bainton has written of him, "He was the father of a household, the moulder of the German people, a new David playing on his harp, an emancipator of certain fetters of the spirit, the divider of the church, and at the same time the renewer of Christendom."

(c) Who was this giant of the church? He was Martin Luther whose 500th birthday is celebrated this year.

II. How did he become a Christian? How did he become one of the greatest Christians in history? Luther was one who fulfilled the words of our text—"to mature manhood, to the measure of the stature of the fulness of Christ." Paul was wishing that every person might come to match the greatness of Christ. Luther defined a Christian as a "little Christ." How you too can become fully Christian is demonstrated by Luther's experience.

(a) Luther became a Christian through baptism. One day only was Luther not a Christian. He was born one day, and the very next day he was baptized. Since it was St. Martin's day, he was named Martin.

(1) Baptism is the initiation into the Christian faith. It is the incorporation into the church, the body of Christ.

(2) It is the time when God adopts a person, infant or adult, as a child of the King. Baptism is a reminder that we are God's children by adoption.

(3) It is the sign and seal that we are saved and going to heaven. Whenever Luther doubted his salvation, he found assurance by crawling on his hands and knees to the baptismal font where God accepted him as a child.

(b) Luther became a Christian by having a thunderous experience that changed the direction of his life. It was a turning point from the secular to the sacred.

(1) At the time he was a law student at the University of Erfurt, Germany. After a vacation at home, Luther was walking back to the university. A thunderstorm came up and lightning knocked him to the ground. Frightened for his life, he prayed: "St. Anne, help me. I will become a monk." This was the beginning of his church life which eventuated in the reformation of the church in the sixteenth century.

(2) Though we are Christians by our baptism, each of us needs an experience that transforms our lives and points us in a God direction. For Paul it was a fall from a horse and blindness. For Augustine it was a voice, "Take and read." For Billy Graham it was an experience in an evangelist's tent of revival. Your experience need

not be that dramatic, but there comes a time when each must make an about face to God.

(c) In becoming a full-grown Christian, we need to understand the experience with God and our faith.

(1) This calls for insight and enlightenment. It came to Luther while he was studying the scriptures in preparing his lectures at the University of Wittenberg where he was a professor and a doctor of theology. The meaning of the gospel came to him. It was his Black Tower enlightenment. He explained: "Night and day I pondered until I saw the connection between the justice of God and the statement that 'the just shall live by his faith.' Then I grasped that the justice of God is that righteousness by which, through grace and sheer mercy, God justifies us through faith. Thereupon I felt myself to be reborn and to have gone through open doors into paradise."

(2) The scriptures urge us to give a reason for the faith we hold. We are not only to know what we believe but why we believe it. A blind faith is no faith at all. The meaning of our faith needs to be understood. The Holy Spirit received in the Word and sacraments gives us insight and understanding.

Topic: Take a Stand!

SCRIPTURE: Eph. 6:10–17.

The one thing most people know about Luther is his stand at the Diet of Worms.

(a) In 1520 the Roman Church excommunicated Luther for heresy. Six months later the Holy Roman Emperor, Charles V, called a Diet to meet at Worms to consider the Luther case. Before the assembly of church prelates and German princes Luther was asked to recant what he had written. Before the top officials of church and state, Luther made this historic and dramatic reply: "Unless I am convicted by scripture and plain reason . . . my conscience is captive to the Word of God. I cannot and will not recant anything, for to go against conscience is neither right nor safe. Here I stand. I cannot do otherwise. God help me. Amen."

(b) Luther obeyed the admonition of St. Paul to take a stand. In Eph. 6 we are told to put on the whole armor of God and then to take a stand. To the church at Thessalonica Paul wrote, "Stand fast and hold the traditions." He urged the Galatians, "Stand fast in the liberty wherewith Christ has made us free." It is a message for our day when, because of compromise and false tolerance, anything goes. There are several ways to take a stand as Luther did in his day.

I. Take a stand against the evils of our day. (a) One reason for the flourishing of evil is the failure of good people to do anything about it. There is a need to take a stand against the evils of our day.

(b) Christians are in a battle against the forces of wickedness. Luther took a stand against the enemies of the gospel. He was against selling salvation by buying indulgences, against mechanically dispensing grace through sacraments, and against putting tradition above the Bible.

(c) In our time we need to take a stand against the evils of our generation. There are heresies to be attacked: astrology, Scientology, and Moonism. We must take a stand against secularism, humanism, and pluralism which flourish in our society. It is a Christian duty to stand against the moral corruption of our times—gambling, drug addiction, sexual perversion, and political corruption.

II. Take a stand for the good. It takes courage to stand for the right and truth.

(a) Luther was a man of courage as he stood for the truth of the gospel. It took courage to nail ninety-five theses to a castle church door and challenge the teaching of the church. It took courage as a simple monk, the son of a miner, to oppose the top dignitaries of church and state at the Diet of Worms. After the bull of excommunication and the ban of the empire, Luther was hidden by his prince in the Wartburg castle. When extremists began to use violence in extending the Reformation, at the risk of his life he came out and took over the leadership of the movement.

(b) To confess the truth of the gospel is to take a stand for the truth. In the Reformation period Martin of Basle was convinced of the truth, but he was afraid to confess it publicly. He wrote his confession on a piece of parchment: "O most merciful Christ, I know that I can be saved only by the merit of thy blood. Holy Jesus, I acknowledge thy sufferings for me. I love thee! I love thee!" Then he removed a stone from the wall of his chamber and hid the parchment. It was discovered 100 years later. Contrast this with Luther: "My Lord has confessed me before men; I will not shrink from confessing him before kings."

III. What we stand against and what we stand for depends ultimately upon what we stand on. Where do we stand and with whom do we stand? God asked Elijah why he was sulking under a juniper tree. Jesus asked Judas at the time of betrayal, "Why are you here?" In Ps. 1 we are told that a blessed person does not stand in the way of sinners. Where and on what does a Christian stand?

(a) Stand on the Word. Here is where Luther stood. "My conscience is bound to the Word of God." It gave him courage and certainty.

(b) Stand on the promises of God. There are over 33,000 of them in the Bible. God can be trusted to keep his word.

(c) Stand on the rock of Christ. We sing, "On Christ the solid rock I stand." He is the rock of ages—stable, secure, and eternal.

IV. There are times when we can do nothing but stand. Evil forces throng around us to undo us. Our problems and enemies are too many for us to handle alone. It is then that we put our destiny in God's hands and let him fight our battles for us. Moses told his people, "Fear not, stand firm, and see the salvation of the Lord."

Topic: The Revolution of the Reformation

SCRIPTURE: Jer. 31:31–34; Rom. 3:19–28; Jn. 8:31–36.

I. "No revolution is to be made for God," said Luther, who is known as a reformer, not a revolutionary.

(a) He was very upset when students at Wittemberg University broke into the parish church, snatched the mass books, and drove out the priests with stones. At the risk of his life he left the Wartburg Castle to put a stop to the radicals who were violently attacking the church. Luther explained his position: "In a word I will preach, teach, write, but I will force or drive no one, for faith must be willing and unconstrained." He was for repairing the house of the church rather than burning it down.

(b) The Reformation of the sixteenth century became a revolution in the strict meaning of the word. Revolution means to revolve. First things must come first. The world is upside down and needs to be turned right side up. It is a matter of having the right priorities.

(1) In church symbolism the church is represented by a ship. A boat can capsize, bottom up! For a boat to sail it must be right side up.

(2) In the course of history there have been times when the ship of the church capsized. In Paul's day the church was seized with Judaizers who turned the gospel into law. In Luther's day the church put works first for salvation rather than grace.

II. Today's church stands in need of a revolution through a new reformation. There is evidence that the boat has capsized. Things have been turned upside down, and we need to turn the boat right side up. A capsized boat throws the cargo overboard. Passengers are threatened with drowning. To right the boat is no easy task. Did you ever try to turn over a capsized sailboat? What today's church needs in being uprighted is found in the lessons for Reformation Sunday.

III. The gospel needs to be up and the law down. Jeremiah reports Yahweh saying, "I will make a new covenant with the house of Israel." A covenant is the result of grace. It depends upon God's initiative —"I will make." God comes with an offer to be the people's God and for them to have him as their God. Grace comes first, and law, as condition of the covenant, comes second. Today we need a revolution because we tend to put law first and grace second. We look at the price tag before we look at the new car we want to buy.

(a) Grace is expressed in God's seeking humanity. It is man who is lost, not God.

As in Thompson's "The Hound of Heaven," God continually seeks us until we surrender.

(b) Grace is in God's choosing us as his children. Jesus said, "You have not chosen me, but I have chosen you."

(c) Grace is God's acceptance of us as we are—sinners unworthy and undeserving of grace. Paul wrote, "While we were yet sinners, Christ died for us."

IV. When the ship of the church is turned right side up, faith is up and works are down. This truth comes to us from Paul: "A man is justified by faith apart from the works of the law." In this area we need a revolution through a reformation. Though we have preached the gospel for almost 2000 years, the average church member still thinks he will get to heaven by his or her good works. Many think they must win God's favor by doing kind acts to the neighbor. If I am good, God will love me. If I obey God's commands, he will bless me. If I repent, God will forgive me.

(a) Forgiveness comes to us without any strings attached. No prior conditions are necessary. It is not a case of "if" but of "because." Because God is good and because Christ died for our sins, we are acceptable to God. Faith is the receptive agent which makes God's acceptance a personal possession.

(b) Works follow faith. Good deeds are an expression of faith. We do good deeds because our hearts have been made good by the gift of the Holy Spirit. In and through the Spirit, God is working in us to make us Christlike.

V. The church needs to be uprighted so that freedom is up and servitude is down. Jesus says, "The truth shall make you free." Today most Christians are not free; they are bound by fear, worry, self-centeredness, and legalism. We think of Christianity primarily as laws and duties.

(a) In *Christian Liberty,* Luther enunciated the paradox of Christian experience: "A Christian man is the most free lord of all and subject to none; a Christian man is the most dutiful servant of all, and subject to every one." Freedom comes first and service comes next.

(b) The truth of the gospel is that Christ has freed us from sin, death, condemnation, and the necessity perfectly to obey the law in order to be reconciled to God. When this freedom is accepted by faith, the Christian voluntarily becomes a servant out of love and gratitude.

(c) In the first century, critics said of the apostles, "These men have turned the world upside down." Today it should be said of us that we have turned the world downside up.

Topic: A Song That Says It All
SCRIPTURE: Ps. 46.

It has been said that Luther spread the Reformation more through music than by preaching.

(a) While other Reformers, such as Zwingli and Calvin, silenced the organs and dismissed the choirs, Luther insisted upon congregational singing and encouraged choirs. For him music ranked second only to theology. He disliked anyone who despised music. An understanding of music he considered a prerequisite for ordination. He was a musician. At age 14 he, with other boys, sang for alms outside wealthy homes in Magdeburg. He played the flute and wrote music for hymns and liturgy. Today's Protestant church with its choirs, great organs, congregational singing, cantatas, anthems, solos, and oratorios is indebted to the fountain of church music, Martin Luther.

(b) "The greatest hymn of the greatest man in the greatest period in German history," said James Moffatt. In 1524, Luther prepared the first Protestant hymnal consisting of thirty-seven hymns for which he wrote both words and music. His "A Mighty Fortress" is considered the greatest hymn used today by Protestants and Roman Catholics since Vatican II. Many Protestant martyrs died joyfully with this hymn on their lips. Gustavus Adolphus' army went into the battle at Leipzig singing this hymn as "the battle hymn of the Reformation." In 1717, J. S. Bach developed it into a cantata. Mendelssohn used it in his "Reformation Symphony." Richard Wagner used the tune in his "Kaiser March." Luther, writing both words and music of "Ein Feste Burg" in 1529, based it upon Ps. 46, a psalm of the confidence we have in God to overcome the evil in the world. His famous hymn says it all about our faith in God.

I. The first stanza shows us the Christian's foe. Luther in the hymn begins with our existential situation. We are in a world of "the flood of mortal ills prevailing, for still our ancient foe doth seek to work us woe." Who is he? Our chief foe is Satan because "his power is great, and, armed with cruel hate, on earth is not his equal."

(a) The devil is a reality for the Christian. He was real for Jesus who confronted him during the forty days in the wilderness. Paul wrote that we do not wrestle against flesh and blood but "against the wiles of the devil" (Eph. 6:11).

(b) How do we know there is a real devil? We recognize him for his works—crime, corruption, and perversion. We see his works in our lives, our churches, and our world. According to Luther in this hymn, he is a fierce, terrible, and cruel enemy who is out to get us.

II. The second stanza presents the Christian's champion. Luther presents Christ as our advocate in this struggle with the devil. We have "the right man on our side, the man of God's own choosing." Who is this man? Luther explains, "Christ Jesus, it is he," and "he must win the battle" against Satan.

(a) Jesus came to us through his incarnation: "The Word became flesh." He took on Satan in a mortal conflict on the cross where a cosmic battle took place, and Jesus won it for us.

(b) His resurrection confirmed the victory. Now we are sure of the ultimate outcome in this present conflict, for when Jesus returns, Satan and the powers of wickedness will forever be destroyed.

III. Christians are involved today in this battle with Satan. The third stanza tells us of the Christian's weapon. That weapon is the Word. With full confidence, Luther wrote, "One little word shall fell him." In Eph. 6 Paul tells us that we should take "the sword of the Spirit which is the word of God." One night Luther became aware of a terrifying, cold, and sinister presence in his room. He saw the devil sitting in a corner, and he said, "Oh, it's you!" He turned over in bed and went to sleep. He said: "The devil is a toothless bulldog. He looks fierce, but for the Christian, he has no bite." "One little word shall fell him," and that one little word is Christ.

IV. The final stanza gives the Christian's hope. We have hope that God will prevail over Satan's power. The hymn assures us: "That word above all earthly powers . . . abideth, God's truth abideth still, his kingdom is forever."

(a) The hymn closes with a mighty crescendo of confidence, assurance, and hope. God will win out. The cause of truth, righteousness, and peace will ultimately succeed. We Christians are on the winning side of this cosmic conflict.

(b) Until final victory comes, we may have to suffer and sacrifice. Luther was a realist. It is not pie in the sky nor peaches and cream on this earth. To be a faithful Christian in these devil-possessed days may mean to "let goods and kindred go, this mortal life also." Even "the body they may kill." Any sacrifice is worth it now, for tomorrow brings victory over the world.

SECTION IX. Resources from II Kings

BY JAMES W. COX

Topic: How Good Is a Promise?

TEXT: II Kings 8:19; see 7; 13:23.

Why was II Kings written? Here is one reason. God's people were in exile. They had every reason to doubt God's promise and faithfulness. Had he not promised great things to David and his descendants? As a captive people they saw no evidence that God would fulfill his promise. II Kings took facts from the past history of these exiled people to show that in spite of wrong—violence, idolatry, etc.—God kept his promise. If he did it then, he could and would do it now and in the future in spite of all that had recently gone wrong for his people. God, not human circumstance, controls the outcome of his promise. Thus God's promise is highly significant.

I. The promise of God is a revelation of God. (a) What does the promise reveal?

(1) It tells us something of the nature of God. A sincere promise implies the ability to carry it out. What is required is not blockbusting violence but total resourcefulness to fit the need. It asserts God's lordship and his sovereign right to do as he wills. But his will is not exercised in an arbitrary manner. Saul would not obey God, and he and his descendants were excluded. David was a man after God's own heart, and he was accessible to God. (See I Sam. 13:13–14.) The promise to David was a matter of God's grace, not of David's deserving.

(2) The promise indicates something of the purpose of God. What that purpose contained was to a degree shrouded in mystery and still is. Yet it was a purpose of grace for all the world and comes to full expression in Jesus Christ. Thus it is a revelation of God's love. (See Eph. 1:9–12.)

(b) God gives us hints of what he is and what he intends to do. (1) Nature points us to God (Rom. 1:19–20).

(2) Persons point us to God. Prophets and others close to God often speak clearly for him.

(3) Special acts of God in history—ancient or recent—remind us of his power, his righteousness, and his mercy.

II. The promise of God suffers many setbacks. (a) Nature often betrays us. We may go quickly from sunset to cyclone, from bird song to earthquake, from gracious rainfall to flood and from sunshine to drought.

(b) Prophets prove false. The best of the false prophets are people who are impatient with God's ways or timetable. They prescribe scenarios for him or become enamoured by numerology and set dates for him to perform his promises. They set the stage for even sincere believers to ask, "Where is the promise of his coming?" (See II Pet. 3:4.)

(c) What God allows may prove tragic. What saved the Israelites in their exodus through the Red Sea destroyed their Egyptian pursuers and brought sorrow to many homes.

III. God keeps his promise. (a) God is always in final control. (See Rev. 11:15.)

(b) At this very moment God is working through the ambiguities of our lives to achieve his ultimate victory. Edward Schweizer has written: "What astonishes us about the Old Testament is that it in no way tries to gloss over the wrong. . . . [It] recognizes that God was with Israel in the midst of all this utter humanness—in suffering, war, and wrong." (See Ps. 76:10.)

(c) The fulfillment of God's promise may be better than the promise as it was first understood. When the Christ came "in the fulness of time," his reality shattered the limited expectation of his people. God regularly does "exceeding abundantly above all that we ask or think."

Topic: Who Says It's Right?

Text: II Kings 21:2.

Fourteen times in II Kings we are told that certain people—mainly kings of Israel—did that which was evil in the sight of the Lord.

(a) How many of those persons believed that what they did was right under the conditions in which they found themselves? Perhaps most of them.

(b) How many of those whose crimes we deplore today can rationalize their behavior? Perhaps most of them.

(c) How many of us who constantly "come short of the glory of God" defend our delinquencies? Perhaps most of us.

I. Often wrong is right in our own eyes. Why? (a) Perhaps we do not know any better. There is vast ignorance of the scriptures and their teachings and of the ethical heritage of the church as well. We may simply take as our guidelines such fractured Bible verses as "Do unto others before they do unto you" or such homely proverbs that sanctify human frailty as "Every man has to sow his wild oats." Proverbs reminds us, "There is a way which seems right to a man, but its end is the way to death" (14:12, rsv).

(b) Someone may have deceived us. Authority figures or glamorous personalities often overwhelm unsuspecting, trusting souls. Politicians, educators or even parents can lead us astray. Well-known and admired women and men in entertainment, sports, and fashionable society sometimes commend lifestyles that are attractive and that lead to imitation and ultimately to disappointment or sometimes to tragedy. The tempter said in effect to Eve, "The reason that God does not want you to eat the fruit of that tree is because, if you do, you will be as wise as he is—and free!" Up to that point Adam and Eve had had no experience with the tempter. So they fell, and great was the fall thereof.

(c) Perhaps we deceive ourselves. There is such a thing as believing a thing to be right because of a deep wish for it to be right. It is possible that praying it through is only a matter of struggling to convince oneself that a wrong thing is right. The apostle Paul said of the heathen that God had revealed to them in nature enough to show them a good way but that "God gave them up . . . because they exchanged the truth about God for a lie" (Rom. 2:24–25, rsv).

(d) When we read that "love is the fulfilling of the law" (Rom. 13:10), we are face to face with what is called situation ethics. But this way of deciding right and wrong can be disastrous if our judgment is overwhelmed by wishful thinking or blind passion.

II. Many times a wrong thing in us may be approved by others for the same reasons for which we do it. But there are other reasons that should put us on guard.

(a) Wrong seeks solidarity. "In unity there is strength" not only against a real enemy but also against the finest traditions, against the most wholesome customs, and against God. Every person with strong opinions seeks those who will agree with him. Misery loves company, and so does guilt or megalomania. Camaraderie may be a camouflage for corruption.

(b) Others may approve wrong in us because they want something from us. It could be something as simple as our approval of them. They want to please us, and they do not want us to reject them. Their approval could be to their financial advantage or could serve some other purpose.

III. What looks good to us and to others may be wrong in the eyes of God.

(a) When we bring God into the picture, we may wonder if we could ever do anything to please him. We know he is Lord and what he says goes. He is supposed to be perfect, and if that is true, what would he tolerate in us? Adam and Eve were suspicious of God's good intentions toward them, so they went their own way, not caring at first whether they pleased him. Could it be that we project what we imagine to be the impossible demands and coldness of our parents on God? The psalmist had a different picture both of a parent and of God. "Like as a father pitieth his children, so the Lord pitieth them that fear him. For he knoweth our frame; he remembereth that we are dust." (103:13–14.)

(b) Because of our human plight—our self-will, our temptation to take refuge in the faulty opinions of others, and our suspicions of God—and because we do what is wrong in God's eyes, God opposes everything that will truly hurt us.

(1) He gives us rules and principles to guide us. The ten commandments have been set in a new light in Christ, not abolished. The law of God is embedded within his grace.

(2) God disciplines us, using the lash of conscience and perhaps even physical suffering to bring us into line. "Whom the Lord loveth, he chasteneth" (Heb. 12:6).

(3) God offers us new beginnings. As we learn more and more about what God expects of us because he cares for us, we are increasingly willing to embrace his will as our own. What he who is our Creator, our Judge, and our loving Father thinks becomes more important than what has seemed right in our own eyes or in the eyes of those whose approval we have coveted.

Topic: Choice and Consequences
Text: II Kings 3:2; see also 13:2, 11; 14:24; 15:18, 24, 28.

Judas, Benedict Arnold, Quisling—all are names signifying treachery and conjure up disdain and revulsion.

(a) The name of Jeroboam the son of Nebat came to suggest something even more sinister. The writer of II Kings compared more than a half dozen evil kings to Jeroboam, each time saying that Jeroboam "made Israel to sin."

(b) One would not have believed that his name would ever have been so besmirched. He was a rising star during the closing days of Solomon's reign. (See I Kings 11:26–14:20.)

I. God gives at least some of us, like Jeroboam, the chance for vast influence.

(a) No person is without some possibilities of influence for good.

(1) Fortunate is the man or woman who is captured by a vision of "the will to meaning."

(2) Finding meaning or making life meaningful can be a driving force for great achievement.

(3) It can be a sustaining power, even if amid frustration and failure, we have only a modest amount.

(4) It can be a matter of sheer faith in God when all evidence seems to deny any meaning in life.

(b) The possibilities of evil influence are also vast. (1) It is easier to do great evil than great good.

(2) Great good is rarely achieved apart from some definite or even strenuous action. But evil triumphs not only through diabolical planning and hazardous action but also when good men do nothing.

II. Responsible choice makes the difference in what our influence will be, whether good or evil.

(a) When life is at a crossroads, we can count on two tremendous facts. (1) God has a plan for us. He has made us for himself, as Augustine said. Exactly what God wants us to do is not always clear to us, but it can become clear to us that only in his will can we find true peace.

(2) God will back us if we undertake to do his will. All the resources of heaven are behind the man or woman who says yes to God. For Jesus this did not mean a takeover of power from the high priest, from Pontius Pilate, or from Caesar. It did mean resurrection after he was crucified.

(b) We can spoil the plan. (1) We can forsake God. (See Jer. 2:13.) Sometimes it is success in terms of money or power that becomes the great temptation.

(2) We can lead others away from God. Jeroboam and the other kings of Israel reinforced their own apostasy with other vulnerable and agreeable people. Users of unethical drugs seek company in their indulgence. "As thick as thieves" exemplified the principle.

(3) God is merciful and forgiving. He attempts to bring us back to his purposes

when we have gone astray. Chastisement follows us. Yet we can refuse to learn from our experiences. (See I Kings 13:33.)

III. We cannot begin to measure the final results of our choices.

(a) Like a rolling snowball, evil compounds itself. (See Exod. 20:5.)

(b) The reverse is true also. (1) The church is adorned with the names of those who have not only kept the commandments but who have also truly loved the Lord from their earliest days.

(2) The church is adorned with the names of those who, like Saul of Tarsus, have changed course and served God as zealously as they had fought against him.

(3) To each of us comes the possibility of sinning and leading others to sin or of obeying God and leaving behind us a luminous trail that will lead others to God.

Topic: Day of Desperation or Day of Salvation

TEXT: II Kings 7:3.

The time of desperation may be the time of salvation. It was so with the starving lepers.

I. Their desperation.
II. Their dilemma.
III. Their decision.
IV. Their discovery.
V. Their day of good tidings.

Topic: Eyes to See the Invisible

TEXT: II Kings 6:8–23.

The ability to cope with our hardest problems depends on a recognition of God's resources.

I. Our human needs are real and often even greater than we know.

II. Our ability to cope is surprising yet limited.

III. God's resources are real and unlimited and can banish our fears, and our eyes are opened to see that "they that be with us are more than they that be with them" (v. 16).

Topic: Is Obedience Too Hard?

TEXT: II Kings 5:13; see also Deut. 30:14; Rom. 10:8.

Salvation comes through simple response to what God requires.

I. *Situation.* (a) A great man, Naaman, was brought down by a dread disease (v. 1).

(b) A surprising providence gave him hope of healing (vv. 2–4).

(c) He set out to find this salvation (vv. 5–6).

II. *Complication.* (a) The king of Israel did not know what to do (v. 7).

(b) Naaman was angered by the prophet Elisha's command and turned away (vv. 8–12).

III. *Resolution.* (a) Naaman listened to the voice of love and concern (v. 13).

(b) He simply obeyed (v. 14).

(c) He committed himself to God to serve him the rest of his days (vv. 15–18).

Topic: Real Security

TEXT: II Kings 2:12; 13:14.

When the prophet Elijah and later the prophet Elisha died, the same confession was made in a lament: "My father! My father, the chariots and the horsemen of Israel!" The words actually said more about God than about the prophet. They said what Proverbs asserted: "Where there is no vision [prophetic vision, in which God's message comes to expression], the people perish" (29:18). Isaiah wrote: "The grass withereth, the flower fadeth: but the word of our God shall stand for ever" (40:7) and "My word . . . shall not return unto me void, but it shall accomplish that which I please" (55:11). The word of the Lord is the strength of his people.

I. Those who speak for God have a decisive role in the fortunes of a people.

(a) Rulers have always had gurus to whom they looked for guidance. Some have consulted astrologers and made decisions by the juxtaposition of the stars. Others have consulted prophets from whom they awaited favorable reports before going to battle. Gurus, astrologers, and prophets have often led the people astray.

(b) People who speak for God, if listened to, can make a difference in the well-being of a people. Military success and political power do not always gain that well-being.

II. The uniqueness of the word of God's true spokesmen lies in the fact that the word comes from outside. It is not born of the selfish and shortsighted aims of arrogant and greedy people.

(a) Micaiah was the first of the classical prophets. Contrary to the court chaplains who told the king what he wanted to hear, Micaiah spoke the truth to the king's displeasure and was imprisoned for it.

(b) Micaiah spoke the word—God's word—from outside. That is why Ahab said, "I hate him; for he doth not prophesy good concerning me, but evil" (I Kings 22:8).

(c) It has been demonstrated again and again in the history of nations that the voices of reason, right, and prudence have been ignored at the nations' peril.

III. The true and saving word often comes when least expected and where least wanted. The time is never quite right. The people are not ready for it. Unjust social customs can be so deeply entrenched and unjust economic practices can be so time-honored that a word from God comes as a rude interruption. The spokesman is a pest. He must be silenced at all costs.

IV. The word from God comes because God cares. "But though he cause grief, yet will he have compassion according to the multitude of his mercies" (Lam. 3:32). God loves his people too much to abandon them forever to their destructive ways.

V. This caring, saving word of God may come in various ways. (a) It may come in an event. "The Lord sent a word into Jacob, and it hath lighted upon Israel" (Isa. 9:8). A word or an act of judgment is in the end redemptive. Simeon said to Mary of Jesus, "Behold this child is set for the fall and rising again of many in Israel" (Luke 2:34).

(b) It may come in the scriptures. So it came in the time of King Josiah (II Kings 22:8–23:3) and in the experience of Timothy (II Tim. 3:14–17).

(c) It may come in a deepening conviction which one interprets as the voice of God.

(d) It may come through the words of one who speaks in God's name. (1) Sunday by Sunday faithful ministers perform a prophetic task. Their work must not be underrated because of the high visibility of the individual prophet who commands universal attention.

(2) God has put forth some individual persons such as Moses, Jesus, Paul, Augustine, Luther, Wesley, and Pope John XXIII, as well as Elijah and Elisha, who have so enacted or spoken his word as to leave the world forever different.

(3) The words of Hebrews are especially appropriate here: "In the past God spoke to our ancestors many times and in many ways through the prophets, but in these last days he has spoken to us through his Son. He is the one through whom God created the universe, the one whom God has chosen to possess all things at the end. He reflects the brightness of God's glory and is the exact likeness of God's own being, sustaining the universe with his powerful word." (Heb. 1:1–3, TEV.)

SECTION X. *Children's Stories and Sermons*

January 2. The Two-Faced Man (New Year's Sunday)

Can you imagine a man with two faces? Well, once upon a time it was supposed that there was a man who had two faces, one where your face is and one where the back of your head is. Just think of having two faces, one in front of you and one behind you. You could look in front of you and behind you at the same time, and no one would be able to talk behind your back without your seeing him. But think also of all the trouble this would be. It would mean two faces to wash, two noses to blow, four sets of teeth to clean and to ache!

This storybook man with the two faces was very real to the ancient Romans. They were so fond of him they told their children about him, put a picture of his head on a coin, and built a temple where people could worship in his honor. His name was Janus, and they named the first month of the year January after him because with his two faces he could look forward and backward at the same time.

No person with two real faces has ever lived. There are two-faced people whose faces are not honest and who do not tell the truth, but God has not made us with a face in front and another behind because we don't need an extra face. God wants us to look ahead, and it is easier to look forward with one face. Of course, he wants us to look back on the mistakes that we have made but only so that we will be able to live better lives in the future.—Ralph Conover Lankler.

January 9. Treasures in the Earth

Our beautiful earth that we enjoy so much has a storehouse of gifts within it. The earth is a ball of rock some 7,900 miles in diameter. It weighs about 6.6 sextillion tons. It contains a hard center as heavy as iron and several massive rock layers. Out of our earth has come a wealth of minerals and stones that add to our economic life. God not only told us to till the land but to use with care and gratitude the gifts inside the good earth.

When we pick up a rock or precious gem, we hold in our hands a part of God's world. If we could go through the center of our earth, we would discover more rock than anything else. If you have toured a cave, you have noticed the colors and shapes of stone and crystal that make the underground passageway look like a cathedral.

The story within the earth tells of God's inestimable riches, beauty, faithfulness, and love for his people. When we use these gifts rightly, we are helping God tell the world.—Harold A. Schulz.

January 16. Four Apples

A circuit rider brought home only four apples at a time. Apples were a rare fruit on the almost orchardless frontier. The preacher's wife gave an apple to each of her three sons and placed hers on the mantle. When the boys finished eating their apples, the mother saw them observing hers. She divided hers into three pieces for them. The boys munched the fruit and discussed how strange it was that their mother did not care for apples.

When one of the sons was an old man, he explained that he had come to understand that it was not because his mother disliked apples but because she loved her sons better.—Adapted from William A. Quayle.

January 23. What Can I Do?

"What can I do?" Have you ever heard those words—coming from your own lips? Theodore Roosevelt had an apt answer. "What can you do?" he would say. "Do what you can, with what you have, where you are."

Most people are prone to underestimate their abilities. That means you're probably one of them. The opposite is sometimes true, but most of us tend to think too little of our capacities rather than too highly of them.

"What can I do? What's the use of competing with those who easily leave me far behind?"

Jesus told a story about a man who talked like that—a man entrusted with a sum of money but so afraid he might lose it he didn't even collect simple interest on it. Instead, he hid it in the ground. The bottom line was he was so fearful of not measuring up to what others could have done with that same amount and was so overwhelmed by the ability of others and embarrassed by what he considered his own lack of ability, he refused to do anything.

Jesus was trying to show by his story— in which this man was soundly rebuked— that even those of marginal ability have important roles to play.—Arthur McPhee.

January 30. Working Together

In Rudyard Kipling's story, *The Ship That Found Herself,* the proud skipper said when she was christened: "It takes much more than christening to make a ship. She's all here, but the parts of her have not learned to work together yet." On her first voyage in the Atlantic, she ran into foul weather. The little ship pitched and rolled, swung and dipped. Her funnels grumbled, her beams creaked, her rivets chattered, and her engines puffed and snorted. After she had weathered the gale for fourteen days, all her parts finally seemed to work together. The ship, wrote Kipling, had found herself, so that, if she had been hailed, she might have replied in one unified voice, "I am the *Dimbula.*"— Jesse Duncan in *The War Cry.*

February 6. Carrying the Load

An oceangoing ship began to complain about the job it was called on to perform. "I have to carry such burdens," it complained. "They just load tons and tons of cargo on me. No one else has to carry such a load. Some day I'm just going to quit." The ocean overheard the ship complaining and replied: "True, they do place heavy burdens on you, but, remember, it is I who bear you up and support you. Suppose I quit supporting you. Where would you be then?"

Some Christians are like that ship. They complain about the heavy burdens they have to carry. They fail to realize that Christ is the one who really supports them. What a source of strength for all those who labor and are heavy laden!— John Wade.

February 13. The Legend of the Web (Brotherhood Week)

A man cried out from the depths of hell, pleading with the gods for relief from his pain and torture. The gods asked what good he had done while on earth. After thinking a long time, he told how one day, while walking through the woods, he saw a spider, and instead of stepping on it, he stepped aside and let it live. At once the silvery thread of a spider web was let down to him in hell. Seizing it, he was lifted slowly out of his unhappiness. His fellow sufferers, seeing him about to escape, grabbed his clothes and his feet, and all were lifted together. Then this man, fearing that the web might break, called out to the others: "Let go. The web is for me, not for you." But, alas, when they all had let go, then and only then the thread broke, and all fell back together into the pit of hell. The tiny thread was strong enough to lift all together, but it could not bear the weight of one selfish person who cared more about himself than he cared for his fellow human beings.—Winfield S. Haycock.

February 20. Our Sensuous Faith

Bible writers regularly choose simple human experiences to explain the wonders of faith. We "hear" the word of the Lord and "see" what God has done. We learn that God "touches" the hearts of people (I Sam. 10:26), that we spread the "fragrance" of the knowledge of God (II Cor. 2:14), and that we can "taste" and "see" that God is good (Ps. 34:1). God in Christ is communicating with us through our human senses. Ours is a sensuous faith. We are persons who can affirm with Peter that we have "tasted the kindness of the Lord" (I Pet. 2:3).—Douglas Bacon in *These Days.*

February 27. The Voice of God (Lent)

A little boy liked to hear the thunder. He would run to the window and look out. If the window was open, he would stick his head outside. His mother thought that this was queer, so she asked him why he did it. He said that he wanted to hear God speak and explained that his Sunday school teacher had told him that God spoke to Moses in the thunder and lightning.

Well, this mother was very happy that her little boy was not afraid of the thunder and the lightning, but she was most pleased that he wanted to hear God speak to him. She told him a story about a prophet named Elijah, who had to run for his life in order to escape the soldiers of a wicked queen named Jezebel. He found a place to hide in a cave in a mountain called Horeb. He waited there to see if God would speak to him and tell him what he should do next. After a while a mighty wind that shook the whole mountain came up, but God was not in the wind; then an earthquake, but God was not in the earthquake; then a fire, but God was not in the fire; then a still small voice, and God was in the still small voice.

God has spoken in the thunder and lightning, but most of the time he speaks in the still small voice—the voice of conscience. We can hear him speaking to us every day. He tells us what is right and what is wrong to do. If we listen to the voice of conscience, we will hear God speaking to us.—Ralph Conover Lankler.

March 6. Around the Table (Lent)

Mealtime! Just hearing the word gives us a good feeling. Most of us like to eat. And if we are eating with friends, so much the better. Conversation seems to flow more freely as we sit around the table.

Jesus must have enjoyed eating. He was certainly a sought-after dinner guest in many social circles. He ate with Pharisees. He ate with publicans and sinners. He ate with Mary, Martha, and Lazarus. He ate on the road with his disciples and at wedding feasts.

He placed special importance on his last meal with the disciples. At this supper Jesus gave his disciples—and us—a new commandment. "Love one another, even as I have loved you." We pledge this love as we meet with other Christians around the Lord's table for Communion. As we love one another, we proclaim the Lord's death until he comes again.—Betty Harmon in *The Upper Room.*

March 13. Reaching Out in Love (Lent)

She rises at 4:30 each morning, prays, eats a simple meal, and goes to the city to work. It is some of the most difficult and heartbreaking work in the world, but she does it gladly. Her name is Teresa; the city is Calcutta.

Although the work Mother Teresa began many years ago has spread all over the world, the heart of it is still in Calcutta, a city where thousands live in the streets—malnourished, clothed in little more than rags, consumed with the one task of somehow surviving until tomorrow.

For thirty years, Mother Teresa and her friends have sought out these destitute ones, providing what food and clothing and shelter they could.

The world needs more Mother Teresas—persons, who because they have known the love of Christ, feel compelled to reach out in love to the lost, the hungry, the destitute, the dying.

Jesus said that his disciples would be known by their love. Jesus' ministry on earth was a ministry of spiritual and physical healing. He wanted to make people whole again, and he still does—in part by reaching out in love through those who seek to follow him.—Arthur McPhee.

March 20. How Close to the Cross? (Passion Sunday)

In the account of the events of Jesus' crucifixion, Luke is careful to note the location of various persons in relation to the cross. The two thieves were crucified "one on the right and one on the left." "The people stood by, watching." The soldiers came up and offered him vinegar. "All his acquaintances and the women who had followed him from Galilee stood at a distance and saw these things." His friends stood at a distance.

Perhaps there is a message for us in the location of those about the cross. Sometimes the most unlikely, even criminals, find themselves closest to Jesus, while those best acquainted with him find themselves distant from him.—S. T. Kimbrough, Jr.

March 27. Forgiving and Forgiven (Holy Week)

In that ancient time when human beings were creating the letters of an alphabet from word pictures, their words had a picturesque quality. They made boats from reeds woven together, very much like our wicker baskets. Moses was hidden in such a craft. These basket-boats were waterproofed with a covering of pitch—which we call tar. And a word which meant thus "to cover" in the ancient Hebrew came to be a word meaning to forgive.

An old leaky boat became waterlogged and useless, no longer able to carry a load. And the ingenious inventors of words had observed lives ruined and burdened by a sense of guilt—able to bear no weight. But, like an old boat which had become new by being given a new coating of pitch, so forgiven people could become new. People's lives, ruined by a sense of guilt, became as new with the experience of forgiveness.

One who said, "Father, forgive them," also said, "Your sins are forgiven." You too may be whole again and your life renewed if you will forgive and be forgiven.—Orval H. Austin in *These Days.*

April 3. Good Morning! (Easter)

"Jesus himself met them, and said, 'Good morning!' " This is Goodspeed's translation of Matt. 28:9. Sometimes we greet other people without putting much meaning into the words, but what a "Good morning" that was following the resurrection!

This greeting of Christ has a special meaning for us every day. His personal "Good morning" assures us he is near enough for every situation we face.

The risen Christ says, "Good morning," and every dawn breaks in glory. Joy and victory brighten our lives and fill our hearts with hope and praise.

This is the new life which Paul wrote about and which has been experienced by countless Christians across the centuries. It can be ours too.—Laren Spear in *The Upper Room.*

April 10. Hearing God

Playing along the Gulf beach in Florida, a little boy found a large shell. He took it to his father, who helped him clean it of sand and silt. The father then put the shell to the child's ear and told him to listen. "What do you hear?" he asked. The little boy listened intently for a minute and then replied, "I think I hear God!"

The voice of God is heard in his creation. His presence makes itself known through his handiwork. We are prone to become so busy that we shut out God's voice. We do not see his wonders about us. Our senses become dulled, and we fail to find him in our world at all.

Certainly God manifests himself in more than nature alone. God is in the smile of a child, the hands of the aged, the stroke of the artist's brush, and the healing art of the surgeon's scalpel. Wherever God may announce his presence, we must be sensitive to see and to respond by attuning our own nature to his.—Paul K. McAfee in *The Upper Room.*

April 17. Parable

Two frogs fell into a jar of cream. The top of the cream was far from the jar's top, and though the frogs struggled, they could not leap out. In despair one frog began to think negative thoughts of defeat. "I know I can't get out. I know I have to die. So why not get it over?" In resignation he sank and died. The other frog, courageous and undaunted, assumed a positive attitude. "Sure, I may die, but if I do, I'll go down kicking." With great vigor he began to swim, thrashing about and kicking with all his might. His continued activity churned the cream into butter, and feeling solid footing under him, he leaped out of the jar.—Richard B. Grenell.

April 24. Can You Love Bats?

Brother Leo and St. Francis were walking along a pathway at dusk. Suddenly two bats came so close that the wing of one of the bats got tangled in Francis' hair. Francis says, "What was that?" Brother Leo responds, "A damned bat, Brother Francis, a plague on it." Then Francis responds to Brother Leo: "All living things have their history, Brother Leo. You must never speak ill of any of them. The moment you know the history of a man, a wild animal, or a bird, your ill feelings will turn to love. Do you know the bat's history?"—Nikos Kazantzakis.

May 1. Try-Outs

A little boy, Jamie, wanted to have one of the lead roles in a church play so badly he couldn't sleep. On the Saturday of try-outs he was up before anyone in the house. Through his persistence, his mother got him to the church exactly on time. When they called for boys and girls to try out, Jamie was first in line. His mother waited anxiously. Fifteen or twenty minutes went by. Finally the doors burst open and out ran her Jamie, eyes shining and grinning from ear to ear. With great joy he said: "I made it! I've been chosen to clap and cheer."—Craig Biddle III.

May 8. It Shines! (Mother's Day)

The ancient Hebrews had a verb which meant to shine which in the process of time gave us a word and an idea—home.

Picture a tribe living in tents, moving herds from oasis to oasis, traveling unbroken stretches with no map or compass. See such a group, tired after a long hot journey away from camp. They are unable to find their way back to camp and may wait for night and the help of stars. The sun is sinking in the west. Suddenly one cries: *"Awhal, awhal!* It shines, it shines! The slanting rays of the setting sun, glinting on their mohair tents back in camp, give them a leading light.

The story behind the word is that the next time they pitched a tent they called it *ohel,* a derivative of *awhal,* that which shines, a beacon to wandering folk. And when they wanted a word by which to call the tabernacle of the Lord, there it was—that which shines, that which guides us when we are lost.—Orval H. Austin in *These Days.*

May 15. Stick-to-itiveness

People who have left significant tracks in the sands of history have not always been the most healthy or the most brilliant. Many of them left their mark primarily because they did not press the eject button when the going got rough. They had a characteristic called stick-to-itiveness.

Thomas Edison's teachers told him he was too stupid to learn.

F. W. Woolworth at twenty-one years of age was not permitted to wait on customers at the store where he worked because he was told he did not have enough sense.

Lou Gehrig was asked to quit his boyhood team because he was such a poor player.

Napoleon was an epileptic.

When Walt Disney submitted his first drawing, the editor told him that he had absolutely no talent.

Beethoven was deaf when he composed much of his most famous music.

The pistol-shooting champion of the 1952 Olympics lost his right arm six months after winning his gold medal. He trained for the next three-and-a-half years with his left arm and then won his second gold medal.

Mozart's publisher told him he would never get a penny for his music.

Louisa May Alcott, author of *Little Women,* was told by an editor that she should stick to sewing because she had no writing ability.

Homer, the poet, was blind.

Fanny Crosby, the songwriter, was blind.

Walter Scott had a club foot.

Woodrow Wilson did not learn to read until he was ten.

Heb. 11 gives many other examples of those who stuck to it.—Knofel Staton in *The Lookout.*

May 22. Taming the Tongue

A man had a trained fish. When he whistled the fish would jump out of the bowl into his hand. I've heard of trained fleas and a flea circus, but the only kind of fleas that I have seen were not trained.

It seems that if they can train the elephant, which is the largest animal in the world, and the flea, which is one of the smallest of insects, we should be able to train anything. But the Bible mentions one thing that cannot be trained. In the epistle of James we read: "For every kind of beasts and birds, of creeping things and things in the sea, is tamed, and hath been tamed by mankind; but the tongue can no man tame."

What James meant is this: No man can tame the tongue except the person who owns it. I cannot train your tongue, and you cannot train my tongue. Each one of us must learn to train his own tongue.

We can train our tongues not to tell lies but to tell the truth. We can train our tongues to say kind and pleasant words and not to utter mean and bitter words. We can train our tongues to speak correctly, to recite, or to sing. One of the hardest things to do with our tongues is to train them to be quiet. We do not want them to be too quiet because we like to hear little boys and girls talk, sing, and even shout, but quiet enough so you won't seem to have a tongue that wags at both ends.—Ralph Conover Lankler.

May 29. Second Choice

Do you always get what you want? When you make your plans and choose your preference, does it always work out that way? Of course not.

Then don't cry about it. If you can't have first choice, be ready for second choice. Make the best of second best.

A midwestern farmer was happy with high hopes for the future. His crops looked great. Prosperity was just around the corner.

Then came a devastating plague of grasshoppers. Everything changed for the worst—except his attitude! He offered a classic demonstration of making do with the leftovers of broken plans.

"Well, they got most of my crop. But I gathered about ten tons of the critters, dried and stored them in the barn. I'll feed them to the chickens this winter. If I can't raise a crop, I can raise chickens. Reckon I'll come out ahead somehow."

God works that way too. Perhaps you rejected his first choice for your life. Those opportunities may be past and beyond fulfillment now. But he still has the second choice for you. Make the best of it! —C. W. Bess.

June 5. We Can Help

Paganini was walking down a London street one cold night when he came upon a blind beggar with blue fingers sawing away on a cheap violin. The great violinist took the instrument and played such divine notes that a crowd gathered. The beggar's hat was passed, and he had a hot meal and a warm bed that night. We cannot all render services this way, but we all can be on the alert to share what we can with those less fortunate than we are.—A. Barton Brown.

June 12. Let Your Light Shine

During vacation we drove to the Cape Hatteras National Seashore in North Carolina and climbed 268 steps to the top of Hatteras Lighthouse, 191 feet above the mean high water mark. Built in 1870 at a cost of $150,000, Hatteras Light is a warning to ships at sea, reminding seamen of the treacherous shoals which extend nine miles out to sea. More than 500 ships of many nations have foundered at or near Cape Hatteras, earning for the area the reputation of "Graveyard of the Atlantic."

Hatteras Light today, thanks to a lamp system producing a beam of 250,000 candlepower, is visible twenty miles to sea, and under especially favorable atmospheric conditions has been observed fifty-one miles at sea. That is some beacon!

Our Lord spoke of his followers as beacons of light, as candles lighted and placed upon a stand, not hidden under a bushel. We who believe in Jesus Christ are expected to radiate light and hope to those who are wandering, lost, and adrift on the seas of life.—Roger A. Nicholson.

June 19. Buried Talents

A fellow bought new hubcaps for his car. He was afraid someone would steal them, so each time he parked his car, he'd remove the hubcaps and lock them inside. Well, many people live their whole lives like that. By burying their talents, their entire existence becomes nothing more than protection of the chrome.

Suppose Sir Winston Churchill had done that. Sir Winston was a slow starter, a disappointment to his parents and his teachers. But because he was willing to put his, as yet, undeveloped talents on the line, he grew into one of the great leaders of the century.

Or suppose Albert Einstein, who was also a slow and disappointing student, had kept his ideas about relativity to himself. Would men have walked on the moon? How would we view the universe today?

Using our abilities and resources well is of great importance to our friends, family, everyone. But not only to them—to God also.—Arthur McPhee.

June 26. People and Dogs

A man, planning a trip, wanted to take his German shepherd dog with him. He wrote ahead to the motel to see if dogs were allowed. The manager wrote back: "I have been in business for more than thirty-five years. I have never had a dog set fire to a bed with a cigarette. I have never had to call the police to have a disorderly dog ejected. I have never had to search a dog's suitcase for stolen towels or blankets. No dog has ever left whiskey bottles in the bathtub or a ring on the dresser. I have never had to check up on dogs to be sure that they were man and wife. Sure, the dog is welcome, and if he will vouch for you, you can come along too."

July 3. God's Rainbow

Wonder fills our hearts when we see God's bow in the clouds. What is a rainbow? It is the light of the sun split up into all its beautiful facets of color. The countless droplets of moisture in the atmosphere reflect the rays of the sun. Then we see the beauty of color that light contains.

So it is with God. He is invisible, but when he came to our world in the person of his Son, people could behold him in all the beauty of his character. In Jesus we see love, holiness, compassion, truth, faithfulness, and mercy. When we see the tears of Jesus, we see God's sympathy. When we see Jesus smile on little children, we see his gentleness. When we see him calming the tempest by his word, we know his power. When we see him suffering and dying for us on Calvary's cross, we know God's great, eternal love for us.—William Montgomery in *The Upper Room*.

July 10. God's Sunshine

Nothing is more beautiful than bright rays of sunshine filtering through tall green trees, glistening on crystal water, or sparkling in the hair of a child. It's as if God is smiling down on his beloved creation. What a warm, fulfilling feeling! We too are filled with sunshine—the sunshine of God's love. It fills our bodies and its rays shine from our eyes and radiate through our smiles. What a shame to hide such beauty! God's sunshine is for sharing so that all who see it may also be filled. So let your sun shine brightly and share the love of God with which you are filled. Keep in mind the words of the song, "This little light of mine, I'm gonna let it shine, let it shine, let it shine."—Andrea Arnold in *The Secret Place*.

July 17. The Goose That Couldn't Fly

A flock of wild geese had settled to rest on a pond. One of the flock had been captured by a gardener, who had clipped its wings before releasing it. When the geese started to resume their flight, this one tried frantically but vainly to lift itself into the air. The others, observing his struggles, flew about in obvious efforts to encourage him, but it was no use. Thereupon the entire flock settled back on the pond and waited even though the urge to go on was strong within them. For several days they waited until the damaged feather had grown sufficiently to permit the goose to fly.—Albert Schweitzer.

July 24. Hearing the Corn Grow

In tall corn country, people often say that they can hear the corn grow. I'm not sure that I have ever actually heard corn grow, but in good, warm growing weather one can recognize with each new day that the corn is taller. Of course, we don't expect it to get shorter. Corn grows. That's its nature. That's the nature of all living things. It is this process of dependable growth that encourages the farmer. He has faith in the process. His livelihood depends upon it. We all depend upon it.

Growth in the knowledge of our Lord Jesus Christ is a process too. No one is born into the kingdom in full strength and maturity. From year to year we should be able to mark our Christian development in those qualities of the spirit that define the nature of his people.

The world around us realizes the vital, living presence of Christ in the growing, maturing personalities of Christians. It is a real testimony to his power when others see and hear Christians grow.—George Adler.

July 31. What the Lungs Need

The lungs need to be filled with air. There have recently been installed in Japan machines from which by inserting a coin one can obtain a supply not of fruit or chocolate but of oxygen. Thank God we do not normally need to pay for air. It would cost us a fortune. Every twenty-four hours each of us breathes on an average some 23,040 times, inhaling in the process some 3,000 gallons of air. In the course of an average lifetime we breathe about 600 million times, deriving 75 percent of our vitality from the atmosphere.

The spirit also needs to be filled with God. Just as it takes the material to satisfy the material and the mental to satisfy the mental, so it takes the spiritual to satisfy the spiritual. The spirit of man is empty until filled with him.—Ian Macpherson.

August 7. Growing Power

Over 100 years ago Rutherford Platt, a Massachusetts farmer, got interested in the growing power of apples, melons, and squashes. He harnessed a squash to a weight-lifting device which had a dial like a grocer's scale to indicate the pressure exerted by the expanding fruit. As the days passed he kept piling on counterbalancing weights. He could hardly believe his eyes when he saw his vegetables quietly exerting a lifting force of 5,000 pounds per square inch. When nobody believed him, he set up exhibits of harnessed squashes and invited the public to come and see. The experiment was reported in the Annual Report of the Massachusetts Board of Agriculture in 1875.

This growth power is amazing. I possess an even more amazing growth potential than a squash. I am searching for what really nourishes and sustains life. I have a restlessness and a guidance system to fulfill an amazing destiny.—Joe A. Harding.

August 14. Moses' Horns

At the main entrance of our sanctuary sits a replica of Michelangelo's *Moses.* A remarkable feature of the famed statue is the pair of horns on the prophet's head.

Exod. 34:29–35 states that when Moses returned from Mount Sinai with the tablets of the law in his hands, the skin of his face shone—so much so that he had to veil his face before anyone would dare go near him. The verb which scholars now translate "shone" is a rarely used one which caused earlier translators, like Jerome, no end of trouble. Its only other occurrence in the Bible (Ps. 69:31) is an unmistakable reference to a bull displaying its horns. Quite naturally the Vulgate—Jerome's Latin translation which was all Michelangelo had to go by—gave "horned" as the strange word's meaning in Exodus too.

That is why Michelangelo put horns on Moses. Often we are victims of faulty data and inadequate knowledge.—Ralph Cannon.

August 21. Greatest Need

"Which is your favorite doll?" the visiting grandfather asked the shy little girl, trying to draw her out. "Will you promise not to laugh?" she requested, solemn blue eyes looking up at him. Reassured, she ran to her room. Soon she was back, a tattered, broken doll tucked protectively under her arm. "This one," she said. Trying to keep his end of the bargain, the grandfather asked gently, "Why?" To which the little girl replied quickly: "Because it needs me to love it. If I don't love it, nobody will!"—Alma Gordon Dole.

August 28. Life-Giving Water

Hezekiah's tunnel is an intriguing place in modern Jerusalem. About 100 years before Christ's birth the Assyrians massed against Hezekiah and the Jews. The Jews covered up the spring outside Jerusalem's walls and dug a 1700-foot underground tunnel in the city. When the Assyrians attacked, Hezekiah's forces had a secret source of water, "a river whose streams make glad the city of God." The secret source of water not only quenched thirst, but it also was a symbol of the presence of God. "The Lord of hosts is with us." The enemy could not see the water or God, but both were there.—John T. Randolph in *Family Devotions.*

September 4. Looking Up

When you go out at night, do you look up at the sky? Do you turn your eyes up to see all the shiny dots that we call stars? If you do, you undoubtedly wonder how far they are away from us, how large they are, and what they would be like if we could travel to them. There are millions of them, millions of miles away, and some of these bright spots in the sky that we call stars are planets much larger than our earth.

The trouble with most of us is that we do not look often enough at the sky. We walk around with our heads bent over looking at the ground. A dog spends most of his time looking at the ground because he buries his bones there. His treasure is in the earth, and he looks at the sky only to bark at the moon. It is good for our souls to look at the sky and think about the wonders of God's universe, and it is good for our bodies. To look up is to raise our shoulders and chests and to fill our lungs with air. It seems to pull the whole body up into the proper shape.—Ralph Conover Lankler.

September 11. Light in the Church

In a certain mountain village centuries ago, a nobleman wondered what legacy he should leave his townspeople. At last he decided to build a church.

When the people gathered for the unveiling of the new church, they marveled at its beauty and completeness. Then someone asked: "But where are the lamps? How will it be lighted since there are no windows?"

The nobleman pointed to many brackets recessed in the walls. Then he gave to each family a lamp which they were to bring with them when they came to worship.

"Each time you are here, the area where you are seated will be lighted," said the nobleman. "When you are not here, the area will be dark. This is to remind you that if you do not come to church some part of God's house will be dark."—John M. Drescher.

September 18. Sticking Your Neck Out

Have you ever watched a turtle closely? If so, you have probably noticed that the creature has two typical poses. First, at any sign of danger, he draws his neck safely into his shell and stands still. Later, when he is ready to move on, he sticks his neck out, stretches his crooked little legs and goes slowly forward. Instructive little habits these are—and typical of some human beings.

There are people like that. Some, at any indication of danger, will draw within themselves, without exposing themselves to any attack from the outside. There are others who, though they recognize the peril of criticism or censure, are willing to stick their necks out and dare to move ahead to stand out and speak out on unpopular causes.—Emil Kontz.

September 25. Lantern-Bearers

Robert Louis Stevenson recorded the memory of a summer that he spent in Northern Scotland as a boy of twelve. Toward the end of September, when school time was drawing near and the nights were already black, Stevenson and his friends would equip themselves with tin bull's-eye lanterns. They would buckle the lanterns to their waists and button their top coats over them. The lanterns smelled of blistered tin, never burned right, and would always burn their fingers, but the boys didn't mind. When the boys met in the darkness of the night, there would be an anxious, "Have you got your lantern?" and a gratified "Yes!" Then the boy would open his coat, pull down the slide on his lantern, and let his light shine. Stevenson entitled the story that described his boyhood experience, "The Lantern Bearers."

Jesus wants you and me to be lantern bearers. He wants our lives to shine as Christian lights that reveal God to others. —John T. Randolph.

October 2. Somebody's Something

Leslie Weatherhead was an air raid warden during the terrible days of the London blitz in the 1940s. Making his rounds one night after an unusually heavy attack, he found an eight-year-old boy sobbing amid the smoking ruins of a building.

Weatherhead asked the boy if he were lost. The boy nodded yes. "Where does your father live?" Weatherhead asked. "He's overseas in the service," the child answered. "What about your mother, brothers, sisters?" "I don't have any" was the boy's reply. "They have all been killed." "Any relatives, grandparents, anybody?" The boy responded negatively.

Weatherhead then stooped down nearer the child's face and asked, "Son, who are you?" Sobbing convulsively, the boy said with a quivering voice, "Mister, I ain't nobody's nothing."

The words of that boy aptly describe the spiritual state of thousands of persons today. "I ain't nobody's nothing." Because of God in Christ, we are not "nobody's nothing" but "somebody's something."—*Proclaim.*

October 9. Out of Sight

What's out of sight is often more significant than what's in view. Take an iceberg, for instance. I've seen several up close, and they are impressive. But when you see one of those marvelous sculptures, all you really get to see is one-tenth of it.

Just as ninety percent of an iceberg is hidden beneath the surface, so ninety percent of the potential of most of us lies beneath the surface and is never realized. Few of us use as much as a tenth of our mind power. Few of us realize our physical potential. But why not?

One reason is lack of insight. If we could see the unlocked potential within us as God sees it, we'd never be content to settle for second best again. That is unless we also suffer from a lack of ambition. Everything worthwhile involves work. As da Vinci once said, "O Lord, you give us everything at the price of an effort."

But there's another obstacle that often gets in the way of our being all we can be —lack of direction. Maybe that one is the most destructive of all to the fulfillment of our potential. If you don't know where you're going, how are you going to get there?—Arthur McPhee.

October 16. A Little Girl's Pennies

Years ago in Philadelphia a little girl went to a Sunday school and asked to be taken into one of the classes. The class was full, and the church was so small that there was no place for her. Her desire to find a place in that Sunday school fired her with a zeal to see the church made bigger to provide room for more children like herself.

Without speaking to anyone, she began saving pennies to help build that bigger church. Death came to the little girl, but under her pillow was found an old, red pocketbook in which were fifty-seven pennies and a little scrap of paper on which was written the reason why she was saving her pennies.

The pastor who conducted the funeral told the story of those fifty-seven pennies, and it got into the newspapers. What could a little girl's fifty-seven pennies do? They did more than you could have imagined. The tide of gifts which her example inspired flowed with increasing strength, and in six years the fifty-seven pennies had become $250,000. This amount of money became the nucleus of the Philadelphia Baptist Temple and its Good Samaritan Hospital, as well as the Temple University with its thousands of students. All this came into being as the marvelous harvest of a little girl's devotion.—C. Thomas Hilton.

October 23. Rooted in the Word

The great skyscrapers of our cities have foundations that descend almost as far beneath the ground as the building rises into the air. Their towering mass requires a system firmly rooted. Such a structure withstands powerful wind currents, storms, and the erosive forces of the years. Our lives in Christ are similar to such a structure, yet they bear one difference. Our lives require firm rooting in the basic elements of the Word of God. We must let our roots be deep in God's Word in order to be the great edifice that we can be. The difference between our lives in Christ and the skyscraper lies in growth. We have both the ability and the responsibility to grow in Christ and to enlarge our edifice. Our building was not destined to remain the same size.—John C. Wakefield.

October 30. The Teacher Who Bowed (Reformation Sunday)

Years ago in Germany there was a teacher named Dr. Staupitz. When formality and discipline were considered an important part of school life, Staupitz had an unusual custom. Upon entering the classroom he would remove his professor's cap and bow to the students. He was not only bowing to the students as they were but also acknowledging their potential. He realized that some of the students would become doctors, lawyers, and theologians, and his bow was a sign of respect for what they would become. His action was well taken. One of his students was Martin Luther.—John T. Randolph in *Family Devotions*.

November 6. Invisible Boundaries

Cecille Bechard, a citizen of Canada, sleeps in that country every night but enters the United States every time she goes to her refrigerator or makes tea at her kitchen stove. The borderline between the two nations runs through her house. Dozens of times a day she steps across the dividing line without even thinking about it.

A similar circumstance might occur with a person in the middle of the Pacific Ocean. If one were aboard a ship or plane traveling along the International Date Line in a northerly or southerly direction, it would be possible to step back and forth between today and tomorrow.

There are many unseen spiritual boundaries which present an intriguing challenge to our Christian skill and wisdom. In these matters too it is easy to overstep borderlines which have no clear and precise markings.—James R. Webb in *Wesleyan Christian Advocate*.

November 13. Answering Prayer (Stewardship Day)

A wealthy man had a reputation for being very pious. He never missed a church service and always prayed at great length in the midweek prayer meeting. On one occasion he prayed especially for an old couple living near his mansion who were quite poor and not in good health. On their way home from church the man's young son said, "Dad, I wish I had some of your money." "What would you do with it if you had it?" asked the father. "Well, Dad," replied the boy, "I'd start answering some of the prayers you said for the old people who live down the street."—John Wade.

November 20. A Task for Everyone

From time immemorial ants have survived through all the wars, floods, and physical upheavals, still building their wonderful ant cities all over the world from the tropics to the arctic. An anthill is organized almost as well as any human city. One striking thing about a community of ants is that everyone has a job to do and does it. There are worker ants, soldier ants, nursemaid ants, and even ants that keep other insects and "milk" them for honeydew to feed the colony. Each has been fitted for a particular task and goes about it industriously.

God has provided a task for each believer. He will fit us for it as we yield to his control. The ants do their different tasks automatically. They have been doing the same thing for thousands of years. God wants us to do ours voluntarily because we love him. There are many kinds of work to do, but he will fit each of us mentally and spiritually for the work to which he calls us.—William Montgomery in *The Upper Room.*

November 27. Guided by the Star (Advent)

A legend from China tells us that two surveyors were crossing a trackless desert. They had a map showing certain trees, streams, and contours of land they were to follow. But one night a terrible storm came, and they hid in a cave. When morning came all the landmarks had been washed away. They were lost. Both of them were desperate. Their maps were useless, for every landmark shown on them had been destroyed by the storm. All day long they tried to find a way to safety. They dared not go far from the cave. About midnight one of them looked out of their place of hiding and called to his friend: "We're saved! We can find our way out of this desolation!" "How?" asked his bewildered friend. The reply, "Because the stars are still there!"—Homer J. R. Elford.

December 4. Your Purpose in Life (Advent)

Charles Dickens in his story, "The Christmas Carol," after introducing several cheerful, lifelike characters, presents Scrooge. He is all work and no play, all business and no pleasure, all money and no people. He answers his critics crisply that business is his life. To which they report: "Business? Mankind should be your business!" And after a scary adventure he discovers just that. So he was changed into a kind and generous person, loving people. And that's how he found his happiness.

What is the reason for our existence? What is it that gives meaning and dignity to our living? These and similar questions need our thoughtful attention and serious consideration.—Emil Kontz.

December 11. God's Gifts (Advent)

Christmas is a time of sensory delight as well as spiritual joy. How we love the smell of turkey roasting and of ginger cookies baking.

Smells are fine, but taste is even better —dressing and gravy and mince pie. Appetite itself is a wonderful blessing.

Our ears are delighted with the well-loved carols. The choirs and choruses, the TV programs demonstrate the joy of music. The angels love music. They sang on that holy night.

Seeing the beauty of Christmas is another blessing—the sparkling ornaments, shining lights, the colors of the red berries and bright poinsettias.

How much joy in life comes from our God-given senses! Too bad if they become jaded and no longer give us pleasure. When Jesus told us we should become as little children, did he mean we should cultivate a child's joy in the common wonders of life?

That must be part of it, though the sensory delights of Christmas must never replace the spiritual meanings. Our Lord became flesh and shared the physical pleasures which are God's gifts. What good and perfect gifts God has given us! —Margaret Buell Allen.

December 18. A Russian Tale (Advent)

The Russian peasantry for centuries had propagated a curious tradition. It is about an old woman, the Baboushka, who was at work in her house when the wise men came from the East and passed on their way to Bethlehem to find the child. "Come with us," they said. "We have seen his star in the east, and we go to worship him."

"I will come, but not now. I have much housework to do, and when that is finished, I will follow and find him." But her work was never done. And the three kings had passed on their way across the desert, and the star shone no more in the darkened heavens.

Baboushka never saw the Christ Child, but she is still living and still searching for him. And though she did not find him, out of love for him she takes care of all his children. It is she who in Russian homes is believed to fill all the stockings and dress the tree on Christmas morn. The children are awakened with the cry, "Behold, the Baboushka!" And they jump up, hoping to see her before she vanishes out of the window. She is like the Santa Claus of the

Western world. The tradition has it that she believes that in each poor little child whom she warms and feeds she may find the Christ Child whom she neglected long ago. But she is not doomed to disappointment, for the divine child said, "He who receives one of these little ones in my name receives me."—Fulton J. Sheen.

December 25. Christmas in Other Lands

In Zimbabwe (Rhodesia) an old tribal custom has become a significant part of Christmas celebrations. One family gives a chicken to another family as a sign of good will. It must be alive when given. The family receiving the gift kills and plucks it and returns it to the givers. It is then roasted over an open fire and the meal is shared. Zimbabwean tribespeople greet each other at Christmas with the words *Kristo wazvarwa farayi!* (Christ is born—rejoice!).

In Guatemala Christmas begins with the tradition of "La Posada." Symbolizing Mary and Joseph's search for shelter, families go to a different house each December night carrying a figure representing the baby Jesus. Though refreshment is served to all who join in, the "Holy Family" is ceremoniously considered to have been turned away. On Christmas Eve, everyone stays up after evening mass for a celebration at midnight, which is thought to be the hour Jesus was born. At that time firecrackers are lit and people gather for prayer and reading of the Christmas story. Then they eat "tamal," a traditional Christmas food, and exchange gifts. Some families make a nativity scene before Christmas, keeping the image of the baby covered until Christmas morning. That night the image is "stolen" and hidden until January 6, the day which commemorates the arrival of the three kings.

In India children decorate their homes with paper streamers, and often a star is hung outside the house. Fireworks announce the arrival of Christmas Day. In rural areas families visit each other to exchange trays of fancy foods. The walls of the homes are whitewashed and the earthen floors are decorated with rice-flour designs called *kolam.*

In Israel many people journey to Bethlehem on Christmas Eve for a service of carols in the Shepherds' Field outside the town. There, accompanied by the bleating of lambs and the ringing of sheep bells, they hear Luke's account of how the good news came first to the shepherds. Other Christians attend Christmas Eve services at the ancient Church of the Nativity in the center of Bethlehem. It is built over a grotto believed to be the spot where Jesus was born.—*World Vision.*

SECTION XI. *Sermon Outlines and Homiletic and Worship Aids for Fifty-Two Weeks*

SUNDAY: JANUARY SECOND

MORNING SERVICE

Topic: Gifts That Cannot Be Exchanged (New Year)

Text: Rom. 6:23.

After Christmas we go through the ritual which we call "Christmas swapping." Merchants have come to accept this as a normal part of the Christmas season, but there are some gifts which cannot be exchanged.

I. *The gift of life.* (a) No one of us had responsibility for our coming into existence. Yet few among us would choose not to have been given this gift. Some might have chosen a different heritage or station in life if this were possible. We know that the misfortunes of birth have precluded the possibility of some talents being developed or some dreams being realized. Consider a person, for instance, who could have unlocked the secret of one of the dread diseases, discovered that hidden road to a lasting peace, or helped to find the solution to the problem of hunger.

(b) That person may never have the opportunity due to the circumstances of his or her birth—too poor to ever hope to develop his or her latent talent or too rich to ever let go of the responsibilities thrust upon him or her by being born to wealth.

(c) Life comes "as is." To make the most of the life that has been given to us—as it is—is to respond to God in the highest and noblest way.

II. *The gift of the world in which life must be lived.* (a) Perhaps this could be better described as the age or the time in which we live. Some of us would wish to exchange this gift. We may have preferred to live in a different time—a thousand years hence or 100 years ago.

(b) Someone has said that the beginning of this century was the ideal time for living—after plumbing and before the wars. No age of humankind's existence has come close to perfection.

(c) This is all the time we have. The best thing that any person can then do is to try to be sure that he or she is part of the answers rather than part of the problems of this age which has been given to us.

III. *The gift of the land in which we live.* (a) We are the wealthiest and most privileged people on earth. The poorest among us—and there are many—are rich compared to most of the others in this world.

(b) Insulated by this affluence, we often forget what John Donne said nearly 400 years ago: "No man is an island. Every man is part of the main." This English clergyman was writing out of the background of his Christian faith, reminding us that as long as one person is enslaved, by that much are all persons enslaved, as long as one person's mind is in darkness, by that much do all persons live in darkness, and as long as one person is suffering, by that much are all persons suffering.

IV. *The gift about which Paul wrote to the*

church at Rome—"the free gift of God . . . eternal life in Christ Jesus our Lord."

(a) This is a gift that cannot be exchanged. It must simply be accepted as it comes to us on God's terms and in God's way.

(b) Malcolm Muggeridge, describing the experience of being reborn in Christ, said, "Seeing with new eyes, I see a new world; understanding with heart and mind and soul, truth breaks upon me." Who, indeed, can doubt?

(c) When we accept this new life, all other gifts fall into proper perspective, and we are able to live as God intended that we should. What better way is there to begin this New Year than to accept this free gift of God and thereby fulfill God's hope and promise for our lives?—Monroe C. Lewis.

Illustrations

FACING THE NEW YEAR. We pledge ourselves to follow through the coming year the light which God gives us: the light of truth, wherever it may lead; the light of freedom, revealing new opportunities for individual development and social service; the light of faith, opening new visions of the better world to be; the light of love, daily binding brother to brother and man to God in ever closer bonds of friendship and affection. Guided by this light, we shall go forward to the work of another year with steadfastness and confidence.

BETWEEN YESTERDAY AND TOMORROW. An American explorer made an interesting discovery on one of his journeys. He was Admiral Richard E. Byrd, the explorer of the South Pole. *The National Geographic* reported the fascinating story of Byrd's second trip to the South Pole. The 180th meridian is an imaginary but important marker. It is the International Date Line. When a traveler crosses it, he either adds a day or subtracts a day, depending on his direction. Admiral Byrd wrote of his experience in flying southward to the Pole: "All the time we continued flying as closely as possible along the 180th meridian. Even without wind drift—for which adequate correction can be made—it is obvious that no navigator can fly exactly along a mathematical straight line. Consequently, since this is the International Date Line, we were zigzagging constantly from today into tomorrow, and back again into yesterday."

At this season of the year our minds are crowded with recollection of the past year, some cheering and some sobering. But before long we find our minds occupied with anticipations of the coming year, some hopeful and some fearful. At this time the past and the future wrestle for dominance in our thinking. In this period between the years there is a strange mingling of memory and hope.—Emil Kontz.

Sermon Suggestions

TIME IN THREE DIMENSIONS. Text: Matt. 6:34. (1) Don't worship the past; build on it. (2) Don't criticize the present; live in it. (3) Don't fear the future; believe in it.

WHAT WISE MEN KNOW (Epiphany). Scripture: Matt. 2:1–12. (1) Wise men know how to be patient. (2) Wise men are persistent. (3) Wise men look for providence.—Mark Trotter.

Worship Aids

CALL TO WORSHIP. "Ye shall know the truth, and the truth shall make you free, God is a Spirit: and they that worship him must worship him in spirit and in truth." John 8:32; 4:24.

INVOCATION. O God, we thank you for leading us until this hour. Direct us in the days ahead through the difficult places of decision. When the call seems clouded and the road is in poor repair, grant the boldness to face the future in faith and to fortify ourselves in truth. Help us to be ready to recognize our own inadequacy and your sufficiency.

OFFERTORY SENTENCE. "Thou crownest the year with thy goodness. . . . Samuel took a stone, and set it between Mizpeh and Shen, saying, Hitherto hath the Lord helped us." Ps. 65:11; I Sam. 7:12.

OFFERTORY PRAYER. Dear God, help us to become unobstructed channels that thy love may flow through us to others and our gifts may be used for the proclamation to all men of thy saving goodness.

PRAYER. O God, who amid the vast and swift changes of our times abidest ever the same, we confess our inability without thee to deal with either progress or decay. We pray for the steadying presence of thy Holy Spirit with all who are confused or in any wise afflicted as new powers, new methods, and new needs unfold before us.

We pray for all who fear change and all who find their secure ways threatened. Give them faith and courage and the spiritual and material resources to find newness of life within in the midst of newness of life without.

We pray for all who in impatience long for change and who seek escape from present boredom or hardships. Give them faith and courage and the discernment not to embrace in their bewilderment a change for the worse.

We pray for all who accept change and endeavor to make of it progress and growth. Give them faith and courage to meet every temptation with integrity, all hostility with love—each difficulty with a reasoned determination to serve God and man.—E. Paul Conine.

EVENING SERVICE

Topic: Facing the Unknown

SCRIPTURE: Josh. 6:1–21.

Josh. 5 reveals how Joshua, facing the unknown as the new leader of the people of Israel, had a meeting with "the captain of the host of the Lord." The result of the interview was submission, power, and direction for his life and that of his people as they were to capture the city of Jericho. We stand before the unknown as did Joshua and we too need a meeting with the divine Captain. We need to submit our lives to him that we may enjoy and possess his power and know his direction for our lives. In three ways this "captain of the Lord's host" revealed himself to Joshua.

I. *The compelling one.* (a) Josh. 5:15 tells us that the Captain said: "Loose thy shoe from off thy foot; for the place whereon thou standest is holy." When Christ appears to any man, it is always with the effect of bringing him to his knees in reverence and in humility with a recognition of his sinfulness. Then there follows the acknowledgment of God's holiness and a spirit of obedience to do his will.

(b) Will we be ready and willing during this new year, as the Spirit of God deals with us, to respond as did Joshua? The record states, "And Joshua fell on his face to the earth, and did worship, and said, What saith my lord unto his servant?" Here was contrition, adoration, and submission.

(c) As Joshua knelt before the Lord, the revelation of his will could be received and acknowledged. The directions for the future, including the plan for taking the city of Jericho, were revealed.

II. *The complete one.* (a) When Joshua inquired of him as to the capacity in which he had come, he replied, "As captain of the host of the Lord." He had not come to supplement the great military leader Joshua but to supplant him. When Christ comes to reveal himself as our Lord, it is not just that he might be a great help to us in our own efforts but that he might control, direct, and command our lives and decide the procedure we are to follow.

(b) When we are willing to accept him in this sovereign way, he will be to us exactly what we in our own individual lives need. He will come to us to defend us and to equip us. Jesus Christ waits to be sovereign in our lives.

III. *The competent one.* (a) A wonderful promise was given to Joshua: "See I have given into thine hand Jericho, and the king thereof, and the mighty men of valor" (Josh. 6:2). The plan of attack was given to Joshua with the promise that if he followed it, victory would be his. To capture the city simply by walking around it once a day for six days in complete silence, to encompass it seven times on the seventh day and to shout loudly on the final time around, and then expect the city to be captured—this was complete foolishness as far as military strategy was concerned. But it was God's way and it worked.

(b) Life is to be lived on God's level,

according to God's plan, and in keeping with his divine will even though this may not seem to us the way things should be done. Joshua took the city because he brought obedience and faith and surrender to God.—C. Reuben Anderson.

SUNDAY: JANUARY NINTH

MORNING SERVICE

Topic: Go, Tell It!
Text: Acts 26:16–18 (neb).
Few of us have had an experience similar to Paul's on the Damascus Road, but we do know that this experience contains all the ingredients of every Christian's call and commission. We have had our visions and conversions along life's pilgrimage. Some have been ordinary and some have been epochal.

I. Where does it all start? (a) It all starts with an apprehension from beyond us. Here is where all meaningful experiences in life begin. Revelation takes place; response is elicited.

(b) This stirring captivation of consciousness commands one, as it did Paul, to stand on his feet. One is moved to attention and into new areas of experience. So it was with the apostle: "I have appeared unto you for a purpose: To be somebody, my servant; to do something, to witness. Out of your new being you shall tell what you have already seen of me and what you will yet see of me in the future. I am the living Christ in your life, in the life of Christian people, in the life of the church, and in the life of the world. I am the one who came, is coming, and will come in every larger and maturing revelations. All that has gone on before is prelude and foundation. Greater things than I did you will do. And you shall witness not only here but to the ends of the earth."

II. What shall I tell? (a) Tell the world that there is a light that shines in the darkness of the world. It has not been extinguished.

(1) To be associated with the Jesus of the gospels will put you into an atmosphere of clear and unpolluted air. Your mind will become clearer, your insights and perception will become sharper, your life will be set in the light of God, and you will see the fuller potentialities of your existence.

(2) The dayspring from on high has dawned. He has brought the light of life into the world. And his light dispels the darkness of error, ignorance, superstition, and falsehood. The person who walks in this light does not stumble in darkness. Light is clarifying, light is therapeutic, and light brings out all the colors of life and the world. Jesus speaks of himself as the light of the world. He came to open eyes and unstop ears. Those who have really seen and heard him have seen and heard the Father.

(b) Tell the world that there is a power that can direct, center, and fulfill life.

(1) It provides the dynamic for meaningful living. It is the same power that caused Jesus to speak with authority. It gave him the power to fulfill his ministry. It filled him with the power to love the unlovely, to forgive his crucifiers, to make a good witness before Pilate, and to commit himself to his faithful Father in his pain and suffering.

(2) This power is the present tense of Jesus available even now to as many as crave it and ask for it. "You shall receive power after the Spirit is come upon you and you will be witnesses."

(c) Tell the world that there is a love that will never forsake us or let us go. Nothing can separate us from that love in this world or the next. The heart of evangelical Christianity is the amazing grace of God in Jesus Christ. It frees us from crippling and imprisoning guilt and frustration. It arouses us to stand on our feet and affirm life in a new rightness before God, others, and the self. When that forgiveness is accepted in honest self-criticism, it creates the free person who can accept himself or herself in real dignity.

(d) Tell the world that there is a place and a status for everyone in God's community of mission and destiny.

(1) We may have a sense of belonging to something larger than ourselves.

(2) The author of Ephesians, writing to

Christians, reminds them that once they were outsiders, now they are insiders; once they were aliens, now they are members of the family of God.

III. How shall I tell it? Go, tell it everywhere! Tell it in your lifestyle, in the integrity of your work, in your relations with others in the daily round, and in your acts of love and service. Tell it in conversational words of comfort and encouragement, in homiletical and educational words, and in pastoral or literary words. Tell it in cartoon, film, and drama. Tell it in sculpture, painting, and music. Tell it with every means of communication available in the ordinary pursuits of life.—Elmer G. Homrighausen.

Illustrations

DO IT AGAIN!   In Nottingham, England, there is a little chapel, and on the wall is a bronze plaque marking the spot where William Booth is said to have received his call from God. One day an African Salvationist went to that little chapel. He saw the plaque and stood transfixed. Looking around, he saw the custodian and asked, "Is this the spot where William Booth knelt and prayed?" The custodian said, "This is it." The African asked, "Can a man be permitted to kneel down here?" The custodian said, "Yes, it is a place for prayer." The African, falling upon his knees prayed, "Lord, do it again, do it again, do it again, Lord!"—*The War Cry.*

GUIDING SPIRE.   On the southeast coast of England, high upon the bluffs, was a church whose slim spire reached almost to the clouds. A hurricane destroyed the church. The congregation, being poor, felt they could not rebuild the church and so made arrangements to worship elsewhere. One day a representative of the British Admiralty inquired of the congregation when they planned to rebuild the church. When he was informed the congregation could not rebuild it, he said: "The British Admiralty will rebuild it for you. That spire was on all our charts. Every one of His Britannic Majesty's ships set its course by that spire."—Warner L. Hall.

Sermon Suggestions

LET'S PRAISE THE LORD!   Text: Ps. 102: 18. (1) For the greatness of his love. (2) For the wonder of his grace. (3) For the sufficiency of his power. (4) For the certainty of his promises.—S. Robert Weaver.

JESUS IN THE MIDST OF THE CHURCH. Scripture: John 20:19–23. (1) He gives the command to preach the gospel (v. 21). (2) He gives the message. (a) A message of peace (v. 21). (b) A message of pardon (v. 23). (3) He gives the power (v. 22).—Henry J. Eggold, Jr.

Worship Aids

CALL TO WORSHIP.   "O love the Lord, all ye his saints: for the Lord preserveth the faithful. Be of good courage, and he shall strengthen your heart, all ye that hope in the Lord." Ps. 31:23–24.

INVOCATION.   As we begin another day, most gracious Father, make us to know that we never drift out of thy love and care. Faces may change and conditions may alter, but thou are never so near to us as when we need thee most.

OFFERTORY SENTENCE.   "Verily, verily, I say unto you, he that believeth on me, the works that I do shall he do also; and greater works than these shall he do. And whatsoever ye shall ask in my name, that will I do, that the Father may be glorified in the Son." John 14:12–13.

OFFERTORY PRAYER.   Help us to remember, O Lord, that a life is a more persuasive testimony than words, that deeds are more effective than argument, and that these gifts are only a portion of the loyalty thou dost require of us.

PRAYER.   Open our hands today, O God. They have often been closed or clenched when they should have been open and extended. May our hands be used to relieve suffering this week, to convey friendship, to do a full measure of service for those who employ us.

Open our eyes, O God. We are so blind to eternal truth. We have looked at good men and condemned their cause because we were hostile within. We couldn't see God's presence in them or their cause because we were blinded by our guilt. We have condemned sinful men and enjoyed it, not because of their sin but because it seemed to excuse our sin. Forgive us.

Open our minds, O Lord. Sometimes our human nature seems so fixed and so unmovable that we give up in our search for moral truth. It often seems to be a losing battle. Our patience is thin and our vision is so limited that we are willing to condemn quickly.

Stretch our understanding so that we will not fall as victims of littleness, pettiness, or a judgment that has never examined the facts. "O Spirit of the living God, thou light and life divine, descend upon our hearts once more and make them truly thine."—Earl F. Lindsay.

EVENING SERVICE

Topic: The Duty of Self-Giving
SCRIPTURE: I John 3:11–24.

If the greatest word on the self-giving of God is to be found in John 3:16, then the greatest word on the self-giving of man is to be found in I John 3:16. We dare not quote the one and neglect the other. If we have eternal life through faith in the self-giving God, as revealed in Jesus Christ, then we are committed by the very possession of that life to love our fellowmen and particularly believers in the Lord. The duty of self-giving is the duty of possessing and practicing:

I. *A spiritual love.* (See v. 11.) (a) Three words in the Greek describe the term love: *eros*—animal attraction, *phileo*—human affection, and *agapao*—spiritual love. This latter quality is unknown to the man outside of Christ because "the natural man receiveth not the things of the Spirit of God: for they are foolishness unto him: neither can he know them, because they are spiritually discerned" (I Cor. 2:14).

(b) This is dramatically illustrated in the life of Cain, who, though having the advantages of a religious upbringing, followed the natural course of a fallen, sinful nature and killed his brother in a moment of religious jealousy.

(c) Though the love of God is the greatest power of attraction in the world, it is also the greatest cause of antagonism. The devil hates the word "love" and will do everything in his power to stamp it out. This presses upon us the tremendous obligation to possess and practice spiritual love.

II. *A sacrificial love.* (See vv. 16–18.) It is of the very nature of divine love to sacrifice; therefore, as believers, promoted by spiritual love, we must be willing not only to lay down our lives for the disposal of others but to give ourselves for the Master to use in any way he sees fit. Likewise we must demonstrate our spiritual love in deed and in truth by sharing with others of that which we have received.

III. *A satisfying love.* (See v. 19.) Love is not only a sacrifice. It is a satisfaction, and the proof that love is satisfying is evidenced by the fact that we have confidence toward God (v. 21), know the contentment of proving and pleasing God in every aspect of our lives (v. 22), and experience a fellowship of love with the Father, Son, and Holy Spirit as we lead obedient lives (vv. 23–24).—Stephen F. Olford.

SUNDAY: JANUARY SIXTEENTH

MORNING SERVICE

Topic: Good News to Share (Missionary Day)
TEXT: Matt. 9:38.

What moves us as Christians to send missionaries abroad? If it is so expensive and if there are already Christian churches in nearly every country, why do we continue the work of overseas missions? What motives compel us?

I. We engage in mission because good news must be shared. (a) If you found a cure for cancer, you couldn't keep it to yourself; you'd just have to share it. The news would be too good not to tell it. If you have experienced the grace of God in Jesus Christ, then you want to share it.

(b) God is a loving God! That's good news. The creator loves every one of us. No other religion has precisely that message as its central theme. That good news must be shared for good news is to share.

II. We engage in mission because Jesus Christ is unique. (a) It is the heart of our faith that for us human beings and our salvation God Almighty became a man in Jesus Christ of Nazareth, that he lived and died and rose again from the dead, and that he is present in the world by his Spirit, giving power to all who will receive him. Christ's birth, death, and resurrection are unrepeatable acts. They happened once and will not happen again.

(b) The very uniqueness of all that requires those who believe it to tell it. Other religions have their holy leaders, but none of them is identical with Jesus Christ. The wonder and glory of his life require us to tell about it and to witness his story—and to tell about it is mission.

III. We engage in Christian mission because Jesus Christ our Lord lived and breathed a missionary spirit.

(a) He was himself a missionary. He came to us with a message, and that is what a missionary is. His message was for all people. He did not say, "I am the light of Palestine"; he said, "I am the light of the world." He did not say, "God so loved the Jews"; he said, "God so loved the world." He certainly did not say, "My message is for the people of the United States but not for the people of Indonesia." His message was for all people.

(b) While on earth Jesus took the initiative in giving his message to others. Some religious teachers are content to sit in contemplation with only a close-knit group around them and are not concerned to give their message to the whole world. Not so with Jesus. His was a missionary spirit. He said, "I am come to seek and to save the lost." He said, "Other sheep I have which are not of this fold, them also I must bring." His footprints were in the countries round about—Samaria, Gadarea, and Perea. He sent his disciples out two by two as messengers. His last words before he was taken up from them were, "Go ye into all the world and preach the gospel." If he is our example and if we are his body,

we too will possess a missionary spirit.

IV. The needs and nature of the human animal call for Christian mission.

(a) Human beings need something to be committed to—a tribe, a country, a business, a leader, a god. Being finite, we humans require an object of loyalty, and invariably we find one. There is a God-shaped void in each of us, and those people who say they do not need a religious faith have usually substituted something or someone as the object of their supreme devotion.

(b) Every person today needs a religious faith that is tenable in a science-oriented world. We have given the people of developing countries our televisions, our C-grade movies, and our weapons of destruction. We have given them our worst. We have an obligation to try, at least, to give them our best. And our best is Jesus Christ.

V. We engage in mission out of a desire to fill up what is lacking of the body of Christ.

(a) We are called to enrich the glory of our Savior by the insights of all the people of the earth. Each people, nation, and race has a contribution to make to the mosaic which is the body of Christ, the church.

(b) Imagine a large stained-glass window with its countless bits of glass of different shapes and colors—blue and red and green and yellow. Each part adds to the beauty of the window. If any part is missing, the glory of the window is diminished by that much. Each has a contribution to make.

(c) Black Americans made a marvelous contribution with their spirituals. Anglo-Saxon people brought their concept of law. The people of India have added their insights into mysticism. And it will take the gifts and insights of all the peoples of the world to portray the full glory of Jesus Christ.

(d) Asian, African, and Latin American Christians have much to teach us, for anyone who has experienced Jesus Christ has unique insights into him and something to share with other Christians and with the world.

VI. We engage in mission because Christ commanded us to do so. "Go ye into all the world and preach the gospel." "Ye shall be witnesses unto me . . . unto the uttermost part of the earth."

(a) These commands have not been completely accomplished. There are still millions of villages around the world where no one has ever witnessed to Jesus Christ. Not having been fulfilled and not having been countermanded, the great commission is still valid. The order still stands.

(b) Christ has commanded his followers to go and witness unto him unto the ends of the earth. So that is the end of the matter. The question is not whether but how. The question is: where and in what capacity shall I participate? There is something each one of us can do. We cannot all go, but we can pray and give and engage in work at the local level. Such support activities are absolutely necessary if the enterprise is to continue to succeed. Your support activities at home are as important as the work of the missionaries abroad. Each of us should find his or her place in the total missionary effort of the church.—Ben Lacy Rose.

Illustrations

DECISION.   Mahatma Gandhi in his student days was touched by reading the New Testament. Gandhi seriously considered conversion to Christianity, feeling that the teachings of Jesus would solve racial problems and caste differences. One Sunday in South Africa Gandhi went to a church, planning to ask the minister afterward for instructions in the faith. As he entered the building, ushers objected to seating him. "Why don't you visit the colored people's church?" one asked. Gandhi never became a Christian. "If Christians also have differences, I might as well remain a Hindu," he remarked.—Cecil B. Murphey.

FULFILLMENT.   An eight-year-old girl was riding one day with her father through the slums of an American city. Depressed by what she saw, she said to her father, "One day I am going to build a house among the poor people so that the children can play in my yard." Her mother had died when the girl was two years old. The child suffered from a spinal curvature which gave her much pain in later life. She went to a medical school to become a doctor, but she had to give up school due to her health. A little later she went to a university to take a course in social service in order to understand the problems and the needs of the poor. Much of those years was spent as a patient in a hospital. Then at the age of twenty-nine she secured a house among the underprivileged in a slum area of a great American city. She opened her home to the poor and the needy of every race, creed, and color. After some years she won the Nobel Peace Prize, and at the age of seventy-five she could say that she had never lost sight of her purpose. So Jane Addams of the Hull House in Chicago wrote her name into immortality.—Joseph R. Sizoo.

Sermon Suggestions

THE COMMUNICATING OF THE BIBLE. Text: Isa. 29:18. (1) The communication of the Bible is a matter of translating the words and idioms of the Bible into language now used anywhere. (2) The communicating of the Bible is a matter of relating the world of the Bible to our world. (3) The communicating of the Bible is a matter of understanding. (4) God communicated himself through the events that the Bible records for us and through the fellowship of the church.—Charles L. Seasholes.

OUR REASONABLE SERVICE.   Scripture: Rom. 12:1–8. (1) We present our bodies. (2) We are renewed in our minds. (3) We use our gifts as well as we can (vv. 7–8) and for the good of others (v. 5).—Gerhard Aho.

Worship Aids

CALL TO WORSHIP.   "Sing unto the Lord, sing psalms unto him. Glory ye in his holy name; let the heart of them rejoice that seek the Lord." Ps. 105:2–3.

INVOCATION.   Lord, lift us out of private-mindedness and give us public souls to work for thy kingdom by daily creating that atmosphere of a happy temper and generous heart which alone can bring the great peace.

OFFERTORY SENTENCE.   "Therefore, as ye abound in every thing, in faith, and in utterance, and knowledge, and in all diligence, and in your love to us, see that ye abound in this grace also." II Cor. 8:7.

OFFERTORY PRAYER.   O Christ, may we walk constantly in thy way and work fervently for those causes which are dear to thee.

PRAYER.   Lord God, our heavenly Father, we know that thou art even now looking upon us with eyes of understanding and compassion, more eager to bless our lives than we to ask thy blessing. We turn to thee with earnest prayer that a channel may be opened into thy grace through which we may receive thy love.

We come into thy presence with happy and glad remembrance of times past when thou hast dealt with us according to thine infinite wisdom and mercy for our own good. Especially we thank thee for the glorious life of deliverance thou hast given us through Jesus Christ, for the light that has come into our lives through the opening of the Holy Scriptures, and for the glory that has been given to our daily existence through our life of prayer when each day we speak with thee. We thank thee for the way our lives today are strengthened by these glad experiences of yesterday and for the hope thou dost give the morrow because thou art steadfast and dependable in thy compassionate character. Thy righteousness is unchanging from day to day and from generation unto generation, and thy presence as our living God is the mighty foundation on which we can surely rest our hopes. We ask that thou wilt lift us above the vicissitudes of the current events of our earthly life. Grant that we may find a higher hope and a deeper foundation for our assurance in the unchanging wonder of thy character of goodness and love and wisdom and strength. As we rest our lives in thy care and in thy keeping, may we know in our heart of hearts that all is well.—Lowell M. Atkinson.

EVENING SERVICE

Topic: Jesus the Discipler

TEXT: John 8:31–32.

Jesus was the master at discipling. When he selected his apostles, he taught them the way to live. The text indicates what Jesus felt would be essential to live in true discipleship.

I. Discipleship begins with belief. The beginning is when a person accepts Jesus as Savior. The basic meaning of belief is commitment. If you believe in somebody or something, you commit yourself to that somebody or something. Too frequently a person accepts Jesus as personal Savior and fails to grow spiritually beyond that initial experience. Many do not trust Jesus to the point of committing all of life to him. Belief in Jesus as Savior is the beginning only.

II. Discipleship means constantly remaining in the Word. The Word and Jesus are the same. "The Word became flesh and dwelt among men" (John 1:14). Being in residence in the Word of Jesus involves four things. Listening, learning, penetrating, and obeying are essential involvements that must be experienced by the individual believer if he is to grow in discipleship.

III. Discipleship issues in knowledge of the truth. Jesus said, "You will know the truth." The truth Jesus reveals allows the believer to know the real values of life. Paul gave us insight into this spiritual principle in Col. 1:25–27. The mystery learned by believers is the truth that "Christ in you is the hope of glory." What a difference living would be for every believer if he were aware that Christ Jesus were in him constantly.

IV. Discipleship results in freedom. A true disciple is free from the bondage, guilt, and penalty of sin. This freedom allows the believer to become what Christ Jesus wants him to be. Jesus teaches us how to live for him.—Lewis Sewell.

SUNDAY: JANUARY TWENTY-THIRD

MORNING SERVICE

Topic: What Are Your Credentials?
SCRIPTURE: Matt. 21:23–32.

I. What are your credentials? (a) The religious elite asked that question of Jesus. He intruded on their turf. He offered forgiveness, promised hope, attacked religious institutions, and worst of all, attracted crowds. "Who gave you authority to do this?" they asked. "Who are your references? Have you a sponsor? Your credentials, please."

(b) Jesus bewildered them with a question about the authority of John the Baptist. They could not answer without shaming themselves or fostering revolt among the faithful. "We do not know the source of John's authority," they replied. "Then," said Jesus, "I'll not tell you about mine." But he told them the parable of a father and two sons.

II. What is he saying? (a) Our credentials as Christians go far beyond conventional goodness. When our Lord speaks of the son who said yes but did not go, he is warning against good intentions which frequently mask the cost of discipleship. He cautions us against flippant "Yes, sirs" and casual tips of the hat to the vital matter of doing the Christian life.

(b) Jesus is the model for the discipleship he seeks. When the father requested Jesus to go to the vineyard, he replied, "I will, sir," and he went. What did that mean? Three years on the road, no fixed address, the religious establishment at his throat, and companions who never got the point of it all. It meant touching cripples, embracing enemies, and feeding souls. It meant a life shaped, ruled, and released by love.

(c) Our task is of a similar order. Our credibility in a skeptical world rests on our throwing our lives into his cause. Our words of assent can be important and our good intentions valuable. But what really are Christian credentials? A life immersed in healing, giving, and freeing. "Go work in the vineyard today." "I will, sir." And we go. That is discipleship.

(d) Are healing, giving, and freeing the credentials you carry? A life radiant with hope and service—is that the authority you bring to human life? Too many of us are like that first son—a good intention to work in the vineyard, a respectful reply, "I will, sir," perhaps even the mobilizing of tools, the arrangement of our calendars, but a million buts. "This far and no farther, Lord."

III. Churches are vulnerable to the amputated Christianity of the first son.

(a) How respectfully we answer the invitation to the vineyard. Our doctrine is concisely stated, our clergy well-trained, our balance sheet in the black, and our building a rare antique and numbers are holding steady.

(b) Numbers, doctrine, and facile clergy are not authenticating marks of the church. This building could crumble and our balance sheets go up in flames, but the core of courage and compassion would remain untouched. Aside from our institutional vital signs, where are our credentials?

(c) Are we true to the invitation, "Behold, I set before thee an open door"? Are we available to the people who sleep in our alley, lean on our wall, and retreat to our sanctuary? Do we nurture the young, cherish the old, and tell the story of Jesus Christ? As a church we are invited to work in the vineyard. How do we answer, "I will, sir"? And do we go?

IV. The churches are only an extension of our own discipleship, and some of that is amputated.

(a) "I'll work in your vineyard, Lord, study the Bible, sing the hymns, and say the prayers," but for many Christians the religion of Jesus and failing cities have nothing to do with one another and faith in the living Christ and merchandising weapons to the world never dovetail. Attendance at Communion and equality in education are in separate worlds. "I will, sir," we say with deep respect, but only up to a point.

(b) Are our human relationships, our search for friends, and our marriages amputated from our faith? "I'll go to the vineyard, Lord, but my relationships and how I manage them are my business."

(c) Going to the vineyard these days is more than a "Yes, sir" and a pledge to the church. Going to the vineyard involves sustaining, nourishing, supporting, and cementing relationships. "I will go, sir." But do we?

(d) The Father urges us to work in the vineyard. He beckons us to invest all that we have for Christ's sake in wiping tears, standing for convictions, and laying ourselves on the line for others. He implores that our deeds be as good as our word. He yearns that each of us with mind and heart, vision and will be consecrated to this service.—James W. Crawford.

Illustrations

MISSION OF LOVE.   Each one has a mission to fulfill, a mission of love. At the hour of death when we come face to face with God, we are going to be judged on love—not how much we have done but how much love we have put into our actions.—Mother Teresa.

TESTIMONY.   Chrysostom's motto was "Glory to God for all things." In Antioch he was popular and preached to as many as ten thousand, but later in Constantinople the Empress turned against him, and he was driven into exile. When soldiers dragged him through the winter snows and he was about to die, his last words were, "Glory to God for all things."—A. C. Braun.

Sermon Suggestion

MOSES AS A LEADER.   Text: Heb. 11:27. (1) His faith. (2) His integrity. (3) His vision. (4) His decisiveness. (5) His obedience. (6) His responsibility.—Ted W. Engstrom.

Worship Aids

CALL TO WORSHIP.   "We are laborers together with God: ye are God's husbandry, ye are God's building. Let every man take heed how he buildeth. For other foundation can no man lay than that is laid, which is Jesus Christ." I Cor. 3:9–11.

INVOCATION.   Grant, O God, that because we meet together this day life may grow greater for some who have contempt for it, simpler for some who are confused by it, happier for some who are tasting the bitterness of it, safer for some who are feeling the peril of it, more friendly for some who are feeling the loneliness of it, serener for some who are throbbing with the fire of it, and holier for some to whom life has lost all dignity, beauty, and meaning.

OFFERTORY SENTENCE.   "The end of the commandment is charity out of a pure heart." I Tim. 1:5.

OFFERTORY PRAYER.   Our Father, we thank thee that thou art so generous to us. All that we have is a gift from thee. Help us to serve one another so that we may reflect thy spirit and goodness.

PRAYER.   O Lord our God, each time we worship thee we are more sensitive to the spiritual poverty of the lives we offer thee. We have not loved thee with all our hearts. We have loved ourselves too much and our neighbors too little.

The life we live, we honestly confess, is not like the life of Jesus nor is our mind like his mind. We have at times sought the spirit of the Master that we might be of that spirit. But it is to our shame and regret that the word has not been made flesh in us to the point that others can see Christ in us and through us.

We have come seeking the light of thy truth so to shine in our lives that we shall see ourselves as you see us that it may make us all the more eager to be transformed by Christ's grace and love.

We ask you to prick our consciences awake to the heroic needs of the day in which we live. Set our sights on higher ways and thoughts so that we may not be satisfied with our lives as they are. We seek the wisdom and strength to live as we know thy children ought to live.—William C. Swygert.

EVENING SERVICE

Topic: Four-Letter Words

TEXT: Prov. 15:23.

I. *Love.* It has been so twisted and tainted by some people that others are somewhat embarrassed to use it. All its beauty and strength are restored by reading what Jesus said: "Love the Lord your God with all your heart, with all your soul, with all your mind. That is the greatest commandment. It comes first. The second is like it: Love your neighbor as yourself. Everything in the law and the prophets hangs on these two commandments" (Matt. 22:37, NEB).

II. *Hope.* This is one of the things Paul said would last forever and he was right, but it's hard to keep it in mind in the midst of today's complex, confusing, pressure-cooker, roller-coaster world. Despair and frustration seem more reasonable reactions than hope, but hope is still the quickening breath of the human spirit, and men with apparently little to live for reach out to the future with optimism.

III. *Heal.* So much in our world is sick— sick minds, sick bodies, sick humor, sick morals, sick literature, sick hearts. There are wounds in our social structure that can't be patched up with band-aids. There are festering sores in our environment that may already be past healing. Down at the root of most of our ills is a sickness of the spirit, a disease that yields only to him who came "to heal the brokenhearted."

IV. *Care.* Involvement has been talked about so much that the word has become a cliche. But the approach generally has been on the basis of duty or self-fulfillment. Maybe a simpler word, care, and a simpler idea would be better. The good Samaritan was a man who saw another man in trouble and cared enough to do all he could to help him. Public response to disasters, from neighborhood fires to major calamities like earthquakes, indicates that people still care and still help.

V. *Give.* Our way of life is geared more to taking than to giving. As long as a man's morals and conduct are motivated by "What can I get?" rather than "What can I give?" sooner or later he will find life empty and stale. Jesus said, "For what is a man profited, if he shall gain the whole world, and lose his own soul?" (Matt. 16: 26).—Philip E. Collier in *The War Cry.*

SUNDAY: JANUARY THIRTIETH

MORNING SERVICE

Topic: A Basketful of Miracles

TEXT: John 6:12–13.

The feeding of the five thousand speaks of the grace of God. After everyone had been fed, there was still more than enough. This is a quality of the grace of God; there is always an abundance.

I. Grace means receiving. (a) Jesus ordered the people to sit down and receive the bread and fish. How difficult it is for us to sit back; we think that all of life's goals must be obtained by effort and work. If life is to maintain any balance, it has to have that receptive spirit. And receiving is not taking.

(1) There are a lot of takers in the world, and the takers take to use and the receivers receive to give. The true receiver humbly realizes that what he receives is a gift.

(2) There are those who don't feel they should accept any gift at all. We would like to feel that we deserve something when it is given to us. If we feel that we don't deserve it, the receiving of something makes us terribly uncomfortable.

(3) Receiving something that we don't feel we deserve makes us feel indebted, and we don't like such a feeling because to feel indebted makes us feel dependent, and feeling dependent makes us feel vulnerable. When we are vulnerable, we have to admit how finite and limited we are. Everything we are is due to someone's suffering and charity. This breaks our self-sufficiency, and we don't like to be so vulnerable.

(b) Receiving means that in a sense you know you can never repay. Being Christian is to be willing to receive without any feeling of deserving.

II. Grace has an extra quality. (a) The graceful person has a reserve of charm and kindness. He is able to give without any calculating manner. There seems to be an abundance from which he draws. Once in a while we are exposed to that person, and he has an overflowing life.

(b) The boy in our story was gracious. He gave what he had and wasn't seeking recognition. Graciousness has lost its grace when it calls attention to itself. This quality is altogether unpretentious.

(c) How often in our conversations an extra word can mean so much. A right word can change the direction of a day. We take so much for granted. But what a word of appreciation can do for a person! A thank you note only takes a minute to write, but many people will accept favors and never say thank you. That extra note is missing.

(d) He that soweth sparingly shall reap sparingly, and he that soweth bountifully shall reap bountifully. It is one of the strange paradoxes of human experience that he who gives himself away most completely has more of himself to give. He finds that extra quality we call grace.

III. Grace is always full of surprises. (a) It is not always easily charted; it is not always predictable. Perhaps that is why we often say unconditioned grace because grace is free of conditions and rules.

(1) This disturbs many people about the Christian faith. It is not based on merit alone. The prodigal son, coming home after a smashing time, is loved as much as the elder brother who was so discreet.

(2) The grace of God is not easy to define. We can only point to the way it seems to act. Grace is something that God does rather than we. Usually it is hidden or gradual and not easily seen or measured. All of us have had experiences that defy descriptions, and the best thing we can say is "grace."

(b) The God of grace is continually doing for us what we need to have done, whether we know it or not, whether we understand it or not, whether we appreciate it or not, whether we are worthy or not. Read Isaiah, Zephaniah, or any of the others, and you are struck by the note of holy expectancy running through them. They were certain that a momentous spiritual surprise would take place. God lived and was merciful and righteous in all his way.

He would act and in ways astonishing to his creatures. He would come when men least expected him and always for their true welfare.

(c) Grace surprises us by the support it gives us. A long distance swimmer, asked how she endured the many hours in the water, answered, "I always think of the water as my friend, and I never fight it." We have seen some swimmers that fight at the water, and it is a pitiful sight. Yet others stroke the water with firmness and confidence as if to say, "I know you will support me, and I will not struggle against you." Something like that has happened to those who have known the grace of God in Jesus Christ. They have found a confidence and trust that even in the face of death do not waver. They speak of the grace of the Lord Jesus Christ.—C. A. McClain, Jr.

Illustrations

TUNED IN.   When I was a boy, radio was just coming of age. We would gather around a crude homemade set and twist the three tuning dials in an effort to establish contact with the transmitter. Often all the sound that came out of the amplifier was the squeak and squawk of static, but we knew that somewhere out there was the unseen transmitter, and if contact was established and the dials were in adjustment, we could hear a voice loud and clear. After a long time of laborious tuning, the far distant voice would suddenly break through and a smile of triumph would illuminate the faces of all in the room. At last we were tuned in. In the revelation that God established between himself and us, we can find a new life and a new dimension of living, but we must tune in.—Billy Graham.

GOD'S GLORY.   In the Music Hall in Vienna in the year 1808 a rendition was made of the renowned oratorio "Creation" by Haydn. Several celebrated artists, assisted by an equally celebrated orchestra and a great chorus of well-trained singers, participated. Haydn was there, having been brought into the hall in a wheelchair. The performance began, and as it proceeded line by line it carried the audience into a transport of almost irrepressible enthusiasm. As the passage "and there was light" was reached and the chorus and orchestra burst forth into full power, the vast assembly, keyed to a higher pitch by the presence of the venerable author, could no longer restrain itself. The enraptured throng by one spontaneous impulse leaped to its feet. The aged composer was seen struggling in an effort to rise from his wheelchair. With the rapturous applause of the people ringing in his ears, he motioned for a moment of silence, and lifting his hand high toward heaven, he cried with all the strength he could muster, "No, no, not from me, but from thence comes all." When he had so cried out, giving to God the glory and the praise, he fell back in his chair weakened and exhausted and was taken from the hall before the moistened eyes and solemnized hearts of the admiring crowd.—*Sunday School Times.*

Sermon Suggestions

TEMPTING GOD. Text: Luke 4:12. (1) We are not to put God to the test of meeting the conditions which we lay down. (2) We are not to put God to the test of proving himself by miraculous and spectacular demonstrations. (3) We are not to put God to the test by counting on his providence in lieu of our preparation.—Ralph W. Sockman.

HOW SHALL WE PRAY FOR THEM? Text: Col. 1:9–10 (RSV). Paul's formula for our prayers for others: (1) That they may know God's will. (2) That they may live out his will. (3) That they may bear fruit and grow in their work for God.—John C. Wakefield.

Worship Aids

CALL TO WORSHIP. "Let all those that put their trust in thee rejoice: let them ever shout for joy because thou defendest them: let them also that love thy name be joyful in thee." Ps. 5:11.

INVOCATION. Our heavenly Father, we thy humble children invoke thy blessing upon us in this hour of worship. We adore thee, whose nature is compassion, whose presence is joy, whose word is truth, whose spirit is goodness, whose holiness is beauty, whose will is peace, whose service is perfect freedom, and in knowledge of whom standeth our eternal life. Unto thee be all honor and all glory.

OFFERTORY SENTENCE. "Upon the first day of the week let every one of you lay by him in store, as God hath prospered him." I Cor. 16:2.

OFFERTORY PRAYER. Accept, O Lord, these offerings thy people make unto thee and grant that the cause to which they are devoted may prosper under thy guidance, to the glory of thy name.

PRAYER. O God our Father, in this hour of worship we wait for some word from thee that will set our lives upon new paths. We are sinful men seeking salvation. We are lost men seeking direction. We are doubting men seeking faith. Teach us, O God, the way of salvation. Show us the path to meaningful life. Reveal to us the steps of faith. Quicken our hearts and purify our minds. Broaden our concerns and strengthen our commitments. Show us duties left undone. Remind us of vows unkept. And reveal to us tasks unattended. Lead us, Father, through worship to a new and rich experience in Christ. Then send us from thy presence to live as thy children.—C. Neil Strait.

EVENING SERVICE

Topic: Jesus and Self-Pity

SCRIPTURE: John 5:1–18.

Jesus meets the problem of self-pity through the miracle at the pool of Bethsaida, where a man who had been crippled for thirty-eight frustrating years was wallowing in self-pity. This miracle took place at a place called Bethsaida. In this particular town was located a famous pool which was so important to many empires as a place of healing that it was called "the house of mercy." People believed that an angel came and troubled the water at particular times. When this occurred, the first in the pool would be healed.

I. When Jesus met the man, his first words were "Do you want to recover?" Jesus didn't ridicule the man about his superstition concerning the angel. He looked at the man with his 20-20 vision, saw his problem, and sought to meet the crippled man's need.

(a) Jesus knew that the one who uses sickness as an excuse or escape from responsibility or as an attention-getter really needs help. So without entering into a theological debate or argument with the man, he healed him by telling him to get his eyes off himself and the water's so-called magic and look to him.

(b) Jesus knew that the man enjoyed and was comfortable being sick. That is why he asked the man the pointed question, "Do you really want to be healed?" Jesus knew that self-pity can be very comfortable for the crippled man and for some of us today.

(c) One reason why self-pity is so seductive and appealing is that it allows us to see ourselves as the one who is not at fault but simply the recipient of undeserved misfortune. That's why the crippled man said, "I've tried to make it to the water, but others get there ahead of me . . . no one will put me into the water."

(d) Self-pity can destroy us, just as it did to the crippled man for thirty-eight years. The problem keeps growing when we look at life's situations with eyes of self-pity. We begin to see all things as a plot to destroy us. Soon we become paranoid with short tempers and feel that everyone is out to hurt us.

II. Jesus instructs the man to "Rise, take up your bed and walk." Why was it necessary for the man to pick up his bed? Perhaps Jesus thought that the bed reminded the crippled man of the day-dreaming hopes that he fostered through self-pity. Jesus knew the true symbolism of the bed, and it could no longer support him.

(a) Jesus was removing the reminders and the means of retreat that the man had laid on for thirty-eight years. Jesus was saying that if you are to be healed you must roll up all the what-might-have-beens and stop lying down on the bed of self-pity.

(b) Jesus says the same to you and me. "Walk, do something! Don't just sit there and look at the magical pool and its superstition as answers to life's problems. Look to me!" We waste our time in waiting for just the right breaks or the right opportunity. Get up and do your best in the situation in which you find yourself.

(c) In the middle of suffering or hardship, God will sympathize with us and give us the power to be healed. If you are sitting by the pool and grumbling, look up. Here comes Jesus, and hear his words, "Arise, take up your bed and walk!"—Philip D. Dicks.

SUNDAY: FEBRUARY SIXTH

MORNING SERVICE

Topic: Proclaim Liberty

Text: Lev. 25:10.

I. Freedom is God's gift to man. Man's very capacity for freedom is from God. Created in the image of God, man's likeness to the creator consists in his freedom. For man was created not for slavery but for freedom, and it is this native freedom which distinguishes man as being in the image of God and exalts him above all other creation. The psalmist declared, "Thou hast put all things under his feet" (Ps. 8:5).

(a) In terms of biblical faith, freedom is born out of a person's relationship to God. Hence freedom is primarily an inner state in which no external authority may exercise control over a person. In this sense freedom is an inner state of being which does not depend on external conditions. Christian martyrs were never more free than when they chose to be faithful even unto death.

(b) Freedom is rooted in God. To be truly free is to be at one with God, for freedom is where God is present. Paul wrote, "Where the Spirit of the Lord is present, there is freedom" (II Cor. 3:17). Thus the hope is expressed in the scriptures "that creation itself would one day be set free from its slavery to decay, and share the glorious freedom of the children of God" (Rom. 8:21).

(c) To proclaim liberty is to affirm God's gift for all mankind. The declaration, "Christ set us free, to be free men" (Gal. 5:1), is near the heart of the gospel.

II. This inner freedom, so integral to biblical faith, is the basis of a person's right to religious liberty. For this reason, religious liberty may be viewed as the outward expression of one's inalienable right to this inner religious freedom.

(a) Religious liberty is the inherent right of a person in public or private to worship or not to worship according to one's own understanding or preferences, to give public witness to one's faith including the right of propagation, and to change one's faith—all without threat of reprisal or abridgment of one's rights as a citizen. The human right to religious liberty is the right to give outward expression to or manifestation of the inner freedom one has found in God.

(b) While this inner Christian freedom does not require civil or political freedom, civil and political freedom are vital as a means of creating that kind of environment which will allow an unhindered expression of religious faith and commitment without civil or political advantages or disadvantages. Persons are to be free in matters of conscience and religion without hindrance and coercion in order that God may be sovereign of their lives and that in turn they may freely respond to that sovereignty and bring about the ordering of their lives according to the will of God.

III. One of the foundation principles of religious liberty to be derived from the Bible is that religion, like God, must wait upon the voluntary responses of persons.

(a) The will of the human person is too sacred to be violated by religious coercion and enforced conformity, which are a denial of the sacredness of human personality and of God's ways of dealing with mankind. The state has no right to intrude on God's dealings with man or to invade the inner life of man.

(b) Religious liberty, if it is to be rooted in principle and properly understood in its biblical context, must be universally espoused by the church for all mankind.

(1) To grant privileges to a particular church or religious community, while denying these privileges to other churches or religious communities, is a denial of religious liberty, no matter how limited this denial may be, and of the fundamental right upon which religious liberty is based.

(2) Discrimination based upon religion is a contradiction of religious liberty, which by its very nature is an equal and inalienable right of all members of the human family.

(c) If the ultimate goal of God's work in history is reconciliation, then religious liberty, both in principle and in practice, must be zealously championed and vigilantly defended by the churches throughout the world.

(1) Each church must see religious liberty not only as its inherent right but also as the right of all churches, all faiths, and all persons.

(2) Even more important for the church, it must see the exercise of religious liberty as the very channel through which the church seeks to fulfill its mission throughout the world.—James E. Wood, Jr.

Illustration

JUMPING FOR JOY.   If a person could look into the future and see what God has planned for his life, he would jump for joy. The life God has planned for you is full of adventure, achievement, courage, and love. He plans for you to be useful in the service of Christ and in ministry to the world's needs. No dull moments and no purposeless days are blueprinted for you. —Perry Tanksley.

Sermon Suggestions

CHRIST'S LEGACY FOR OUR DAILY LIVING. Text: John 13:15. (1) Christ's joy. (2) Christ's love of life and people. (3) Christ's sympathetic and caring heart. (4) Christ's great dream of what life may become in fellowship with God. (5) Christ's courage. (6) Christ's humility and lowliness of spirit. (6) Christ's trust in God and his trust in his disciples to whom he passed on his message and his work.—Frank A. Court.

DARING TO BE DIFFERENT.   Text: Matt. 6:8 (RSV). (1) The sermon on the mount is a call to be different in our attitudes. (2) The sermon on the mount is a call to be different in our behavior. (3) The sermon on the mount is a call to be different in our comprehension.—James M. Dodson.

Worship Aids

CALL TO WORSHIP.   "We have thought of thy lovingkindness, O God, in the midst of thy temple. According to thy name, O God, so is thy praise unto the ends of the earth." Ps. 48:9–10.

INVOCATION.   O God, in glory exalted and in mercy ever blessed, we magnify thee, we praise thee, we give thanks unto thee for thy bountiful providence, for all the blessings of this present life, and all the hopes of a better life to come. Let the memory of thy goodness, we beseech thee, fill our hearts with joy and thankfulness.

OFFERTORY SENTENCE.   "For ye know the grace of our Lord Jesus Christ, that though he was rich, yet for your sakes he became poor, that ye through his poverty might be rich." II Cor. 8:9.

OFFERTORY PRAYER.   Our Father, take us with all of our failures and develop us after thine own heart. Give us more of the mind of the Master, more of his spirit of compassion, and more of his sacrificial and loving heart.

LITANY.   O God, who hast so curiously made us that from whatever heights we climb we see yet loftier heights before and, forever being thus dissatisfied, behold what we ought to be outreaching what we are, strengthen in us this divine discontent.

We lift up our hearts unto thee, O Lord.

From all manner of self-complacency, from pride in the actual and forgetfulness of the ideal, from the cowardice of time-serving and the contented living of mediocre lives on common levels,

We lift up our hearts unto thee, O Lord.

We confess our temptation to measure our lives by the standards of the crowd and to excuse our disordered behavior by appeal to common practices. O Christ, who didst demand of thy disciples, "What do ye more than others?" grant us such clarity of vision, independence of mind, and courage of will that we may live according to our best conscience, without fear or favor of the multitude.

We lift up our hearts unto thee, O Lord.

Grant us humility, knowing that we have not yet attained. Shame us from our pride by a fresh vision of our possibilities. Since what we are is but the seed of what we may grow to be, grant us the inspiration of his Spirit, who gives to them that receive him power to become the sons of God.

Lord, have mercy upon us and grant us this blessing.

Disturb us with visions of a juster social order. From being contented ourselves while poverty and ignorance, lack of labor, and destitution of soul afflict our fellows,

Good Lord, deliver us.

From complacency with political corruption, racial prejudice, the hardships of unfair industry, the disunion of the churches, and the insanity of war,

Good Lord, deliver us.

O God, who without our asking it hast set us in this mysterious scheme of circumstance, give us light in the same that we may know the path to walk in. Confirm in us the dreams of seers and the hopes of prophets, let not cynicism blight nor faithlessness uproot our confidence in thy coming kingdom of righteousness upon the earth, and at the fire of our faith let courage be kindled that we may live as we pray.

Lord, have mercy upon us and grant us this blessing.—Harry Emerson Fosdick.

EVENING SERVICE

Topic: Four Anchors That Hold
TEXT: Acts 27:29.

Life is not all calm sea and prosperous voyage. Sooner or later we all face storms. Sometimes the storms are so violent and prolonged that we lose our bearings and find ourselves being driven toward the rocks. At such times the best thing we can hope to do is to cast out all the anchors we have and pray that the anchors will hold through the night. There are any number of anchors that people have used when they have found themselves drifting on a lee shore, but since the story of St. Paul's shipwreck speaks of four, let me limit myself to that number in speaking of the anchors that hold.

I. The first anchor is light in weight, and for that reason it will not hold indefinitely. But because it is light in weight, it is the easiest one to throw overboard. It is the knowledge that no matter how dark the night may be, the day is bound to follow. There is truth in the old adage that it is always darkest before the dawn. The worst experiences that we have are usually short in duration. The bitterest pains we bear are not permanent. The worst tragedies that smite us may seem unendurable when they come, but in time we live beyond them, and they recede into the past. The darkest nights of suffering are always followed by the day.

II. The second anchor is heavier in weight and holds longer. It is forged of the kindness of people.

(a) Trouble teaches us two lessons about people. The bitter lesson is that some of the people you think are your friends can let you down. That discovery can be the heaviest blow imaginable, but it is far outweighed by the discovery that quite ordinary men and women are capable of love and loyalty and self-sacrifice for which they ask nothing in return except the knowledge that they have been of help to someone who needed them.

(b) The story of the shipwreck provides a beautiful example of this. (1) Some of the sailors, after the anchors had been thrown out, began to let down a lifeboat. They had decided to desert the passengers and make for the shore themselves. Some of the soldiers of the guard, fearing that the prisoners might escape or turn on their captors in the confusion, began to talk of murdering them forthwith.

(2) At that point the centurion achieved real stature as a man. Without thinking of his own danger or of the heavy responsibility of guilt he would have to bear if the prisoners were allowed to escape, he walked to the side of the ship, cut the lifeboat free, and watched it drift away empty. Then he gave orders to the soldiers that the prisoners were not to be harmed.

(3) That man rose to the occasion when trouble came. He proved himself not only a brave man but a large-hearted human being. People often rise to the occasion like that.

III. The third anchor is the knowledge that God always remains the same, steadfast and immovable. The sailors on Paul's ship could not see the stars above the clouds. All around them was raging water. But they did not forget that the bottom was solid. Beneath the churning sea there was something steadfast in which the anchors could take hold. When trouble comes, it is not always easy to be conscious of the nearness of God. Underneath the raging waves of such storms of life there is a solid bottom, and the bottom is firm.

IV. The fourth anchor is the knowledge of Jesus Christ. To know the story of Jesus is the most wonderful thing that can happen to a man or a woman. That story says two things.

(a) The first is that God cares enough for men to have sent his Son into the world to die for them.

(b) The second is that a human being can suffer the worst misfortunes that life can inflict and still turn defeat into victory. Jesus knew physical and mental suffering as you and I will never know it. He knew the ultimate agony of soul that asks, "My God, my God, why hast thou forsaken me?" Yet he was capable not only of refusing to be broken by the heavy load of suffering that was his but of offering that suffering to God as a willing sacrifice in order that God might use it to help other people.

—Charles H. Buck, Jr.

SUNDAY: FEBRUARY THIRTEENTH

MORNING SERVICE

Topic: Jesus Identifies Our Neighbor (Brotherhood Week)

TEXT: Luke 10:37.

Jesus asked gently, "Which one of the three turned out to be a neighbor?" In a whisper the young intellectual replied, "The one who helped him!" "Go," Jesus said, "and do likewise." This is a different way to define a neighbor. It does not start with where a man lives but with how a man lives. It has more to do with attitude than with residence.

I. *A neighbor is someone who is responsive to another person's need.*

(a) That was the essential difference between the priest and the Samaritan. There were many other differences between them. Jesus did not spell them out, but they are clearly implied in the story. One man was religious; the other man wasn't. One man was respectable; the other was not quite respectable. One man was educated and cultured; the other man was rather non-descript. One man was careful about his language; the other was not. The priest was one of the town's leading citizens; the Samaritan probably couldn't even rent a locker in the YMCA. The differences did not have to be catalogued for the people who heard the story. They knew how to tell the difference between a priest and a Samaritan.

(b) The difference that finally determined which was the real neighbor was in how they reacted to a fellow human being in trouble. It was a difference in basic instincts. The priest saw the victim and drew back in horror and revulsion. The Samaritan saw the victim and responded to him with compassion and love. The reaction in each case was not premeditated; it was spontaneous. They were not playing to an audience; each man was alone with the victim and his own conscience. They were not competing for a Good Citizen Award; they were simply revealing what they were really like on the inside.

(c) To be a neighbor, Jesus said, means responding to another human being with love and compassion.

II. *A neighbor is one who uses his own resources to alleviate the needs of others.*

(a) Someone read this story with a slightly different accent. Ordinarily we read it this way, "When the priest *saw* that he had been robbed, he passed by on the other side." This man put the accent in a different place: "When the priest saw that he *had* been robbed, he passed by on the other side."

(b) All kinds of motives are at work when a man relates to his fellowman, and sometimes people do respond to others for ulterior purposes because they expect to gain something by doing so. The Samaritan had nothing to gain. No one was going to pin a medal on him. No one was going to write him up in the *Jericho Gazette.* He did not expect to be paid back for his investment with a little bonus on the side for his effort.

(c) It was a free and genuine outpouring of his own means. He was willing to tear up his own garment to make a bandage. He was willing to let the victim ride on his donkey while he walked. He was willing to assume the expenses that might be incurred at the inn. He translated his compassion into dollars and cents and paid the bill.

(d) J. B. Phillips has just the right expression in his translation: "The man who gave him practical sympathy!" That's what it takes—a compassion that gets involved in the most basic and elementary way at the point where the need is the greatest.

III. *A neighbor is someone who comes to stay.*

(a) It was not hit-and-run charity such as many of us practice. It was not just making a donation and then erasing the incident from your mind. It was accepting a continuing responsibility for the welfare and recovery of a fellow human being. The first thing the Samaritan did was to bathe and cleanse the wounds of the victim. But he did not stop there. He tore strips from his robe and used them as bandages. But he did not stop there. He put the man on his donkey and got him to a place of shelter. But he did not stop there. He told the innkeeper to provide anything the man needed and then said that he would return and cover any expense that was involved. He projected his practical sympathy into the future and assumed a personal obligation that did not end at sunset.

(c) This is hard when it comes to ministering to the needs of others. It is especially difficult when it comes to civil rights. Our sympathy is aroused; we even give some practical expression to our generous impulses. But beyond that we do not want to get involved.

(d) The real question for America today is not "Guess who's coming to dinner!" Guests come and go, and most of us are equal to these casual and semi-informal encounters. The real question is "Guess who's coming to stay!" An ethnic minority individual is moving into our neighborhood not just for an overnight visit but to stay. An ethnic minority individual is moving up into equal employment opportunities not just for a trial period but to stay. An ethnic minority individual is coming to church not just for Brotherhood Sunday but to stay. That's the heart of the matter, and that is the background for the final test of our willingness to love our neighbor as ourselves.—Clarence J. Forsberg.

Illustrations

BROTHER.   The Russian novelist, Ivan S. Turgenev, was stopped one day by a decrepit old beggar. "I began to feel in all my pockets," wrote Turgenev later. "No purse, no watch, not even a handkerchief. I had taken nothing with me. And the beggar was still waiting, and his outstretched hand shook feebly and trembled. Confused, ashamed, I warmly clasped the filthy shaking hand. 'Don't be angry, brother. I have nothing, brother.' The beggar stared at me with his bloodshot eyes. His blue lips smiled, and he in his turn gripped my chilly fingers. 'What of it, brother?' he mumbled. 'Thanks for this too. That is a gift too, brother.'"

ONE MAN'S INFLUENCE.   In Piccadilly Square in London stands a statue of Lord Shaftsbury. On it are inscribed the words, "The reforms of this century have been chiefly due to the presence and influence of Shaftsbury." What is back of that? It was a man representing the noblest ancestry, wealth, and culture who became the voice for the poor and the weak. He gave his life to reform acts such as emancipating enslaved boys and girls who were toiling in factories and mines. He exposed and made impossible the horrors of the inferno in which chimney sweeps lived. He founded forty industrial and trade schools and established shelters for the poor. When they carried his lifeless body through the streets where he had devoted his life, peddlers lifted a sign on which they had scrawled, "I was sick and in prison and ye visited me." Boys, now attending schools which he had started for them, had their banner too. It read, "I was hungry and naked and ye fed me."

Sermon Suggestion

WHAT MAKES A CHRISTIAN?   Text: I Cor. 12:3 (RSV). (1) Acknowledgment that Jesus is Lord of one's life in some significant ways. (2) Loyalty by responding to his will and his claim. (3) Resemblance by loving and honoring him so that other people can see his spirit in us.—Edward C. Dahl.

Worship Aids

CALL TO WORSHIP.   "Worthy is the Lamb that was slain to receive power, and riches, and wisdom, and strength, and honor, and glory, and blessing." Rev. 5: 12.

INVOCATION.   Merciful God, forgive the halting nature of our discipleship. We confess that so little of thy love has reached others through us and that we have borne so lightly wrongs and sufferings that were not our own. We confess that we have cherished the things that divide us from others and that we have made it hard for them to live with us. And we confess that we have been thoughtless in our judgments, hasty in condemnation, and grudging in our forgiveness. Forgive us, we beseech thee.

OFFERTORY SENTENCE. "Verily I say unto you, inasmuch as ye have done it unto one of the least of these my brethren, ye have done it unto me." Matt. 25:40.

OFFERTORY PRAYER. O eternal God, may these gifts represent an inner commitment to love thee above all else and to love our brethren in need because they are loved by thee.

PRAYER. Eternal God, our Father, thou who art the Father of every race, culture, and creed: may the day come when we shall not be bound by racial differences but regard all thy children as members of one great human family, when all cultures shall blend into one culture of the soul, and when man-made barriers shall give way before thy overwhelming love of humanity.

Keep us aware of injustices whether in our own land or elsewhere. O God, our Father, may we never rest while any human being anywhere is shackled by any form of slavery and until everyone is free, for we recognize that no one is free until everyone is free.

Help us to learn how to distribute the world's goods in order that everyone may have enough and that none may be without life's necessities. Cause those of us who have so much to remember how many millions of thy children, our brothers, do not ever have enough to eat and to realize that freedom and peace cannot become realities on empty stomachs.

May we not only be concerned about them, but may we also do everything in our power to alleviate their hunger and misery in the spirit of our Master, who calls upon us to resolve the conflicts of life, to create better and more wholesome relationships, to strive for a world order dedicated to peace and justice, and to build bridges of service and love that ultimately we ourselves may become bridges of reconciliation.—Chester E. Hodgson.

EVENING SERVICE

Topic: What Is Caring?
TEXT: John 13:35.

I. Caring involves loving someone as we love ourselves. It is more than liking, comforting, showing sympathy, or having an interest in what happens to another person. Caring involves a concern that spills over into loving, compassionate acts.

II. Caring is trying to understand another person. When we care we seek to know the other person's needs, resources, and ability to cope. We try to see things from the other person's perspective before we try to offer specific help.

III. Caring is showing respect for another person. It does not involve giving rigid advice, criticizing, or talking about someone in a manner that approaches gossip. Instead, caring involves willingness to bear burdens. It looks for ways to help the other person grow, even if such growth means that in time our help may no longer be needed.

IV. Caring means that one is willing to take risks. It is not easy to care for another person. When we care for people we risk being misunderstood, rebuffed, criticized, and even harmed physically. For the Christian, however, failure to take these risks is to ignore Bible passages, especially in the book of James, that emphasize that faith in Jesus Christ must lead to works of compassion.

V. Caring involves us in being willing to accept help. Jesus said that it is more blessed to give than to receive (Acts 20: 25). He would agree that it is easier to give than to receive. In our culture we like to solve problems on our own and are reluctant to accept help. Caring, however, involves at least two persons: the one who needs and accepts care as well as the one who sees a need and gives the care. If we are serious about bearing one another's burdens (Gal. 6:2) and about caring for one another, then we must be willing both to reach out and care and to accept with gratitude the caring that other people bestow upon us.—Gary R. Collins in *Christianity Today.*

SUNDAY: FEBRUARY TWENTIETH

MORNING SERVICE

Topic: The Seven Pillars of Wisdom's House

Text: Prov. 9:1.

I. The first pillar is purpose. A high and noble purpose is to a successful life what the drive wheel is to the locomotive or what the rudder is to the ocean liner. It produces a willingness to toil and sacrifice; it drives the soul and keeps it right on course; it refuses to be defeated in its quest for achievement.

II. The second pillar is courage. (a) The onward march to success and power must ring with the note of courage. The spirit of courage melts mountains, spans seas, conquers storms, slays giants of opposition, and fights its way to victory.

(b) Courage that counts does not depend on time or place or circumstance. It is the quality that moved Caleb to say to Joshua, "Give me this mountain," where he could win his inheritance from the giants and the walled cities. Christian courage is one of the scintillating jewels of the Christian faith, and God's command, repeated over and over in scripture, is "Fear not."

III. The third pillar is genuineness. Purity is the dynamic of success. The world soon sees through a camouflage. A sign in the window of a London jeweler read: "Artificial gems set in real gold." No gold setting can make paste jewels genuine. If you are counterfeit, the world will find it out. Paul's injunction to Timothy was "Keep thyself pure."

IV. Wisdom's fourth pillar is unselfishness. No worthwhile life can stand on a foundation of selfishness. In God's order of things, only that which gives, lives. Palestine has its sea of life, the Sea of Galilee, and its sea of death, the Dead Sea. The difference is that the one receives and generously gives, while the other receives and keeps all it gets.

V. The fifth pillar is work. (a) Americans are worshipers of genius, forgetting that genius is often only another name for hard work. Asked to define genius, Thomas A. Edison said, "Genius is one percent inspiration and 99 percent perspiration." Carlyle said, "There are two things necessary to a life of success; one is to find one's work and the other is to do it."

(b) Theodore Roosevelt was offered sympathy by a friend because of the tremendous demands made upon him as the President. He replied with a smile, "No, I like my job. I am glad that I can have a part in the world's work." The first blessing that God bestowed upon Adam outside the Garden of Eden was the blessing of work.

VI. Right thinking is the sixth pillar of wisdom's house. There is no crown of enduring success that is not purchased by high and noble thinking. "For as he thinketh in his heart," says the writer of Proverbs, "so is he." Life will gravitate toward its ideals. We become like the things with which we keep company in our thoughts. It is said that when Michelangelo completed his statue of David, the hard lines in his own face had softened.

VII. The last and crowning one of the seven pillars in the house that wisdom built is faith.

(a) In the window of an art store in Paris was exhibited the statue of a medieval knight, clothed from head to foot in chain armor, a broadsword hanging by his right side and his shield at the left. On his face was a look of high resolve, and in his outstretched hands was a scroll bearing the inscription, "Credo—I believe." The man who believes is the man who accomplishes.

(b) A musician went into a china shop and asked for some goblets pitched to the key of C. The proprietor threw up his hands and said, "You have it on me, sir." Said the musician, "I will take care of that," and going to a table in the center of the room, he struck his tuning fork. Immediately every goblet in the room pitched to the key of C trembled into song.

(c) Faith is the tuning fork that brings singing to our hearts, the music of heavenly assurance that Jesus Christ, through his atoning death, is ours; that we, through his redeeming grace, are his; and that we are saved through his precious blood and kept evermore by his power.—*The War Cry.*

Illustrations

PREVISION. Man alone of God's creatures has the power of prevision. Bees store honey against the day when no flowers bloom. Squirrels hoard nuts to keep them through the winter. Birds build nests for eggs not yet laid. But this is instinct, not conscious foresight. Man plans for years, builds for centuries, sacrifices for generations unborn. He alone has dreams of a Utopia, a new Jerusalem, "when earth shall shine among the stars, its sins wiped out, its captives free," and of a life of larger scope and permanence than earth affords when his life here is done. Foresight is one of his highest faculties for it enables him to set up goals and then patiently, steadily, to work toward them through the years.—Frank Halliday Ferris.

FAITH AND MORALITY. Moral endeavor without belief lacks power to persevere. Ethical stamina depends ultimately on the dynamic of faith. Morality by itself cannot give the power to perform what it demands. He who would act greatly must also believe strongly. The power of ethical movements is determined by their religious force. Perhaps it is this most of all which brings men to recognize the need of faith. They are aware that the ethical glow fades unless it is maintained by religious fervor.—Edgar P. Dickie.

Sermon Suggestions

WISDOM FOR DECISION MAKING. Text: Prov. 3:13. (1) Wisdom to appreciate. (2) Wisdom of humility. (3) Wisdom as perspective. (4) Wisdom to discern.— Herschel H. Sheets.

QUESTIONS JESUS ASKED. Text: Luke 11:9. (1) A question of devotion (Mark 10:36). (2) A question of self-appraisal (Matt. 21:40). (3) A jolting question (Matt. 26:50). (4) A question of faith (Matt. 14: 31). (5) A question about true gain (Mark 8:36). (6) A question of understanding (Luke 12:56). (7) A question of gratitude (Luke 17:17). (8) A question of stewardship (Matt. 15:33). (9) A question of loyalty (John 6:67) (10) A question of one goal (Mark 5:9).—Thomas White Currie, Jr.

Worship Aids

CALL TO WORSHIP. "They that wait upon the Lord shall renew their strength; they shall mount up with wings as eagles; they shall run, and not be weary; and they shall walk, and not faint." Isa. 40:31.

INVOCATION. Almighty God, who hast given us minds to know thee, hearts to love thee, and voices to show forth thy praise, we would not know thee if thou hadst not already found us. Help us to know thee with pure minds and to praise thee with a clear voice.

OFFERTORY SENTENCE. "Therefore, as ye abound in every thing, in faith, and utterance, and knowledge, and in all diligence, and in your love to us, see that ye abound in this grace also." II Cor. 8:7.

OFFERTORY PRAYER. O Lord, who hast given us the privilege of life, help us to magnify eternal values and to show forth by our lives and our tithes the Christ, whom to know aright is life eternal.

PRAYER. O God, teach us to die to anger which divides nation from nation, race from race, class from class, family from family and rise to that forgiveness which unites, restores, and knits heart to heart.

O God, teach us to die to covetous desires and to possess what is not our own and to rise to generosity that is patient and content to work and achieve its goals and dreams.

O God, teach us to die to gluttony which exploits the labors of others and lays waste the earth and rise to temperance that honors and conserves the blessings of men and creation.

O God, teach us to die to envy of the welfare and happiness of others and rise to love that seeks not its own and is not selfish or rude.

O God, teach us to die to sloth which ignores the call and the needs of others and rise to diligence in service that dignifies life and glorifies thy name.

O God, teach us to die to lust which would use for ignoble ends the bodies and lives of men and women and rise to purity, the crown of all virtues, in our body, soul, and spirit.

O God, teach us to die to pride which trusts only in ourselves and rise to humility and our need of the power of the resurrected life which you have given us through Jesus Christ our Lord.—James D. Furlong.

EVENING SERVICE

Topic: The Gates of New Life

Text: Ps. 118:19.

When Rome, the proud city of the seven hills, was falling before its invaders, Augustine saw another city not made with hands, the dwelling place of the Most High. This city God invites us to enter. His hand opens to us the gates of new life, the gates of devotion and happiness, the gates of peace and security, the gates of faith and service, and the gates of fellowship and love.

I. *The gate of faith and insight.* (a) A pupil sits before his teacher, listening attentively and trying to grasp the teacher's thought. At first the pupil's understanding is vague and confused, but presently the gate seems to open and the pupil now enters into the real meaning of his teacher's thought. The ideas take fire in his mind, and he knows he is now grasping the truth his teacher seeks to convey. "You shall know the truth," said the great teacher, "and the truth will set you free." Jesus was referring to his revelation of God and to the new life experienced in the love of God.

(b) The pure in heart see God. The singleminded are those whose hearts are set on accepting and obeying God's will. The rich young ruler who came to Jesus possessed fine qualities that made him lovable. He had position and wealth and youth, but in the presence of Jesus he was conscious that he was missing something. "What do I still lack? Where do I fall short?" Jesus swung open to him the gates of a new life, but he refused to enter.

(c) God opens to us the gates of a new life of faith and consecration to his kingdom. It is in this context of God's approach and our glad response that we come to know God.

II. *The gate of righteousness.* (a) Righteousness means what is right in God's sight. Only in God's will, living by God's rule, can our lives find their true measure and be directed toward their true focus.

(b) One of the most crippling things about life is no settled aim, no steady drive, no consistent purpose, and no far-off divine event. Too many of us live unfocused lives—what William James called double-minded—and are never able to keep a steady course like a boat without a rudder, tossed and whirled about by conflicting wind and wave.

(c) Jesus affirmed that the supreme focus for our lives is the kingdom of God. "Seek first the kingdom of God and his righteousness." The hand of God will open this gate to the earnest seeker. You don't see life's true direction or its real meaning until through the light of God's Spirit, your heart becomes focused on what is right.

III. *The gate of a new life.* (a) Life becomes cramped and dwarfed without God. We are made for fellowship with him which is what the Bible calls eternal life—life rooted and grounded in the love of God. Christ opens the gate that leads you out of your self-centeredness and into the broad places of true living and consecrated service.

(b) When Luther grasped the truth that on the grace of God alone the salvation of men depended, a new joy and exhilaration broke over the life of Europe. Out of this sense of God's love men found "confidence instead of fear, liberty instead of bondage, gratitude instead of the desire for reward, love for others instead of thought of self."

(c) Christ shares with us the inexhaustible riches of his grace. We can possess those riches only as we share them with others and only as we become channels of the love of God. When we share our loaves and fishes with the multitude, the loaves and fishes are multiplied. Our lives are not impoverished but enriched. We shall receive "good measure, pressed down, shaken together, running over."—Richard E. Gosse.

SUNDAY: FEBRUARY TWENTY-SEVENTH

MORNING SERVICE

Topic: Mercy Divine and Human
SCRIPTURE: Luke 18:31–43.

A blind man is calling to Jesus for relief from his misery, "Jesus, Son of David, have mercy on me!" It is the desperate cry of men who are down and out, and who among us has not experienced the need to utter this cry when everything seems to be going wrong and there is no one to turn to except God?

I. The begging of the blind man was most certainly well known to those on the road to Jericho.

(a) They had probably heard such wailings from this man before. Many a time he had probably asked for a crust of bread or a garment to clothe himself. How often they had heard him say, "Benjamin, Ben Jacob, have mercy on me!" or "Simon, son of Jared, pity me!"

(b) Undoubtedly several of them had heeded his requests begrudgingly or in genuine compassion, while others treated him like a dog. When he heard Jesus of Nazareth was passing by, he called out, "Jesus, son of David, have mercy on me!" It probably sounded to them like more of the same sort of moaning they were accustomed to hear from him.

(c) Those in the front of the crowd turned to rebuke him. This was no time for beggars. They were more concerned about this Jesus of Nazareth passing by. Many undoubtedly thought him an important, if not unusual man. He was becoming famous. Many considered him a potential leader of men, while certain leaders of the people in Jerusalem already considered him a threat to their security.

II. The blind man evidenced a deeper insight into the person of Jesus of Nazareth than any of them.

(a) He must have heard reports about Jesus before. When he cries out, "Jesus, son of David, have mercy on me," he seems to be asking for more than a mere crust of bread. It's as if he were asking for more than he had ever asked before. He is acting as if this were the Messiah, the chosen one of God, sent to redeem Israel from all her troubles. When Jesus stops near him, he asks for a miracle, the recovery of his eyesight.

(b) It must have been a shock to those who had known the man. After all, he had been blind for a long time, perhaps for his entire life. The best that they had been able to do for him was to pity him for his disability. Men and all their optimistic notions about their ability to help their fellowmen could do no more than this. They could show sympathy, but they could not get to the root of his misery. Man at his best cannot restore human life that is apparently beyond repair. Man's ultimate weakness and cause for despair is that he cannot redeem himself from death.

(c) The blind man looked upon Jesus with eyes of faith that discerned him to be far greater than anything man could imagine to come from the hands of God. He saw in him God's chosen vessel to bring restoration and healing to human life. He saw in the man they called the Christ the depth of God's mercy for fallen man. For in him God demonstrated his power to restore life among those who were fallen and in need of his help. In acknowledging his weakness and availing himself to God's help, the man is healed. Jesus tells him, "Receive your sight; your faith has made you well."

(d) You would have thought that we would have learned the lesson of the text. You would have thought that by now we would always avail ourselves of God's aid, as this blind man did, by facing up to our weaknesses and turning to God for his power to renew us when we are feeling low and painfully aware of our inadequacies. Our problem is that we are slow to discover our sins. How many of us would have felt more at home with the crowds as they cheered when Jesus of Nazareth passed by? But to fall on your knees, as this blind man did, is asking too much. After all, it is an admission of our weakness and the need that we have for the mercy of God.

III. God expects far more of men than mercy as it is set by worldly standards. What men call mercy is often much less than the standard of mercy that God has set.

(a) The subtlety of sin is that at the very moment we may think we are showing mercy and kindness to our fellowmen we are actually dominated by motives of condescending pride which enjoys the idea of playing god toward men we consider inferior. Men often take pleasure in patronizing others when they are only feeding their own sense of superiority. The people on the roadside in our text thought they were showing mercy to the blind man when the most merciful thing they could have done was to take him to the front of the procession to receive the mercy of God through Jesus, the mercy of God which is far greater than anything man can do.

(b) We stand before Jesus of Nazareth, as the blind man did, in need of God's mercy and help. We stand before our fellowman, as the blind man did, in need of God's forgiveness for the things that we do. We stand before our fellowmen, as the blind man did, with no reason to boast that we are more or less than they. We stand before our fellowmen with the commission from God to reveal to them mercy and love according to his standards. We are called to love as he has loved and to forgive even as we are forgiven.

(c) This incident on the road to Jericho ultimately leads to Jerusalem. Jesus has just announced to his disciples that he is about to suffer and die for the sins of men. While he contemplates his own suffering, he turns to the suffering of another man and so reveals the depth and the mystery of God's mercy which has no interest in itself but rather the healing and mending of all that is broken among men. He shows that the only meaning that mercy can have

for us is the redemption of all that has separated us from God and from our fellowmen. God in Christ has shown that he can accomplish far more than we could ever offer in return. This is the depth of his mercy which goes beyond the mercy of men.—Richard Kraemer.

Illustrations

BEGINNING AGAIN. When he created man, God gave him a secret—and that secret was not how to begin but how to begin again. It is not given to man to begin; that privilege is God's alone. But it is given to man to begin again—and he does so every time he chooses to defy death and side with the living.—Elie Wiesel.

THAT WHICH BINDS. What Christ is saying always, what he never swerves from saying, what he says a thousand times and in a thousand different ways is this: "I am my Father's son, and you are my brothers." And the unity that binds us all together, that makes this earth a family, and all men brothers, and so the sons of God, is love.—Thomas Wolfe.

Sermon Suggestions

FIVE QUESTIONS ABOUT PRAYER. Text: I John 5:14. (1) Is your prayer rational? (2) Have you done all you can to answer your prayer? (3) Do you believe you are asking for what God wants? (4) Do you believe God has the power to answer your prayer? (5) Have you turned your need to God, relinquishing yourself?—Edgar M. Arendall.

STANDING IN THAT DAY. Scripture: Luke 21:25–36. (1) Pray to be alert. (2) Pray to remain clearheaded. (3) Pray to be found worthy.—Norbert H. Mueller.

Worship Aids

CALL TO WORSHIP. "Wait on the Lord: be of good courage, and he shall strengthen thine heart: wait, I say, on the Lord." Ps. 27:14.

INVOCATION. O Lord, who hast taught us that the love of money is the root of all evil, teach us to care for what money cannot buy—not security but opportunity, not withdrawal from the world but a full participation within it, and not prestige but use. Help us to handle all the goods of life in the spirit of thy Son who out of his poverty made many rich.

OFFERTORY SENTENCE. "It is good to give thanks to the Lord, to sing praises to thy name, O Most High; to declare thy steadfast love in the morning, and thy faithfulness by night." Ps. 92:1–2.

OFFERTORY PRAYER. We pray thee, O God, to give us sight to see the Christ, the insight to chose him, the steadfastness to follow him, and the stewardship of loyalty represented in these gifts offered in his name.

PRAYER. Let us pray for the company of all faithful people, for the followers of the way of the cross; for those who are asking honest questions, lest they lose the way; for those who know all the answers, lest they become proud; for those who withdraw from all fellow travellers, lest they become arrogant; for those who are disappointed and discouraged, lest they give up in despair; for those who will not accept changes, lest they become inflexible; for those who change with every passing fad and fancy, lest they lose their direction; for those who have the spirit but neither the will nor the power; for those who have the will but not the imagination, the faith but not the love; for all those, hear our prayer, O Lord, and let our cry come unto thee.

For those who can withstand everything that life can do to them and be neither downcast nor bitter; for those who follow the way even though they see it only dimly; for those who shine like stars in a dark world; for those who stagger not at the uneven motion of the world or censure their journey by the weather they meet or turn aside for anything that befalls them; for those who by their steadiness keep us in the way when we are tempted to drop

out, we are thankful, O Lord.—Theodore P. Ferris.

EVENING SERVICE

Topic: The Dangerous Gospel of Love
TEXT: Mark 11:18.

Why did those in authority, the men of power and prestige in first-century Palestine, fear Jesus who had never harmed anyone, who had walked before the people in simple humility and meekness, who had taught that love is the supreme law of life?

I. They feared his frankness. (a) His outspoken denunciation of the accepted but unjust practices in Jerusalem society made these men exceedingly uncomfortable. As we read the seven woes recorded by Matthew, Jesus' blistering excoriation of the high-caste religious leaders, we marvel that they did not then and there pick up stones to silence him. (See Matt. 23:13–26.) Across the twenty centuries that separate us, we still smart at the sting of his cutting lash on the back of hypocrisy.

(b) Christian history has yielded many leaders who, following the example of their master, put truth above privilege, justice above self-interest, and right above personal comfort. Stephen, the first Christian martyr, was stoned to death outside the walls of Jerusalem. William Lloyd Garrison, in the middle of the last century, goaded America's drowsy, sluggish conscience against the heinous crime of human slavery. "I will not be silent. I will not excuse. I will not equivocate. I will not retreat a single inch, and I will be heard."

II. The chief priests and the scribes feared Jesus' simplicity. (a) It was openly rumored throughout Jerusalem that this man did not observe the ceremonial washings before each meal. He did not follow the prescribed periods of fasting or adhere to the elaborate sacrificial system established over the centuries. Moreover, he was accused of failing to honor the Sabbath, the keystone of Jewish observances.

(b) When they asked him which of the six hundred and thirteen commandments he considered the most important, he answered: "You shall love the Lord your

God with all your heart, and with all your soul, and with all your mind" and "You shall love your neighbor as yourself." He insisted that it is just as important to love your fellowman as it is to love God. To the Pharisees this was blasphemy.

III. The chief priests and scribes feared Jesus' gospel of love. (a) The danger of this doctrine was not that Jesus taught that men should love all God's creatures but that he actually applied it. If we love our fellowmen merely in broad, sweeping generalities, the gospel of love is perfectly harmless. Love of this vague, amorphous type is dangerous to no one. Charlie Brown put it with a great deal of wisdom: "I love all mankind. It's people I can't stand."

(b) When Jesus applied his gospel of love to specific areas of conflict and unrest in the social life of first-century Palestine, the national leaders concluded that it was a subversive doctrine. The Jews of Jesus' day had their prejudices, deep-grained, blind, unshakable, just as people have them today. This Galilean teacher not only advocated that the Jews love their half-breed brothers to the north, but he actually went to live with them in their villages. He insisted on telling stories in which Samaritans were portrayed in a more advantageous light than his own countrymen. Had he no loyalty, no patriotism?

(c) We fear the gospel of love more than we fear the gospel of hate.

(1) Hate we know how to handle. We can resist that. We can call out military forces, and with rifles and mace put down an uprising of those who hate.

(2) How do you resist the gospel of love? How do you deal with people who insist on loving you, who do not fight back, who pray for you when you club them over the head? No matter what you do to fight them, you cannot shake off the inevitable sense of guilt. It makes you very angry with yourself and robs you of your peace of mind. It calls into question all the values of your way of life.

(d) The religious hierarchy of Jesus' day had little to fear in his teachings about love, the way of the abundant life, and the kingdom of God on earth. His teachings are not dangerous—except when applied.
—Milton B. Eastwick.

SUNDAY: MARCH SIXTH

MORNING SERVICE

Topic: The Stewardship of Jesus (Lent)
SCRIPTURE: John 17.

The figure of the exhalted Christ is so vivid in our minds that we sometimes forget that Jesus was, on the human side, subject to the principles of stewardship like any other man. In his great intercessory prayer Jesus knew that his earthly life was at an end. He felt that he must, in prayer, render an account of his stewardship. Jesus was a responsible steward. This is his report.

I. *Work.* "I have glorified thee on earth, having accomplished work which thou gavest me to do." Jesus was annointed, appointed, commissioned to do the work of the Father.

(a) His calling was to be the messiah. His understanding of his calling grew with the years. How to fulfill his messiahship was a problem to him from the first day of his public ministry to the last. He was constantly being pressured by his disciples and others to proclaim an earthly kingdom.

(b) His vocation was to lead men back to God and thus to secure for them eternal life in the Father. To Jesus was entrusted the good news that God is love. Never did any man have so heavy a stewardship entrustment. Never did any man so completely fulfill his calling. He is the only man who could say: "I have accomplished the work which thou gavest me to do."

II. *People.* "I have manifested thy name to the men whom thou gavest me out of the world."

(a) The disciples, with all their faults, were God-given. "Thine they were, and thou gavest them to me, and they have kept thy word." The Father gave Jesus a work to do and the people necessary to carry out that work.

(b) Many things are necessary to get things done in the world: money, machinery, power, food, minerals, and the rest. But the most important is people. A leader no matter how great can only supervise about seven to ten to twelve colleagues.

(c) Leadership must be expressed through trained and creative followers. Jesus taught his disciples, but mostly the training consisted in being with them. After the resurrection and Pentecost they began to put it all together. Jesus indeed had manifested God's name to them.

III. *Words.* "I have given them the words which thou gavest me." (a) Jesus was a man of prayer and earnest searching to find and do the will of God. All the great crises of his life found him on his knees in prayer: the temptation, the selection of the disciples, the night before the crucifixion.

(b) Jesus spoke with the authority of the Father. His purpose was always to lead people to God, and this required that they believe that he was sent from God.

(c) This also was the purpose of John in writing this Gospel: "That you may believe that Jesus is the Christ, the Son of God, and that believing, you may have life in his name." John as a writer was conscious of the power of words. He described Jesus as "the Word made flesh." Jesus had received the words of God and had faithfully given them to all who would hear.

IV. *Glory.* "The glory which thou hast given me I have given to them."

(a) Jesus had just witnessed the departure of Judas. He was aware of the weakness of the disciples and their probable behavior at the time of his crucifixion. The cross was the worst of deaths. Yet Jesus spoke of glory.

(b) The disciples and all true followers of Jesus were likely to suffer a fate similar to that of their Lord. Where then the glory of which Jesus prayed? It was in the joy of knowing that they were doing the Father's will. It was the same glory "which thou hast given me in thy love for me before the foundation of the world." There is a glorious joy in Christian stewardship of the kind Jesus lived and taught.

(c) When Jesus had finished this prayer, he went out with his disciples across the Kidron valley where he often met with his disciples. Judas knew the place and led the soldiers there to arrest Jesus. In a few hours he would be hanging on a cross and giving his life as a ransom for many.

(d) In this prayer Jesus used the word "given," indicating entrustments from God, seventeen times. So great was his consciousness of what God had given to him which he in turn was to give also to his followers—including those of the twentieth century.—T. K. Thompson in *The Clergy Journal.*

Illustrations

OVERCOMING EVIL. If evil were stronger than God, he would never have sent his Son to show us how to overcome it. God in his wisdom knew that evil could be defeated. God in the person of his Son faced the cruel facts of evil and pain and death unflinchingly for us. The resurrection tells more about God and his power to overcome evil than any other event in history.—Helen Smith Shoemaker.

GOD'S PLANS. God alone has secret plans, and what he'll do we'll find out when it happens. We'll leave things in his hands and cast all our cares on him, for it's his cause that is at stake, and he will advance it.—Martin Luther.

Sermon Suggestions

WHO CARES? Text: I John 1:9. (1) Christ cares about your salvation. (See John 3:16.) (2) Christ cares about your needs. (See Phil. 4:19.) (3) Christ cares enough to hear you. (See Heb. 4:15–16.) (4) Christ cares enough to give you the Holy Spirit as your comfort. (See John 14:15–18.) (5) Christ cares enough to prepare a place for you. (See John 14:2–3.)—Robert W. Proctor.

WAY, TRUTH, AND LIFE. Text: John 14:6. (1) Christ is the way by which we must go. (2) Christ is the truth to which we come. (3) Christ is the life in which we ultimately must abide.—St. Bernard.

Worship Aids

CALL TO WORSHIP. "It is good for me to draw near to God: I have put my trust in the Lord God. God is the strength of my heart, and my portion for ever." Ps. 73:26, 28.

INVOCATION. Our heavenly Father, who by thy love hast made us, through thy love hast kept us, and in thy love wouldst make us perfect: we humbly confess that we have not loved thee with all our heart and soul and mind and strength and that we have not loved one another as Christ hath loved us. Thy life is within our souls, but our selfishness has hindered thee. We have not lived by faith. We have resisted thy spirit. We have neglected thy inspirations. Forgive what we have been, help us to amend what we are, and in thy spirit direct what we shall be, that thou mayest come into the full glory of thy creation in us and in all men.

OFFERTORY SENTENCE. "Of every man that giveth willingly with his heart ye shall take my offering [saith the Lord]." Exod. 25:2.

OFFERTORY PRAYER. Our heavenly Father, help us to remember that, though Christ offers his companionship, to us belongs the decision as to whether or not we will follow him. May we through these gifts and our witness share with all the world the blessedness that comes to us through thy grace.

PRAYER. Father, we come to worship mindful of the many gifts you have given us. Of all the gifts we have received, we most remember the gift of thy Son. On this Sunday in Lent we commit ourselves to the task of being the people we are called to be in Christ. Forgive us, Father, when we stray, and cleanse our lives this day.

Father, as we pray this prayer of forgiveness, we know that by the giving of your Son for forgiveness of our sins, they are forgiven. As we pray this prayer we cannot help but be humbled and conscious of thy great love at work in our lives. Not only do we feel humbled, but we also feel strengthened, empowered, and ready to face the challenges of a new day.

Let us not forget the suffering and pain which Christ faced that we might be free. Let us not forget the people this day who suffer in hunger, sorrow, and affliction. Help us to remember that we are the answer for the problems of the world only when our lives reflect the message and wisdom of the one who has come before us. As Christ is revealed to others through us, then the world may know the peace and love and joy of life we find in thy kingdom.—James R. Rosenburg.

EVENING SERVICE

Topic: Matthew Presents the Master
TEXT: Matt. 1:1.

The genealogical tree presented by Matthew clearly shows that Jesus came to earth through all kinds of people. In the larger sense Jesus is the contemporary of all. Why did God direct Matthew through the Spirit to preserve the human genealogy of Jesus? The tracing of Jesus' family line is illuminating proof that our Lord is part and parcel of both heaven and earth. He is God's man in the world of mankind.

I. *Jesus the achiever* (Matt. 5:17–20). (a) The old law presented types that showed what could come following the law. Jesus nailed the old statutes to his cross. At the same time he fulfilled the types of the former dispensations and the predictions of the prophets.

(b) The Pharisees personified righteousness as they calculated it, but they were imperfect models that left much to be desired. Jesus pointed out that those who became a part of his kingdom would need to live out a righteousness superior to the conduct of the Pharisees.

II. *Jesus the caller* (Matt. 9:9). (a) Matthew describes what happened to him when Jesus stopped by the place of tax collection. Jesus summoned Matthew to a higher calling. The Pharisees regarded Matthew as a sinner and an alien, but Jesus saw in him the writer of one of the gospel narratives.

(b) Jesus used the imperative mood in addressing Matthew, even as he so commands us today. He does not offer options. His directives are issued out of a gracious intent. He sees in us what we do not see in ourselves. He dares us to take him at his word of assurance.

(c) The name "Matthew" means "Jehovah's Gift." But as an officer of Herod, Matthew took instead of giving. Then came the day when Jesus called him, and he followed Jesus. It took only a minute to decide to answer that invitation, although the time of his reporting for duty was undoubtedly later. He became a personal attendant of Jesus. In Matthew, Jesus reproved the social narrowness of that age.

III. *Jesus the expositor* (Matt. 13:51–52). (a) In seeking to advise his disciples of the character of the kingdom of heaven, Jesus spoke three parables—the hidden treasure, the beautiful pearl, and the fisherman's net filled with fishes. He then made sure that his disciples understood clearly what he had offered to them.

(b) He illuminated the thinking of those disciples through old truths adorned with fresh applications. The teacher instructs the learner by offering the bread of truth. At the banquet table of the Master we satisfy our hunger for heaven's word. Jesus is the great expositor.—Ard Hoven.

SUNDAY: MARCH THIRTEENTH

MORNING SERVICE

Topic: What Do We Know for Sure? (Lent)

Text: Rom. 8:38–39.

There is but one fundamental affirmation we can make and upon which we can stake our very lives. That affirmation of the apostle Paul is our text. In an age no less vexing than our own, in a world sorely in need of an abiding faith, Paul enunciates the central affirmation of the Christian faith. To understand that rightly we must begin with Paul's conclusion and then move to his assumption.

I. The love of God in Christ Jesus our Lord. How in the name of heaven can one be sure of that at any time and especially in a world like ours?

(a) Certainly we cannot be sure of God's love by observing nature. There are times when we may think we can—when we have stood on some seashore and watched the sun dip into the golden horizon, when we have beheld the towering grandeur of Mt. Shasta or Mt. Hood, when we have gasped at the wonder of a garden or a meadow, a riot of color and symmetry. These speak to us of beauty and order and design, of a creation behind which there must be a loving Creator. But what shall we say of nature when the hurricane sweeps in, a fury of wind and rain, leaving death and destruction in its wake? What shall we conclude from nature when the earth's crust convulses and bricks and timbers come

tumbling down upon innocent victims? That too is nature. Nature cannot of itself assure us of the love of God.

(b) Can history assure us? History is peopled with great men and women, benefactors of the race, agents of the love of God. But history is not only St. Augustine and Joan of Arc and Abraham Lincoln; it is also Genghis Khan and Torquemada and Adolph Hitler. History is not only the Declaration of Independence; it is Valley Forge and Ticonderoga. It is not only the Gettysburg Address; it is Bull Run and Antietam and Vicksburg. It is the ground red with blood and tears. Where in all that is the God of love?

(c) We find God's love displayed in human personality, we may say. And surely we do—in parents and children, in home and friendships. Those of us who are fortunate do. But what of those who were born unwanted, who grow up in homes where there is only tension and hostility, and who are twisted and maimed and disordered by the very absence of love? How talk to them about the love of God in human personality?

II. While we may see reflections of God's love in nature and history and human personality, these are not enough to make us know and to make us sure. Experience and the Bible lead us to conclude that we do not find the love of God, but the love of God finds us.

(a) In the fulness of time Christ came into our world. He breathed the same air which we breathe and walked the same ground upon which we walk. He not only spoke of the love of God—others had done that; he was in himself that love which healed the broken-hearted, lighted despair with gladness, and lifted the weight of guilt by his own forgiveness.

(b) Then, as now, there were those who, in their pride and self-sufficiency, could not understand love, let alone accept it, and so it was that they—or was it we?—crucified him.

(c) Was that the end of God's love, broken and lifeless on a tree? No says the gospel again and again, as if it cannot believe what it is fairly bursting to tell. God's love overcame even the sin and the death, the final enemies of love. Christ and that love are alive forever. Since that living, loving Christ has been meeting men in every place and condition, we have taken that cross and lifted it up that we and all men might see what has become God's signal of victory. A cross is the length and breadth and height and depth of God's love.

III. How more persuasively can God speak than he has spoken? What more can God do than he has done? To what further end can God go than he has gone to show us his love? All this is implicit in the Christian affirmation, as in Paul's words to us, "The love of God in Christ Jesus our Lord." It is that love, he declares, from which nothing can separate us.

(a) Death cannot separate us from the love of God. (1) Death has been conquered. There is the resurrection and an empty tomb for witness. And standing forth is the one who speaks to our trembling hearts as no other: "I am the resurrection and the life. He who believes in me, though he were dead, yet shall he live; and whoever lives and believes in me shall never die."

(2) We are mortal and death is the one surety, except for the love of God which claims us from the finality of death by the sufficiency of Christ. Of death we can be sure, but of the love of God in Christ Jesus we can be even more sure. That love embraces us and illumines the darkness, through which all of us must pass, with an unquenchable light.

(b) Loneliness cannot separate us from the love of God. Our deepest loneliness is a homesickness for God. But because God made us for fellowship with himself our loneliness is the ache of our hearts for the very love in which we were meant to live. We ought, in our deepest moments of understanding, to take comfort in the very ache which drives us to his outstretched arms. Loneliness is finally the surety of our bond with him and him with us.

(c) Guilt and remorse cannot separate us from the love of God. (1) It is of the very nature of love to forgive. It is of the nature of God's love, as we have witnessed repentance. Do you think that you are beyond forgiveness or that you are off there in some far country with no way back? Then read again that parable of another prodigal and of a father waiting, yearning for the sight and sound of a lad who had been away too long. That is the love of God ready to say to each of us when we've come home, as to that other, "This, my son, was dead and is alive again; he was lost and is found."

(2) We may stride manfully off on our own, flinging ourselves into an orgy of self-indulgence, swearing we've seen the last of him. Always there's a cross. What will you do when you look at the cross? You can't escape that any more than you can flee from that love which looks at you from the cross.—George T. Peters.

Illustrations

RAISING THE CROSS.   The small church in a midwestern town was almost finished. The cross at the tip of the steeple had to be welded in place. But the scaffolding would not reach that high. One of the workmen, a tall, broad-shouldered fellow, offered to stand the welder on his shoulders and hand up the melted lead. Breathlessly the small crowd watched. Finally it was finished. The welder crawled down from the shoulders of his husky helper. Then the helper came down very slowly. As he reached the ground he toppled over. His shoulders and arms were covered with terrible burns. What had happened? While the welder was soldering the cross, the boiling lead ran drop by drop onto the shoulders of the man holding him up. Though the pains were intense, he had not moved an inch. Any movement would have plunged the welder to his death. It took weeks for the painful burns to heal.—Arthur Tonne.

GOING SOMEWHERE. In *Alice in Wonderland,* Alice asked the cat, "Would you tell me please, which way I ought to go from here?" The cat replied, "That depends a good deal on where you want to go." "Oh, I don't much care," said Alice. To which the cat responded, "Then it doesn't matter much which way you go." "But I want to go somewhere," protested Alice. The cat answered with wisdom and insight, "Oh, you are sure to do that!"

Sermon Suggestions

GIFTS OF THE RESURRECTION. Text: Rom. 8:11. (1) A gift of presence. (See Luke 24:31.) (2) A sense of destiny. (See John 11:25–26.) (3) A new kind of caring. (See John 21:17.)—John H. Townsend.

THE QUIET HEART. Scripture: John 14: 1–4. (1) The quiet heart is sure of the person of God (v. 1). (2) The quiet heart is sure of the place of God (v. 2). (3) The quiet heart is sure of the presence of God (v. 3).—Bramwell Tripp.

Worship Aids

CALL TO WORSHIP. "I will praise thee with my whole heart, I will worship toward thy holy temple, and praise thy name for thy lovingkindness." Ps. 138:1–2.

INVOCATION. We turn our minds unto thee, O God, that thou wilt give us deeper insight into the meanings of the life of thy Son, our Lord. We turn our hearts unto thee that thy love may flow through them. We turn our wills unto thee that thou may guide us in all that we do and in all that we say.

OFFERTORY SENTENCE. "If any man will come after me [saith Jesus], let him deny himself, and take up his cross daily, and follow me." Luke 9:23.

OFFERTORY PRAYER. O God, who hast given us thy Son to be an example and a help to our weakness in following the path that leadeth into life, grant us so to be his disciples that we may walk in his footsteps.

PRAYER. O God, our Father, who hast given us everything—life and liberty and love—and who requirest nothing of us but our love, we lay before thee our lives with all our faults and all our abilities. Take our faults—our laziness and selfishness and insensitivity—and purge them from us. Take our abilities—our talents and skills and accomplishments—and show us how to put them to higher use.

We lay before thee our wealth as individuals and as a nation. Take the poverty of our imagination that blinds us to a world in need and quicken our sympathies for the desperate. Take the blessings of our productive land that obsess and intoxicate and anaesthetize us, and show us how to use them to thy greater glory and our own deeper satisfaction.

We lay before thee our nation with its paradox of self-interest and high ideals. Take our narrow self-interest that would make us build a fortress America and broaden our concern to encompass all who can be reached with our missiles. Take our ideas of life and liberty and the pursuit of happiness, and help us to share them as we share our bread with a world that hungers for more than bread.

We lay before thee our church with its strange combination of the ridiculous and the sublime. Take our obsession with the trivia and minutiae of the institution and bring it under thy judgment that this is no time to fiddle, for the world is already aflame. Take our untapped capacity for proclaiming the gospel, and compel us to let it loose on the world by the words on our lips and the witness of our lives.—Harry W. Adams.

EVENING SERVICE

Topic: The Cross in Ephesians
TEXT: Eph. 1:4.

I. The cross of wood is a symbol of the cross eternal. The stupendous truth Paul tells us is that the cross was in the mind and heart of God even before the creation of the world.

(a) God's plan and provision for us in

Christ, which includes Calvary, was made before our world was created. God's plan of salvation was not an afterthought. The cross was not a divine expedient to meet an unforeseen emergency. It was conceived in the eternal heart of God when planet earth was merely a blueprint in the divine mind. How inscrutable are the ways of God!

(b) "Before the foundation of the world." The New Testament word for foundation is *katabole,* which means "a throwing or laying down." The word for world is *kosmos,* which refers to "an orderly arrangement" and is opposite from the Greek and English word "chaos." Paul is saying that before God threw whirling stars and orbiting planets into space, he loved us and adopted us in Christ. God's love for us is truly everlasting.

(c) God "hath chosen us in him [Christ] before the foundation of the world . . ." "Chosen" does not refer to setting apart certain persons but rather a historical selection. It is a determination of the divine mind before the creation of man.

II. Our human time frames are very short compared to God's eternity. We usually think in terms of a few thousand years, divided by the birth of Christ, B.C. or A.D. But Paul in our text is speaking of P.W. time—pre-world time, "before the foundation of the world." God loved us and chose us and provided for redemption in Christ that far back in eternity.

(a) There are intimations in scripture of Christ's preincarnate existence. In the breathtaking opening of John's gospel there are declared three great truths about Christ before his earthly life. He was eternal—in the beginning was the Word. He had fellowship with God—the Word was with God. The verse comes to its climax with a declaration of Christ's divinity—he was God. In his prayer in John 17, Christ refers to his pre-world glory: "And now, O Father, glorify thou me with thine own self with the glory which I had with thee before the world was" (v. 5).

(b) In Phil. 2:7 Paul describes the divine condescension—he emptied himself. Jesus put aside his eternal glory in that moment of history when he became man to fulfill God's plan of the ages in his going to the cross.

(c) Our salvation not only cost Christ the terrible sacrifice and ignominy of Calvary. It also cost the impoverishment of the Godhead. Even before God created man, in his foreknowledge he knew that man would disobey him, would sin and fall. But back somewhere in the eons of time before our world came into being, God loved us with an everlasting love and chose us in Christ to become his children. Back then he planted the spiritual potential that we should be holy and without blame before him in love.

(d) Paul prays later in this epistle that his readers "may be able to comprehend with all saints what is the length of God's love." Could he have been thinking of how long God has loved us? With the psalmist we praise God because his mercy is everlasting (Ps. 100:5). Jeremiah expresses this truth in immortal words: "I have loved thee with an everlasting love: therefore with lovingkindness have I drawn thee" (Jer. 31:3).

III. Divine anticipation is written on every page of human experience. God knew that man would be cold, so he put coal in the earth. He knew that man would dread the dark, so he put electricity in the air. He knew that man would be hungry, so he put seeds in every piece of food. He knew man would be thirsty, so he put water in the clouds. He knew that man would be lonely, so he put family instinct in him. He knew that man would sin, so he provided a savior. The staggering truth of God's everlasting love is far beyond the grasp of my finite mind. But such love of God constrains me to give my little all in response.—Henry Gariepy.

SUNDAY: MARCH TWENTIETH

MORNING SERVICE

Topic: The Man Who Obeyed (Passion Sunday)

TEXT: Heb. 5:8.

I. Jesus learned obedience through what he suffered, and he in turn became the source of salvation for all those who believe in him.

(a) In terms of his being the second person of the trinity, this son never had to learn obedience. The thoughts, the ideas, the communications, the desires, the will of the Godhead are one. There never was and never will be any tension or confusion within the mind of the triune God. The sentence from the book of Hebrews acknowledges that there is something strange about the fact that this person had to learn obedience. That is why the sentence reads, "Although he was a Son. . . ."

(b) Jesus had to learn obedience because he became a man. The moment he entered humankind, he became one with a race of men who were not totally in tune with the will of God. Mankind had fallen into sin, and so there was a tension between what God wanted man to be and to do and what man wanted to be and to do. Jesus became part of this. But he became part of this in a very special way.

(c) When Jesus became a man, he had to become obedient to the laws of God, and he did that. He fulfilled the law of God perfectly, and he resisted the attacks of Satan successfully. But when Jesus, the Son of God, entered our race, he not only had to be obedient to God's law, but he also had to be obedient to God's way of achieving salvation.

(d) Jesus came into our world to become the source of salvation. He came as the savior, and there was only one way for man to be saved. God knew that way; man didn't. The only way that man could be saved was by having sin paid for through the suffering of the Son of God. (See Heb. 2:10).

II. The only way man can be saved is through a savior who has become the perfect savior through suffering.

(a) That Jesus became the perfect savior through suffering means that the only begotten Son of God was not the perfect savior prior to his incarnation. To be sure, he was perfect, for he was God; but he was not as such able to be the savior. The perfect savior came into existence when he took on the nature of his people, became their brother, and endured suffering on their behalf. The perfect savior is the person who was the only begotten Son of God who came into our world to become one of us and who in our world became obedient.

(b) Jesus' obedience to the will of his Father in heaven was absolute and total. He said, "My food is to do the will of him who sent me, and to accomplish his work" (John 4:34). His obedience was expressed in his laying down his life for his people. (See Phil. 2:7–8). This means that when we look at the crucified savior, we are viewing the most intense and absolute expression of obedience ever to occur in the history of the world.

(c) Don't think the obedience of Jesus Christ was easy. We are apt to think that way about it because we know the entire story. We not only know about Jesus' eternal sonship and about the way he came into our sin-stricken world, but we also know that finally Jesus rose from the dead, victorious over the grave. We know that, and he knew that too, even while he was plunging ever deeper into the depths of agony. He knew that he was walking a road that would ultimately lead to glory. As we think of this, we are inclined to discount the reality of his suffering.

(d) Jesus' suffering was the most intense anyone has ever gone through, and it was the intensity of his suffering that made him the perfect savior. If suffering was necessary so that Jesus could become the perfect savior, we must acknowledge the reality of his suffering.

(e) At every point in his life his obedience was sustained by his will to obey his Father in heaven. It was his obedience that caused him to say in the garden, "Not my will, but thine, be done." Doing the will of his Father in heaven was his meat and drink.

(f) Just as the eternal Son of God was not the perfect savior until he had been perfected by agonized suffering, so the great plan of God had to be actualized in our time and on our earth, and that happened when God suffered in the person of his only begotten Son.

III. As we observe the perfectly obedient savior give himself totally for the sins of man, we are called to obedience ourselves. The Bible says that when Jesus became the perfect savior, he became the source of salvation for all those who obey him. Jesus, the obedient Son of the Father, now calls us to obedience.

(a) What does this mean? (1) It means that we must believe in Jesus Christ and we must do his will. (See John 3:23.)

(2) This means that we must learn to love. We must learn to submit ourselves to others in loving service.

(b) It is obedience that holds our world together. At the center of the Christian faith there is the man who was perfectly obedient. Those who obey him discover that their lives are made whole by his re-creating power. Those who obey Jesus are saved, and they discover that this salvation changes for the good everything about their lives.—Joel Nederhood.

Illustrations

BEGINNING.   And he uttered a triumphant cry: "It is accomplished." And it was as though he had said, "Everything has begun!"—Nikos Kazantzakis.

THE STEADY HEART.   Frances of Sales in the country districts of France in which he lived had often seen a servant going across a farmyard to draw water from the well. He noticed that before she lifted the full pail of water the girl always put a piece of wood into it. One day he asked, "Why do you do that?" She answered: "To keep the water from spilling. To keep it steady." Writing to a friend later, the bishop told this story and added, "When your heart is distressed and agitated, put the cross into its center to keep it steady."—C. Jarrell Tyson.

Sermon Suggestion

THE NEW COVENANT OF JESUS CHRIST. Scripture: I Cor. 11:23–26. (1) A clear covenant. (2) A gracious covenant. (3) A responsible covenant.—Gerhard Aho.

Worship Aids

CALL TO WORSHIP.   "Hereby perceive we the love of God, because he laid down his life for us: and we ought to lay down our lives for the brethren. Let us not love in word, neither in tongue; but in deed and in truth." I John 3:16, 18.

OFFERTORY SENTENCE.   "Greater love hath no man than this, that a man lay down his life for his friends." John 15:13.

OFFERTORY PRAYER.   Awaken us to the claims of thy holy will, O God, and stir us with a passion for thy kingdom, that we may respond at this time with our gifts and also with our lives.

PRAYER.   Once again our Father, we step aside at the beginning of another week, turning from the tasks that only consume us, to regain a perspective on the truth that sustains us. We come from the realities of life as men have made it to remember the dimensions of life as you intend it. As we come we cannot offer you any more than what we are, but we know we dare not confess or express to you less than what we have been.

You have made us little less than God and crowned us with glory and honor. But we see for ourselves that we have become captives of the common ways, creatures of conformity, and living biographies that are only histories of habits we have formed. Made with the distinction of what is acceptable in your sight, we confess that too often we have buried what is possible for us in the grave of what is more acceptable in others' eyes. We are they who too willingly substitute what has been for what ought to be.

Here we offer you this mixture of minds

that dream but hearts that cling to lesser things. Here is the mixture of the great and the commonplace that has shaped our lives as men. Still, you have promised that our weakness in your hands is sufficient strength. And you have said whoever leaves behind the common or acceptable to take up the way of the cross will discover in its carrying the joy of life. Lord, we believe! Help our unbelief.—Paul E. VanDine.

EVENING SERVICE

Topic: Gethsemane and Calvary

TEXTS: Matt. 26:36; 27:33.

Two phrases in the gospels should be joined in our thinking—the first "to a place called Gethsemane" and the second "to a place called Golgotha."

I. The place called Gethsemane was the anticipation of the place called Calvary. It was the inner cross at Gethsemane that explains and anticipates the eventual cross on Calvary.

(a) What was the cup which Jesus prayed first that it might pass from him? Not a cup of fear, for that would not have been worthy of him. Not just a cup of physical pain.

(b) George A. Buttrick wrote: "This was a soul agony. It was a cup of rejection in that he saw his whole word and work eclipsed in failure. Through what was done by Judas and the others, Jesus saw that the whole race of men had chosen a way which would lead to destruction, and there was no one to understand, let alone to share, his poignancy of grief."

(c) We find here the agony of soul of one who would not debonairly invite an issue or relish its coming to a head, nor would he cravenly shrink from it. He faced it in deep concern and travail of soul. He agonized not over what they would do to him but what they would reveal about themselves and do to themselves in what they did to him, and he saw in this, humanity in all its alienation from God.

(d) That was the cup, and he prayed if at all possible it might pass. When it could not pass, he uttered his prayer that has made Gethsemane the world's shrine, "Not as I will, but as thou wilt." This was Gethsemane as Calvary anticipated, and the inner victory won.

III. The place called Calvary was the consummation of the place called Gethsemane. There was carried out in actual events what had been anticipated in agony of soul in Gethsemane.

(a) Jesus had prayed, "Thy will be done." Was what was done to him at Calvary God's will? Were the evil deeds of men as they wrought their work upon him God's will that he had prayed should be done?

(b) We do well always to remember Leslie D. Weatherhead's distinction between what God permits and what God intends. What men did to Jesus on Calvary was because of God's permissive will in giving men their freedom, even to work such dastardly things. But God's intentional will is found in what Jesus did about what was done to him. In his prayer for forgiveness for his enemies and in his whole self-giving on the cross, we find God's intentional will being done through him. They took his life, but he gave his life.—Charles L. Seasholes.

SUNDAY: MARCH TWENTY-SEVENTH

MORNING SERVICE

Topic: The Road Less Traveled By (Palm Sunday)

SCRIPTURE: Luke 19:28–40.

"Two roads diverged into a yellow wood," Robert Frost wrote, "And I—I took the one less traveled by and that has made all the difference." The choices before Jesus on that first Palm Sunday are the choices that each of us must face.

I. The first choice before Jesus is the pressure of the crown versus the purposes of God. Every Jew could tell you what the messiah would look like. When the messiah came, he would be a kingly figure bringing in God's rule. He would re-establish the throne of his father David. Rome and its tyrannizing legions would be put to flight. A new era of peace and brotherhood would be ushered in.

(b) Jesus knew the role model to which he was expected to conform. (1) He was surrounded with disciples who urged him in this direction. James and John anxiously awaited the day when Jesus would establish his kingdom so they could sit as his minions on his left hand and his right (Mark 10:37). Judas and Simon were Zealots, members of the extreme and violent Jewish nationalist party which sought to drive the Romans out of Palestine by revolution and guerrilla warfare.

(2) There were pressures from friends and family members who urged him to turn back, to cease and desist, and to steer clear of danger. "Stay in the safety of Galilee," they counseled, "instead of venturing into perilous Jerusalem."

(3) This is what the authorities encouraged him to do by opposition and intimidation. It would have spared them a great deal of trouble and would have spared Jesus' life.

(c) In Mark 8:31–35 he told his disciples that the son of man must suffer many things and be rejected and be killed. "And he said this plainly." Peter began to rebuke him, and Jesus said, "Get behind me, Satan, for you are not on the side of God, but men."

(d) Jesus agonized over the pressures of the crowd versus the purposes of God. It's all there, climaxing with that scene in the garden.

(1) He could have saved his life, but that would have meant the loss of all he had lived for. "He that saveth his life shall lose it."

(2) He would not buy their idea of a power-wielding messiah but instead accepted the role of a suffering servant.

(3) He would not capitulate to their pressures, but he would turn his face steadfastly toward Jerusalem.

(e) If you don't stand for something in life, you'll fall for anything. Take heart if you are resisting the pressures of the crowd because you're in good company. You are walking the road less traveled by with your Lord and Savior.

II. The second choice Jesus faced was personal integrity versus public popularity.

(a) Social commentators remind us that of all of the fantasies people engage in none is stronger than the fantasy of fame. T.V., radio, the movies, magazines and newspapers, sports, politics, advertising, and even religion thrive on fame and the personalities of the famous. Fame even has its own rituals: Miss America pageants, Academy Awards, political elections, and the Nobel prizes. Fame has its high priests who make their living merchandising the famous. Fame has its committed disciples waiting offstage to make their one appearance in the footlights.

(b) Jesus didn't come to make a name for himself. He always pointed beyond himself to his heavenly Father. He took no credit for his mighty acts but gave the credit and the glory to God. He was strangely indifferent to human accolades.

(c) Jesus possessed what psychologists call "congruence." (1) A congruent person knows who he is, what he is here for, and where he is going. A congruent person has self-respect, self-esteem, self-worth, and self-dignity. He doesn't need the public's approval.

(2) So few people we know are congruent and so many others are not congruent and must look to others to confirm their dignity and worth. I want to suggest that you become congruent. You are a person of worth, dignity, and value because you know you are a child of God.

III. A final choice Jesus faced was success versus service. (a) Jesus' ministry was a failure in the eyes of his contemporaries. The successful were like Caiaphas and Pilate. The dominant motif of Jesus' life was not success but service.

(b) The world instinctively accepts the values of service. The world knows a good person serves humanity. The world may respect and fear someone who wields power, but it will love someone who serves. The doctor who comes any time night or day, the pastor who is always among the people, the employer who takes an active interest in the lives and troubles of employees, the person to whom we can unburden our hearts and feel accepted, and the business person who tutors at an elementary school are people who are loved and in whose lives is seen the reflection of Jesus Christ.

(c) In service lies true greatness. The world may assess your greatness by the number of people you command, by your intellectual standing, by your academic excellence, or by your bank balance. But in the assessment of Jesus Christ all these are irrelevant. His assessment is how many people have you helped.—Terry V. Swicegood.

Illustrations

ALWAYS GREATER. When the Venetian painter, Tintoretto, was in his last years, he wanted to see the sea again before he died. He was carried to the ocean. As he took a long look at the Adriatic Sea, he said, "The sea always grows greater." When we look repeatedly at the cross, it grows greater in our minds.—John R. Brokhoff.

LAST WORD. The purpose of God in the history of man was accomplished when Jesus breathed his last upon the cross. The cry "It is finished" was not the mere gasp of a worn-out life; it was not the cry of satisfaction with which a career of pain and sorrow is terminated; it was the deliberate utterance of a clear consciousness on the part of God's appointed revealer that now all has been done that could be done to make God known to men and to identify him with men.—Marcus Dods.

Sermon Suggestions

THE INEXHAUSTIBLE CHRIST. Text: John 21:25. (1) Christ Jesus is inexhaustible in his winsomeness. (2) Christ Jesus is inexhaustible in his saving power. (3) Christ Jesus is inexhaustible in his provisions.—H. Hansel Stambridge, Jr.

WHERE IS OUR PEACE? Text: Luke 19:41 (RSV). When Jesus looked at Jerusalem long ago and when he looks at our city today: (1) He sees that we tend to be confused about the things which really make for peace because when our affairs seem to be going reasonably well we easily become self-satisfied. (2) He sees that we tend to be confused about the things which really make for peace because when our affairs become difficult to handle we are prone to

discouragement and despair. (3) He laments over our confused way of understanding life's meaning.—Charles D. Kean.

Worship Aids

CALL TO WORSHIP. "Lift up your heads, O ye gates; even lift them up, ye everlasting doors; and the King of glory shall come in. Who is this King of glory? The Lord of hosts, he is the King of glory." Ps. 24:9–10.

INVOCATION. Our Father, thou who wast received amid the shouts of an earlier day, open our hearts and journey into our inward parts. Help us to lay aside all prejudices, forsake all sins, and overcome all biddings that might bar thy entrance. Let thy entrance into our hearts be triumphant. Conquer our fears, silence our unbelief, and quicken our faith. Lead us through thy Spirit to spiritual victory and conquest.

OFFERTORY PRAYER. As thy faithful disciples blessed thy coming, O Christ, and spread their garments in the way, covering it with palm branches, may we be ready to lay at thy feet all that we have and are, and to bless thee, O thou who comest in the name of the Lord.

PRAYER. Eternal Father, who art the same yesterday, today, and forever, whose throne is established in righteousness, whose mercies are new every morning, and whose love knows no end nor change: lift the light of thy countenance upon us, pilgrims as all our fathers were, that remembering all the way by which thou hast led us, we may take heart and hope as we face the duties and demands of a new week.

We acknowledge with penitence the blessings we have received with too little gratitude, the difficulties and trials in which our courage has deserted us and our faith grown weak, and our absorption in our own concerns and our indifference to the joys and sorrows of others. We thank thee for the gifts thou dost bestow upon us, for health of body and mind, for the care and shelter of home, for the joys of friendship, and above all for thine inestimable love in the redemption of the world by our Lord Jesus Christ.

We would not weaken our souls with vain regrets and idle musings and with murmuring and resentment, but rather, believing that all things work together for good to those that love thee, we would seek to learn thy will and to be made strong to perform it, sure that in thy will is our peace. Preserve us from fretfulness and impatience and from depression and anxiety. Increase our faith, strengthen our judgment, quicken our zeal, and deepen our affections. Open to us the meaning of life, and reveal thyself as our companion and friend as thou art our Lord and Master.

Hear our prayers for a confused and anxious world. Send thy light into our darkness. Bestow upon the President of the United States and upon all in every land who bear rule special gifts of wisdom and understanding that they may uphold what is right and follow what is true, and help establish a world in which the ills of this time may disappear and a glad day of brotherhood and peace may dawn.

Look with thy favor upon this congregation. Uphold our hands in every good and serviceable work, deliver us from indolence and unbelief, fill us with ardor and zeal and sustain us in sacrificial devotion to Christ that the ministry of this church may be empowered and enlarged. So may our labors, begun, continued, and ended in thee, be honored by thy benediction, furthered by thy grace, and crowned at the last by thy "Well done!"—Robert J. McCracken.

EVENING SERVICE

Topic: The Great Reversal (Good Friday)

SCRIPTURE: Matt. 27:62–28:10.

Jesus was proven wrong on Good Friday in the eyes of the world and his followers. The characters of our scripture tell the story.

I. The Jewish leaders were right. Jesus had been marching out of step—not them. He was a liberal, trouble-making activist. Things had been going on the same way in Israel for as long as any living person could remember. Why should they change? The Sanhedrin was in power, not Jesus. How dare he suggest improvements? He was only in his thirties. He was even a newcomer—an outsider to Jerusalem.

II. Pilate was right. Smart too. He saw trouble coming. He knew how costly a religious dispute could be in Jerusalem. He saw the injustice, and he washed his political hands. He turned his eyes so he could not watch it.

III. The Roman guard was right. They symbolized the power of Rome. Might makes right. Roman power was right. It nailed Jesus to the cross of torture, and he died in disgrace while Rome ruled on.

IV. The disciples of Jesus were right in their efforts at self-preservation. There was no need for the whole movement to go down with Jesus. Why should they die for ungrateful people? Perhaps Jesus did not know what he was talking about anyway. Best to lay low until the heat was off. The one who spoke of the glory of giving one's life for others died horribly and disgracefully on a cross on Friday. The one who said, "Don't worry about the world, for I am victorious," was dead wrong because he died on Friday.

V. Popular opinion was right. On Palm Sunday the crowd sang Hosannah, Hosannah to Jesus. If he had even been scratched by Roman or Jew, there would have been riotous chaos as the masses proclaimed their godly, right opinion. And on Good Friday the same crowd was right again as they shouted in unison, "Crucify him." Popular opinion was right because Jesus was crucified.

VI. Chapter 27 ends with a quite final note. He was dead, buried, and sealed in forever.

(a) On Sunday morning Mary Magdalene and another Mary were the first to discover the unexpected, good news. The guards were shocked to behold the amazing, mysterious, unpredictable power of God. The angel of God shared the news with the women: "You are looking for Jesus . . . he is not here; he has risen, just as he said."

(b) For two days Jesus was wrong in everybody's opinion. By all measures this world can use he was dead wrong because on Friday he died. He clashed with all the selfish, distorted values and morals of fallen humanity, and he died because no one can fight a monster that big and win.

(c) Because he lives he has been proved right after all. Because he lives we can stand against all that is wrong and be assured of eternal victory. For two days Jesus was proven wrong by the world, but for all eternity the third day found him right. For this reason we can have hope in our world so full of problems and despair. So often evil seems to win, but the truth is Jesus Christ, raised from the dead and victorious over the world. Because he lives, evil cannot win.—Robert B. Clemons III.

SUNDAY: APRIL THIRD

MORNING SERVICE

Topic: The Emotions of Easter (Easter)
Text: Matt. 28:8.
There are many ways to approach the resurrection. (a) You can approach it philosophically and try to analyze it. You can approach it biblically and try to understand the context out of which it came. You can approach it critically and discuss the rational reasons for believing or not believing in it. You can approach it pragmatically and seek to discover what it all means. Or you can approach it experientially and feel the impact of this event upon your life.

(b) At times we place too much emphasis on feelings in matters of religion, but the gravest problem in the church today is not that we feel too much but that we feel too little, not that we are too emotional but that we are not emotional enough, and not that we are so captured experientially with the message of the gospel but that we never get caught up in experience at all.

(c) Two emotions were expressed in the first Easter experience.

I. The first emotion evoked by the Easter event was wonder. (a) In our text the writer says, "And they departed quickly from the tomb with fear" (v. 8).

(b) Mark's account tells us that when the women saw the stone was rolled away "they were amazed" (16:5). Then Mark tells us, "They went out and fled from the tomb, for trembling and astonishment had gripped them" (v. 8).

(c) Luke tells us that when the women saw the empty tomb they "were terrified and bowed their faces to the ground" (24: 5). The Emmaeus travelers told of the news that the women had brought to them about the empty tomb with these words: "Also some women among us amazed us" (v. 22). When Jesus later appeared to the disciples, Luke says, "They were startled and frightened" (v. 37).

(d) Three Greek words are used in these passages to describe the emotional reaction of the disciples and the women.

(1) The word used in our text is the word *phobeo* from which we get our word "phobia." It means to be frightened so much you want to run away. The basic idea is fear.

(2) The word used in Mark 16:8 is *ekstasis* from which our word "ecstasy" comes. It means holy frenzy or enthusiasm. The basic idea is astonishment.

(3) The word used in Mark 16:5 is *ekthambeo.* Basically this word means amazement or wonder.

(e) Confronted by an event their minds could not comprehend and their experience could not explain, these first witnesses were filled with astonishment and amazement. Something extraordinary happened that day, and the emotional reaction was wonder.

(1) We have lost this sense of wonder. The familiarity of the facts and the commonness of the custom have robbed us of the sense of amazement at the awesome activities of God.

(2) We listen to a recital of the facts of the resurrection with total indifference and contemplate instead about what we are going to have for dinner. But what happened the first Easter is the most stupendous event in all of history.

(f) I want you to feel again (1) the wonder that gripped the women as they approached the tomb and saw the stone rolled away (Luke 24:2), (2) recapture the astonishment of Peter as he peeked into the tomb and saw the face cloth and the linen burial wrappings neatly rolled up but no body (John 20:7), (3) sense the awe which touched the Emmaus travelers as they realized they had been talking with the risen Lord and their hearts burned within them (Luke 24:32), (4) relive the ecstatic enthusiasm which erupted in the hearts of the disciples when Jesus appeared to them in the upper room and said, "Peace be with you" (John 20:19), (5) identify with the holy hush that fell upon the heart of Thomas as Jesus invited him to put his finger in the holes in his hand and to put his hand in the wound in his side (John 20:27), and (6) walk again where they walked, see again what they saw, feel again what they felt, and experience again what they experienced.

II. A second emotion in the narratives about the resurrection is joy. (a) Matt. 28:8 says, "And they departed quickly from the tomb with fear and great joy and ran to report it to his disciples."

(b) Luke concluded his narrative by saying, "And they returned to Jerusalem with great joy, and were continually in the temple, praising God" (24:53).

(c) John tells us that when Jesus showed them his hands and his side, "The disciples therefore rejoiced when they saw the Lord" (20:20).

(d) In John's account twice Jesus said, "Peace with you," to his disciples, once to quell their fear and once to quell their joy. The darkness of Good Friday had been invaded by the light of the resurrection. The defeat of Calvary had been reversed by the victory of the empty tomb, and the emotional reaction was joy.

(e) We have lost this sense of joy. (1) We hear again of God's victory over death, sin, and the powers of evil, and we yawn with indifference. But that was the most stupendous victory that has ever been won.

(2) If there is no enthusiasm in your soul when you hear again about the resurrection, it is because you do not understand what was at stake—the ultimate outcome of the struggle between good and evil, between God and Satan, between light and darkness, and between life and death. On Friday it seemed as if the victory belonged to the forces of evil. But the resurrection event changed that. Since the first Easter, we have lived in the assurance that the ultimate victory belongs to God. That is the reason for our joy.—Brian L. Harbour.

Illustrations

REMINDER. At the funeral of Louis XIV, the cathedral was filled with mourners who had come to pay their final tribute to the king, whom they all considered to be great. The room was dark save for one lone candle which illuminated the gold casket which held the mortal remains of the monarch. At the appointed time the court preacher stood to address the citizens. As he rose he reached from his pulpit and snuffed out the one candle which had been put there to symbolize the greatness of the king. Then from the darkness came just four words, "God only is great."

NOW AND FOREVER. The great Easter truth is not that we are to live newly after death—that is not the great thing—but that we are to be new here and now by the power of the resurrection; not so much that we are to live forever as that we are to and may live nobly now because we are to live forever.—Phillips Brooks.

Sermon Suggestions

BELIEVING EASTER. Text: John 20:8. What will convince us that Easter is a reality? (1) The certainty which possessed Jesus' friends. (2) The birth and continued existence of the church. (3) The power of the New Testament. (4) The experience of persons in our own time who have met the living Christ.—Charles E. Ferrell.

THE GREAT DISCOVERY. Text: Mark 16:6. (1) They believed. (2) They witnessed. (3) They rejoiced.

Worship Aids

CALL TO WORSHIP. "Blessed be the God and Father of our Lord Jesus Christ, which according to his abundant mercy hath begotten us again unto a lively hope by the resurrection of Jesus Christ from the dead, to an inheritance incorruptible, and undefiled, and that fadeth not away, reserved in heaven for you." I Pet. 1:3–4.

INVOCATION. O God, we thank you this Easter morning for the eternal beauty and everlasting power of the resurrection of Jesus. We pray that these days shall see our Christ emerging from the tomb in which our generation has placed him—a tomb which we have closed with the stone of our selfishness and sealed with our hardness of mind and heart. Fill us this day with the spirit of reverence and humility because we are permitted to sing your praise. Help us to remember that we are your children living in your divine presence in our human lives. Make us faithful to duty and worthy of your love, through Jesus Christ our risen Lord.

OFFERTORY PRAYER. We give thee thanks, O Father, that through our tithes and offerings thou dost give us an opportunity to illuminate the dimness of the future and to glorify our present life with the word of him who is the light of the world.

PRAYER. Lord Jesus, as you made yourself known first at Easter to the people who most loved you and missed you, make yourself known on this resurrection day to any who have felt cut off from you, who are burdened by guilt and do not understand how much you love them, and any who feel that joy has gone out of their life forever. And as you dealt patiently with the problems of Thomas, deal patiently with all people who are handicapped by closed minds, all who fear that the resurrection news is too good to be true, and all who are held back from faith by intellectual barriers of doubt. Make yourself known to them too and set them free.

Truly you have risen, O Lord! Let the gospel trumpets speak and the news as of holy fire, burning and flaming and inextinguishable, run to the ends of the earth.

You have risen, O Lord! Let all creation greet the good tidings with jubilant shout. Its time of release has come, and the long night is past. The Savior lives and reigns in triumph now and throughout all the ages.—Church of Scotland.

EVENING SERVICE

Topic: The Empty Tomb
TEXT: Matt. 28:6.

I. The empty tomb proclaims that Jesus is God and that life comes from him. He boldly proclaimed to the Jews, "I lay down my life, that I might take it again . . . I have power to lay it down, and I have power to take it again" (John 10:17–18).

(a) Only God could do that. The scripture speaks of people coming back from the dead to life, the Shunammite's son under the stretched-out Elisha, the widow's son at Nain, and Lazarus. They all had life restored. But it was given, not taken back, by their own power.

(b) Jesus awoke of his own accord and by his own power. There was no voice calling, "Jesus, come forth." No one stretched out upon him. No hand touched him. He was and is self-existent. The empty tomb attests his divine claim that he is God. As I Tim. 3:16 declares, "God was manifest in the flesh."

II. The empty tomb is assurance that he has power to raise us. In Col. 1:18 Paul proclaims him to be "the firstborn from the dead." In I Cor. 15:20 he says Christ has "become the first fruits of them that slept." His resurrection was a prelude to our own.

(a) No longer does the Christian view the grave as the end but rather the beginning. Jesus turned the tomb into a womb—from a place of death to a place of life, from sunset to sunrise. The question through the ages has been, "If a man dies, shall he live again?" The empty tomb speaks to that question majestically: "Because I live, ye shall live also."

(b) The cemeteries have become fields of immortality. Sown as corruptible, we shall be raised incorruptible. Sown as mortals, we shall arise as immortals. The graves shall become the arena of one of his greatest victories. Death shall be defeated by life. "O grave, where is thy victory?" (I Cor. 15:55).

III. The empty tomb speaks of real life here and hereafter. It gives a touch of glory to life and moves it from a mere existence and terrible monotony to a meaningful experience.

(a) To the disciples it became a window through which they looked back on their experiences with Jesus. Confused, baffled, and in despair, they now saw and understood with a new hope and a new light. Things fell into place. There was a new clarity and a new purpose. Life was made full.

(b) Believing brings this eternal life, according to John 3:36: "He that believeth on the son hath everlasting life." This was the whole purpose of Christ's coming, to rescue men from spiritual death. "Whosoever liveth and believeth in me shall never die" (John 11:26).

IV. The empty tomb speaks to the person who has chosen the lower way. He who is suffering from moral paralysis and has become a slave to sin and its habits is offered life and hope.

V. The empty tomb speaks to the person who had drifted from God, who is undergoing a process of degeneration, who is becoming more and more content with things as they are, who realizes he is suffering spiritual decay but in his spiritual stupor accepts it, who is slowly losing his awareness of God. The empty tomb offers him hope of eternal life. It proclaims to all who will listen that death is not the final event. Death is only the gateway to a larger, more beautiful life, not a door out of life but a door into life.

VI. The empty tomb is our guarantee that nothing, not even death, can separate us from an eternal habitation with God. He is our life. "Come, see the place where the Lord lay." He is not there. He is alive. He is risen.—E. M. Abbott.

SUNDAY: APRIL TENTH

MORNING SERVICE

Topic: Life Without Living
Text: John 11:25–26.

Easter confronts us with the two basic realities of human existence—life and death. On the first Easter the women went to embalm a dead body, but they were surprisingly confronted with life. An angel asked, "Why do you seek the living among the dead?"

I. In our text Jesus says that he is the personification of life. "I am the resurrection and the life . . ." At another time he said, "I am the bread of life." In explaining his purpose on earth, he said, "I came that they might have life and that they might have it more abundantly." How can Jesus personify life?

(a) It is because he is the second person of the trinity. The resurrection from the dead on Easter proved this. He is the divine Son of God. As God's son, Jesus is life and gives life. After all, God is life. He is the creator of all living things. He gives life to every person. Since Jesus is the life, our life is in him. Jesus said he was the vine and we are the branches. If a branch is torn off a vine, it soon withers and dies. As long as we branches stay in the vine, the life of the vine comes into our very beings and we have life.

(b) Jesus is the life because of the resurrection. By his resurrection he conquered death and life became eternal.

(1) Here we must pause to clear up a popular misconception of resurrection. Most people think of it in terms of resuscitation. Resuscitation is just a continuation of earthly life after an interruption called death. It is like Lazarus who was raised from the dead by Jesus. Lazarus resumed living, but in due time he died again.

(2) Resurrection involves the fact that every man is born under the dominion of the evil powers, Satan, and sin. Under the dominance of Satan we sin and sin leads to death.

(c) When Jesus died on the cross he broke the power of Satan. By his resurrection he proved that he overcame death. He died that he might defeat death; there was no other way to do it.

II. Jesus tells us in this text that we might share in his life. His resurrection does not mean that automatically all mankind has life after death. There is a price to be paid. There are conditions to be met to get this life as a gift from Christ.

(a) One condition to receive this life is to believe in Christ.

(1) The way to heaven is not by works but by faith. Often at a funeral we hear it said, "I am sure he is in heaven because he was a good man." This is not necessarily so. We do not get to heaven because we lived a good life. Character does not count when it means getting life. It is faith and faith alone that counts.

(2) This life does not come to those who have plenty of possessions, for the rich young ruler was rich but he lacked eternal life. It does not matter whether your head is as full of knowledge an an encyclopedia; it is not enough to get life.

(3) To believe in Jesus is much more than intellectual assent. It involves complete trust in Jesus, and out of that trust comes obedience. When you and I truly believe in Jesus, we are one with him, and through that union the life of Christ flows into our lives and we have Life.

(b) Another condition for receiving life is to live in Jesus. Jesus said, "Whoever lives and believes in me." To live in Jesus implies involvement and participation in Christ. Before we can live in Jesus, we must die with him. There can be no resurrection without a prior death. There can be no Easter without a prior Good Friday. Jesus bids us to deny ourselves and die with him. We must truly die to self, sin, and selfish desires. As Paul said, we must be buried with Christ in baptism. Then we shall rise a new man. We shall rise with Jesus out of the grave of our sinful selves into the life of a new person.

III. Life comes to those who live and believe in the risen Christ. Our text tells us that this life in Christ is permanent. Jesus said, "He who believes in me shall never die."

(a) Jesus did not mean that we would not physically die. Death is a part of living. All creatures were meant to die physically. Only man was made to live eternally in Christ. Resurrection or no resurrection, we shall die. Faith or no faith, we shall die. Whether we are good or bad, we shall die.

(b) Jesus meant this in a spiritual way. He who lives and believes in the risen Lord will never taste of death. This means that we can have life while living. Eternal life begins now, not after death. Jesus told the repentant thief on the cross, "Today you will be with me in paradise." Eternal life is a present possession; its permanence begins the moment you believe and live in Christ. If you do not have eternal life now, you will not have it after death. If you are not in the kingdom of heaven now, you never will be.

(c) The permanence of life in Christ makes it possible to say that you can have life without living. You can physically die and still have this same life. That is because death cannot touch, curb, cancel, or nullify this life in Christ. Paul assured us of this when he said, "I am persuaded that neither death nor life, nor angels nor principalities, nor things present nor things to come, nor height, nor depth, nor any other creature shall be able to separate us from the love of God which is in Christ Jesus our Lord." Physical death cannot touch this life we now have in Christ. It goes beyond the grave.

(d) Doesn't this bring us worlds of comfort and peace? It takes away the sting of death. Why then should we fear death? Death for a Christian is nothing more than a higher step toward a closer relationship with Christ and a clearer vision of God. So Paul could truthfully say, "For me to live is Christ and to die is gain." As Christians we actually gain when we die. We gain in joy, peace, and love. There is nothing more wonderful than to be closer to Christ and participate more fully in his life and love.—John R. Brokhoff.

Illustrations

LIVING DEATH.   Sinclair Lewis and William Stidger engaged in a debate in a Kansas City church. Stidger spoke on the theme "Why I Believe in God," and Lewis took the negative of the proposition. At the conclusion of his address, Lewis said with dramatic suddenness, "If there is a God, let him strike me dead now." Then, as if he had proved God a sentimental illusion, Lewis marched from the platform.

The morning after Lewis made his dramatic address, the *Kansas City Times* remarked editorially that God did strike Lewis dead, but Lewis didn't seem to know it. His untimely death was evident in his contempt for people, in his sneering egotism, in his conviction that living is futile, and in his declining literary powers.—Harold Blake Walker.

GRIEVOUS TAXES. Taxes are indeed very heavy, and if those laid by the government were the only ones we had to pay, we might more easily discharge them; but we have many others, and much more grievous to some of us. We are taxed twice as much by our idleness, three times as much by our pride, and four times as much by our folly; and from these taxes the commissioners cannot ease or deliver us by allowing an abatement.—Benjamin Franklin.

Sermon Suggestions

GOD AND OUR TRIVIAL TROUBLES. Text: Ps. 46:1. God is a very present help in our trivial troubles. (1) God swings our littleness out into his greatness. (2) God helps to free us from our trivial troubles by giving us a bigness of purpose. (3) God is a very present help in our little troubles by imparting a bigness of spirit.

A PASTOR'S PRAYER FOR HIS CONGREGATION. Scripture: Eph. 1:16–23. (1) Know God personally (v. 17). (2) Know the hope to which God calls you (vv. 18–21). (3) Know that God's plan for this world is in the hands of the church.—Bruce J. Lieske.

Worship Aids

CALL TO WORSHIP. "Thou wilt keep him in perfect peace, whose mind is stayed on thee: because he trusteth in thee. Trust ye in the Lord for ever: for in the Lord Jehovah is everlasting strength." Isa. 26:3–4.

INVOCATION. O heavenly Father, who hast given us a true faith and a sure hope: help us to live as those who believe and trust in the communion of saints, the forgiveness of sins, and the resurrection to life everlasting; and strengthen this faith and hope in us all the days of our life.

OFFERTORY SENTENCE. "Give unto the Lord the glory due unto his name: bring an offering, and come before him: worship the Lord in the beauty of holiness." I Chron. 16:29.

OFFERTORY PRAYER. We praise thee, O God, for thy countless blessings and pray that thou wilt accept these gifts in gratitude in Jesus' name.

PRAYER. Father, we come to worship this day, praising thy name and saying "Hallelujah." The joy of spring is around us and glory of the risen Christ fills our souls. We remember the cross, the pain, and the suffering. The resurrection has been made vivid in our minds. Challenge us this day to carry these memories of Christ's love with us every day.

O God, we do humbly come expressing our gratitude for thy Son. We ask thy forgiveness for the many sins we have committed. We give thanks for the many blessings that you have given us. May the reality of the Easter message not be a one-day reality in our lives, but may we always have the deep feelings of thy love for us and know thy power over sin and death.

We have celebrated the joy of the resurrection. On this day we need thy continued strength to keep us mindful of who we are in the light of the resurrection. We need to see that thy resurrection power is a power we can draw upon every day. Through the resurrection we are, through Christ, heirs of life eternal.

Help us, Lord, through your love to show the power of the resurrection to others through what we say and do. Help us, O Lord, to respond in times of need, conflict, and adversity in ways that represent your will. Help us, O Lord, to be accepting, loving, and responding followers of your Son. For it is his life that is our key, his love that is our strength, and his Spirit living through us that gives our lives meaning.—James R. Rosenburg.

EVENING SERVICE

Topic: More Than a Day (Low Sunday)
TEXT: I Pet. 1:3.

I. Easter does not come and go. It comes and stays. Liturgically, it is more than a day; it is a season. Spiritually, it is more than a season. Resurrection is the concept that embraces and supports our life in Christ, his living presence among us, and our communal sharing through his church.

II. We've called it Low Sunday, that Sunday coming a week after Easter Day. Some still do. What did Low Sunday bring to mind?

(a) Letdown after the excitement of the big congregations, special music, potted lilies, and general bustle of Easter Day.

(b) Conclusion of the liturgical and spiritual momentum that had been developing during Lent, reaching its climax on the Feast of the Resurrection.

(c) Inactivity with many clergy and others taking post-Easter holidays. All of which seems to me to be out of order.

III. Our lectionary now refers to those Sundays after Easter Day as Sundays of Easter. Not "after Easter," but "of Easter," stressing the truth that Easter is a season and not merely a special day, the "Queen of Seasons" as we sing in that hymn, "Come, ye faithful, raise the strain."

(a) What do the Sundays of Easter bring to mind? (1) Continuation of the experience, the spirit, the message, and the joy that result from proclamation of Christ's resurrection.

(2) Personal visits to those "Easter only people" to talk with them about their lives and the new life we have heard about on Easter.

(3) Enthusiasm resulting from the knowledge that by our baptism we have been incorporated into the life of Christ through his church.

(b) Easter is not just a day but a season. Easter is not only a season but a truth that lives with us each day of our lives.—John M. Allin.

SUNDAY: APRIL SEVENTEENTH

MORNING SERVICE

Topic: This Is the Day

Text: Ps. 118:24.

I. *Today is all you have.* (a) We have heard, "There is no time like the present." That is incorrect. We should say, "There is no time but the present." The apostle Paul recognized the importance of making a mountain of the moment. To the Ephesians he wrote, "Making the most of your time, because the days are evil" (Eph. 5:16). "Making the most of your time" is sometimes translated "redeeming the time." The idea is to buy up opportunity. The businessman knows the value of an item. He sees how he can use it. He buys it up.

(b) The Christian grasps every opportunity to present Christ to a world lost in sin. The prevalence of evil days may cool the enthusiasm of the Christian. Therefore, we must eagerly watch for the opportunity to do good unto all men.

(c) You don't waste time. You waste yourself. Even though the fish is in the sea, we never say that the fish wastes water. The water is there for the fish to enjoy and perpetuate its life. You are in the now today. You don't waste time; you waste yourself.

II. *Today is all you can manage.* (a) Many live frustrated lives because they are trying to manage two days at a time. One of those days is yesterday.

(1) Some people are glad yesterday is gone because of broken health and aborted dreams. But most of us view yesterday wistfully. We talk of the good old days.

(2) We worship yesterday because yesterday we were young. We have been taught in America: "Have fun when you are young. You won't have any fun when you're older." That is a stupid lie. Teens tell me that high school days are best. My response is simply: "How do you know? I've tried some other ages and they are great too."

(3) Or I want yesterday back because I messed it up. Hairy old Esau sold his birthright, sobbing, "I threw away my yesterday." He sought it diligently with tears. We say that we will do better next time, but so many big things never get a next time.

(b) The other day we try to manage is tomorrow. (1) If we know God as Creator, loving Father, and Lord, worrying is absurd. We can orient our lives on him, invest our assets with him, rest assured that "God shall supply all your needs according to his riches in glory in Christ Jesus" (Phil. 4:19).

(2) Tomorrow is beyond our immediate control. The sun will rise tomorrow, either in splendor or behind a mask of clouds, but it will rise. Until it does, there is nothing we can do about the day, for it is yet unborn.

(c) Today is all you can manage. Can you be agreeable for one day? Or endure pain for twenty-four hours? Surely you can. Put yourself in the middle of God's will and eliminate reminiscing about the past or worrying about the future.

III. *Today is all you need.* (a) When tomorrow comes, today will be gone forever, leaving in its place something for which I traded it. Today God will fit you for the door of tomorrow.

(b) Get ready today for tomorrow. Perhaps then you will enjoy marriage, advance in wisdom, rejoice in a feast of music. But don't waste today worrying about tomorrow. Use today to its fullest, and tomorrow may bring more than you've dreamed.

(c) A poster said, "When walking along the paths of life, pause to smell the flowers along the way." That's the secret. Slow me down, Lord. Let me look around. See the flowers and the bees. Examine the cloud formations. Gaze at the elderly couple, obviously just married. Eat slowly, enjoy the food, and the company about the table. Sit and talk to your spouse or children or close friends. Express gratitude to a fellow worker.

(d) Now is the most important time in your life. It is too late for yesterday; it is too early for tomorrow. Today is the first day of the rest of your life. Devote it to God.—Max R. Hickerson.

Illustration

THE FUTURE IS NOW.   We cannot act in the future tense—we can only contemplate. And because the future is unknown, we are forced to contemplate a universe of alternatives. But here is the crucial point: we contemplate not only possible options but also preferred options. This involves deciding and choosing. And once we cross this magic-like barrier something dramatic happens. We are instantly transported back to the world of the present tense where we must consider the impact of our day-to-day actions on that future. Hence, in a tremendously real sense, the future is always now. And to deal responsibly with the present requires contemplating the future and deciding in which directions we would prefer to move. This is freedom in its most fundamental dimension. The act of choosing a preferred future also implies a future step—commitment. The opposite of surrender—commitment—is giving power to the direction in which one decides to move.—Edward B. Lindaman.

Sermon Suggestions

THE THINGS THAT CANNOT FAIL.   Text: I John 2:17. (1) In the midst of all life's flux there is an essential integrity at the heart of the universe that will not fail us. (2) There is the moral beauty of Jesus and the redemptive love of his heart for a world of men. (3) There is the destined victory of the good. All these things are possible because the Christian believer is aware that he has eternal life in himself.—Aaron N. Meckel.

NEW POSSIBILITIES.   Text: Acts 13:38–39 (RSV). (1) New ways of thinking. (2) New ways of acting. (3) New ways of relating.—Harold R. Fray, Jr.

Worship Aids

CALL TO WORSHIP.   "O come, let us sing unto the Lord: let us make a joyful noise to the rock of our salvation. Let us come before his presence with thanksgiving, and make a joyful noise unto him with psalms." Ps. 95:1–2.

INVOCATION.   Grant, O Lord our God, we beseech thee, that now and every time we come before thee in worship and in prayer we may be vividly aware of thy presence, become conscious of thy power and a sense of thy protection, and finally know in our hearts and minds and souls the wonder and the grace of thy peace.

OFFERTORY SENTENCE. "Every man shall give as he is able, according to the blessing of the Lord thy God which he hath given thee." Deut. 16:17.

OFFERTORY PRAYER. Dear Father, help us to be ever concerned to find thy way for our lives, and may we never be satisfied to give thee our second best in return for thy great gift of love.

PRAYER. O Father, thou hast promised that we may come to thee with our burdens. We come now with loads of care, heaviness of heart, and weights of carelessness and sin that withhold us from assuming our proper duties. We come with anxieties about tomorrow, with worry over events that never happen, with pride of self that has no foundation, with unloving thoughts that have no spiritual backing, and with false fears that paralyze our true senses. Receive these mountains and toss them into the ocean of thy love to be dissolved into nothingness. In place of this unnecessary baggage, show us the lily which toils not and which has no care, nor which is worrisome and anxious for tomorrow. Show us the humility, purity, and innocence of a child that passes our way in faith and trust. Show us the trustfulness of sheep such as those which were tended by the shepherd of old. For of such is the kingdom of heaven. Receive us as new creations in thy sight. Receive our refreshed spirits, our renewed minds, our purified hearts, and our templed bodies. Receive our whole self made whole for thy service and for thy sake.—Harold A. Schulz.

EVENING SERVICE

Topic: The Surprises of Grace

SCRIPTURE: John 5:2–9.

I. The grace of God often comes from an unexpected source. (a) The man beside the pool was waiting for an angel. The man apparently did not know who Jesus was or his reputation as a healer. After the miracle had taken place, he could not even identify his benefactor.

(b) It is always possible for a man to fail to recognize the grace of God when it comes. We look for a conventional angel, and sometimes the grace of God comes through very ordinary human beings.

(c) The tragedy is to be so close to the help you are seeking and miss it. Sometimes it can be on your own doorstep, but in your preoccupation you cannot see it. It is a tragedy which takes place all too often in our lives. We are so busy looking for an angel that we miss the one whom God sends to us.

II. The second surprise is that the grace of God comes when we least expect it.

(a) In the story help could come only when the waters riled up. On this day there was not a ripple on the surface of the pool. No one was predicting that anything would happen. It was a day for saving your strength and visiting with your friends and speculating about when the time would be more favorable. And then Jesus came along to change what had started out to be a very ordinary, mundane, uneventful day into a day to be remembered.

(b) That's how it can happen for you. You live with a problem for years and get to the place where one day follows another in an endless monotony of routine. And then, when you least expect it, God's grace breaks into your situation to change everything completely around.

III. The grace of God comes into our situation in an unexpected way.

(a) If Jesus had told the man in the story that he could have anything he wanted, what do you suppose he might have asked for? Maybe he would have asked Jesus to help him get into the water at the right moment. Or maybe he would have asked Jesus to arrange things so that he could be a little more comfortable while he waited. Or perhaps he would have asked Jesus to see to it that no one would ever deprive him of his right to lie there by the pool.

(b) Any one of those requests would have been less than Jesus was prepared to offer him. The last thing he might have thought of asking was for a miracle by which he could stand on his own feet and walk under his own power, and that is exactly what happened.—Clarence J. Forsberg.

SUNDAY: APRIL TWENTY-FOURTH

MORNING SERVICE

Topic: Faith in the Furnace

SCRIPTURE: Dan. 3:13–26 (LB).

I. This is a picture of men who had formulated a conception of a God who was personal.

(a) They were instructed to fall down before an idol, and this they could not do because they were convinced that the idol was nothing more than the materials of which it consisted.

(1) To many people God is no more than an idea. He may be the grandest idea one has ever had, but he is still a remote theory to many people. To the rest of those people the idol in the plains of Dura was symbolic of many things, but to these men it symbolized nothing. They saw it for what it was, and it could not command their devotion.

(2) When we talk of God as being real, what do we mean? We mean that God is more than the grandest idea men can have. It is more than saying that God is the greatest power or the prime source of energy in the universe.

(b) Many people have never moved to the experiential position of thinking of God as a person.

(1) The idea "personal" is to be differentiated from a thing in only one way. That way is communication. One can't communicate with a thing. One can't communicate with an idea. You can only wrestle with some aspect of it, but your relationship stops there.

(2) These three men saw the idol as something they could not relate to nor communicate with. They talked of their God as "he" not "it." They said, "If he wishes to deliver us he will."

(3) For God to be personal simply means that one thinks of God as one thinks of persons. It means that we think in terms of being able to communicate with him, and this is where Christian praying differs from the worship of idols or the musing over lofty ideals. Jesus taught us to pray, "Our Father." This is praying to a person as one talks to a person, and in many unmistakable ways Christian experience has taught us that God speaks to us in return.

(c) They actually said that their God would and could act in their behalf if he so desired, and they displayed this assurance.

(1) Knowing God in a personal relationship was what Jesus was talking about when he said, "No man comes to the Father but by me." By believing and committing oneself to Jesus Christ, he will show one the Father. As they knew Jesus as a person, they could know God in something of the same manner.

(2) God was real to them because they had cultivated this relationship through prayer. There is no better way to learn about a person than to talk to the person. There is no better way to learn about God than to pray to him.

II. This is the account of men who served God because it was part of their very being and not for some utilitarian purpose.

(a) They served their God regardless of what happened to them. This is a positive denial of the kind of religion which flourished in that ancient world. A god was supposed to undergird and, if needs be, vindicate his people. One would then choose the god that could do the most for him, and one changed his allegiance when it was obvious that there was a more powerful and benevolent god to be offered.

(1) Many church-going people serve God because he is better than Blue-Cross —the best insurance they can get and they want to stay on good terms.

(2) They go to pieces when trouble comes. They are the persons who use prayer not as the communication of confidence that all will be well because God is present but who require a miracle of healing as proof of God's presence.

(b) These men rested their case before the trial ever began. They said: "If God so desires to free us then he will. If he does not, it will not shake our faith, we will continue to serve him." That is real maturity. They were not going go manipulate and use God as one uses a light switch to light a darkened room.

(c) The Christian plateau is to love God and to serve God because he is God. Paul said, "The person who truly loves God is the one who is open to God's knowledge" (I Cor. 8:3). These men served God because this was dear to their hearts. Faith is committing oneself to God regardless of what happens or how hot the fire is.

III. This is a classic portrait of men who were free. (a) They were delivered yet still in the furnace. They only appeared to be bound as they were cast into the furnace. These men were truly free in the only real way men can be free.

(1) One can be bound with the shackles of fear, distrust, or pagan and idolatrous ideas and still think himself to be a Christian.

(2) One can be bound with superstition, with tradition, and even with much Bible reading and prayer, but it is slavery until he is wrapped up in the kind of confidence these men had. They said that they had no need to answer the king.

(b) There used to be a tradition, and may still be, that at sunset four bugles sound from the castle rock at Edinburgh. Tradition says that after the fourth bugle one can hear on the streets below a fifth, a bugler who was slain long ago. The kind of religious faith which is meaningful for all circumstances is like this. When we walk through the fires, out of the unseen comes the clear and unmistakable note of another trumpet. It is the assurance that Christ is with us and that the outcome is not so important after all. The important thing is that he is there. When the king looked in, he saw not three men but four, and one looked like a son of God.—Merle Allison Johnson.

Illustrations

DON'T RUN AHEAD.　In her autobiography Corrie ten Boom told of the experiences of her Dutch family during the Nazi occupation. Defiantly they hid Jews in their home and helped them escape certain death. The ten Booms knew they themselves were risking capture and probably death, so one day young Corrie blurted to her father: "I need you. You can't die, you can't." Her father responded, "Corrie, when you and I go to Amsterdam, when do I give you your ticket?" The child replied, "Why, just before we get on the train." "Exactly, and our wise Father in heaven knows when we are going to need things too. Don't run ahead of him, Corrie. When the time comes that some of us will have to die, you will look into your heart and find the strength you need, just in time."

LETTING GO.　There is a secret in the Christian life. It is the secret of letting go, of being willing to will what God wills, of being willing to let go of all our particular prescriptions of how he ought to deal with us. Without this we haven't really learned what divine love is. The Christian spirit in the face of death is "Whether we live or die, we are the Lord's. Our life is hid with Christ in God." God will do with every life what an infinitely wise and caring God can and will do with it. And this is enough to live by and by which to die.—Daniel Day Williams.

Sermon Suggestions

WE ARE IN THIS TOGETHER.　Scripture: Phil. 1:3–5, 19–27. (1) We need each other's support. (a) Paul was thrilled to receive support from the Philippian Christians. (b) We too need spiritual encouragement. (2) We can help each other. (a) Paul was sure that he could assist the Philippians in their faith. (b) We can help our fellow Christians grow in the faith.— Dwight O. Weber.

HOW TO WALK ON WATER.　Text: Matt. 14:22–23. How can we go from where we are to where we want to be when there's deep water between? How can we do that which seems impossible? (1) There must be a tremendous desire on our part. (2) We must not ignore the obstacles we must face. (3) We must identify our strength. (4) We must get out of the boat.—Jerry Hayner.

Worship Aids

CALL TO WORSHIP.　"We have thought of thy lovingkindness, O God, in the midst of thy temple. According to thy name, O

God, so is thy praise unto the ends of the earth." Ps. 48:9–10.

INVOCATION.   Eternal and ever-blessed God, grant this day light to the minds that hunger for the truth and peace to the hearts which yearn for rest. Grant strength to those who have hard tasks to do and power to those who have sore temptations to face. Grant unto us within this place to find the secret of thy presence and to go forth from it in the strength of the Lord.

OFFERTORY SENTENCE.   "Give unto the Lord the glory due unto his name: bring an offering, and come before him." I Chron. 16:29.

OFFERTORY PRAYER.   Not by words only, O God, would we offer our thanksgiving for so many loving expressions of thy concern for us but also in Christ's name we dedicate these gifts that through them we may participate in the work of thy ever-widening kingdom.

PRAYER.   Eternal Father, let us not be hesitant to stop the swift pace of our living. May our racing thoughts slacken their speed and for this moment let all our strivings cease. Let us center down to the reality that is behind all the phenomena of our existence. And in this worship experience may we feel the sense of wholeness. Let this be a moment when all the pores of our soul are open and the portals of our mind are flung wide in receptivity. And in receiving we shall be made strong again and recapture the courage to embrace life.

O God, we confess that so often we have been afraid to live fully and vibrantly. There has always been this smaller self cowering inside of us, wanting to stay in the darkness, afraid of light and of truth, and fearful of being exposed to the strong demands of the actual. Free us from our imprisonment. As we glimpse the Son of Man again with his courage and his exuberant confidence in life, with his complete trust in the ultimate decency of things, and with his faith that the goodness of God shall prevail. Let us in this time come close to his spirit, and let it infuse our life until we in his fellowship can again walk the road of life with the shackles of fear, anxiety, and fretfulness fallen from us. Grant that we shall find the secret of this free spirit. For whom the Son of Man hath made free, ye shall be free indeed.—C. A. McClain, Jr.

EVENING SERVICE

Topic: Unfinished Business
TEXT: Col. 4:17.

At the conclusion of his letter to the Colossians Paul says, "Tell Archippus, 'Be sure to finish the task you were given in the Lord's service.' " Whoever Archippus was and whatever he was supposed to do, Paul was vigorous in urging the entire Colossian community to see to it that there was no unfinished business left among them. "Tell Archippus to discharge his duty in the full." When Paul wrote as he did, his reference was to some activity or service which related to the well-being of the Christian community. That task needed to come to fruition; the man named Archippus could be expected to do it. One translation of Paul's advice reads: "Archippus, God ordained you to your work. See that you don't fail him!"

I. In our own day and in our own places we are given the charge to finish the task given us in the Lord's service.

(a) In one sense, that task never can be completed. It is ongoing. In another sense, we must not shirk the calling which is ours. We must not fail in exerting every effort to deal with the business at hand.

(b) What is that business? Jesus said: "The message about repentance and the forgiveness of sins must be preached to all nations. . . . You are witnesses of these things." We call this our great commission, our Christian mandate, and our responsibility as God's people. Jesus said, "Go to all peoples everywhere and make them my disciples."

(c) Clearly this is our business, and an unfinished business it is. You and I have a share and a stake in its completion. Extending the message of Christ is the task given us in the Lord's service. We are witnesses of these things. How do we go about this business?

II. The answer begins not with techniques but with priorities. Christ's mission-mandate is intended to take preeminent place in the ordering of our lives.

(a) This requirement disturbs us. There are so many other things competing for first place in human experience.

(1) Making a living ordinarily seems to outrank all other considerations. One's family certainly should be high among our personal priorities. There sometimes is the need for concentrating on a better education and for adjusting to new dimensions of living such as retirement or a vocational change. The list of potential priority concerns is endless.

(2) In the midst of this the biblical word addresses us, saying that over all else our responsibility is that of declaring the Christian good news to every people and nation. It is a perplexing and a disturbing word, for usually our priorities lie elsewhere.

(b) All of life's necessary pursuits can be caught up in the larger framework of Christian commitment.

(1) The daily work we do can become a channel for communicating God's good news. Our family circles can model the ideals of love and caring. The people we meet in other relationships can be given to know of our service in Christ's name.

(2) The whole context of our lives is meant to be infused with the Christian message. That is the obvious thrust of Jesus' teaching when he said, "Seek first [God's] kingdom and his righteousness, and all these things shall be yours as well," referring to food, clothing, and security.

III. To priority must be added urgency.

The apostle Paul would wince at our complacency as Christians today.

(a) Urgency is an inescapable scriptural theme. We read: "Now is the acceptable time. Now is the day of salvation." "It is high time to awake from sleep," Paul declared. Not only scripture but experience teaches that we do not have forever. "We must work the works of [God] while it is day; night comes, when no one can work." These are the lessons which repeatedly we have heard but not necessarily taken to heart.

(b) A spirit of keenness, intensity, and urgency needs to be called into our service as Christian disciples.

(1) Elton Trueblood writes, "When people are so enkindled by contact with the central fire of Christ, they in turn set others on fire." This is the point of Emil Brunner's dictum: "The church exists by mission as a fire exists by burning."

(2) Our priorities must be straight, a sense of timeliness and urgency must be invoked, and a vital relationship with Christ must be kindled. His life at work in our lives will enable us to accomplish his purposes to the full.

(c) The mission task starts where always it has started—first where we are and then where we can reach with our appointed representatives and with our resources. Jesus said, "Look to the fields ripe with harvest." Then looking at his friends he asked: "Will you be laborers there? Will you help with the harvest, completing this unfinished business for the glory of the Father and the blessing of the people? Will you be my disciples?"—John H. Townsend.

SUNDAY: MAY FIRST

MORNING SERVICE

Topic: The Unforgotten Debt
SCRIPTURE: Acts 9:26–31.

I. The greatest motivating power you can discover is your remembered debt of gratitude to a host of people.

(a) If you disabuse yourself of any ideas of your own self-sufficiency and your own sole capability of making it to the top of the heap, you will become an instrument of divine power through kindness, love, and faith.

(b) As long as you and I persist in making it to the top alone by pushing others aside and asserting ourselves, we diminish our stature. It is the well-remembered, unforgotten debt that we owe to others that gives us the power to create, to lead, to live fully, and to be our true selves.

II. St. Paul never forgot the debt that he owed to other people. Chiefly there were three persons who developed his spiritual life.

(a) Ananias, a layman who made pottery in Damascus, was sent by the Holy Spirit to give him back his sight and to restore his serenity.

(b) A woman named Priscilla opened the gates in Greece when the itinerant St. Paul went there but had no beachhead. This professional woman, a dealer in fine fabrics, opened her home and her social clientele to give credence to this new convert, whom we call St. Paul.

(c) The more important person is Barnabas. (1) Barnabas is the focus of the unforgotten debt we owe to other people. He was a large, rotund man with a majestic head so that when he was besieged by a crowd on one of his missions they thought he looked like their idea of the Greek god Zeus. Barnabas came from the island of Cyprus and lived on the periphery of the disciples of Jesus.

(2) After the resurrection, when things were difficult for the disciples and they were frugal and penurious, Barnabas went back to Cyprus and sold his farm and brought the income from that to support John, James, Peter, Bartholomew, Mary, Martha, and the rest.

(3) Here was a large-framed man with a large mind and a generous heart who was content to play second fiddle. When St. Paul was first converted, he was rebuffed by the apostles. This wonderful, intellectual Jewish Pharisee presented himself to the disciples for acceptance. No one welcomed the apostle Paul except Barnabas.

(4) He was not pressing to become president of his company, but come what may, he was content to be an ever-growing personality. Barnabas put his arm around Saul of Tarsus and said, "Brother Saul, I stand with you." After that St. Paul was in.

II. Who plays the role of Barnabas in your life? (a) I can name a dozen men and women who have played the role of Barnabas or Priscilla in my life. It is an unforgotten debt.

(b) An even more important question exists in this troubled time—"Whose Barnabas and Priscilla are you?" Write that name down on paper today. If you cannot write someone's name down, then your life is not existing in its plenitude.

(c) If you want to make it to the top, if you want to be a leader, or if you want to be an instrument of God, write down the name of some person who stands alone today, questioned, scorned, unsure, and anxious. Then write down; "I am your Barnabas. I am your Priscilla."

(d) It won't be easy to do. You will have to take the criticism with St. Paul. You will bear the scorn that goes with loyalty, but you will set a character free that may endure and influence the whole of civilization, as St. Paul did.

III. Very few people remember St. Barnabas, but there would have been no St. Paul if there had been no St. Barnabas. Barnabas wasn't his name. Barnabas was only his nickname. Barnabas' real name was Joseph. He was so warm-hearted that he came to be called the Encourager (Barnabas). He was so round and jolly, strong and outgoing, they gave him the title Barnabas which really means "Son of Encouragement."

(b) To whom are you the son and daughter of encouragement? Whom are you turning away from slipping into the abyss by the helpful actions of your personality? This is the age of narcissism. "What's in it for me? Take care of me." But there is more to life than that.

(c) Jesus persuaded Barnabas that he who seeks to save his life will lose it and he who seeks to give his life away in abundance will receive it back as an overflowing spring of eternal spirit coming out of that person. This promise is available to all men and women to give to others today.

IV. I think of all the men and women who have accepted me, influenced me, and loved me.

(a) I think with gratitude of the men and women who have sometimes taken the opposite viewpoint in criticisms. They also have enriched life too. If I started to write a list, it would be like a scroll. Everything I am and have I recognize as a gift. I identify at this stage in life with Paul and Barnabas, who encouraged each other.

(b) Every man and woman has a Priscilla

or a Barnabas or an Ananias in their lives. My hope is that you too will acknowledge that. If you do, it will let loose a motivating flood within your heart and cause you to become a Barnabas or a Priscilla. It will liberate the mystique of kindness in you. It will make you realize that you touch everybody's life for weal or woe. When you touch them for better, you release their personalities and you set them free.

(c) You can do it in a socially acceptable manner in our modern culture by a look or a word. Most people have a very hard time hiding under the facade that we all maintain in this world where we are striving for the illusion of getting to the top. Did you ever try to be realistic with people? Most of the time they want to hear rosy optimism. One writer said: "Don't go to the heights. Go to the depths with people."

(d) It is in the depths of life that Barnabas stands with you. It is in the depths of doubt that Priscilla trusts you. It is in the depths of bitterness that Ananias comes to you in your anger and your blindness and your self-rejecting hostility. Barnabas comes with love, trust, and acceptance to say, "Brother Saul, the Lord has heard your prayer."—Bryant M. Kirkland.

Illustrations

THE MASTER'S LETTERS.   A woman had an unusual and meaningful dream. She was looking into a room crowded with people, all of them obviously deeply distraught. In the dream she intuitively knew the reason for their distress was that they lived and died feeling they had not lived up to what God wanted them to be.

Suddenly the door of the room opened and Jesus Christ walked in. Seeing everyone in such distress, he was moved to compassion, and walking around the room, he stood in front of each person in turn.

"My child, why are you crying?" he asked the first one.

"I'm crying, Lord, because my husband died when we were so young, and from then on I was just lost without him. I wanted to serve you, but I was too lonely and upset all those years to do anything."

"But didn't you get my letter?" His voice was heavy with concern.

"What letter, Lord? Did you write me a letter?"

"Oh, yes," he said, "I wrote you a letter and told you not to worry, that you believed in God, believe also in me, and that I would not leave you comfortless."

The woman looked surprised. "You know," she said, "the minister read that letter at my husband's funeral, but I didn't know it was personal, from you to me."

Jesus stepped to the next person in the room. The man said, "Lord, I couldn't live for you because there were too many things I always had to be worrying about."

"Oh, then you didn't get my letter either?"

"No, Lord. Did you write me a letter?"

"Yes, my son, and in it I told you about the birds of the air. They don't worry about their next meal, and yet they are fed. I told you to put me first, for I had work for you to do, and I'd give you everything you really needed."

"Oh, Lord, I remember reading about that, but I didn't know you meant it for me!"

Around the room the master went. For every malady that was represented, there were words of healing and help from scripture. But no one had taken his words to heart.—Colleen Townsend Evans.

ON TRIAL.   Long ago a chieftain completely defeated detachments of Cyrus' army. Finally the king amassed his whole army and captured him and took him to the capitol for trial and execution. On the day of the trial his wife and two children were brought to the judgment hall. Cagular was a fine looking man over six feet tall. His wife was a noble woman, and golden ringlets hung around the childish faces of the children. Cyrus, impressed with the appearance of the four, asked Cagular, "What would you do should I spare your life?" He answered, "I would return home and ever remain your obedient servant." Again he asked, "And if I spared your children?" Cagular declared that he would take his troops and lead them to victory for the king. And what would he do if he spared his wife? Cagular replied, "I would die for you." The king was so moved that he set all four free. When they returned home, Cagular asked his wife if she noticed the marble of the mansion, the tapestries, and the golden throne of the king. She said she did not notice them. He continued, "Well, what then did you see?" She replied, "I beheld the face of the man who said he would die for me."—John R. Brokhoff.

Sermon Suggestions

THE PATTERN FOR MARRIAGE. Scripture: I Cor. 7:1–11. (1) The purity of married life (vv. 1–2). (2) The partnership of married life (vv. 3–5). (3) The permanency of married life (vv. 10–11).—Stephen F. Olford.

THE WAY OF THE CHRISTIAN. Text: Jas. 2:7. (1) Faith makes a man a Christian. (2) His life proves he is a Christian. (3) Trials confirm him as a Christian. (4) Death crowns him a Christian.

Worship Aids

CALL TO WORSHIP. "Be strong and of a good courage, fear not: for the Lord thy God, he it is that doth go with thee; he will not fail thee, nor forsake thee." Deut. 31:6.

INVOCATION. Heavenly Father, we come before thee in trembling because we are conscious of our many sins and yet boldly because we know that thou dost love us. Forgive us our sins, and help us to become more worthy of thy goodness and love. May we gain that strength from communion with thee which will enable us to walk humbly and righteously before thee and uprightly before the world, manifesting in life's every experience that faith and courage which befit thy children.

OFFERTORY SENTENCE. "And whatsoever ye do in word and deed, do all in the name of the Lord Jesus, giving thanks to God and the Father by him." Col. 3:17.

OFFERTORY PRAYER. O God, in whose sight a contrite heart is more than whole burnt offerings: help us with these our gifts to dedicate ourselves, body, soul, and spirit, unto thee, which is our reasonable service.

PRAYER FOR A WEDDING. Our heavenly Father, who hast willed the holy estate of marriage and who hast taught us the way of love, we ask that thou wouldst bless this union. As this home is established, may it be endowed with true devotion, spiritual commitments, and personal initiatives.

Give to this man and this woman the ability to keep the vow and covenant between them made. Where selfishness would show itself, give love; where mistrust is a temptation, give confidence; where misunderstanding intrudes, give gentleness and patience.

Give, our Father, times of joy, peace, and happiness. May this husband and wife in such moments acknowledge the source from which such privileges come. We realize, our Father, that life does not unfold without its bitter moments. We ask that thou wouldst give to this union the patience to endure affliction. When suffering becomes their lot, give them a strong faith and an abiding hope. Should tragedy be woven into the fabric of this marriage, give them substance wherein they can comfort one another. May they not demand of thee a reason for everything, but may doubt give way to trust. Help us to realize that thou dost teach us in many ways.

If thou shouldst bless this home, our Father, with children, give to this couple the qualities of true parenthood. Make this home a shelter from that which corrupts and destroys, and may it be a school wherein they may be fitted for life and service in the kingdom of God.—C. Neil Strait.

EVENING SERVICE

Topic: A Good Word for Church People
TEXT: Phil. 1:3, 5.

So many books written condemn the local church for excluding people from parish life, for being concerned only with their own needs, for being too denominational, for rejecting the single, for hypocrisy and dishonesty, and for apathy to the anguished human condition surrounding them as well as in the larger world. In the parish I have found a wealth of faithful, sincere, thoughtful, generous, and open-minded people who are working very hard.

I. Instead of hypocrisy I have found hundreds who attend worship in all kinds of weather and at all times of the day and night, who seek out books to read, biblical and theological courses to take, and means to live out their faith to the best of their understanding. They willingly participate in new liturgies, lead worship when asked, and attend even when the worship leadership is poor.

II. Instead of dishonesty I have found hundreds who will speak up directly, challenge when necessary pastor and neighbor, and defend the church against critics.

III. Instead of exclusiveness I have found the parish to be one of the few places where all individuals are welcomed, the place where all of society's outcasts—the alcoholic, the unemployed, the unwed mother—can be made to feel loved and cared for.

IV. Instead of narrowness I have found parishioners who are open-minded and willing to listen and to try, as long as the trust level between them and their leaders is well established. I have seen many go along with new ideas, new programs, and new liturgies because the majority wanted to try. They will admit it when new ideas work.

V. Instead of laziness I have seen parishioners with exhausting jobs take themselves out to weekly meetings, special worship, and weekend retreats without complaint. I have seen people in their seventies, with at least fifty years of hard work already behind them, give of themselves without complaint because they believe that is what the church is all about.

VI. Instead of selfishness I have found parishioners more generous than any other group of people I have ever known. They have asked only, "How much is needed?" I have seen them respond to disaster victims in their own neighborhoods, to the hungry and ill-clothed in their own towns, to the poor and distressed in their state and nation, and to the oppressed and starving in the world. I have seen factory workers and farmers give away clothing, food, and hard-earned cash to hundreds of strangers. I have seen them give large purses to pastors who have been sick or who are leaving them. I have seen them give away hours and hours of free time to the elderly, the young, and the disabled. I have not heard them say no to any need. —Emily Preston in *A.D.*

SUNDAY: MAY EIGHTH

MORNING SERVICE

Topic: Focus on the Family (Mother's Day)

SCRIPTURE: Eph. 5:25–6:4.

I. The purpose of families is to preserve and to teach the values of the Christian heritage to their children.

(a) The church places upon parents the priestly vocation of communicating the heritage of values to the children. That's why, in the baptismal ritual, the church asks the parents to live a life before the children "that becomes the gospel."

(b) The source of much of the alarm sensitive parents have about the family lies in the feeling that they get very little support in their vocation of teaching values. If our age is different from others, it's different in the number of influences children are exposed to. Parents are no longer the sole models for children of what is right and wrong. The mass media, the peer society, and the schools teach values to our children. When you measure the time that children spend in those institutions over against the time they spend with their parents, it's no wonder that parents feel embattled, and they feel there is a crisis in the family.

(c) Parents ought to assert their responsibility to communicate and to demonstrate the values of our heritage. More than three hundred thousand parents were interviewed in a survey on what they felt was the greatest threat to the family.

The number one issue was not television, drugs, alcohol, permissive sex, divorce, or women working outside the home. The greatest threat to family life today was identified as inattentive parents.

(d) Children are great learners. Some parents think the children are just playing, but they are learning all the time. They are learning what it means to be a man or a woman and what it means to be an adult. Parents are still the primary source of learning for children. There is a myth that the primary learning experience for children is from their peer groups, but it is true only if parents forfeit their responsibility to be the primary source of learning for children.

(e) Most children will go their own way. And when they do, it may be painful. But often after going their own way they will come back to the values of their parents. Many adolescents reject the values of their parents in order to test them. They have to find out for themselves if they work. It's painful and uncomfortable, but it's not a crisis. The crisis occurs when parents forfeit their responsibility to stand for something and communicate values to the children and yield to some other source in the society to instruct their children.

(f) Parents can give children an appreciation for right and wrong and for what is good and true and beautiful and equip their children to find their own way.

I. The Christian family is a community of love and caring. (a) The deepest meaning of the baptismal vow is to live before the children a life that becomes or demonstrates the gospel.

(b) Christian families can take many forms and styles, but one thing that distinguishes them from all other families, the one distinctive Christian quality in a family, is that they are communities where, in spite of human sin and error, one can be received with forgiving love and care as a human being.

(c) The greatest gift that a family can give individuals is the assurance that they're important. Russ Campbell called this "focused attention." It emphasizes that the quality of the time we give one another is more important than the quantity of time. In our age it is very difficult to give great quantities of time to the family, but we can still give one another focused attention.

(d) Loneliness is not a matter of isolation. Loneliness is a matter of being ignored. You can be lonely in a crowd if nobody speaks to you or acknowledges your existence. Loneliness is a matter of having the sounds of your life dissipate for the lack of a hearer. That's why the most redeeming experience that we can ever have is to know that somebody hears what we're really saying and understands us. Children need to be listened to more than they need all the things we give them. We achieve a sense of worth in this life not by receiving things but by being received.

(e) Families let us know that we are wanted, that we're important, that somebody cares for us, and the assurance that we are important.—Mark Trotter.

Illustrations

COMPLAINT BOX. A newly married couple were determined that they would solve their problems without fighting. So it was agreed that if either one noticed anything in the other that was irritating, anything at all that carried the seeds of future trouble, he or she would write a note about it and put it in the "complaint box." At sometime each one would go alone to the complaint box and take out the notes with his or her name on them. In an atmosphere of calmness and self-examination they would read the note and do their best to change. The plan seemed to work perfectly. One month rolled into two, two into three and four, and they were as happy as they had been during the honeymoon. At the end of the year they were discussing their marvelous invention for happy homes and discovered that neither had ever opened the complaint box. Each one had been so certain that he or she was innocent of all fault that neither one had looked in the box.— W. E. Borne in *Christianity Today*.

MY MEAN MOTHER. I had the meanest mother in the world. While other kids ate candy for breakfast, I had to eat cereal, eggs, and toast. When other kids had cokes, cupcakes, and potato chips for lunch, I had a sandwich, an apple, and carrot sticks. I won't tell you what I had for dinner, but I bet you can guess!

My mother had to know where I was at all times and what friends I ran around with. She even went to teacher's conferences and PTA meetings. If that wasn't enough, I had to be in bed by 9 o'clock each night.

My mother even had the nerve to break the child labor laws. I had to work—wash the dishes, pick up my clothes, make my bed, and mow the lawn. There were times when I felt like I was on a chain gang. I just knew that she laid awake nights thinking up mean things for me to do.

By today's standards my mother was a complete failure. I was never arrested, studied hard, and went to college to learn. I traveled the world because she made sacrifices for me. I was expected to go to church; there was never any excuses for not worshiping on Sunday.

I am trying to raise my two sons in this manner. Hopefully, I can stand a little taller before my children because when they call me mean, I am giving them standards to live by, a God to worship, and respect for family, friends, and nation. All this, because I had a mean mother.—Lanny Arrowsmith.

Sermon Suggestions

A MODEL MOTHER.　　　Scripture: Luke 1: 39–56. (1) Mary was amenable to God. (2) Mary was attentive to the needs of her son. (3) Mary was aspiring. (4) Mary was affectionate.—Brian L. Harbour.

THE PARENT'S HANDS.　　　Text: Gen. 21: 17–18 (RSV). What God said to Hagar he says to us: "Hold him fast with your hand." To do this takes two hands. (1) The hand of firmness. (2) The hand of friendship.—Carol Wilson.

Worship Aids

CALL TO WORSHIP.　　　"Delight thyself also in the Lord; and he shall give thee the desires of thine heart. Commit thy way unto the Lord; trust also in him; and he shall bring it to pass." Ps. 37:4–5.

INVOCATION.　　　God of all life, we have come here today alone as persons, together in families, all joined in the community of Christian faith. Though we seek your face in the world of life, we ask your blessing in these moments of withdrawal. Take us not from the world, but prepare us for life in the world. Let us not imagine special privilege for ourselves, but let us encourage common opportunity for all. Give us not love for ourselves alone, but make us instruments of your love in the midst of every human place.—Richard D. Bausman.

OFFERTORY SENTENCE.　　　"He that hath a bountiful eye shall be blessed; for he giveth of his bread to the poor." Prov. 22:9.

OFFERTORY PRAYER.　　　As we bring our offering today we thank thee, O God, for the happiness of our earthly life, for peaceful homes and healthful days, for our powers of mind and body, for faithful friends, and for the joy of loving and being loved. We pray that these blessings may come to abound throughout all the world and to all people.

PRAYER.　　　Thank you for the newness of this day. May we receive it in all of its freshness. May we enter fully into its possibilities. No man needs to stay the way he is. No church needs to be impotent in the face of the world's great need. In thy house there is bread enough and to spare.

Thou art here, O God, in the fullness of your love, joy, and peace. We thank you for your coming in Christ that we might know what true manhood is. We thank you for your coming in the presence of your Holy Spirit. May this day be an experience of your aliveness today in this time and place. May we catch visions of the new thing that you are doing in our day. May we not be disobedient to these visions when they come.

Be with those who are our comrades-on-the-way, for we realize that "no man is an island, but each is a part of the main" and what distresses one, distresses all. Be with all those suffering distress of mind, body, or spirit. Grant to them a quiet confidence in thee that can mean their health. Be with thy church. We pray that even in its brokenness it can be used to lead men and nations to thy wholeness.

We pray for our congregation and the greater church in which its life is set. May we so experience your love and share it with one another that we may "dwell together in the unity of the Spirit and the bond of peace," calling the nations of the world and the peoples of the earth to thy reconciling love in Christ.

Bless all those who are bridge builders in the cause of world community. Through the power of your Spirit that makes all things new, may we live this day and all days in the experience of a perennial springtime.—John Thompson.

EVENING SERVICE

Meditation: How Loose, How Soon?
TEXT: Prov. 22:6.
On a supermarket parking lot a child was screaming mad, his face red and purple. His mother was holding him by the hand, and he was pulling with all his might to get away, tilted at about a 45 degree angle, pulling the opposite direction from his mother's hand.

The child wanted loose and thought his mother wanted to prevent him. In reality she was trying to turn him loose but couldn't get him into a position in which he could be set free without bashing his brains out on the pavement, toward which he was already well slanted.

The scene illustrates the problem of the rearing of the child and the releasing of him to be free and on his own at some proper time and circumstance of life.

Children usually think their parents are trying to hold them too tightly. Parents have as their goal that of turning the children loose as soon as they can stand on their own feet. The question is, How loose, how soon?

The child's hand needs to be held until he learns where to go and where not to go. He needs to be turned loose at a time when he is upright, in good balance, and able to walk alone. There are times when to turn him loose just because he wants loose would result in his destruction.

The apostle Paul declared that the law was a schoolmaster under which the people of God were appropriately ruled until they could stand in Christ without the necessity of law. Parents play somewhat the same role as the law. They hold the children on leash until they gain wisdom and poise to walk on their own without parental control. They must not be held too close, too long, nor turned loose too early, too suddenly.—Frank Owen.

SUNDAY: MAY FIFTEENTH

MORNING SERVICE

Topic: Receiving What We Need from God
TEXT: Phil. 4:19.
How do we receive what we need from God?

I. *We must ask with humility.* From the psalmist, to Isaiah, to David, to the apostle James, the message continues to ring forth: "The Lord will not forget the cry of the humble," "The Lord dwells with the man of a humble and contrite spirit," and "A broken and contrite spirit he will not despise." We do not command God. He is sovereign! We do not approach God arrogantly with demands and alternatives. God is to be approached with humility.

"God resisteth the proud, but giveth grace unto the humble" (Jas. 4:6).

(b) When we come to God with a petition, we do not make demands of God; he is omnipotent. We do not order God; he is omnipresent. We do not bargain with God; he is all righteous. We humble ourselves under the mighty hand of God that he might exalt us in due time.

II. *We must ask in faith.* (a) Jesus said, "What things soever ye desire, when ye pray, believe that ye receive them, and ye shall have them" (Mark 11:24). He also said, "If ye have faith . . . nothing shall be impossible unto you" (Matt. 17:20). Again he says, "If thou canst believe, all things are possible" (Mark 9:23).

(b) The central theme of the New Testament is grace through faith. God has made his grace available on the basis of simple faith. "Whosoever believeth in him should not perish, but have everlasting life" (John 3:16). Repeatedly this theme is echoed by Paul, by the writer to the Hebrews, and by all New Testament spiritual leaders. If we are to receive from God, we must ask in faith.

III. *We must ask with expectancy.* (a) It perhaps could be argued that faith and expectancy are the same. Admittedly there is a thin line between the two. It is one thing to have faith that God can do what you ask him to do and quite another to believe that God will do it. Faith says God can; expectancy says God will. Expectancy is faith in action.

(b) Today is the only opportunity we have to claim the promises of God. (1) For those who are unregenerate and in need of the saving grace of God, today is the day of salvation. It is their only day. Tomorrow is not promised.

(2) For those who need cleansing by the sanctifying blood, today is the only promised opportunity.

(3) For those who need the indwelling presence of the Holy Spirit, divine healing or a miracle, and for every person with a need, today is the only day. We have no promise of tomorrow.

(c) If we are to receive what we need and if today is the only day we are promised, we should ask in expectancy, believing that God will provide the need today.—James E. Cossey.

Illustrations

FLICKERING LIGHT.   We walk by faith, but let us remember what faith is for. That little candle flame, lighted at the altar of the Most High, was given us that, guarding it from the wailing winds of doubt and the shuddering earthquakes of pain, we might hold its flickering light close to the ground where we must daily walk—not to hold aloft in a vain attempt to peer into things too high for us lest from the darkness between the stars we hear the mocking laughter of God.—Kenneth J. Foreman.

EXPRESSING THANKSGIVING.   Is being thankful enough? Perhaps we could live our thanks by doing God's bidding. In return for spare time, we can use more time in sharing Christ. In return for heaping tables, we can fast a few meals each month and send the savings to a world hunger fund. In thanksgiving for our lifestyle, we can share our material goods with needy neighbors—shoes, clothes, blankets, and other necessities. In thanksgiving for our knowledge of God's love for us, we can provide Bibles, Christian literature, and fellowship to the spiritually hungry.—Rosalie C. Black.

Sermon Suggestion

GOD'S SELF-DISCLOSURE.   Text: I Cor. 1:9. (1) Man encounters the God of creation through the world of nature. (2) Man encounters the God of history through the medium of human experience. (3) Man encounters the God of the covenant through salvation by redeeming love. (4) Man encounters the God of the resurrection through the living Christ and his promise of the ultimate victory of life over death.—Hoover Rupert.

Worship Aids

CALL TO WORSHIP.   "Bless the Lord, O my soul: and all that is with me, bless his holy name." Ps. 103:1.

INVOCATION.   Father God, we come to this place to ask for a new vision of your presence and a resurrected spirit of life within history and beyond history. We come as humble pilgrims, none of us possessing all faith and knowledge but all of us seeking your truth as it lives in our midst. Be with us now, we pray, that we may be aware of you in a special way and, being thus aware, that as we live in the world we may be aflame with your joy.

OFFERTORY SENTENCE.   "Unto whomsoever much is given, of him shall be much required: and to whom men have committed much, of him they will ask the more." Luke 12:48.

OFFERTORY PRAYER.   O living Christ, help us to know the ecstasy of thine everlasting lordship that we may more perfectly become cheerful givers.

PRAYER.   O God, you are the Lord of life, the Giver of breath and pulse. From you we sprang; throughout our wanderings it is to you that we long to return. Yet instead of joyfully moving through our journey, we tend to hold fast like crusty barnacles as waves of change crash over us and then return to the sea. Sometimes we wish we could let go, join the rhythm, and trust in your future. Lord, deliver us from our grasping. Help us to meet change. We know that you forgive our fears and our failures and that even now you invite us into a new life. We thank you that you have made trust possible, that while nothing remains unchanged, some things are dependable—the rhythm of day and dark, rest and work, comradeship and solitude, seasons and tides high and low, and the constant love of Christ. You have kindled in our hearts a desire for depth in our living. We come to you earnestly seeking to participate in the fullness of life. Where we block and deny ourselves, grant that we may become free. As we extend our hearts and minds across continents and oceans, we pray that all men may come to know your love and to possess a sense of peace and wholeness.—*Forward.*

EVENING SERVICE

Topic: The Strength of Weakness
TEXT: I Cor. 2:3.

When we are depressed, full of a sense of our own unworthiness and incapacity, and overwhelmed with a sense of failure, we may know that we are not alone in our experience. It is common to all those who have striven to attain some lofty ideal. The winning of strength is nearly always the result of conquering weakness. Nobody was ever born a saint. Saints are not born. They are developed. They become saints by being patient when it is hard to be patient, by pushing forward when they wanted to stand still, by keeping silent when they wanted to speak, by being agreeable when they desired to be disagreeable, and by being cheerful when it was difficult to be cheerful. A sense of weakness does some good things for us.

I. It keeps us humble and makes us sympathetic. It prevents us from saying: "I did it all alone. Mine own right arm hath gotten me the victory." It makes us sympathetic with the weakness of others. Brilliant students rarely make good teachers; they don't know the difficulties. But we can't despise those who have the same weaknesses that we have had ourselves. Feeling the weight of our own burdens, we want to help others to bear theirs.

II. It drives us to Christ. When all is going well, when we appear to be successful, and when we feel we can do what we want to do and are powerful enough to step over the obstacles which lie in our path, we are likely to forget or ignore Christ. But when we are helpless or prostrate, we can only pray. When our strength is gone, we reach out a hand for his.

III. In reaching for his strength in our weakness, we become strong. This is real strength for it is not ours but his. Then with Paul we realize, "I can do all things through Christ which strengtheneth me." —Ernest Edward Smith.

SUNDAY: MAY TWENTY-SECOND

MORNING SERVICE

Topic: They Changed the World (Pentecost)
SCRIPTURE: Acts 1:1–8.

You don't go far into the pages of the book of Acts to discover that the people who believed strongly that Christianity was unique among the religions of the world and who committed themselves fully to its teaching began to change the world. On the day of Pentecost they got the attention of the people, and that was only the beginning. By the time the book ended, we find that this belief in the resurrected Christ had spread from the upper room in Jerusalem to the palace of Caesar in Rome. Thousands upon thousands of people now called themselves Christians. Here is how it happened.

I. *They waited expectantly.* "And gathering them together, Jesus commanded them not to leave Jerusalem, but to wait for what the Father had promised."

(a) Later we read that their waiting together had several component parts consisting of teaching, praying, and worshiping. Before they went out to change the world, they changed themselves.

(b) The upper room was an important place to them. It was the sanctuary where they worshiped. It was the prayer room where they shared their hopes and dreams, their doubts and fears. It was the classroom where they received instructions. It was their huddle where the directions were given to the team.

(c) No one will become the world changer that God wants him to be if he fails to feed his own spirit in worship, Bible study, and prayer. We come together in order to go out and do our work. It's a picture of a team meeting together in the huddle where instructions, encouragement, and inspiration are given so that they might go forward to face the opponent. We, like the team, need this time together. We need to worship, to study the Bible, to pray together, to encourage one another, and to support one another.

II. *They received gratefully.* "But you shall receive power when the Holy Spirit has come upon you."

(a) Lloyd Ogilvie said that there were four characteristics which expressed the emptiness of the disciples prior to the coming of God's power into their lives—discouraged, dejected, disabled, and depressed. The death of Jesus greatly discouraged them. Their hopes and dreams were shattered with his last cry from the cross. They fled in disbelief and hid behind the closed doors of their old sanctuary. Dejection was a natural response to the death of Christ. It was as if their hearts had been cut out. Their disappointment knew no limits.

(b) Have there not been times when you felt as if your world had come to an end and that the sun would never be as bright or as warm again? Helen Keller said, "I have known the depths where great dark-

ness was." Down in the cellars of our human existence we have groped in the darkness, dejected and depressed. Discouragement, dejection, and depression are disabling emotions.

(c) "But you shall receive power from the Holy Spirit." I don't know anyone who doesn't want power in his or her life—power to live a victorious, fulfilled life and power to get, as we say, on top of life. The kind of power that caused those early Christians to change their world had four facets.

(1) They had intellectual power. When God's spirit filled their lives, they became smarter people. On the day of Pentecost God's power gave them the ability to do things and to understand things that they did not have within their own strength.

(2) They had emotional power. They had power to love people in a way they had never known before. That's one way you and I can know if we are possessed by the Spirit of God. Do you have the ability to love? If you and I are out to change the world and to change the lives of our friends and family members, we must do it through the power that love generates.

(3) They had great physical power. They went beyond human endurance and beyond human strength. They had excess energy with which to do the work they felt compelled to do. Paul survived a shipwreck. The disciples survived beatings and stonings. They drove themselves to reach the top. They had a vision of a world that was not yet but ought to be.

(4) They had spiritual power. Their faith was increased. They believed that nothing was impossible for God to do. If God could bring forth Jesus Christ from the dead, he could resurrect others too. They believed in a God who had no limits. When Jesus said, "All power is given to me in heaven and in earth," they believed he meant it.

III. *They submitted cheerfully.* "Jesus said to them, 'It is not for you to know times or epochs which the Father has fixed by his own authority.' "

(a) Right in the middle of Jesus' teaching about how God's Spirit was going to come and give great power to each of them, the disciples blurted out, "Lord, is it at this time you are restoring the kingdom to Israel? Is this the time when Israel, our beloved nation, is going to reassert itself as the leader of the world? Is this the time when our flag is going to wave above every flag, our army winning victories over every army?" Their poorly timed question allowed Jesus to tell them how to trust God in the present and in the future. "You are not going to be told about the times and epochs which the Father has in his authority," said Christ, "but you are to go into all the world as if you knew every detail of every answer."

(b) Those people who were out to change the world knew that change would come through their commitment to the God who can make all things new. "Go in my name and because you believe others will know that I live."

(c) The disciples were thinking about the good ole days, and Jesus was saying to them, "God has the power to make those days pale." Sometimes our problem is that we want to reproduce yesterday when God wants to give birth to something that has never been. "Greater things than I have done shall you do," said Christ. But if those greater things are to be realized, we must submit ourselves cheerfully to the God who holds the past, the present, and the future in his hands.

IV. *They witnessed faithfully.* "You shall be my witnesses." (a) Nothing you and I ever do will be more important than to be Christ's witnesses. The worshiping, learning, praying, and the time spent together should inspire us and prepare us to share God's love in word and deed with those who need it.

(b) The infilling which we receive of God's power within our own lives should cause us to want others to know of that power and experience in their lives. In a world where people are held captive by their past, where they are afraid of the future, and where they are defeated by the present, when Christ enables us to trust God, we should want to help others to trust him too.

(c) Wouldn't it be foolish for a football team to spend sixty minutes huddling in the middle of the field and never play the game? Wouldn't it be shameful for a doctor to have the cure for cancer but never share the remedy with the medical world? Wouldn't it be dreadful for someone to have information which could help people to rest their minds without fear and not share that information? How much worse it is for you and me to keep silent about the best news ever announced in the history of man.—Jerry Hayner.

Illustrations

FAITH AND LOVE.   Faith is a living, daring confidence in God's grace, so sure and certain that a man would stake his life on it a thousand times. This confidence in God's grace and knowledge of it makes men glad and bold and happy in dealing with God and with all his creatures, and this is the work of the Holy Spirit in faith. Hence a man is ready and glad, without compulsion, to do good to everyone, to serve everyone, to serve everything in love and praise of God, who has shown him this grace.—Martin Luther.

MAD PEOPLE.   In Bernard Shaw's play *St. Joan,* some soldiers are talking about Joan of Arc. One of them says: "There is something about the girl. Her words and her ardent faith in God have put fire into me." The captain replies, "Why, you are almost as mad as she is." And the soldier stubbornly says: "Maybe that's what we need nowadays—mad people. See where the sane ones have landed us."

Sermon Suggestions

COMPONENTS OF PENTECOST.   Texts: Acts 2:2. (1) Historicity. (2) Unity. (3) Spontaneity. (4) Certainty. (5) Curiosity. (6) Inquiry. (7) Mockery. (8) Opportunity. (9) Efficacy.—Harold J. Ockenga.

LET THE FIRE FALL.   Scripture: Acts 2:1–4. (1) The fire of God fell, and the church became one in the spirit. (2) The fire of God fell, and the church became mission centered. (3) The fire of God fell, and the people began to sacrifice to reach their world.—John Dunaway.

TOGETHER IN COMMUNITY.   Text: Acts 2:1 (RSV). Penecost pinpoints the community of Christians, and we have our identity both in our individuality and in our membership in the community called the church. (1) Our sense of belonging to a worshiping community whether in formal worship or in informal groups in homes. (2) Our continuing to study and learn together for personal growth and corporate strength. (3) Our outreach to the living community around and beyond us not only in dollars but also in human involvement.—Robert P. Patterson.

WORSHIP AIDS

CALL TO WORSHIP.　　"Lord, who shall abide in thy tabernacle? Who shall dwell in thy holy hill? He that walketh uprightly, and worketh righteousness, and speaketh the truth in his heart." Ps. 15:1–2.

INVOCATION.　　Almighty God, who of thy great mercy hast gathered us into thy visible church: grant that we may not swerve from the purity of thy worship but may so honor thee both in spirit and in outward form that thy name may be glorified in us and that our fellowship may be with all thy saints in earth and in heaven.

OFFERTORY SENTENCE.　　"We then that are strong ought to bear the infirmities of the weak, and not to please ourselves." Rom. 15:1.

OFFERTORY PRAYER.　　God of our fathers, dearly do we cherish the blessing which thy church brings to us and dearly do we covet the privilege of sharing through these gifts the proclaiming of thy word until all of the earth shall praise thee.

PRAYER.　　O God, our Father in heaven, we give thee thanks for this opportunity to come together in this holy place as Christian people and to draw nigh unto thee in spirit and in truth. Our Father, we thank thee for Jesus Christ, thy Son, our Lord, the one who hast shown us that thou art indeed the God of great love and compassion. We thank thee for him who is our way to thee, who gives us life that is abundant and beyond death, and who is the truth that frees us from that which is false and hateful and unloving.

O God, we are a Christian church, a part of the church created by our Lord Jesus Christ that now extends in every land and among every people. We pray that as a church we may be always faithful and trusting and obedient to thee.

Our Father, we are different in so many ways. We are all individuals with our own particular backgrounds and our own peculiar needs. And yet, our Father, we recognize how much alike we are in so many ways. We know that we are all sinners, that we have fallen short of the mark thou hast set for us, and that we have been selfish, proud, lazy, and disobedient. We have been fearful when we should have been confident and trusting. We have felt utterly alone and been filled with despair when we should have rejoiced in the still small voice that comes from thee to those who will listen with their whole heart.

We are all alike in our great need of thee. We need to know of thy love for us, the love of the Father for his wayward children. We need thy forgiveness. We need thy companionship and strength as we walk and travel through this earthly life. We need thee, O God, to give us purpose, to give us direction, to take us out of our confusion, to make some deep sense out of our days, and to give us understanding and hope.—Gordon H. Reif.

EVENING SERVICE

Topic: The Holy Spirit and the New Order

TEXT: John 16:13.

I. Jesus proclaimed, demonstrated, and was a new humanity. (a) A new order for society was to be made of new folks, the first of which was Jesus. Jesus' life revealed the truth of the human condition. We who were made for God and the greatness of being human are convinced by Jesus' life that we have all fallen short, missed the mark, and are lost from God and the life he wants to give. When we are moved to try to do something about it, we discover that our power is just not enough to get the job done.

(b) We can't recover our humanity on our own, but God can and will do it for us. Jesus by his life, death, and resurrection speaks to our need. He opens the way to God. He can say, "I am the way, the truth, and the life." A new order has arrived in Jesus, a new order of life, manifesting itself in love, the very nature of God.

(c) Jesus came and then Jesus left. His work was finished. In his own infinite wisdom and power, God would now effect the work of Jesus in the lives of humanity. It was expedient that Jesus leave that the Spirit of Truth might come and accomplish the redemption Jesus provided. And on Pentecost the Holy Spirit came.

II. Before men would ever desire God, the Holy Spirit would begin to stir their hearts. He would work in hearts to make belief possible. He would join the bride, Jesus, saying "Come," inviting men to life. He would convince them of their sin and true righteousness. He would bear witness to all that Jesus said and did. He would deliver men from sin and its consequences, creating within them a new heart. He would intercede for them in prayer. He would comfort them in their trials. He would equip them for service in the new order and empower them for life as children of God. He would assure them that they really are God's people, and he would keep them for all eternity. He would be both the creator and the sustainer of new folks who would make up the new order. Jesus' work was finished; the Holy Spirit's work began on Pentecost.

III. We live in a confused age. Is this Holy Spirit a gift of God to all believers or just some believers? Do some receive more of the Spirit than others who believe? What is evidence that a believer has for the presence and activity of the Spirit in his life? The Bible answers these questions.

(a) The gift of the Holy Spirit is to all believers. The prophet Joel said, "In those days I will pour out my Spirit on all flesh." It is recorded in Acts that "he fell on all who heard the Word." St. Paul taught us, "By one Spirit we were all baptized into one body, and all were made to drink of one Spirit." The Holy Spirit is not a special possession of some believers. He is the gift of God to all believers. While he may give special gifts to some believers, he gives himself to all believers! "Whoever confesses that Jesus is the Son of God, God abides in him and he in God," declared John.

(b) Some have confused the gifts of the Spirit with the Spirit himself, and some see the gifts as evidence that the Spirit abides in their lives. Did Jesus say, "By their gifts you shall know them"? He said, "By their fruits you shall know them." Evidence of God as Holy Spirit in the lives of believers is not the gifts he gives but the fruit he produces. Our Lord said that some will continue to claim they belong to God because of his gifts even on judgment day. They'll talk about working miracles and speaking prophesies, but they did not bear fruit. They did not manifest the works of love. Therefore, they did not know God and were still separated from him.

(c) If you believe, then you can thank the Holy Spirit for bringing you to faith. And if you believe, then you can rejoice that you have received the gift of the Holy Spirit from God. You have been grafted onto the vine. The Holy Spirit is the life principle of that vine and the branches, producing fruit. The more you yield to the life in the vine, the more fruit he produces. —Jack Barker.

SUNDAY: MAY TWENTY-NINTH

MORNING SERVICE

Topic: Let's Be Human!

SCRIPTURE: Eph. 1:3, 5, 9–10.

I. Humanist may refer to someone who does not believe in God, but it may also refer to someone who is passionately concerned with what it means to be human, someone who believes that human beings are sacred and of great importance.

(a) In this regard, God was the first humanist. He created humanity and said, "It is good!" He considered human beings so sacred that he issued a commandment not to kill them.

(b) Jesus placed a supreme value on persons. Confronted by a religious system that tried to make its rules and regulations into matters of ultimate importance, he said bluntly, "The Sabbath was made for man, and not man for the Sabbath" (Mark 2:27). Nothing—no thing, no place, no day, and no rule—is more sacred than persons. In this regard Jesus Christ was also a great humanist.

(c) We celebrate the incarnation, when "the Word became flesh and dwelt among us." J. B. Phillips translates: "The Word of God became a human being." The incarnation invested humanity with a dignity not known before. Christians should never be afraid of anything truly human, for God was not. Christ was truly human, and he calls us to be truly human.

(d) From a prison cell in Hitler's Germany, Dietrich Bonhoeffer wrote, "To be a Christian does not mean to be religious in a particular way but to be a man." That is, a genuine human being. Bonhoeffer clearly specified what he meant by humanity. "Not just any type of man, but the man Christ creates in us." Jesus Christ is God's definition of what it means to be truly human.

(e) Karl Barth said: "Man is the creature made visible in the mirror of Jesus Christ" and "Christ stands above and is first, and Adam stands below and is second. So it is Christ that reveals the true nature of man."

II. If Christ reveals the true nature of man and if he is humanity as God intended it to be, then what went wrong?

(a) Before Christ we stand in awe and confess that we have fallen short. We say with Simon Peter of old, "Depart from me, for I am a sinful man, O Lord" (Luke 5:8). And so the real question is not "Is Christ human?" but rather "Are we?"

(b) St. Paul spoke of Christ as the Second Adam, that is, God's pattern of humanity as he intended it to be. The first Adam rebelled against God, and the image of God became defaced in him. It became necessary for God to issue a revised version of what it means to be human. That is why the ancient creeds spoke of him as true God and true man. He is the plumbline which God has let down to help us measure our humanness.

(c) Christ's coming is not merely judgment; it is also promise. It not only shows us how far short we have fallen: it also shows us how high we may rise. Christ is God's goal for us and for the world and what Pierre Teilhard de Chardin called "The Omega Point," the goal toward which all creation is moving. Christ is the end of all humanity. He is God's definition of what human means. In Christ we see two things—what God is like and what we were created to be like.

III. Humanness is not something we are born with. It is something we grow into.

(a) Being human is more than merely walking upright instead of on all fours, more than being able to oppose thumb and forefinger, more than possessing an intellect superior to the rest of the animal kingdom, and more than possessing the power of speech. That's biology, and we are more than biology.

(b) To be human is to possess the freedom of will and the spirit to direct our lives, to become children of God, living in right relationship with God who is the ground and source of our being and with one another.

(c) To be human is to affirm the dignity of each person, to assume responsibility for our lives and not be driven to and fro by circumstance, to be loving and kind and compassionate in all our relationships, and to commit ourselves to the social task of making our world and all of its institutions more human.

(d) To be fully human means to follow Christ. He is the image of the humanity that God had in mind for us. To be Christlike is difficult business. It is always being on the edge of things, always carrying love a little too far, giving forgiveness a little too much, and always being a little more caring and compassionate than others and more aware of the pain and hunger and suffering of the world.—Donald B. Strobe.

Illustrations

KNOWING CHRIST.   The father of a family in Idaho had been converted to Christianity. At every opportunity he talked about Christ. One day an atheist neighbor challenged him with this question: "Do you really know anything about Christ?" "Yes, I do," replied the convert. "When was he born?" asked the atheist. The new Christian was not exactly sure. Then came another question: "How old was he when he died?" Again the new follower of Christ could give no answer. He had feeble and even incorrect answers for most of his neighbor's questions. Finally the godless one exclaimed, "See, you don't know very much about Christ, do you?" "I know very little," replied the convert firmly, "but I do know this: two years ago I hit rock bottom; two years ago I was a drunkard; two years ago I was hopelessly in debt; two years ago my wife seldom smiled; two years ago my children feared my footsteps. But today I am a sober man; today I am out of debt and even making payments on a new home; today my wife smiles often; today my children run to greet me. All this Christ has done for me. That much I do know."—Arthur Tonne.

DIARY.   The life of every man is a diary in which he means to write one story and writes another, and his humblest hour is when he compares the volume as it is with what he hoped to make it.—James M. Barrie.

Sermon Suggestions

THE SPIRIT IN THE FLESH.   Text: Joel 2:28 (RSV). When is the spirit of God poured into our flesh so that young people see visions and old people dream exciting dreams? (1) When we keep faith in all of the possible richer meanings in our lives. (2) When we at any age accept the challenge of educating ourselves. (3) When we create a more human church and world.—Winfield S. Haycock.

CHILDREN OF THE TRIUNE GOD.   Scripture: Rom. 8:14–17. (1) We can call God our Father. (a) We do not have to fear him. (b) He made us his children. (2) We are led by the Spirit. (a) The Holy Spirit leads us to spiritual life. (b) The Holy Spirit leads us to live as God's children. (c) We are heirs with Christ. (d) Then we shall be like Christ.—Gerhard Aho.

Worship Aids

CALL TO WORSHIP.   "God hath exalted him, and given him a name which is above every name: that at the name of Jesus every name should bow, of things in heaven, and things in earth, and things under the earth; and that every tongue should confess that Jesus Christ is Lord, to the glory of God the Father." Phil. 2:9–11.

INVOCATION.   Lord God Almighty, holy and eternal Father, who dwellest in the high and lofty place, with him also that is of a humble and contrite spirit: we come before thee, beseeching thee to cleanse us by the grace of thy Holy Spirit, that we may give praise to thee, now and forever.

OFFERTORY SENTENCE.   "To do good and to communicate forget not: for with such sacrifices God is well pleased." Heb. 13:16.

OFFERTORY PRAYER.   Dear Father, help us to be ever concerned to find thy way for our lives, and may we never be satisfied to give thee our second best in return for thy great gift of love.

PRAYER.   O God, in this time of worship be real not only to our minds but to our affections, our wills, our consciences. Stir our gratitude for all the blessings and comforts of this life, yet let us not be too dependent on them. For the inevitable and the unpredictable give us courage. Show us how to take a stand for the things in which we believe and to play a worthy part in the life of our times. Give heavenly wisdom and understanding to all in every land who occupy positions of leadership, and by thy grace incline the peoples of the world to the ways of righteousness and peace.—Robert J. McCracken.

EVENING SERVICE

Topic: Name Above All Names
SCRIPTURE: Heb. 1:2–9.

Hebrews makes six mighty assertions which in the case of any other than Jesus would strike one as the height of absurdity.

I. Christ is "the heir of all things." We find in him the clue to the direction in which history is moving. The love of God manifest in Christ finally will be supreme in all the universe.

II. He is the creator of the world. As

James Denny put it, "The mediation of creation through Christ is a legitimate way of putting the conviction, that in the last resort and in spite of appearances the world in which we live is a Christian world, our ally, not our adversary." The love of God manifest in Christ is back of the creation of the world, the source from which it has come as well as the goal toward which it moves.

III. He is the light of the world. As the Jerusalem Bible translates, "He is the radiant light of God's glory and the perfect copy of his nature" (1:3). It was put more simply by Jesus when he said, "He who has seen me has seen the Father."

IV. He is the sustainer of the world. Human history is not in the grip of blind fate but in the hands of one who died and rose again. In the cross and its aftermath we see the divine power and love that sustains the universe and every-one who puts his faith in Christ.

V. He is the redeemer of the world. Purification of sin refers to Christ's redemptive work which is the main theme of Hebrews. "Since the object of the divine revelation is fellowship between God and man, it must culminate in one who can deal with sin as no prophet could do" (Moffatt). As no statesman, philosopher, or scientist can do. Acceptance of Christ's love and surrender to his demands frees us from the guilt and power of sin.

VI. He sits at the right hand of God. The life, death, and resurrection of Jesus are affairs of supreme importance in the history of mankind. Jesus is not one who once lived and remains now only a memory but one through whom God's presence, love, and power become available to us in life, death, and after death.—Ernest Trice Thompson.

SUNDAY: JUNE FIFTH

MORNING SERVICE

Topic: The Way of Forgiveness
TEXT: Matt. 6:12.

I. Jesus made it clear that we can be forgiven only as we forgive. He taught his disciples to pray, "Forgive us our trespasses as we forgive those who trespass against us." This is not a legalism in which we are required to do something in order to get something. It is expressing a fundamental psychological law which says we cannot accept forgiveness until we are ready to give it. Note the development of the idea of forgiving others as outlined in the Bible.

(a) The first possible reaction is unlimited vengeance. This is the ethical credo of the barbarian. Unfortunately unlimited vengeance is not merely the belief of the historic stage of civilization called barbarism. It is the barbarian in every man, even sophisticated modern man.

(b) Higher in the scale of morality than unlimited vengeance is limited vengeance. Its clearest statement is "It shall be life for life, eye for eye, tooth for tooth." We must confess this is far from being the convic-tion of only primitive men. It is widely echoed in our time.

(c) A third step is limited forgiveness. Peter knew that forgiveness was a virtue, but he wanted to know how long he must be governed by it. He asked Jesus, "Lord, how often shall my brother sin against me, and I forgive him?" When Peter had reached the specified limit of forgiveness, he was then going to do what he had wanted to do all along.

(d) Towering high above the ideal of limited forgiveness is the full Christian conception of unlimited forgiveness, the ideal and the goal of Christian ethics. When Christ said to Peter, "Seventy times seven," he was using the scriptural symbol of infinity. Nor is this an isolated statement of the principle. It underlies his admonition that we are to turn the other cheek, go the second mile, and give our cloak as well if our coat is asked for. The attitude of forgiveness is necessary if we are to be able to accept forgiveness.

II. Jesus made it clear that confession is necessary. In I John 1:9 we read, "If we confess our sins, he is faithful and just, and will forgive our sins and cleanse us from all unrighteousness."

(a) There are many misconceptions as to what is meant by confession. Confession is not necessarily the sharing of some lurid experience. It is the revealing of ourselves to God and to ourselves through communication, possibly with a person who understands and represents God to us and us to God, but it may also be opening the self in honesty to your wife or a trusted friend. How often I've heard couples say, "We haven't really talked to each other for years."

(b) Confession is a liberating grace. An old proverb says, "An honest confession is good for the soul," and how true this is. When a man wrongs or injures his neighbor, his parents, his children, his employer, or his wife, he carries with him a sense of guilt from which he is not delivered until he makes a free and full confession to the one harmed.

(c) Confession is usually difficult and we feel awkward, but how life is opened and made free when we gain the courage to accept full responsibility for our own acts and decisions. This is the only way we can stand before God as truly human. But the temptation is always there to say as did Adam: "I'm not responsible. It's this woman you gave to me."

III. Repentance is the third step. (a) There are over 100 references in the Bible to repentance and its necessity. It implies a regret at having done something we ought not to have done and an experience of growth in which harmful attitudes and desires are renounced. It implies a willingness to make amends and restitution to the best of our ability. Its importance in the eyes of Jesus is made clear in Luke 13:3 when he said to his disciples, "Except you repent, you will all likewise perish."

(b) Making amends to the one injured is not always possible, but we can do our best to restore and make new. When we have done all we can, then what is God's part in this? He forgives but not as a judge who can extend pardon to a man and then go home and forget it. God is a father who suffers with us through the cost of our mistakes and sins and brings us back to the old atmosphere of love and trust and friendship. A cross is a dramatic reminder that sin is a serious matter and forgiveness is not light-hearted.

(c) God offers forgiveness. We sometimes say, "It is his business to forgive." But let's not chatter about any light-hearted attitude which condones sin and makes forgiveness cheap and easy, confusing tolerance with indulgence. God's grace is not cheap. It cost a cross. He suffers with us in our sin that the broken bond may be restored. That's what Jesus is saying in the parable of the prodigal, and that's what the cross symbolizes.—Emerson S. Colaw.

Illustrations

RECONCILIATION.   From ancient Greece comes the report that Aristippus went to his enemy Aeschines and said, "Shall we never be reconciled until we become a table talk to all the country?" Aeschines answered that he would most gladly be at peace with him. Then Aristippus said, "Remember that though I were the elder and better man, yet I sought first with thee." Aeschines replied, "Thou art indeed a far better man than I, for I began the quarrel and thou the reconcilement." Aristippus started the process of forgiveness by going first to his enemy. So far so good. But he almost spoiled the reconciliation by reminding Aeschines that he had been the first to forgive. It is not good enough to say, "I'll forgive, but I can't forget." That keeps resentment alive in my mind. And it is even worse to say, "I'll forgive, but I won't let him forget." That keeps the resentment alive in both minds. —Ralph W. Sockman.

LAST WORDS.   Sir Thomas More, Lord Chancellor of England, having been condemned to death in a high-handed court on specious grounds, addressed his judges thus: "More have I not to say, my lords, but that St. Paul held the clothes of those who stoned Stephen to death, and as they are now both saints in heaven, and shall continue their friends forever. So I verily trust, and shall most heartily pray, that though our lordships have now here on earth been judges to my condemnation, we may nevertheless hereafter cheerfully meet in heaven in everlasting salvation."

Sermon Suggestion

PRISONERS OF HOPE.   Scripture: Zech. 9:9–13. If we are prisoners of hope in God (1) we will refuse to call wrong right and right wrong, (2) we will forgive even as we must ask God to forgive us, and (3) we will be guided and strengthened by prayer.—David W. Richardson.

Worship Aids

CALL TO WORSHIP.   "And we declare unto you glad tidings, how that the promise which was made unto the fathers, God hath fulfilled the same unto us their children." Acts 13:32–33.

INVOCATION.   O Lord Jesus Christ, who art the truth incarnate and the teacher of the faithful: let thy spirit overshadow us as we meditate on thy word and conform our thoughts to thy revelation that, learning of thee with honest hearts, we may be rooted and built up in thee, who livest and reignest with the Father and the Holy Spirit, ever one God, world without end.

OFFERTORY SENTENCE.   "Bring ye all the tithes into the storehouse, saith the Lord, [and I will] open the windows of heaven, and pour you out a blessing." Mal. 3:10.

OFFERTORY PRAYER.   Our Father, help us to trust thee more fully and to accept our responsibility toward thy work and thy children who are our brethren in Christ.

PRAYER.   Eternal Spirit, whom the heaven of heavens cannot contain, much less these temples which our hands have builded, but who dwellest in the humble and contrite heart, we worship thee. From the violence of the world and the turmoil and confusion of our busy lives we turn to thee for an hour of quiet thought, meditation, and prayer. Let the roiled waters of our lives settle. After the rapids and waterfalls of another week, grant our spirits a tranquil pool, and then send us out in a fresh direction and on a better course.

Ah, Lord, the mystery of life is very deep; we cannot fathom it. The explanation of this vast and varied universe does not lie within the comprehension of our minds. Today we pray humbly for light enough to walk by. Lead us in paths of righteousness for thy name's sake. Give us the eyes of faith that can see the way despite life's mystery and the world's discordant noises.

To that end lift us above the immediate and set our lives in the wide horizons of abiding verities. Our eyes grow too accustomed to man's ugliness and sin and to the world's tumult and disorder. Today remind us of the goodness that is here, of the beauty that our eyes have seen in nature and in human life, of friendliness that has been visited upon us, love that has sustained us, character that has undergirded us, and of thy goodness that has been patient with us. Today put Christ in our remembrance and those strong and radiant lives who have followed in his steps. Awaken gratitude in the hearts of some of us who have forgotten to give thanks, and around the evil that depresses us throw great memories and wide hopes. —Harry Emerson Fosdick.

EVENING SERVICE

Topic: Four Goals for Living (Baccalaureate)

TEXT: Prov. 4:18.

I. In trust, keep God central in your life. The nature of being human is that there will be moments of high joy and moments of deep pain for you, but most of your life will be lived on a plateau somewhere between extreme joy and great hurt. If you walk with God regularly on the plateaus, you will be able to find God at all times, including the moments of pain and joy, and you will be sustained.

II. Risk loving people of all ages. Humans are so created that we develop our full potentials only in a variety of relationships with other persons. God intends that such relationships grow. There are risks involved in loving. When those you love suffer, you will suffer with them. And when those you love reject your love, you will suffer. But if you do not give your love to others, you cannot be the complete person God intends you to be, and your life will be empty. Risk loving and be fulfilled.

III. Believe in yourself without being egotistical. You have many genuine abilities. When you function in the areas of your skills, do so with confidence but without arrogance. Remember that all humans also have weaknesses. Try to know what your weaknesses are and find ways to grow, especially in areas where weaknesses reduce your effectiveness as a servant of God or impede your feeling secure when with your associates.

IV. Live up to your highest standards. There will be many who will try to pull you down to their level. Resist such attempts. Remember that it is easier to lose your self-respect than to regain it. You have to live with yourself. Try always to be the kind of person you want to live with.—Elmer A. Thompson.

SUNDAY: JUNE TWELFTH

MORNING SERVICE

Topic: God's Unexpected Ways
Text: John 6:42.
I. The New Testament says that Jesus surprised his countrymen. Perhaps more accurately one should say he shocked them. When he went home to preach in Nazareth, the neighbors were incredulous. One said in a kind of stunned puzzlement, "Is this not Joseph's son?" The longer Jesus talked, the more their surprise turned to anger. At last they drove him from town and would have flung him from a cliff.

(a) Apparently Jesus surprised the people because they were unprepared to find anything they could call prophetic in the form of a son of a carpenter's family in the local village.

(b) He surprised the people by what he taught. In a culture that valued legality among themselves and retribution against their conquerors, he surprised them by honoring grace and love and forgiveness.

(c) Jesus surprised his friends and neighbors and countrymen by his associations. He lived among peasants and fisher folk, speaking and ministering to sinners, or those identified as sinners. He illustrated the good neighbor with the story of the hated Samaritan who responded to human need.

(d) He surprised his followers by claiming no special privileges of immunity from those who opposed him. He tried to advise his followers, but finally they were left in shocked disarray when he went to the cross and risked everything upon their understanding of his words and his life.

II. A few people in that time began to reflect on what Jesus said and did. They came to see that his life represented, in the words of Paul, "a more excellent way." His teachings provided a new set of values. They provided a new way of looking at reality and of ordering society.

(a) For those who heard of him and believed that in some wondrous way God revealed his purposes in Jesus, there was a need to find a metaphor to express their sense of gratitude. From the analogy of human experience and with a sense of what would be the most precious human gift came these beautiful words: "For God so loved the world that he gave his only begotten Son."

(b) What a surprise that the Creator of this universe, who made light shine out of darkness, is the same God who revealed in the face of Jesus Christ that he cares about each of us. He invites us, does not coerce, and asks us to learn and follow the teachings of Jesus to find a new life of harmony with God and man.

(c) In the spirit of God's own gift we ought to find ways to surprise others with acts of kindness, concern, and love. Each of us, made in the image of God, gives good gifts, surprising our neighbors and friends and the stranger who is in need. If we are to respond to the spirit of God's surprising gift our challenge is to surprise others with kindness, generosity, and love.
—Allen K. Jackson.

Illustrations

GIFT OF HEALING. We are all familiar with the medallion on the back of a physician's car showing the sign of the snake entwined around a staff. It is the symbol of the god Aesculapius. The Christian uses the snake as a symbol of sexuality or evil, but the Greeks used the snake as a symbol of healing. Their myth recognized that the mind affects the body. They had developed a whole process whereby one could go to the temple of this god and undergo a period of purification and reorientation.

The myth behind it is interesting. A person supposedly had all the attributes of life except immortality. If he found and ate a certain substance he would have his immortality. He found it, but being tired from the pursuit of seeking it, he fell asleep. While the man was asleep, a snake came and ate this precious substance. He woke up and cried, "I have lost my immortality." But according to the myth, at that moment the snake shed its skin and said, "But I give to you the healing of the renewing of your mind, your spirit, and your body, year after year. You do not have immortality, but you do have the power of renewal."

This great truth of renewal is in both the Old and New Testaments and in modern science. The human being has a gift from God in being able to renew itself by the action of mind over body.—Bryant M. Kirkland.

BEHOLD! George Washington Carver was a devout Christian, and each day he made it a point to have a quiet time. He began his prayers with one word: "Behold!" The theme of his meditation was always the same: "Behold! What will God show me?" It was his way of opening his mind to God's wonderful world. Quietly, passively he waited in faith for God to reveal something new. He was in a sense letting go of his own world-view to let God lead him. Patiently and with trust he waited. One day, as he began his quiet time, Carver happened to be holding a sweet potato. And God said to him: "Behold! What can you do with it?" Today, if you visit Tuskegee Institute in Alabama, you can see samples of the 118 things that Dr. Carver did with the sweet potato. Actually he redefined the sweet potato. He saw this creation of God from a new perspective, and in doing so he unlocked some of God's secrets.—Richard F. Grein.

Sermon Suggestions

DISCIPLINE IN THE HOME. Texts: Prov. 29:15, 17. (1) Discipline is necessary. (2) Discipline and love are not antithetical. (3) Discipline can be administered in many different ways. (4) Our discipline must be consistent. (5) The goal of our discipline must be eventually to lead our children to the point of self-discipline. (6) Discipline must be given in the context of love.—Brian L. Harbour.

WHAT IS A CHURCH FAMILY? Text: Gal. 6:10. (1) A church family is people eating together. (2) A church family is children. (3) A church family is music. (4) A church family is sharing. (5) A church family is laughter and tears. (6) A church family is one body in Christ.—Jeannette N. Lohner.

Worship Aids

CALL TO WORSHIP. "Both young men, and maidens; old men, and children: let them praise the name of the Lord: for his name alone is excellent; his glory is above the earth and heaven." Ps. 148: 12–13.

INVOCATION. Eternal God our Father, who art from everlasting, thou hast made us and not we ourselves. Thou hast set us never far from thee, that we, thy children, may learn the ways of freedom and choose thee with all our hearts. Grant us now thy Holy Spirit that, confident in prayer, we may worship thee with gladness and become as little children before thee.

OFFERTORY SENTENCE. "If ye then, being evil, know how to give good gifts unto your children: how much more shall your heavenly Father give the Holy Spirit, to them that ask him?" Luke 11:13.

OFFERTORY PRAYER. O Father of our Lord Jesus Christ, we dedicate these offerings to the fellowship of him, whom to know aright is life eternal.

PRAYER. O thou whose promise is to us and to our children, we thank thee for the constant renewal of life through the coming of children into the world and for the new hope and joy their advent brings.

Here at thy altar thou hast heard the solemn promise of men and women to whom thou hast entrusted the care of innocent and precious little lives. Who save thyself knoweth the divine possibilities which, when trained by them to Christian manhood and womanhood, they may disclose? O thou great parent of us all, give to human parents wisdom and strength to fulfill their vows.

Thou knowest the frailty and uncertainty of our mortal life. To thy fatherly protection we commend our children. May they, like Jesus, grow in wisdom and stature, in favor with God and man. May they become such men as other men will honor and women trust and children love and such women as will make glad the homes in which they dwell.

We care not ask that they be kept from sorrow, strife, and temptation, but we pray thee to cleanse and heal their sorrow that there may be no bitterness in their pain, to arm them for the strife that they may be able to withstand in the evil day, and to make temptation their opportunity to win the moral victory and go from strength to strength and come off more than conquerors.—Frank Halliday Ferris.

EVENING SERVICE

Topic: A Call for Christian Manhood
TEXT: I Cor. 16:13–14.

I. *Strong physical manhood.* (a) God is interested in our bodies as well as our souls, for the body is the temple of the Holy Spirit. The Bible stresses the sacredness of physical manhood. It is becoming increasingly evident that as a nation we are going soft. The health of manhood is being ruined by the sins against the body —intemperance, harmful habits, lust, and all that goes with these vices.

(b) When God made all of creation, it is recorded, "And God saw that it was good." But man has taken so many of the good things which God made and has spoiled and desecrated them. He has taken the good gifts and has put them to foolish uses.

II. *Strong moral manhood.* (a) The admonition of Paul, "Quit you like men," refers to moral strength as well. Morality is at the bottom of all permanent strength and lasting progress. A man cannot be physically and mentally strong for very long if his moral and ethical codes are faulty. Immorality weakens the body and destroys manhood. God said to Joshua when he was getting ready to lead the people of Israel across the Jordan River, "Be strong and of good courage." God cannot use a coward.

(b) Our text pleads for the kind of courage that will stand up for principle rather than have popularity, that would rather be right than rich, that would rather die than lie, and that would rather starve than steal. The moral code of America and that of the nations of the world is on the skids. History shows what happens to men and nations when they forget God and morality. Wealth, affluence, education, and armaments have never saved a nation.

III. *Strong spiritual manhood.* (a) Most important is strong spiritual manhood. Only men and women who speak the mind and will of God can restore the world to sanity. Intellectualism will not do it. Materialism cannot do it. Only the power of God in Christ will change men's hearts and lives.

(b) There is abroad in our nation disrespect and disregard for law and order which can only lead to chaos and confusion. Before it becomes too late, we have to come back to faith and confidence in God. Fathers must find, uphold, and defend the ideals of applied Christianity for their families and for our nation.—C. Reuben Anderson.

SUNDAY: JUNE NINETEENTH

MORNING SERVICE

Topic: A Lost Christian Virtue

TEXT: Ps. 51:17.

I. What do you think is the most important Christian virtue? Would you say love? Or would you choose spiritual wisdom? Perhaps you think leadership ability is paramount. Maybe you feel purity is the greatest virtue for a Christian to possess.

(a) All of these are good ideals. But none of them remotely approaches the basic element that is the most important virtue in the Christian life. Not even love, you ask? That's right, not even love. Without this virtue, real love cannot exist. This virtue is called brokenness.

(b) David gained this knowledge through the pain of being broken in heart himself. In contrition he cried out for God to forgive his unholy actions against Uriah, and God forgave him. David knew what brokenness really was.

II. Where is the brokenness that characterized the giants of the Bible?

(a) Isaiah knew what a broken spirit was. When he saw God, he cried out, "Woe is me!" A conviction of personal and national sin overwhelmed him. He stood in absolute awe before the Lord on his throne and realized his own utter unworthiness. It was through the mercy of the Lord that he was cleansed from sin.

(b) Peter knew the reality of a broken heart. He had boastfully declared his loyalty for the Master. Others might deny him, but he never would. Yet the night had not passed before Peter did deny Christ, not once but three times. "And the Lord turned, and looked upon Peter. And Peter remembered the word of the Lord. . . . And Peter went out, and wept bitterly" (Luke 22:61–62). Truly Peter repented with a broken heart.

(c) Perhaps the greatest New Testament example of brokenness is that of Saul— Saul the destroyer who ransacked the believers' homes and threw men and women alike into the unspeakable horror of the Roman prisons and persecuted the Chris-

tians with all his might because he believed he was right. On the Damascus Road, when Jesus personally confronted him, Saul's reaction was one of brokenness. "And he trembling and astonished said, Lord what wilt thou have me to do?" (Acts 9:6). From this repentance came a life so changed that he was no longer known as Saul the destroyer but as Paul the worker.

III. Brokenness results from conviction of sin, repentance, and conversion. It characterized the life of every godly biblical person. It should characterize the life of every true believer.

(a) Perhaps the spirit of the age—the world's concept of self-sufficiency—has made it unpopular to be broken before the Lord. Nowadays church people are supposed to be go-getters, able to deal with people, and educated. These things are good, but they cannot substitute for brokenness.

(b) A broken spirit must be learned through the experiences of life. There is a broken and contrite heart that results from conversion when one honestly admits he cannot stand before God without a savior. Too often this is as far as it goes. One admits his need for God in the hereafter but denies any need for him in this life.

IV. When brokenness comes, there is no mistaking it. There is a gentleness now, a humility, and a teachable spirit.

(a) There is a strength of character resulting from knowing and doing God's will instead of one's own. There exists an objective admission of one's faults. No longer does pride, ambition, or a desire for power hold sway in the believer's life. Such things are identified as sin and are repented of instead of being ignored, denied, or excused and condoned. The cross is no longer merely historical. It now has a very personal meaning.

(b) Brokenness leaves its mark on one's life, not just as a one-time experience but as a continuing attitude of life. A broken life has the sweet and holy power to draw men to the Savior. Brokenness is the vital necessity for a life empowered by God. It springs from one's realization of his vital need for God.

(c) Brokenness has many names—death to self, sanctification, surrender, the lordship of Christ. Yet it is strangely indefinable. The world cannot understand it. The shallow Christian is afraid of it. But to one who has tasted of its fruits, brokenness is his most precious possession. In his need he has found God, and he glories in it.—Martha Lou Farmer.

Illustrations

TEARS.   A child was very upset at bedtime, and his father came into his bedroom to comfort him. His father lay next to him and listened to him share his broken heart. Finally the son had talked it out and cried it out, and he was ready to go to sleep. At this point the father eased his way out of the bed and went back to his own room. In readjusting himself for sleep, the boy moved over where his father had been lying and found that that part of the pillow was wet also. His father had been crying with him.—Thomas C. Short.

ONE CONDITION.   Some botanists were looking for a rare flower on land that was owned by a man who had a son. They found a very fine specimen of this rare flower growing on a ledge far down a steep cliff. They asked the boy if he would allow them to tie a rope around his waist so they could lower him over this precipice to fetch this rare specimen of the flower. The boy said he would go on one condition. They must let his father hold the rope.—Clarence J. Forsberg.

Sermon Suggestions

OUR GREAT HIGH PRIEST.   Scripture: Heb. 4:14–5:10. (1) Jesus sympathizes with us as no other can. (a) With our weaknesses. (b) With our sufferings. (2) He offered a sacrifice no other could. (a) A sacrifice to end all sacrifices. (b) A sacrifice that is the source of eternal salvation.—Gerhard Aho.

GIFTS A FATHER CAN GIVE.   Text: Matt. 7:9–11. (1) The gift of time. (2) The gift of love. (3) The gift of a positive, joyous faith in Jesus.—Joe A. Harding.

Worship Aids

CALL TO WORSHIP.   "Great is the Lord, and greatly to be praised; and his greatness is unsearchable. One generation shall praise thy works to another, and shall declare thy mighty works." Ps. 145:3–4.

INVOCATION.   Almighty and everlasting God, who givest to all who desire it the spirit of grace and supplication, deliver us, O Lord, from all coldness of heart and from all indifferent wandering of the mind, that we may fix our affection upon thee and upon thy service. Fill us with holy, peaceful, and beautiful thoughts, that with steadfast minds and kindled affection we may worship thee in spirit and in truth.

OFFERTORY SENTENCE.   "If there be first a willing mind, it is accepted according to that which a man hath, and not according to that which he hath not." II Cor. 8:12.

OFFERTORY PRAYER.   O heavenly Father, we pray that thy blessings, which are as countless as the stars, may be so used as to bring light and love to thy children everywhere.

PRAYER.   O God of all the earth and every creature, we rejoice and give thanks for thy mercy which is more varied even than our need; for the way over which we have come and all that was good in it; for the way that still lies before us and the opportunity to call it thine own; and for men and women in whose living we have seen no death and for those great persons who, having died, live in our memory and spirit forever.

O God of our fathers and our future, by all our conflicts, by all our hopes, by all our happiness and all our sorrow, move through us and in spite of us to bring alive the joy of the Lord in the souls of all who watch and wait. And when the time thou hast given us is ended, grant that we may commend into thy keeping both ourselves and those we love and also those we do not know or, knowing, have not loved, that we may rest in thy care without fear and without regret.—G. Stewart Barns.

EVENING SERVICE

Topic: Responsible Fatherhood (Father's Day)
TEXT: Luke 11:11.

I. As a father I must be responsible for the livelihood of my family. I have an obligation to provide the very best I can for my family.

II. As a father I must be responsible for the spiritual welfare of my family. I am the spiritual leader. I must pray with my family and for my family. I must be an exemplary Christian. I must read the Bible with them and urge them to read the Bible. I must set the example of Christian service and urge them to be faithful servants of Christ.

III. As a father I must be responsible for the morale of my family and help provide a happy atmosphere in our home. This means I must smile and be pleasant even during times when I don't feel like smiling and when it is not easy to be pleasant. It means I will not impose upon my family problems and situations which will disturb and worry them unnecessarily.

IV. As a father I must be responsible for family fellowship and recreation. This means I must provide time to relax with my family and to enjoy various family activities.

V. As a father I must be responsible for encouragement when it is needed. This means I must carefully observe my family, and when one of the members is discouraged or disheartened, I must be there to assist.

VI. As a father I must be responsible for celebration when it is called for. This means I must be happy when one of my family members is successful in an endeavor or is recognized for some accomplishment. It is important that my family members know I am proud of them and want to share their joys with them.

VII. As a father I must be responsible for their recovery when they are sick. This means I will go to the greatest extent possible to provide for their health and physical well-being.

VIII. As a father I must be responsible for guidance to my children in education, career-choosing, marriage, and in their becoming parents. This means I may have to sacrifice personal pleasure to be of assistance, yet, as a father, I want to help them.—O. W. Polen in *Church of God Evangel.*

SUNDAY: JUNE TWENTY-SIXTH

MORNING SERVICE

Topic: The Early Church Set the Pattern
TEXT: Heb. 12:2.

I. The early church was a small, solitary church—just 120 to begin with, but they did not feel they had to play it big or have an inferiority complex just because they were not as large or as mighty as other established religions. We need to be ourselves and not try to depend on size for our power. If we are empowered from on high we can fulfill our mission and become an integral part of the kingdom of God.

II. The early church was an obedient, expectant church. It was a praying church. The church expected something to happen. They believed the scriptures. They knew they needed a power that would get them out of their hiding place to witness. They were free to be instruments in the hands of the Lord and were not even worried because those outside said they were drunk. Those outside of the church want to see fire upon our heads, hear us glorify God, and hear the message of salvation in their own languages.

III. The early church sought the direction of the Holy Spirit in making their decisions. The Holy Spirit helped them in choosing the one to take the place of Judas. The Holy Spirit helped them choose the first foreign missionaries. They did not ask physicians or psychiatrists if they thought the candidates were eligible for the mission they were to fulfill, nor did they ask the heathen nations what type of missionary would be the most acceptable to them. (See Acts 13:2.)

IV. The early church was of one accord. God never works in the place of strife and confusion but in the place of harmony and unity. We have hundreds of different personalities in our church. Some of us can be sons of thunder like James and John, while others can be sons of reconciliation and consolation like Barnabas. But when it comes to the final endeavor to do God's work, we must be of one accord. We cannot succeed at building the church when we have those who foster factions and divisions. We need cooperation and not strife.

V. The early church took murmuring with graciousness. Acts 6 tells us that the Grecians murmured because their widows were being neglected. The twelve apostles knew that the accusations were against them because they had been so busy with preaching, baptizing, and performing miracles that they had left something undone. I can almost hear Peter saying, "It is not good for the church to be divided over this question and the devil wants to divide us, but we will not let him split us and hinder us from being instruments for people to be saved." The apostles did not say: "We are the heads of the church, and no one else knows how the church should be run. If you Grecians continue to murmur against us, we will excommunicate you, and you know we can do it." I can almost hear John say, "Brethren, I am sorry this thing has come up, and we must correct this situation. Let's call the whole congregation and see what all of us can come up with." The church could not afford to allow little sentimentalities to get in the way of reconciliation. When the devil can manage to get us to split, the world will laugh at us and the Lord's work will suffer.

VI. The early church was a materially poor church. (See Acts 3:6.) They might have been poor in material things, but they were rich in spiritual power. There is no blessing in being poor or condemnation in being rich. The danger is to lose the power to make men walk. They were not rich, but there were no needy ones among them because they all shared with each other what they had.

VII. The early church had a wide range of activity and witness. They went from house to house. They were not confined to the four walls of the temple. They broke bread together. Wonders and signs took place. They prayed for people and things happened. They rejoiced and were not afraid to be criticized for witnessing what the Lord had done for them.

VIII. The early church broke many barriers—the sex barrier between men and women, the social barrier between slaves and free men and between rich and poor, the racial barriers between Jews and Gentiles and between whites and blacks or yellow and Indians, and the international barrier. Paul never knew when he crossed from one country to another, from one language to another, and from one culture to another. He was a debtor to the wise and to the unwise, to the Greeks and to the barbarians.—Jose D. Fajardo.

Illustrations

PERSUASIVE FRIENDSHIP. Dyonisius of Syracuse was a cruel despot. He once condemned a man named Pythias to death. When Pythias begged leave to visit his aged parents before submitting himself to the cross, his friend Damon stepped forward and offered himself as a hostage to be held until Pythias returned. For some reason Dyonisius consented to the arrangement, and after a lengthy absence involving a long sea journey, Pythias at last returned to be executed, and Damon was spared. Dyonisius was touched by this scene, his cynicism and hard-heartedness dissolved. "Let me become a party to this friendship," he said, "and I will free you both."—Bruce Robertson.

PRAYER. My God and my Lord, take me away from my own self, and let me belong completely to you.

My God and my Lord, take away from me everything that keeps me apart from you.

My God and my Lord, grant me everything that draws me closer to you.—St. Nicholas of Flue.

Sermon Suggestions

BUILDING UP THE CHURCH. Scripture: I Cor. 3:10–11, 16–23. (1) God commissions us to build up the church. (2) Jesus Christ provides the foundation for building up the church. (3) The Holy Spirit dwells in those who build the church.—Harold H. Zietlow.

WHY CHURCHES GROW. Text: Acts 16:5. (1) The people hear the word. (2) The people tell others. (3) The people follow their leaders. (4) The people warmly love.—Bailey Smith.

Worship Aids

CALL TO WORSHIP. "How beautiful upon the mountains are the feet of him that bringeth good tidings, that publisheth peace; that publisheth salvation; that saith unto Zion, Thy God reigneth!" Isa. 52:7.

INVOCATION. Almighty and everlasting God, whom the heaven of heavens cannot contain, much less the temples which our hands have built, but who art ever nigh unto the humble and the contrite: grant thy Holy Spirit, we beseech thee, to us who are here assembled, that cleansed and illumined by thy grace, we may worthily show forth thy praise, meekly learn the word, render due thanks for thy mercies, and obtain a gracious answer to our prayers.

OFFERTORY SENTENCE. "I will freely sacrifice unto thee: I will praise thy name, O Lord; for it is good." Ps. 54:6.

OFFERTORY PRAYER. Our Father, help us to love thee so well that we shall have all thy kingdom interests and all thy children at heart.

PRAYER. For all the things for which we have never given thanks to thee, O Lord, we humbly bow our hearts. For common things of earth which sustain our bodies in health and strength, though we pay scant attention to them, we give thee thanks. For far-off things in the ages past or in lands distant from us which enlarge our heritage and expand our horizon, we give thee thanks. For invisible things of heaven and earth which sweeten life with beauty and grace, we give thee thanks. For things of the spirit which disclose to us the beauty of thy holiness and sanctify the passing time with eternal meaning, we give thee thanks. For things bought with a great price, given to us without cost, by which we are deepened and heightened to the measure of Christ our Lord, we give thee thanks. Though there be no end to thy gifts, help us to number them as they are revealed to us day by day.—Samuel H. Miller.

EVENING SERVICE

Topic: Sharing the Continuing Ministry of Jesus
TEXT: Acts 1:1–2.

I. Acts opens with an arresting statement. Luke calls the attention of Theophilus to the previous book he had written about "all that Jesus began to do and to teach, until the day he was taken up."

(a) The gospel of Luke sets forth the earthly ministry of Jesus from the time of his birth until he was raised from the dead.

(b) The words, deeds, and personal presence of Jesus represent the mightiest act of God in history in which he visited mankind with the light of his truth, the warmth of his love, and the integrity of his righteousness. This ministry of Jesus Christ is the culmination of the ministry of Israel and the fountain of the ministry of the Christian movement in subsequent history.

II. What Jesus Christ began to do and teach was continued. (a) The discouraged disciples entered into a new phase of the ministry of Jesus Christ. They thought the ministry of Christ was finished. Through the night of despair and bewilderment and fear they waited as they were instructed.

(b) Then Jesus returned. This time he appeared in a new form to take up his new body, which is the church. This was the promise he had made but which the disciples never fully understood.

III. Christ was raised from the dead. He now came alive in a new body which was to continue his ministry in a vaster and grander way.

(a) The disciples now shared Christ's ministry. Through their Spirit-inspired and empowered ministry the gospel would be preached, works of mercy and compassion would be effected, the divine-human fellowship would be manifested, and the purpose of God in Christ would make its way through history.

(b) The Christian community is the mission of the living God whose history began after Jesus had completed so perfectly the ministry his Father gave him to do. A clearer realization of this truth would not only dignify the work of the church but also point the church to its crucial and central ministry.

(c) The church is an integral part of God's mission to redeem the world. The acts of the apostles continue. What Jesus began to do and teach we seek to carry on humbly. And in that service we have the fellowship of the Spirit.—Elmer G. Homrighausen.

SUNDAY: JULY THIRD

MORNING SERVICE

Topic: Responsible Citizenship (Independence Sunday)

Text: Rom. 13:7.

I. *The call to respect.* The Bible makes it clear that Christians are called to an attitude of respect for the goals of government. Government is the instrument of God's choosing for the creation of security and the development of minimal rules for all to follow.

(a) Christians are in serious danger of failing to be responsible to the biblical calling when they despise the potential for good which is possible through politics. You and I hear constantly the negative pictures of politicians as crooked, self-interested, and uncaring for others. Such an attitude is to overlook the opportunity for a positive and effective ministry to persons which is possible through government.

(b) Respect requires action. Too often Christians have participated in citizenship concerns in a negative way. They are seldom heard from by political leaders when positive legislation is proposed to enhance life through improved education, more equitable criminal justice, support systems for the mentally ill, consumer protection, expanded employment opportunities, reform of the judiciary, or a reduction in nuclear arms.

II. *The call to protest.* (a) The Bible makes it clear that Christians are not to idolize their governments. Contrary to much biblical understanding, Christians are never called to support oppressive, racist, or God-defying governments. The Bible enjoins an active protest against such behavior.

(1) Rom. 13 has too often been wrongly interpreted to mean love for the state instead of respect for it. Paul admonishes the Romans to support their government to the degree it is deserving of support. Yet in Rom. 13:8 he insists that one must love one's neighbors whether or not he deserves it. It is a different relationship between persons and the relationship of persons to the structures which govern their lives.

(2) John understood this quite clearly in Rev. 13. The Roman state had lost its right to respect by claiming divinity for its emperor and demanding a confession of lordship from Christians who could only protest, "Jesus is my Lord." John heaps the wrath of God's judgment upon this "beast" who would claim power which belongs only to God.

(b) Our nation was born in protest against tyranny and rooted in the rights of the people to replace bad government with good government. Our Declaration of Independence and Constitution are models of the ideals of freedom for oppressed people around the world. How sorrowful we should feel when we fail to live up to our own dream of liberty, justice, and the pursuit of happiness for all.

(c) While we shall never fully embody this impossible dream, we ought to protest every law, every judicial decision, and every administrative action which falls short of the dream by working for improvements in our political life. Let us not be accused of idolatry by allowing our government to fall short of the best of which it is capable.

III. *The call to participation.* (a) The Bible makes it clear that Christians are called to participate in their government. The most explicit form of participation is the payment of taxes. Jesus made it clear that involvement in politics was not optional when he challenged those who would withhold taxes from Caesar. "Render unto Caesar that which belongs to Caesar."

(b) Christians must enter the arena of political power, compromise, negotiation, and decision making to insure the most equitable and just use of tax money.

(1) The power to tax is ultimately the power to govern. It is symbolic of the most fundamental act of citizenship which can be performed. Every Christian has the responsibility of participation in government by paying taxes, by voicing one's concerns to those who levy, collect, and spend taxes, by replacing those who abuse the power of taxation, and by working steadfastly to insure budgets rooted in righteousness.

(2) Christian protest is ultimately a refusal to allow Caesar to use the tax dollar for unrighteous purposes. The American Revolution was fought over a slogan, "No taxation without representation."

(c) The Christian political credo ought to be "no taxation for the destruction of human persons, no taxation for the support of religion, no taxation for the benefit of the few, no taxation for the support of immorality, no taxation to maintain racism, and no taxation for injustice." The call of Jesus to participate in Caesar's work is always tempered by the more powerful calling for every person to render unto God the things which are God's.—Larry McSwain.

Illustrations

CELEBRATION OF DEMOCRACY. Xenophon was a part of a Greek mercenary force of ten thousand troops attached to a much larger Asian force led by Cyrus. The general Cyrus was on an expedition into Asia against a vastly overwhelming force, hoping to steal the throne from his brother Artaxerxes. By great military prowess he overcame the enemy deep in their own territory but died in the battle, leaving his Greek mercenaries with a victory but now no cause since he was to have become king. Accepting an invitation from the Persian general to a conference, all the Greek generals were massacred, leaving the ten thousand leaderless. Xenophon was then elected leader, and this is where the appeal of the story for Greeks was established. Against great odds, deep in enemy territory, harrassed constantly, they fought their way to the Black Sea, built ships, and sailed home.

What fascinated the Greeks about this story was that it demonstrated how free men, voting for leaders, making decisions as a group in the field of contest were more flexible, capable, and motivated than people living under dictatorial despots. The *Anabasis* was for the Greeks a celebration of democracy.—George Alder.

DAWN. In 1833 the British Parliament voted to abolish the institution of slavery in the crown colony of Jamaica, and a certain date was set when the emancipation proclamation would go into effect. On the night before that glorious day the slaves did not sleep. Instead they dressed in their finest clothes and streamed up the mountain sides so that they could catch the first glimpse of the dawning of the new day. When the first rays of light streaked across the horizon, the slaves erupted into unrestrained ecstasy. And on that day a Negro spiritual was born which has been often used today: "Free at last, free at last, thank God almighty, free at last!"—Brian L. Harbour.

SYMBOLS AND SHRINES. When the American colonies began to realize the need of union in their effort to redress the wrongs of taxation without representation, the colonists sent delegates to a Continental Congress. They passed a Declaration of Independence. They adopted Articles of Confederation and finally a Federal Constitution. Thus they had signed statements in black and white.

Were not these enough? No, people are not inspired and sustained merely by documents in black and white. On January 2, 1776, at Cambridge, Massachusetts, Washington displayed a flag of thirteen stripes and with it the Union Jack, from which evolved, about a year later, the flag of these United States, with its stars and stripes. Our flag is only a piece of colored cloth. Yet who can measure the influence of that emblem as school children stand to salute it? What would happen to our morale if we removed all symbols, all shrines, and all monuments from our national scene?—Ralph W. Sockman.

Worship Aids

CALL TO WORSHIP. "Know therefore that the Lord thy God, he is God, the faithful God, which keepeth covenant and mercy with them that love him and keep his commandments to a thousand generations." Deut. 7:9.

INVOCATION. Almighty God, regard, we beseech thee, thy church, set amid the perplexities of a changing order and face to face with new tasks. Fill us afresh with thy spirit that we may bear witness boldly to the coming of thy kingdom and hasten the time when the knowledge of thyself shall encircle the earth as the waters cover the sea.

OFFERTORY SENTENCE. "Every man hath his proper gift of God, one after this manner, and another after that." I Cor. 7:7.

OFFERTORY PRAYER. We thank thee, O God, for another anniversary of our nation's independence and pray that this rich gift may be an opportunity to serve one another in love.

PRAYER. Our God and Father, who art the source of the truth which makes men free, help us to be loyal to the truth we have and humble before the truth we have yet to discover. Help us, we pray, to use more responsibly the freedom we have and to yield to others the freedom to differ from us.

We praise thee, O God, for the humble and the great who over many decades have bequeathed to us a heritage of freedom. For legislators who have established our liberties in law; for lawyers who have defended the just rights of the radical and the reactionary; for teachers who have imbued new generations with a sense of the freedom that belongs to others; for all who in conversation with friends and neighbors and associates have helped to change the attitudes and thoughts of others; for ministers of thy church who have made the freedom which we have in Christ relevant to the issues of liberty in today's world—for all these who came before us we render our thanksgiving to thee.

Our Father, may this be a living heritage for us, like a sharp sword dividing the substance from the pretense of freedom. By thy Holy Spirit within us and among us grant us to become worthy citizens of a nation which proclaims to others that it is the home of the free. May each yield to each the right of hearing as well as of speaking and the freedom to read as well as to write. Apart from the law, may we never deem ourselves wise enough to decide what others should not read or hear or worthy enough to judge another's patriotism or loyalty.—Cameron P. Hall.

EVENING SERVICE

Topic: Christ or Caesar?
TEXT: Matt. 22:21.
For many Christians these words suggest that politics and religion should be kept completely separate. The state must not interfere with the activities of the church. The church must not interfere with the activities of the state. Two separate worlds exist—one ruled by Caesar and the other ruled by God. Since the Christian must live in both worlds at once, he must walk a tightrope as he seeks to avoid giving offense either to Caesar or to God.

I. Most of the time we are able to live without any sense of conflict between these two worlds. When the demands of the state do conflict with the demands of God, the sincere Christian has a problem. For then he must decide whether he will obey God or Caesar. History attests that this can be one of the most difficult decisions that any Christian can be called upon to make.

(a) Some Christians, responding to the voice of their Christian consciences, have opposed unjust, dishonest, and immoral policies of their nation. Many of them have been maligned, smeared, or condemned by many of their countrymen. Citizenship will not guarantee immunity from the condemnation of patriotic neighbors.

(b) There have always been sincere, misguided Christians who, believing that the world of Caesar and the world of Christ are completely separate and distinct, have supported public policies that have run roughshod over everything that Christ and Christianity stand for.

II. Was Jesus actually dividing the world into two spheres—one, physical, social, and political to be ruled by Caesar and the other, religious, spiritual, and otherworldly to be ruled by God? How can any Christian think that Jesus, God's faithful and obedient Son, actually elevated proud, unjust, and immoral Caesar to a position of such power and status that he could stand on the same level with God and rule the political sphere with the same authority and power as that with which God rules the realm of the spirit? Jesus did not mean to designate Caesar and God as co-equal rulers of two separate and distinct dominions.

III. What are some of the implications of Jesus' challenging statement? (a) He reminds us that God alone is the sovereign Creator, Lord, and Ruler of all existence. God comes first. He claims, he deserves, and he must have our first allegiance and our highest loyalty. Since all power comes from God, Caesar must exercise whatever power he has under the rule of God.

(b) No man, no state, and no government can command the Christian conscience. The right of the Christian to follow the dictates of his own conscience is God-given and unalienable. When the policies of the state seem just and fair, Christians should support these policies. When the policies of the state serve unjust, unrighteous, and immoral ends and when they lead to wars of aggression and exploitation, to the oppression of the weak and helpless, and to the denial of human rights and human dignity and human opportunity, the Christian must cry out in protest and work to change them, for he serves as the conscience of the state.

IV. Jesus points us to the true and higher kind of patriotism. There is a form of patriotism that prompts too many of our citizens to give blind, unreasoning support to every law and policy that the leaders of our nation adopt. Caesar speaks!

(a) It is a naive kind of patriotism that is based on the mistaken assumption that our nation and its leaders have always been on the side of the angels and that for one to criticize the state is tantamount to criticizing God.

(b) Jesus calls us to a higher patriotism than this. It is the patriotism of the informed, thoughtful, compassionate, and constructively critical Christian citizen. It is the kind of patriotism reflected in the words, "America: love it and help make it better!"—C. K. Norville.

SUNDAY: JULY TENTH

MORNING SERVICE

Topic: On Loving and Being Loved
TEXT: John 15:12.

That love is needed there is no doubt. The question is how is the need to be satisfied? Is love an art? Or is it, as the Bible suggests, something done, accomplished, an expression of concern by one sensitive to human souls? If so, then it requires knowledge, effort, commitment, and decision. Or is it just a pleasant sensation, a matter of chance, something you fall into if you're lucky and something you fall out of if you're unlucky? It is not that people think that love is not important. They are starved for it. Yet hardly anyone thinks that there is anything that needs to be learned about love. This peculiar attitude is based on several premises which tend to uphold it.

I. The first premise is that most people see the problem of love as that of being loved rather than that of loving and of one's capacity to love.

(a) The problem is seen to be how to be loved, how to be lovable, how to be accepted, and how to be well thought of. The massive pursuit of these aims follows many paths. One, which is especially used by men, is to be successful or rich or powerful. Another, used especially by women, is to make oneself attractive by cultivating one's body, dress, poise, etc. Other ways used by both men and women are cultivating pleasant manners, good conversation techniques, sense of humor, etc.

(b) The goal is to represent oneself to the world as an attractive package, desirable to the world. What most people in our culture mean by being lovable is essentially a mixture between being popular and having sex appeal.

II. The second premise leading to the conclusion that the problem of love is primarily that of being loved rather than that of loving and of one's capacity to love is this: the problem of love is a problem of finding an object to love rather than the ability to love.

(a) People think that to love is simple but that to find the right object to love— or be loved by—is difficult. The procedure then is, first, to make oneself lovable or attractive and, second, to go shopping for an object. In our culture, based upon appetite buying and on the idea of a mutually favorable exchange, this concept is a natural carryover into the area of mate seeking. The man looks for an attractive girl and the girl for an attractive man, the best available, considering one's own exchange values.

(b) It is unfortunate that many a divorce takes place for no greater reason than that the package is now shopworn and unattractive. What is attractive seems to depend on the fashion of the time. The mass media continually preaches the gospel of how to be lovable. They set up the laws and rules to conform to if one wants to be attractive or lovable.

III. Another premise that leads to the conclusion that love is easy and the problem of love is that of being loved rather than loving is the confusion that exists between the initial experience of falling in love and the permanent state of being and staying in love. The first one just happens by chance or by luck. The second requires effort, commitment, and nurture.

(a) Two people meet and they are attracted, the wall drops, they feel close, they feel atone, they feel exhilarated, especially if they previously had felt loneliness and isolation. The miracle of sudden intimacy and the sudden gratification of a deep human need takes them right out of this world.

(b) But the exhilarated state is not lasting, and as they become more acquainted the miraculous disappears. Disappointments and arguments and boredom kill the initial excitement, and they think that love is gone. Lasting love is an art that needs to be worked at continually. It requires effort and commitment.

IV. This attitude that there is nothing easier than love and that the problem of love is making oneself lovable and finding an acceptable object to love and be loved by does prevail despite overwhelming evidence to the contrary.

(a) Hardly any activity or enterprise on earth is started with such high hopes and expectations and fails so regularly as love. In any walk of life we would be suspicious at the regularity of failure. In business we would want reasons for the failure or we would give up the activity as a poor venture.

(b) Since we cannot do the latter, we have only one recourse—to look at the reasons for failure. The source of the problem is an erroneous concept of the nature of love.

(c) The real problem of love is to become a loving person, not to spend one's time making oneself lovable. It is an erroneous concept to believe that there is nothing easier than love, that there is nothing to be learned about love, that it requires no effort, and that it is something that just happens to you if you're lucky.

(d) The same is true of the love of God. Some people just wait until it hits them or happens to them as it did to Paul on the road to Damascus. But the initial experience of falling in love with God is not lasting. It also requires effort and nurture.

Even Paul found it was not lasting and he cried out in despair, "Wretched man that I am."

V. The biblical answer is that love is not easy and requires commitment, self-giving, self-sacrifice on behalf of your neighbor, even the cross.

(a) To be truly human is to become a self-giving, loving person, living a life in the image of Jesus Christ. The answer to the problem of love is not seeking it continuously because, if everyone is seeking, who is to give? The answer is to commit your life to giving love.

(b) You don't have to be beautiful or handsome to love. You have to be committed. Which gospel do you hear? The gospel of the mass media: "A new commandment I give unto you that you make yourself very attractive and you shall receive love." Or the gospel of Jesus Christ: "A new commandment I give unto you that you love one another, even as I have loved you that you love one another."—Bruce H. Brooke.

Illustrations

PERFECTION. The Greek word *teleios* which is translated "perfect" in Matt. 5:48 means "attaining to the end, complete, mature." But here a comparison is made between the believer and God, and so the word implies that we must strive for a godlike, unselfish love for others, especially those who don't deserve our love. This ideal wholeness and perfect love can only come out of a deepening relationship with Jesus Christ, who alone is perfect.—Alma Gordon Dole.

CONQUERING LOVE. Hate cannot destroy hate, but love can and does. Not the soft and negative thing that has carried the name and misrepresented the emotion but love that suffers all things and is kind, love that accepts responsibility, love that marches, love that suffers, love that bleeds and dies for a great cause—but to rise again.—Daniel A. Poling.

Sermon Suggestions

THE PRACTICALITY OF LOVE. Scripture: Luke 10:25–37. (1) Extended to all who need help. (a) With no restrictions based on race. (b) With no restrictions based on acquaintance. (c) With no restrictions based on character. (2) Ready to do anything that needs to be done. (a) Without excuses. (b) With specific aid. (c) With generosity.—Gerhard Aho.

THE ELEVENTH COMMANDMENT. Text: John 13:34–35 (RSV). (1) A fraternal love: "love one another." (See I Thess. 3:12.) (2) A faithful love: "to the end" (v. 1). (See Jer. 31:3.) (3) A forgetful love (v. 35). (See Rom. 5:8.)—Hardy R. Denham, Jr.

Worship Aids

CALL TO WORSHIP. "The Lord is great in Zion; and he is high above all the people. Exalt the Lord our God, and worship at his holy hill; for the Lord our God is holy." Ps. 99:2, 9.

INVOCATION. Great is thy name, O Lord, and greatly to be praised and to be had in reverence of all them that call upon thee. For thou only are God; we are the people of thy pasture and the sheep of thy hand. Therefore we worship and adore thee, Father, Son, and Holy Spirit, ever one God, world without end.

OFFERTORY SENTENCE. "Therefore, my beloved brethren, be ye steadfast, unmoveable, always abounding in the work of the Lord, forasmuch as ye know that your labor is not in vain in the Lord." I Cor. 15:58.

OFFERTORY PRAYER. Dear God, help us to become unobstructed channels that thy love may flow through us to others and our gifts may be used for the proclamation to all men of thy saving goodness.

PRAYER. O Lord God, thou who art the beginning of our yesterdays, the mystery of our todays, and the hope of our tomorrows, hear our prayer.

O Lord, we are thankful. Although our days have pain as well as joy and sickness as well as health, we are thankful for the good gift of life. Although we stumble and falter in mazes without end, we are thankful for thy revelation to us in Jesus Christ.

Although we cannot see beyond the grave, we are thankful simply to feel our way in faith.

O Lord, we are sorry that our vision is so short-sighted, that we feast on prejudice, that we can't seem to get our feet out of our own self-righteous mud, and that we even claim to be Christian when we are so un-Christian in certain concrete relations with our fellow men.

O Lord, we are in need. Give us a little more love for a few more people on the other side of the tracks. Give us more understanding of the oppressed that we may confess, "There but for the grace of God go I." Give us, O God, Christ, lest we become hypocrites of hypocrites, pious lovers of mankind who hate people, for it is in his name that we pray.—Bert E. McCormick.

✓ EVENING SERVICE

Topic: Chasing Donkeys
   TEXT: I. Sam. 9:20.

In I Sam. 9 and 10 we find the first appearance of Saul, son of Kish, and soon to be the first king of Israel. He is chasing donkeys all over the countryside. His father had sent him out to round up the donkeys, but he is having a terrible time. Out of this unusual incident comes positive thoughts for living.

I. Often the greatest blessings will be couched in the menial tasks of life.

(a) It is while Saul is out chasing donkeys that he will meet Samuel and be anointed king. In an unlikely place and doing an unlikely task, God chose an unlikely man to be king.

(b) If your life is ever dull, sometimes routine, unexciting, and commonplace, be careful for you might run right by a great blessing. God's way of using us involves such ordinary things as kitchens and cradles, wrenches and washing machines, desk jobs and field work.

II. Sometimes it takes inconvenience to bless us. (a) Inconvenience is sometimes another way of saying that our status quo has been disrupted. Saul did not like having to chase donkeys, but had he stayed where he was, he would not have met Samuel.

(b) Paul was aware of the doctrine of inconveniences during his many troubles and prison experiences. He kept seeing these inconveniences as blessed opportunities to preach the gospel, to meet new people, and to sing and pray.

III. Regardless of the outward appearance, God is at work for good in our behalf.

(a) Chasing donkeys is good? It was for Saul because God was using the adventure. How very often we think that because the outward appearance is bad that God is doing bad toward us. But it is not so. He loves us and is at work to do good in our behalf.

(b) Job tries to convince his friends that outward appearances do not tell the whole story. The disciples think Jesus has failed them when he dies on a cross. Even when things look bad, God loves us and is working for us.—Jim Futral.

SUNDAY: JULY SEVENTEENTH

MORNING SERVICE

Topic: Called to Be Witnesses
   TEXT: Acts 4:20.

I. *In all the earth* (Acts 1:8). (a) Jesus had completed his mission on earth. He spent forty days with his disciples following his resurrection, revealing that he was alive indeed and teaching them many things relating to the kingdom of God. Then, as he prepared to ascend to the Father, he gave these great words to his followers, "Ye shall be my witnesses."

(b) Our message tells of a personal relationship with him. The words of our Lord on that hillside have the force of a command. There is no option for the Christian. We are witnesses.

(c) Christ gave the content of the message witnesses are to tell. "You shall be witness unto me." The message was to be about the Lord. He had been crucified but had risen from the dead. Their story was his story.

(d) Jesus gave the geographical outline of their mission. They would tell of him in Jerusalem where they were. They were to spread on out into Judea. Then they were to go beyond their own land to Samaria, where the despised Samaritans lived. They would go to the ends of the earth.

II. *To those who search the scriptures* (Acts 17:10–12). (a) On his second missionary journey Paul arrived in Berea under less than desirable circumstances. He and Silas were sent out of Thessalonica under the cover of night to protect them from angry mobs of Jews who resented his preaching (17:1–9).

(b) Paul always went first to the synagogue. He felt a strong compassion for his own people and took the gospel first to them. His great desire was to see them get saved. (See Rom. 10:1.)

(c) The Jews in Berea were devout and noble people (v. 11). They knew the scriptures. When Paul spoke to them they listened with minds ready to receive his words. Then they searched their scriptures to verify his words.

(d) A great thrill comes to the messenger of God when he speaks to people who are familiar with the Bible and who are willing to listen to his words. He becomes more eager to speak as he looks into the eyes of people who are anxious to hear. "Blessed are they which do hunger and thirst after righteousness: for they shall be filled" (Matt. 5:6).

III. *To all people* (John 4:7–10, 42). (a) Jesus set the example for his disciples in witnessing. He and his followers were on their way back to Galilee from Judea. Their route took them through Samaria.

(b) The Jews hated the Samaritans because the Samaritans had intermarried with their captors hundreds of years earlier. The Jews considered the Samaritans impure.

(1) As Jesus and his group of disciples came to Sychar, a Samaritan city, they stopped at Jacob's well. Jesus was tired and sat down by the well to rest (v. 6). The time was about noon.

(2) While Jesus rested, a woman from the city approached the well to draw water (v. 7). Jesus asked her for a drink. He was thirsty as well as hungry. The disciples had gone into the city to get some food (v. 8). Jesus wanted a drink of water but had no jar with which to draw from the well.

(3) Jesus surprised the woman by asking her for a drink (v. 9). She replied quickly with a question of her own. Why would he, a Jew, ask a Samaritan for a drink? She knew well the hatred between the two peoples. They would not speak to each other or have any dealings with each other. She was astonished at his words.

(4) Jesus gave a gentle but firm answer. If the woman only knew who was speaking to her, if she only knew of God's gift of everlasting water to quench her spiritual thirst, she would be asking him for that drink (v. 10). Living water is that which gives life. He spoke of spiritual matters.

(c) People the world over are searching for the physical when the spiritual matters most. They pursue and desire the wrong things. If they only knew of God's gift, they would ask for it instead.

(d) Our Lord's encounter with the woman at the well instructs us that we should cross all barriers with the message of everlasting life. All people, no matter who they are or where they are, need this word.

IV. *To those who seek* (Acts 16:9–10). (a) One of the great moments of Paul's life occurred while he was at Troas on his second missionary journey. He had wished to go into Bithynia, but the Holy Spirit said no. He then went to Troas, and it was there that he learned why the Spirit refused to let him go to Bithynia.

(b) While at Troas Paul had a vision. A man from Macedonia appeared to him and urged him to come over into Macedonia and help them (v. 9).

(c) Today the Macedonian call refers to the call from men in foreign lands for Christians to come and bring them the gospel. There is a need for the message of salvation in all the world.—James L. Heflin.

Illustrations

DIMINISHED GLOW. Sir Edwin Landseer painted a picture showing a fire burning in the grate of a living room. When the painting was exhibited, the fire glowed with such marvelous radiance that visitors were intrigued by it. The artist sold the painting for a handsome price. After a few years the purchaser summoned the artist, saying: "Please come and light your fire. It has gone out." The painter realized then that he had used a brilliant but fugitive pigment. The glow of the fire had faded prematurely.—Raymond M. Veh.

THE ONLY ROAD.   To follow Christ is to set out on an extraordinary new adventure. Your life is no longer your own. You are not any better than you ever were. Certainly no new sanctity or wisdom or power suddenly descends. You are nonetheless on call in a new way. You start moving through the world as a follower of what people see as either the world's oldest and most impossible dream or the holy, living truth itself. In unexpected ways and at unexpected times people of all sorts—believers and unbelievers alike—make their way to you, looking for something that often they themselves can't name any more than you can name it for them. Often their lives touch yours at the moments when they are most vulnerable, when some great grief or gladness or perplexity has swept away all the usual barriers we erect between each other. For a moment you see them as they really are and are stripped naked yourself by their nakedness. But far ahead the road goes on anyway. We must follow if we can, because it is our road; it is his road. When you come right down to it, it is the only road that matters.—Frederick Buechner in *A.D.*

Sermon Suggestions

WHAT CAN WE DO?   Text: II Pet. 3:11. (1) We can go. (See Acts 13:1–3.) (2) We can give. (See II Cor. 8:1–5.) (3) We can pray. (See Eph. 6:18–20.) (4) We can witness. (See Phil. 1:12–14.)—Lloyd R. Humphrey.

THAT WE MAY GROW.   Scripture: Rom. 8:28–30. (1) Our growth is stunted. (a) When we become discouraged. (b) When we become depressed. (c) When we lose confidence. (2) Our growth is assured. (a) When we remember that we were predes-

tined. (b) When we remember that we were called. (c) When we remember that we were justified. (d) When we remember that we were glorified.—Jerrold L. Nichols.

Worship Aids

CALL TO WORSHIP.   "I will instruct thee and teach thee in the way which thou shalt go [saith the Lord]. I will guide thee with mine eye. Be glad in the Lord, and rejoice, ye righteous: and shout for joy, all ye that are upright in heart." Ps. 32:8, 11.

INVOCATION.   O thou who art the light of the minds that know thee, the life of the souls that love thee, and the strength of the wills that serve thee, help us so to know thee that we may truly love thee and so to love thee that we may fully serve thee, whom to serve is perfect freedom.

OFFERTORY SENTENCE.   "God is not unrighteous to forget your work and labor of love, which ye have showed toward his name, in that ye have ministered to the saints, and do minister." Heb. 6:10.

OFFERTORY PRAYER.   Our Father, help us this day to remember that we do not live in our own strength but that thou art our help and that from thee cometh even these gifts which we consecrate in Christ's name.

PRAYER.   O Lord our God, in whose presence we stand, in whose care our restless lives are held, to whose mercy we turn again and again, the voice of thy Spirit calls us to thee. It sounds in our inmost being like a haunted melody and reminds us of the beautiful music for which we were created. Although we are conscious of the blaring discord we have actually made, yet thy voice still calls us, and the deep yearning within us responds.

Here, in thy presence, O holy Lord, we have confessed our failures. Here we have heard thy Word. Here, with clumsy hands ill-accustomed to prayer, we have turned to thee for life and light, for hope and peace, for higher motives and wider visions. Cut through all the tangled undergrowth of the path, and bless us with the cleansing knowledge of thy presence.

With faltering voices, O Lord, we thank thee for thy mercy to us. We thank thee for the undergirding regularity of nature—for light and night, for rain and sunshine, for the beauty of blue sky and the mystery of dark night. We thank thee for the structure of our lives—for the alternation of work and rest, for the welcome shelter of home and the persistent needs of family, for the stimulation of friends. Preserve us from corrupting our thankfulness with conceit or destroying gratitude with complacency.

With persistent voices, O Lord, we come asking for ourselves. Strengthen our grasp on those things in life that are important. Increase our abhorrence of those things that are evil, degrading, and false. Sharpen our appreciation for our families. Blunt our aptness to criticize, scoff, or distort the motives of others. Rescue us from accepting the easy answers to the hard questions of life. Instill in us a new spirit.

With interceding voices, O Lord, we come asking for those who need thy care at this hour—those in hospitals, those in crisis, those faced with major changes in their lives, and those deadened with loneliness.

Grant us the ability to voice not only our needs in prayer but also the willingness to leave our needs in thy care. Save us from piously voicing words while keeping our real needs from thee. Above all, forgive us for demanding of thee that our will be done, and give us the discernment to see thy will in the events of life.—Robert Lloyd Shirer.

EVENING SERVICE

Topic: Paul Said, "I Am"

Text: Rom. 1:14–16.

I. Paul said, "I am a debtor." (a) Every Christian is in debt to everyone without Christ. Paul recognized this debt and spent his life traveling over the then known world telling others about the Savior. His motivation for soul winning was the recognition of his debt to every lost person.

(b) We could call this a debt of position. A man in England was found guilty in court of murder. He never saw the child whose death he was found guilty of causing. It was proved that he heard the child's cry for help in a public swimming pool and did nothing about it. The child drowned. He was in the position to save a life and did not do it. This is the position of every Christian. We too are debtors.

II. Paul said, "I am not ashamed." If a person is ashamed of Jesus and his gospel, he will never talk to others about the Lord. On the margin of an old Bible someone wrote by this verse, "I am proud of the gospel of Christ." If you are proud of someone, you are happy to tell others. This is true of grandparents talking to others about their grandchildren. Paul was proud of Jesus, and he spent his life telling others about him.

III. Paul said, "I am ready." Unless a person can say this, it really doesn't matter if he recognizes his debt or if he is not ashamed of the gospel. Unless we are ready to witness to others, we will never do it. God needs followers who recognize their debt to the lost, who are not ashamed of Jesus, and who are ready to help win a lost world.—John E. Barnes.

SUNDAY: JULY TWENTY-FOURTH

MORNING SERVICE

Topic: Three Things That Jesus Believed In

Text: John 20:31.

I. Jesus believed that the church was an essential part of life. (a) Jesus went to the synagogue every Sabbath to take part in the formal worship of God that was carried on there. Not that he thought the synagogue was perfect. Obviously he did not. He recognized that many of its members were so concerned with preserving the letter of the law as to miss its spirit, and some were downright hypocrites, preaching to others what they did not practice themselves. But he did not turn his back on the institution for that reason. He continued to uphold it and to be a part of it.

(b) He believed in the value and importance of the national church of his day, the temple in Jerusalem. We recall readily enough his anger at those who had defiled the temple by turning it into a place of business—a den of thieves, as he put it—and we also recall that he predicted that the day was coming when the temple would be destroyed, when not one of its stones would be left standing on another. But let us not forget that he spoke these words when he himself had gone to the temple as a pilgrim to worship there, and when he spoke them, he wept.

(c) Jesus was a believer in the value of the church. He founded a church that he intended should be permanent, of a tradition current in his time to the effect that Jesus said that even the gates of hell would not prevail against it.

II. He believed it was necessary to have a Bible. And he seems to have known his own Bible by heart. His teaching in essence is a commentary on the Hebrew scriptures.

(a) He comments on the law—as when he says that what the law comes down to is a pair of commandments each beginning, "Thou shalt love." "Thou shalt love the Lord thy God with all thy heart and soul and mind" and "Thou shalt love thy neighbor as thyself."

(b) He quotes from the prophets—as when he rebukes the Pharisees for their unkindness to social outcasts by reminding them of Hosea's line: "I desire mercy and not sacrifice."

(c) He recalls the great days of the nation's historic past—as when he says of the lilies of the field, "Even Solomon in all his glory was not arrayed like one of these."

(d) He is never at a loss for the example that perfectly illustrates his meaning—as when he reminds those who criticized his disciples for plucking grain when they were hungry on the Sabbath, "Have you never read what David did, when he was in need and was hungry, he and those who were with him: how he entered the house of God, when Abiathar was high priest, and ate the bread of the Presence, which it is not lawful for any but the priests to eat, and also gave it to those who were with him?" Then he added, "The sabbath was made for man, not man for the sabbath."

III. Jesus believed that you can depend on the love that ordinary people bear toward one another.

(a) He believed in the love that one finds in families. The evidence of that is found on every page of the gospels.

(1) His teaching about the fatherhood of God, which revolutionized theology, tells us all we need to know about the regard he had for his own human father, and his teaching about the dignity of women, the liberating influence of which is still at work in the world, tells us all we need to know about the high regard in which he held his mother.

(2) His followers referred to each other as brothers and sisters, which is yet another reflection of the same attitude, as is his choice of the setting for one of his greatest parables, the prodigal son, in which the son is saved when he comes home to the family he has left. Jesus believed in the family. He thought of it as the model of the new society that would one day come into being in the kingdom.

(b) He believed in friendship. The story of his life is a story of friendship—the friendship among his followers that became the fellowship of the church, and the friendship that he and they freely offered to all who would accept it. The parable of the prodigal son is about a family. The good Samaritan is about friendship—a stranger in this case acting the part of a friend and thus saving another man's life. —Charles H. Buck, Jr.

Illustrations

SERENITY. It is difficult, when the outside is hard pressed by the trouble in the world, to keep the inside serene, but it is only difficult when you think that you can make it serene. The serenity will be given you. That is the benediction and the reward for those who sought and knocked and found. You are here at this moment, at this time, at this place, in this Presence, and the Presence is the only reality, and he is thy Shepherd.—*Letters to the Scattered Brotherhood.*

ETERNAL VERITIES. A nineteenth century businessman traveled from New York to Chicago in two weeks by stagecoach; his counterpart today gets there in two hours by plane. When each arrives, he faces the same questions: Do I remain honest in my business dealings? Do I remain faithful to my wife? Where do I find a good meal? Regardless of science and technology, we live with certain eternal verities. What is most important in our lives is precisely that which does not change down through the ages—our familiar quests for justice, friendship, comfort, love, truth, order, for integrity, nourishment, beauty, honesty, and family—the human constants. They are, and will continue to be, the measure of all change.—Stephen Rosen in *The New York Times.*

Sermon Suggestions

THINKING LIKE JESUS. Scripture: Phil. 2:1–11. (1) Think like Jesus about yourself. (2) Think like Jesus about others. (3) Think like Jesus about God.—Lloyd Strelow.

BELIEVING BRINGS BLESSINGS. Text: Matt. 6:33. (1) We who believe in Jesus have no doubt as to God's goodness, and that surely is a blessing. (See Rom. 5:6, 8.) (2) Believing in God has the blessing of stilling our fears. (See Rom. 8:38–39.) (3) Believing in God brings the blessing of knowing we are sent by God. (See John 20:21.)—David W. Richardson.

Worship Aids

CALL TO WORSHIP. "Ho, every one that thirstest, come ye to the waters. Incline your ear, and come unto me: hear, and your soul shall live; and I will make an everlasting covenant with you, even the sure mercies of David." Isa. 55:1, 3.

INVOCATION. O God, whose name is great, whose goodness is inexhaustible, who art worshiped and served by all the hosts of heaven: touch our hearts, search out our consciences, and cast out of us every evil thought and base desire; all envy, wrath, and remembrance of injuries; and every motion of flesh and spirit that is contrary to the holy will.

OFFERTORY SENTENCE. "Every one of us shall give account of himself to God." Rom. 14:12.

OFFERTORY PRAYER. Dear Lord, as we travel the highways of life give us a generous and sympathetic spirit for all people in all circumstances of life.

PRAYER. O Infinite Source of life and health and joy! The very thought of thee is so wonderful that in this thought we would rest and be still. Thou art beauty and grace and power and truth.

Thou art the light of every heart that sees thee, the life of every soul that loves thee, and the strength of every mind that seeks thee. From our narrow and bounded world we would pass into thy greater world.

From our petty and miserable selves we would escape to thee to find in thee the power and freedom of a larger life. We recognize thee in all the deeper experiences of the soul.

When the conscience utters its warning voice, when the heart is tender and we forgive those who have wronged us in word or deed, and when we feel ourselves reborn above time and place and know ourselves citizens of thy everlasting kingdom, we realize, O Lord, that these things, while they are in us, are not of us. They are thine, the work of thy Spirit upon our souls.

Spirit of holiness and peace! Search all our motives, try the secret places of our souls, set in the light any evil that may lurk within, and lead us in the way everlasting. —William C. Swygert.

EVENING SERVICE

Topic: The Mystery of God's Will
TEXT: Eph. 1:9.
The apostle Paul speaks of the mystery of the will of God. One commentator's suggestion is that Paul uses the term

"mystery" to mean something into which one must be initiated before it is fully known. Translate that into life's experiences, and we learn the necessity of trusting the totality of our beings to the will of an all-knowing and almighty God who makes no mistakes with the affairs of our lives. The mysteries of his will can bring the results suggested by Paul in Eph. 3.

I. You will gain knowledge of his power (3:16). "The riches of his glory" is a reference to God's inexhaustible power and grace in times of critical circumstances. In every situation the believer can affirm that he is "able to do far more abundantly than all that we ask or think."

II. The mystery of his will permits a deepening of the knowledge of his presence (3:17). "That ye being rooted" is a very imaginative phrase. We are readily drawn in our thoughts to a large tree in which the roots are deep and firmly imbedded in the soil. When that occurs for the individual in his relationship to God, nothing disturbs his faith.

III. We gain the knowledge of his perfection (3:19). Paul suggests that "to know the love of Christ" is something more than receiving his thoughtful, caring attention. Rather, as a result of his transforming love through redemption, we gain an understanding of his perfect love. He desires excellence of his children in what we are and in what we do, and so he promises the glorious possibility of being "filled with God," enabling the believer to perceive the good in every negative circumstance.

IV. The mystery of his will brings a knowledge of his purpose (3:21). "Unto him be glory in the church." Flesh and blood comprise the real church, not bricks and mortar. We are intended to glorify him. That is essentially the reason for our existence. How better translate the message of an active God than through the experience of a believer who has emerged from life's devastating circumstances as a winner. He then really understands the "mystery of his will," for he has been initiated and therefore comprehends much more adequately the purpose of God for his life.—Israel Gaither in *The War Cry*.

SUNDAY: JULY THIRTY-FIRST

MORNING SERVICE

Topic: Amos Calls for Righteous Living
TEXT: Amos 5:14–15.

I. *Worship without encounter.* (a) Amos had something to say about the worship life of the people.

(1) He could have dealt with regulations for worship, reminding the people to conduct their worship in the prescribed ways. But others were taking care of that, and he felt no need at all to stress propriety in worship.

(2) If he had been living in our day, he might have called for innovation in worship. Tired of being bored, he could have exhorted the priests to try new forms of worship. But forms and rituals were not a major concern of his as he looked at those who were supposed to be the people of God.

(b) One purpose of worship is to facilitate the encounter of persons with God. But this was not happening in Israel, so far as Amos could tell, because the life of the nation did not reflect the character and purposes of God.

(c) The problem at Bethel was not that people were not coming to worship. They were coming in large numbers. The problem was that their worship was not causing them to be confronted by God. So Amos told them that God despised their worship (Amos 5:21–23).

II. *Religion without alterations.* (a) Religion consists of beliefs, attitudes, and practices which are supposed to bind persons to God. Amos did not believe that Israel's religion was having the intended effect, for his conception of God was such that he knew alterations would have to be made in people's lives if they were truly in touch with God. That was not happening in Israel. The people were religious enough, but their religion was not altering their lives.

(b) Change simply for the sake of change is not to be desired or encouraged. But when change is needed and a people's religion retards or prevents that change or simply does not help to effect it, the religion is deficient.

III. *Prosperity without righteousness.* (a) The setting of Amos' ministry throws light on what he expected religion to do. The time was about 750 B.C., near the end of the forty-year reign (786–746 B.C.) of Jeroboam II. This had been a period of relative peace and stability for Israel. Trade with other countries had flourished, and prosperity was being enjoyed by those in positions to take advantage of the opportunities peace provided. But the people had been pushing God further and further toward the periphery of their lives, and this meant that he had less and less influence in and control of their lives.

(b) Apparently they were not aware of what they were doing. They were still diligent in their religious exercises and would doubtless have claimed to be ardently pious. But their conduct belied their profession, and those benefiting least from the prosperity of the times were paying the price. While some were getting richer, some were getting poorer, and in their poverty they were helpless before the ruthless selfishness of the rich and powerful.

(c) They found a champion in Amos. He had watched both the flourishing of religious observances and worship and the decrease of justice and righteousness, and he knew that something was wrong at the very heart of the people's life. So he called for repentance and radical change.

IV. *Covenant without obedience.* (a) The first two chapters of the book of Amos highlight some of the sins of neighboring countries. In chapters three and four, Amos sounds the warning note for Israel, reminding the people of the special relationship they have had with God and emphasizing the certainty of God's judgment because of their unfaithfulness.

(b) In chapter five he begins detailing the sins of Israel, interspersing promises of judgment and calling upon people to right the wrongs they are perpetrating.

(1) The gate of the city was the courthouse of ancient times. Persons who felt that they had been wronged took their grievances there to seek compensation or justice. But they were not finding such there.

(2) Those responsible for establishing justice were more interested in feathering their own nests than in seeing that injustices were ended. Bribery was common, and righteousness (standing for and dong the right) was seldom to be seen. Justice was scarce, and the suffering of the poor went unrelieved.

(c) In Amos' view, worship under those circumstances was mockery of God. It was not that he wanted the people to stop worshiping; it was that he wanted their worship to be authentic, to be based upon the covenant they had made with God and to reflect the moral content of that covenant.

V. *Sainthood without character.* Perhaps some of those Amos condemned so severely were kind, thoughtful, and generous where family members were concerned. They deserved commendation for that. Yet their consideration for loved ones, like their diligence in religious observances, could not excuse nor compensate for the greed, the absence of integrity, and the lack of compassion that characterized their dealings with others. Amos admonished them, "Seek the Lord and live . . . seek good, and not evil . . . hate evil, and love good, and establish justice in the gate" (Amos 5:6, 14–15). He knew that character and right conduct were not options but essential consequences of authentic religion.

VI. *Prophesying without reservation.* Prophets, generally, were practical-minded persons. For Amos this meant bearing down where the problem was. He used several approaches in trying to get the people to recognize the error of their ways and to return to authentic religion.

(a) He reminded them of the graciousness of God's dealings with them in the past.

(b) He emphasized the essential moral content of religion.

(c) He pointed out some specific violations of the laws of God of which the people were guilty.

(d) He warned of the inevitability of the judgment of God.

(e) He offered hope of redemption if the people would seek the Lord and hate evil and love good.

VII. *Justice without interruption.* (a) Amos was not pleading for occasional acts of kindness nor for spasmodic spurts of justice. He was demanding justice without interruption and righteousness without ceasing. "Let justice roll down like waters and righteousness like an everflowing stream" (Amos 5:24).

(b) An everflowing stream is not easily found in Palestine. Most stream beds are empty for several months each year during the long dry season. Then when the fall rains come in September or October, the streams begin to flow again. A stream is especially precious if it has sources that keep it flowing all the time.

(c) Amos meant for justice and righteousness to be like that—not intermittent, occasional, spasmodic but constant, dependable, unceasing. A just and righteous God expected that, and all of their worship and religious observances were futile and meaningless if they were not producing justice without interruption and righteousness without ceasing.—Herschel H. Sheets.

Illustrations

RAISING QUESTIONS. Clearly the church's present calling is not so much to provide the answers as to raise the questions. We proclaim Christ initially not as the solution but as the question about life. He comes to answer our needs once we recognize them, but before that he comes to question how we've settled up with life, to ask whether we may be satisfied for the wrong reasons, whether we've grown complacent in some lesser pursuit than the kingdom of God.—Ralph Cannon.

AWAKENED ASPIRATIONS. Dorothy Thompson in an essay on architecture began with the specifications from a government manual that said all rooms in public buildings should be no higher than twelve feet so nobody would feel insignificant. She recalled the days in World War II when she was a reporter in Europe. She watched GIs awestruck in Salisbury Cathedral and overwhelmed with emotion in witnessing the procession in Canterbury. She saw them go into St. Peter's in Rome and kneel to pray under that immense dome. She said they were not feeling insignificant then. On the contrary, they were awakened for the first time to aspirations and dreams they had never even known before.—Mark Trotter.

Sermon Suggestions

JOHN: THE MODEL FOR PASTORS. Scripture: Matt. 11:2–10). (1) The pastor's need to grow. (2) The pastor's need for perseverance. (3) The pastor's need for integrity. (a) Integrity of principle: "reed [not] shaken in the wind." (b) Integrity of ministry: "one who lives [not] in kings' palaces." (c) Integrity of message: "a prophet, yea more than a prophet."—Robert H. Mueller.

WHAT MAKES A CHAMPION? Text: Phil. 3:13–14. (1) A champion knows the value of time. (2) A champion dares to discipline himself. (3) A champion is willing to sacrifice.—Drew J. Gunnells, Jr.

Worship Aids

CALL TO WORSHIP. "Whatsoever things are true, whatsoever things are honest, whatsoever things are just, whatsoever things are pure, whatsoever things are lovely, whatsoever things are of good report; if there be any virtue, and if there be any praise, think on these things." Phil. 4:8.

INVOCATION. Mysterious God of creation, we are forever awed by the wonder of life here and now, beyond and forever. The more we learn of nature and existence, the more we ponder the puzzle of your conceptions. Through science and technology we have conquered boundaries unimaginable to our father's father. Yet every answer leaves unknown, though sharper in its reality, the inexpressible nature of your word. The more we discover of the discernible, the more we anticipate our need of the eternal.

OFFERTORY SENTENCE. "As we have therefore opportunity, let us do good unto all men, especially unto them who are of the household of faith." Gal. 6:10.

OFFERTORY PRAYER. Help us, dear Father, to be cheerful givers of our time, means, talents, and self to the Master that he may use us in the upbuilding of his kingdom.

PRAYER. Our Father, we have come to this quiet place at the side of a well-traveled road. We have come to wait that unrest may settle and confusions may be lifted and to see more clearly the way that lies ahead. We come to rest from the weariness of the way that we have journeyed, and we come for guidance along the path that is yet to be.

Some of us have left behind far more than lies ahead. For these we ask the faith that joy can be held as richly and as completely in brief moments as in those months and years now growing so short. Some of us have more years that lie ahead than we have found sufficient grace and strength to live. For these we ask the love that makes the years worthwhile.

We ask these things, our Father, in the power of him who captured in his own few years enough of life that we return to him again and again to know what true life is. —Paul E. VanDine.

EVENING SERVICE

Topic: Can You Outgive God?
TEXT: Ps. 68:19.

I. God is the most resourceful being in all the universe. He can outgive us seven times in six. And he is capable of blessing us beyond our ability even to receive (Ps. 23:1; Ps. 84:11; Phil. 4:19).

II. Stewardship is the concrete expressions of our faith response to God's gracious attitude toward us and his graceful actions on our behalf.

III. The stewardship challenge is to live out a new relationship with Christ and others, based on the giving of our heavenly Father. This relationship grows from such gifts as forgiveness, trust, supply, and guidance.

IV. Stewardship can be seen as faith that results in corresponding action, as practical expressions of discipleship, as a responsive relationship to God, and as putting arms and legs, heart and will to the creed.

V. Stewardship is what a person does after saying, "I believe."

VI. Stewardship is what happens when Christ gets into a person's heart and gets into the moving parts of the body.

VII. With a few understandable exceptions, a member or family unit of a local congregation shows exactly where it stands with the Christian faith and the church by its readiness or resistance to demonstrate its faith by financial commitment.

VIII. Christianity is implemented by commitment. Whether the challenge is for dollars or lives or talents or time, the ensuing commitment will be the result of a spiritual process.

IX. Faith is best communicated when there is a living, fervent faith to communicate. As we believe that the most important thing a person can do is to come into a right relationship with God and that there is no loss compared to eternal loss and no gain compared to eternal gain, God abundantly blesses our efforts to communicate our faith.—Hoyt Purcell.

SUNDAY: AUGUST SEVENTH

MORNING SERVICE

Topic: Vanity and Promise
SCRIPTURE: Eccl. 1:1–11, 15; Rom. 8:18–25.

"Vanity of vanities, all is vanity, says the Preacher." What preacher would say that? A preacher is expected to tell us that life has purpose and direction and that work for the Redeemer will itself be redeemed. But this preacher thought differently. He believed that everything was in vain. Why is Ecclesiastes in the Bible?

I. Ecclesiastes is a significant part of our religious tradition. (a) Ecclesiastes legitimizes the experience and expression of despair.

(1) Some Christians believe that it is a sin to worry. When anxiety comes, as it must, anxiety is compounded with guilt, and the result is a crippling anguish.

(2) Don't be afraid to say occasionally, "All is vain." The Lord Christ cried: "My God! My God! Why hast thou forsaken

me?" It is often only as we express despair that we move toward its transformation.

(b) Ecclesiastes provides the background for an honest and mature faith. (1) Let us not be Job's comforters unless we are sensitive to Job's experience, which is the experience of Ecclesiastes.

(2) Written on the walls of a Jewish home in Nazi Germany were these words: "I believe in the sun when it does not shine. I believe in love when I don't have it. I believe in God when he is silent."

(3) This is the mature faith exemplified by St. Paul, who was "afflicted but not crushed, perplexed but not driven to anguish, struck down but not destroyed." It is faith in spite of Ecclesiastes and not understood apart from the experience of Ecclesiastes.

(c) Ecclesiastes provides the strong test for an easy-going secularism.

(1) It is not difficult to understand the person who has examined life, found it vain, and declares himself or herself to be an atheist. It is difficult to respect the person who has never openly questioned the meaning of life but scoffs at religion.

(2) Joseph Margolis argues: "A man who reflects on his own strenuous enterprise must somehow come to terms with the fact that he and others will die. What can be the point, he must ask, of any effort in the face of this inevitability, an inevitability that seems to wipe out the meaning of his own and everyone else's purposiveness?"

(3) This question is, according to Margolis, the basis for a religious concern with life which no rational person can neglect. The experience of Ecclesiastes quickens a secular conscience to consider the religious quest.

II. We admire the writer of Ecclesiastes for his realism and courage but not for his conclusion that "everything is vain." The preacher needed therapy based on New Testament principles. He needed to challenge the assumptions he brought to his encounter with life which led him into three errors.

(a) He was mistaken about himself. (1) He wanted to know, "What can I get from life and never lose?" He focused upon having rather than being and missed the significance of who he was.

(2) He was so concerned with what he could get and keep from life that he lacked appreciation for the rather remarkable person he was. Whenever we focus on having rather than being we court despair. For what we have will either pass away or be surpassed by the possessions of another. Our significance rests in who we are —a presence in the world that we alone can be and express.

(3) St. Paul wrote, "By the grace of God, I am that I am." In the strength of that grace be who you are.

(b) The preacher was mistaken about the world. (1) He began his search for significance in life with the hidden assumption that "there is nothing new under the sun."

(2) The preacher could not overcome his despair because the world, as he saw it, lacked possibility. Vanity was to be endured rather than redeemed, since "the crooked road could not be made straight."

(3) St. Paul was sensitive to the "futility of creation." "The whole creation groaneth," said Paul, "until the day of redemption." Paul believed that God suffers with creation toward the emergence of a new heaven and a new earth. At any time the bondage of futility might be shattered by the liberty of God's presence. In Paul's view even our moments of greatest groaning are filled with redemptive possibilities.

(c) The preacher overlooked the eternal significance of love. He was a preacher without a congregation and without a community of support to remind him of life's possiblities. He suspected that "two persons are better than one" but knew nothing of that love which "bears all things, believes all things, hopes all things, endures all things." He was not open to the love which breaks asunder our morbid self-brooding and energizes us to celebrate the life of another person.

III. Ecclesiastes has a place in our heritage and in our hearts. It expresses our despair and challenges our innocence, but it lacks the higher vision of a New Testament faith. Where Ecclesiastes concludes with the "vanity of all things," the New Testament points us to a redemptive presence which gives us the strength to say, "I am that I am," in spite of all losses, a presence which shows us the open door of possibility in each tribulation, and a Spirit which transforms despair into wonder, love, and praise.—C. Jack Orr.

Illustrations

WISDOM AND KNOWLEDGE. Wisdom is the right use of knowledge. To know is not to be wise. Many men know a great deal and are all the greater fools for it. There is no fool so great as a knowing fool. But to know how to use knowledge is to have wisdom.—Charles H. Spurgeon.

HIDDEN WITHIN. There was a time when all men were gods, but they so abused their divinity that Brahma, the chief god, decided to take divine power away from man and hide it where they would never find it. Where to hide it became the question.

Discussion between Brahma and some of the lesser gods brought them to the conclusion that they would never find a hiding place anywhere in the earth or even under the sea, for eventually man would dig deep down into the earth, explore the depths of every ocean, and find and take again for himself the divine element which they wished to take away from him forever.

At last Brahma said: "Here is what we will do with man's divinity. We will hide it deep down in man himself, for he will never think to look for it there." Ever since man has been going up and down the earth, climbing, digging, diving, exploring, searching for something that is already in himself.—Catherine Anderson.

Sermon Suggestion

HOW TO WALK ON WATER. Text: Matt. 14:22–23. How can we go from where we are to where we want to be when there's deep water between? (1) There must be a tremendous desire on our part. (2) We must not ignore the obstacles to be faced. (3) We must identify our strength.—Jerry Hayner.

Worship Aids

CALL TO WORSHIP. "If a man love me [saith Jesus], he will keep my words: and my Father will love him, and we will come unto him, and make our abode with him." John 14:23.

INVOCATION. Our Father, we thank thee for this opportunity to worship thee and to purify our lives and thoughts by holy fellowship with thee. We ask thee for the grace to forget the rankling past and to press on with joy and confidence to the high calling of God through Jesus Christ. As we strive to be good givers of our lives to others and to thee, help us now to be good receivers of thy grace and mercy.

OFFERTORY SENTENCE. "Seek ye first the kingdom of God, and his righteousness, and all these things shall be added unto you." Matt. 6:33.

OFFERTORY PRAYER. O God, help us so to practice by our gifts and our lives the divine principle of good will that in our homes, our communities, and among all the nations of the earth men may enjoy the boon of peace.

PRAYER. Gracious Father, whose mercy is higher than the heavens, wider than our wanderings, deeper than all sin, we turn to thee. Throw thy vast horizons around our littleness and restlessness. Deal with us one by one in the secret places of our hearts, making us ashamed of our sins, begetting in us the spirit of penitence. Awaken in us the spirit of gratitude for the beauty of the world around us, for the wonder of the world within us, for every gleam of light which turns our minds toward thee. Enlarge our sympathies, broaden our interests, intensify our concerns. Give peace in our time, O Lord, and prosper the labors of all in every land who are seeking to establish it. To thy loving kindness we commend the sick, the sorrowing, all who are fighting a hard battle. Do for them—and for us—more than we can ask or think.—Robert J. McCracken.

EVENING SERVICE

Topic: Life in the Kingdom
TEXT: Luke 17:20–21 (RSV).
Jesus talked about the kingdom in two ways. He said that the kingdom is yet to

come. He also talked much about the kingdom that is here now. Of twenty-seven references to the kingdom in the gospels, eighteen imply that the kingdom is already here in part. Within Jesus' teachings we find certain elements that help us to experience the closeness of God's kingdom.

I. The first is *humility*. (a) Much of Jesus' teaching about humility was in response to the spiritual conceit and hypocrisy of the Pharisees. They would stand on the street corners and pray out loud so others would take notice. They would stand in the temple and thank God they were not like other sinners. They would insist that others should follow their examples of holiness.

(b) Jesus' response was that those who place themselves first will in the end find themselves last. Those who sit at the head of the banquet table may be asked to move further down to make room for others more worthy. Jesus is trying to help us understand that self-arrogance and conceit make it impossible to love God or to love others.

II. A second element of life in the kingdom is *sincerity*. Jesus insisted that our inner selves should agree with our outward acts. We should be honest and real to others. We should practice sincerity.

III. Then comes *compassion*. (a) When Jesus looked over the crowds that followed him, he had compassion on them, and he healed and fed them. He loved them.

(b) A rich young ruler came to Jesus and asked, "What must I do to inherit eternal life?" Jesus responded by telling the story of the good Samaritan, the one who had compassion on a stranger who had been beaten and robbed and left by the side of the road.

IV. Another element of life in the kingdom is *forgiveness*. (a) How hard it is to forgive a business competitor for an unfair deal, a friend for betraying you with a lie, or a marriage partner for breaking the marriage commitment. The Hebrew law allowed revenge in cases where it was warranted.

(b) Jesus challenged the old rules of "an eye for an eye and a tooth for a tooth." He said instead that we should forgive as many as seventy times seven. By the time you get to 490 you have probably lost count. Jesus showed the ultimate forgiveness when, as he hung dying upon the cross, he said, "Father forgive them, for they know not what they do."

(c) Those who don't learn to forgive others can never understand or accept God's forgiveness of them. The very heart of self-worth is to feel forgiven and accepted by God.—Duane M. Gebhard.

SUNDAY: AUGUST FOURTEENTH

MORNING SERVICE

Topic: Love's Activity
Scripture: I Cor. 13:4–7.

There are fourteen aspects of the activity of love in this song of love, and it becomes fairly evident that this double seven is intended to portray the personal mastery of love's activity and the practical ministry of love's activity.

I. *The personal mastery of love's activity.* (a) Love's generosity. "Love envieth not" (v. 4).

(1) Envy is the feeling of ill will toward those who are in the same line as ourselves. It is a spirit of covetousness and dissatisfaction. Love, however, is the very opposite of this. The Lord Jesus wonderfully exhibited this generosity of love when his disciples vied with one another for positions of authority among themselves. We read that "there was a strife among themselves, which of them should be accounted the greatest" (Luke 22:24), but love's answer to this was "I am among you as he that serveth" (Luke 22:27).

(2) How much Christian work is spoiled by the loveless spirit of envy! We do well to test ourselves constantly with this question, "Does the superiority or success of another in the same line as myself stimulate envy or joy?" Whatever others are doing, can I always say, "I am among you as one that serveth?"

(b) Love's modesty. "Love vaunteth not itself" (v. 4). (1) To vaunt oneself is to parade one's imagined superiority over others. In simple language it denotes showing off. Someone has said, "Folk admire the peacock for the grandeur of his plumes, until they are driven away by the discordant tones of his voice."

(2) How modest was the Lord Jesus in all his words and actions before men! Concerning his words, he could say: "My doctrine is not mine, but his that sent me" (John 7:16) and "The words that I speak unto you I speak not of myself: but the Father that dwelleth in me" (John 5:19). Here, surely, was love's modesty in action.

(c) Love's humility. "Love is not puffed up" (v. 4). (1) To puff oneself up is to manifest pride and self-esteem. The Corinthians were not only parading their gifts but were puffed up with their own ideas of importance and knowledge. Without doubt the apostle here was indirectly rebuking this spirit of self-esteem.

(2) How different is the life of the one who personifies all these aspects of love's activity. We read that he "made himself of no reputation . . . he humbled himself, and became obedient unto death" (Phil. 2: 7–8).

(d) Love's courtesy. Love "doth not behave itself unseemly" (v. 5). (1) Love can never be rude, for it is foreign to her nature. Love is always polite, and politeness has been described as "love in the little things of life." Let us never forget that courtesy is not merely a matter of birth; it is a matter of the spirit. It has been well said that "what breeding does by training, love does by instinct."

(2) We are not being irreverent when we say that the Lord Jesus was the perfect gentleman, for a gentleman is a man who does things gently, lovingly, and with a view to pleasing others. Speaking of his Father, he could say, "I do always those things that please him" (John 8:29).

(e) Love's divinity. Love "seeketh not her own" (v. 5). (1) Love is not selfish, but selfless, not self-centered but self-forgetting. Love never seeks her own advantage.

(2) Campbell Morgan said, "Perhaps this is the profoundest word about the self-emptying capacity of love." That is why we have called it "love's divinity," for only the divine nature can empty itself in the interests of others.

(3) Paul could significantly say of the Lord Jesus, "Even Christ pleased not himself" (Rom. 15:3). With us it often has to be admitted, as of the believers at Philippi, "All seek their own" (Phil. 2:21).

(f) Love's civility. Love "is not . . . provoked" (v. 5). (1) The Authorized Version reads: "is not easily provoked." The revisers, however, have rightly omitted the word "easily," for it is not there. The phrase "easily provoked" has been an excuse for many a person getting into a bad temper, but love gives no excuse for bad tempers. Love never gives way to provocation, exasperation, or irritation. Love is never touchy.

(2) F. Y. Fullerton wrote, "The crowning glory of our Lord was that he was never impatient." How exasperated he could have been amidst the pressure of his busy program, but he never answered back, even in spite of the many unpleasant things which were hurled at him by friends and foes. His friends said: "He is beside himself" (Mark 3:21); his foes added: "He hath a devil, and is mad; why hear ye him?" (John 10:20). But he remained unprovoked.

(g) Love's integrity. Love "rejoiceth not in iniquity, but rejoiceth in the truth" (v. 6).

(1) Moffatt's rendering is helpful here: "Love is never glad when others go wrong. She is gladdened by goodness."

(2) This activity of love is revealed to us in the story of John 8. How those critical Jews gloated over the fact that an unfortunate woman had been caught in the very act of sin, and so they dragged her into the presence of the Master for condemnation. But what a surprise awaited them! Instead of siding with the accusers, the Savior challenged them with the searching question, "He that is without sin among you, let him first cast a stone at her" (v. 7). And we read that "being convicted by their own conscience, they went out one by one, beginning at the eldest, even unto the last" (v. 9). Then with grace and love Jesus turned to the self-condemned and embarrassed woman and said: "Hath no man

condemned thee? She said, No man, Lord. And Jesus said unto her, Neither do I condemn thee: go and sin no more" (vv. 10–11). That was love's integrity, acting first in truth and then in grace.

II. *The practical ministry of love's activity.* (a) Love's patience. "Love suffereth long" (v. 4). Here is the long-suffering which waits rather than flares. How beautifully this is revealed in our Lord's answer, when Peter asked him, "How oft shall my brother sin against me, and I forgive him? 'Til seven times?" The Lord laughed at him, and with tender satire replied, "I do not say seven times, but 490 times, or seventy times seven" (Matt. 18:21–22).

(b) Love's benevolence. "Love . . . is kind" (v. 4). Love is always ready to consider others with a view to extending good. Have you ever noticed how much of Christ's life was spent in doing kind things, not merely good things? Think of the occasion when he called his disciples aside to rest awhile, because there were so "many coming and going that they had no leisure, so much as to eat." But no sooner had they departed into a desert place to be quiet, than a multitude of people broke in upon their privacy. The first reaction of the disciples was "Send them away," but the Savior answered, "Give ye them to eat." Then followed that wonderful miracle of the feeding of five thousand (Mark 6:31–44).

(c) Love's lenience. Love "thinketh no evil" (v. 5). Love does not keep an account of evil done and does not reckon up her grievances. In this sense, love is a poor mathematician. How easily the Lord Jesus could have reckoned up the evil done to him throughout that eventful day when he was led from Gethsemane to Gabbatha and then from Gabbatha to Golgotha. But even as the nails were being driven into his hands, he prayed, "Father, forgive them; for they know not what they do" (Luke 23:34).

(d) Love's silence. Love "beareth all things" (v. 7). Love patiently and silently endures, when it has to suffer, without breaking down or telling others of what it has to bear. Recall how Jesus silently endured when subjected to the accusations of false witnesses before Pilate. We read that "he answered . . . never a word" (Matt. 27:14).

(e) Love's innocence. Love "believeth all things" (v. 7). The idea behind this clause has nothing to do with credulity. It is rather the absence of suspicion. Some people are always suspicious, but the love-mastered believer always puts the best construction on things.

(f) Love's reassurance. Love "hopeth all things" (v. 7). Love is always optimistic and undiscourageable. When others have long ago given up, love hopes on. The Lord Jesus never gave up hope for the most depraved of people. Of him it could be truly said, "A bruised reed shall he not break, and smoking flax shall he not quench" (Matt. 12:20).

(g) Love's perseverance. Love "endureth all things" (v. 7). (1) This activity of love is the crown of all that has gone before. It represents love's victory. The writer to the Hebrews tells us that, for the joy that was set before him, the Lord Jesus "endured the cross, despising the shame, and is set down at the right hand of the throne of God" (12:2).

(2) The apostle Paul knew something of the triumph of this love for he could say, writing to these same Corinthians, "Being reviled, we bless; being persecuted, we suffer it; being defamed, we entreat" (I Cor. 4:12–13).—Stephen F. Olford.

Illustrations

LOVE THAT BENDS.   Faith, like light, should always be simple and unbending; while love, like warmth, should beam forth on every side and bend to every necessity of our brethren.—Martin Luther.

VIRTUES.   Love means loving that which is unlovable, or it is not virtue at all. Forgiving means pardoning that which is unforgivable, or it is not virtue at all. Hope means hoping when things are hopeless, or it is not virtue at all.—G. K. Chesterton.

Sermon Suggestions

WHAT'S A HEAVEN FOR?   Text: II Cor. 4:17. (1) It is for making men whole. (2) It is for unifying the fragments of mortal existence into a beautiful design. (3) It is for realizing in fullest measure the Christian ideal of fellowship with God.—John H. Townsend.

LOVE CONQUERS ALL. Scripture: Rom. 5:6–11. (1) The love of God in Christ broke into our lives when we were helpless (v. 6). (2) The love of God in Christ broke into our lives when we were yet sinners (v. 8). (3) The love of God in Christ broke into our lives while we were enemies of God.

Worship Aids

CALL TO WORSHIP. "I will lift up mine eyes unto the hills, from whence cometh my help. My help cometh from the Lord, which made heaven and earth." Ps. 121: 1–2.

INVOCATION. Lord God Almighty, holy and eternal Father, who dwellest in the high and lofty place, with him also that is of a humble and contrite spirit: we come before thee, beseeching thee to cleanse us by the grace of thy Holy Spirit, that we may give praise to thee, now and forever, in the name of our redeemer, Jesus Christ.

OFFERTORY SENTENCE. "Give unto the Lord, O ye kindreds of the people, give unto the Lord glory and strength. Give unto the Lord the glory due unto his name: bring an offering, and come into his courts." Ps. 96:7–8.

OFFERTORY PRAYER. Eternal God, give us a vision of thy glory that no sacrifice may seem too great, and strengthen us in every step we take from selfishness to generosity.

PRAYER. Our heavenly Father, who art present in this moment and every moment of our lives, who art the listener in every conversation, who art the strength for every action of our bodies, and who art reflected in every gleam of our eyes, we bow and recognize thy presence with us.

Forgive us, Father, when we think that thou art present here and not on our job or in our kitchens, when we think that we can worship thee this morning and forget about thee this afternoon, and when we seek to rationalize and love only those we choose to love and forgive only those who make it easy for us to forgive.

Forgive us, O Lord, when we remember thee only when we need thee. Often we have forgotten to thank thee for the breaking forth of a new day, for the tender touch of a mother's hand, for the comforting embrace of a mate's arms, or for the handclasp of a forgiven friend.

Forgive us, Master, when we duck our heads so that we do not have to look into the piercing eyes of a neighbor who might need our help. We confess we are selfish and do not want to share ourselves without expecting something in return. We recognize that sometimes we want to run from life and our responsibilities, from thee and from others. Forgive us, Father, in our running, our selfishness, our forgetfulness, and for our unnecessary concern for ourselves.

Father, we offer to thee just what we are with all our shortcomings, our joys, our sorrows, our fears, our confusion, our love, our concern, and our thanksgiving. Lead on, O Lord of life, in the renewal of our lives, in the recommitment of our actions, and in the rededication of our witness.—Jimmie L. Gentle.

EVENING SERVICE

Topic: False Gods We Have Known
TEXT: Gal. 4:8.

I. *The god of work.* (a) This is the god who proclaims that work is not only edifying but also the way we work out our salvation. Despite our parents' fears, most of us grow up to love working.

(b) We have pushed the work ethic so far that we have come to believe God unfailingly rewards our hard work with large salaries, comfortable homes, and fuel-efficient cars.

II. *The god of time is money.* (a) This is a lesser god than the god of work but is no less false. This god proclaims that every hour a working person spends on a job is worth a certain amount of dollars, or conversely, every hour is worth a certain amount of money. This is certainly an odd way to place value on the amount of time we have to live.

(b) The real God, who promises tomorrow to no one, has indicated the real value of time, and it can't be measured in dollars.

III. *The god of winning.* (a) This god is especially cruel and is well known to all of us. Mother Teresa admitted that there was little indication in her work among the desperately poor that her efforts were successful. "But God has not called me to be successful," she said. "God has called me to be faithful." This is a monumental heresy to most of us.

(b) Our local church budgets are not raised on the concept of faithfulness. They are raised on the concept of winning—giving more than last year, reaching newer and higher goals, digging deeper and deeper in the wallets. To fall short of the goal is to fail. The god of winning, who makes us feel like failures despite our most faithful efforts to serve, is doing us no favors. This god is destroying us.

IV. *The god of beauty.* Not many teenagers have the ego-strength to survive plainness in a world in which beauty is the required standard for success. Even Christians give special honor to the talented and beautiful people who spread the word. "Where,"

Martin Marty asked, after surveying a long shelf of Christian books by the Anita Bryants and Pat Boones, "are the books about fat girls with pimples who sit in wheelchairs?" The god of beauty, whom we worship, has forgotten them.

V. There are other false gods. (a) *The god of power.* Grab it so we can do some good and hope it doesn't corrupt us too soon.

(b) *The god of the status quo.* If we-never-did-it-that-way-before, there's certainly no good reason to do it that way now.

(c) *The god of the electronic church.* Evangelism is much faster and much easier than the old painful one-on-one witnessing.

(d) *The god of our own desires.* The easy assumption that if we desire something to be, it must be God's will.

VI. The insidious thing about each of these false gods is that each represents some element of truth. By the time we discover the falsity among the truths, the false gods may have taken over our lives. The discovery of the one true God is not easy, or Jesus would not have warned us that few can expect to enter by the straight gate. As we follow the well-worn paths pointed out by the false gods, we may discover too late that the path ends.—Philip E. Jenks in *The American Baptist.*

SUNDAY: AUGUST TWENTY-FIRST

MORNING SERVICE

Topic: Why Go to Church?

TEXT: Acts 2:42.

I. Church attendance is a source of strength. Jesus said, "For where two or three are gathered together in my name, there am I in the midst of them" (Matt. 18:20).

(a) When the 120 followers of Jesus gathered together in his name in the upper room, the Holy Spirit baptism was first given. At Cornelius' house, the Holy Spirit was first given to the Gentiles as they came together to hear God's messenger. In Antioch, as the Christians were worshiping God, the Holy Spirit spoke and called forth the first foreign missionaries. God's promise to his people is that when they come together in

his name, he is in their presence.

(b) God's people need to attend church because it is a source of spiritual strength for their lives. When a person fails to attend the worship services of his church, he does not receive the strength and stamina that is made available to him by the presence of the Holy Spirit. Because the person has not received that measure of strength, he will not be able to stand against the enemy of his soul as he encounters him day by day.

II. Church attendance is a source of biblical truth. (a) In his second epistle (II Pet. 3:1–2) Peter was concerned that the Christians of the early church have a good knowledge of the teachings of Christ and of the prophets of God so that their faith would be firmly grounded in the truths of God and not in the wisdom of men. He was also aware that the followers of Christ needed to be reminded of the truths they learned lest they should forget or fail to keep them. Heb. 2:1 says, "Therefore we ought to give the more earnest heed to the things which we have heard, lest at any time we should let them slip." The life of every Christian is only as strong as his knowledge of God's Word.

(b) When a person misses church, he misses the message that God has given the pastor for him. He misses the instruction of God for his life and is missing the biblical truth needed to live for Christ. That person is in danger of forgetting the things which he has learned and letting the most important thing in life pass him by.

III. Church attendance is a source of Christian fellowship. (a) In Acts the new converts felt the desire to fellowship with the church people. This is a natural result of conversion. When a person is born again, he seeks for the things of God, not the things of the world. His desire for fellowship should also change in the same manner. Instead of seeking for the companionship of the unsaved, he should desire to be with God's people. Paul stated, "Be ye not unequally yoked together with unbelievers: for what fellowship hath righteousness with unrighteousness? and what communion hath light with darkness?" (II Cor. 6:14).

(b) When one leaves off fellowship with those of "like precious faith," he will naturally turn to nonbelieving friends for companionship. Bad company leads to a breakdown in principles and to compromise. Every believer needs the fellowship of the brothers and sisters of the household of faith.

IV. Church attendance is a source of growth and maturity. (a) Growth is a natural result of living. Babies grow into mature men and women, sprouts become towering timbers and blooming flowers, and newborn Christians should grow into strong, firmly grounded saints of God. For growth to take place there must be the right food and the right environment. Paul said the ministry of the church is "for the perfecting of the saints . . . unto the measure of the stature of the fulness of Christ" (Eph. 4:12–13).

(b) God's plan for the spiritual growth and maturity of the believer is that he attend the local church where his Spirit provides the right environment and the proper food that he may grow and reach the full stature of the Christian faith. If one fails to attend, he will not have that environment, will not receive the proper food value for growth, and will eventually die spiritually.—F. Dean Hackett.

Illustrations

STRAIGHT AND TALL. A little girl was sitting with her father in the worship service. During the sermon she was drawing a picture of people coming into the church and of others going out of the church. The people coming in were short and stooped. The people going out were tall and straight. When asked for an explanation, she replied, "When we go to church, God helps us to stand up straight and tall."—Donald L. Germain.

STAGE AND AUDIENCE. Ordinarily the congregation thinks of itself as an audience, for whose special benefit the minister and choir give their performance. The relation which God bears to this performance is rather like that of an absentee playwright or producer. But a true picture shows us the church as a stage rather than a theater. The congregation are themselves the actors, and the minister and the choir are but promptors making suggestions and giving clues from the wings. And God? God is the audience.—Søren Kierkegaard.

Sermon Suggestions

GOD'S CALLING. Text: Matt. 28:19. (1) God calls us to service and discipleship in a spirit of adventure. (2) God calls us to bear witness to our faith. (3) God calls us in the church to provide and share in a continuing program of Christian nurture. —Hoover Rupert.

AFTER TROUBLE, WHAT? Scripture: Isa. 6:1–9. When Isaiah's friend, King Uzziah, died, the following transpired: (1) Isaiah went to church (v. 1). (2) Isaiah experienced divine presence (vv. 3–4). (3)

Isaiah was made aware of his spiritual need (v. 5). (4) Isaiah's need was resolved (vv. 6–7). (5) Isaiah found direction for the future (vv. 8–9).—David L. Lemons.

Worship Aids

CALL TO WORSHIP. "O send out thy light and thy truth: let them lead me; let them bring me unto thy holy hill, and to the tabernacles." Ps. 43:3.

INVOCATION. O God of mercy, in this hour in thy house have mercy upon us. O God of light, shine into our hearts. O thou eternal goodness, deliver us from evil. O God of power, be thou our refuge and our strength. O God of love, let love flow through us. O God of life, live within us, now and forevermore.

OFFERTORY SENTENCE. "This is the thing which the Lord commanded, saying, Take ye from among you an offering unto the Lord: whosoever is of a willing heart, let him bring it, an offering of the Lord." Exod. 35:4–5.

OFFERTORY PRAYER. O Lord, upon whose constant giving we depend every day, teach us how to spend and be spent for others that we may gain the true good things of life by losing every selfish trait.

PRAYER. O God, help us find thee. Help us find thee through nature— through a drop of water, the seven seas, massive mountains, high hills, pointed peaks, a blade of grass, the flight of birds, the harmony of flowers, the rhythm of life, and the pulse-beat of growth.

Help us find thee through the arts— through the conflict of drama, the grandeur of a cantata, the cheer of a carol, the joy of a hymn, the colors of a painting, the rhythm of the dance, the flow of words, and the lines of a temple.

Help us find thee through the lives of people—through the laugh of a child, the winsomeness of a lad, the glow of youth, the vigor of manhood, the understanding of womanhood, and the wisdom of age.

Help us find thee through scripture— through the vision of Abraham, the wrestling of Jacob, the purity of Joseph, the strength of Deborah, the conscience of Amos, the faith of a centurion, the vigor of Peter, the humility of Mary, the forgiveness of Stephen, and the love of Paul.

Help us, O God, to find thee most through the life of the Man of Galilee who walked the highways of the holy land, leaving behind pictures of thee, our Father.— Fred E. Luchs.

EVENING SERVICE

Topic: The Empowering of Life

TEXT: John 14:26.

I. The Holy Spirit is the illuminator of the human mind. (a) All Christian ministries must be accompanied by the power of the Spirit if the truth of the gospel is to set people free from ignorance and error and release them into the life-giving light of truth.

(b) Our confused and dark time needs the clean, clear mind of Christ to think straight about God, life, and history. The Spirit clarifies and interprets in current reality who Jesus is, what he can do in a life that receives him, and how the new life in him may be matured by "growing up in every way into him."

II. The Holy Spirit is the regenerator of the human heart. (a) Every person needs a radical change in his nature. The natural man cannot enter the kingdom of God; he must be born again.

(b) Christians have differed on the measure of the Spirit's help, but they have not disagreed on the necessity of that help. The great saints insist that faith and repentance are created by the Spirit. A person is started on the new life in Christ through an action of the Spirit that is as radical and as critical as human birth itself.

III. The Holy Spirit is the re-creator of human life. (a) God's action in Jesus Christ continues to work in maturing the Christian's life. The Spirit's creative power teaches us to pray, gives us assurance of our sonship with God, instructs our consciences, leads us into all of the truth in Christ, and helps us to love and serve our neighbor.

(b) A sure sign of the Spirit's presence in life is this continuous striving of the

Spirit with the human spirit, so that the old man dies and the new man in Christ grows into true personhood.

(c) The Spirit creates a unique community life by bringing about a new relationship among those who share in Christ's life and work. The Spirit creates the community of fellowship, worship, witness, nurture, and pastoral care. The Spirit creates Christian unity. Where the Spirit is, there is the urge of a missionary passion and social compassion which makes the needs of the whole world its concern.—Elmer G. Homrighausen.

SUNDAY: AUGUST TWENTY-EIGHTH

MORNING SERVICE

Topic: Lost in Your Own Backyard

SCRIPTURE: Luke 15:25–32.

Jesus is saying that it is possible to be lost in your own backyard. This chapter is made up of stories about a lost sheep, a lost coin, and two lost sons. One lost himself in a far country in riotous living and in burning the candle at both ends. His sins were those of the harlots and the hogs. But the other son was lost too. Decent, honest, and respectable he was, but he was still lost. And because most of us are more like him than like the other, it may be worth our while to see just where his trouble lay. How could he have gotten lost so close to home?

I. He was lost in jealousy. (a) Even a cursory reading reveals that familiar green-eyed monster. Coming in after a hard day's work, he hears the sound of music and laughter and dancing. He naturally wants to know what is going on. When he finds out, he can hardly wait to upbraid his father: "You never gave me a kid. You killed for him the fatted calf." His sibling rivalry had gotten out of hand, and everyone knows what damage can result from a parent's favoring one child over another.

(b) In the Old Testament there is another picture, drawn from life, of a man lost in jealousy. David was a fast-rising young lieutenant of King Saul. Before long he was getting more attention for his exploits in battle than the king. And straightway Saul "was very angry" and "eyed David from that day on" (I Sam. 18:6–9). Eventually, eaten away by his envy and suspicion and jealousy, Saul lost his mind and his kingdom and died by his own hand.

(c) You don't have to live a licentious or gross kind of a life to be lost in jealousy. You can do it in your own backyard.

(d) Othello was a good, honest, sincere, just, and loving man. Strength and honor were his clothing. But once the cunning Iago plants the seed of jealousy, we see his nobility deteriorate before our very eyes. Trifles are magnified, the most innocent of intentions are distorted, and by the end of the play he is lost like the older brother, like King Saul, and like many another person in his jealousy.

II. This young man was lost in self-righteousness. (a) How holier-than-thou can you get? "Lo, these many years I have served you, and I never disobeyed your command. . . . But this son of yours . . . devoured your living with harlots" (15: 29–30). "What a good boy am I!" He makes no attempt to conceal his contempt —"this son of yours." He is so smug about his moral superiority that it is painful.

(b) Jealousy may be corrosive, but self-righteousness is probably more subtle and more common, particularly among religious people. Paul suffered from a bad case of it; so did Luther; so did Wesley; so do most of us.

(c) Evelyn Underhill observed that in the book of Revelation "it is the saints and the elders nearest God who cast down their crowns to adore him. The lesser fry, further off, are quite content to go on wearing theirs." How often that is true. The great are humble, and the small are lost in their own self-righteousness.

III. This young man was lost in his own backyard and didn't know it.

(a) He was sublimely oblivious to his own failures. He could plainly see that his brother had gotten off the reservation, but he never knew that, in his own way, he had too.

(b) We can see jealousy in others; we can see self-righteousness in others. But it is hard to see them or other faults in ourselves.

(c) The more certain you are about yourself, morally and spiritually, the greater the likelihood that you're wrong. You can be lost and not know it, so "judge not, that you be not judged" (Matt. 7:1).—Raymond E. Balcomb.

Illustrations

JUDGMENT. When man judges man, the accused knows whether he is innocent or guilty; it is for the judge to find out. When God judges man, the judge knows the truth already; it is the accused who has to learn it. Our judgment by God will be an exhibition to ourselves of our own record; in the sight of God that record is already plain to view.—Ronald Knox.

POINTS OF VIEW. A king was engaged in great wars with many countries. To each he sent an army for its conquest. One army was led by his son, the prince; each of the others was led by one of his nobles. When the king's son heard that the nobles were successful in their campaigns, though he himself was not progressing too well, he rejoiced because the will of his father, the king, was being carried out, and his father would take joy in their victories. But when he heard that the nobles were defeated, even though he was winning his own battle, the prince became sad because he knew that this would cause much pain to his father, the king.

The nobles reacted in the opposite manner. Every noble rejoiced when his own army was victorious, regardless of the progress of the others. And if one heard that the other nobles did not strengthen their position but fell back before the enemy and that he alone was the mighty victor, then he rejoiced even more, for he believed that he alone would be exalted by the king. The will and the happiness of the king meant nothing to him. His only concern was his own happiness and what he might receive from the king.—Samuel H. Dresner.

Sermon Suggestions

TAKING FROM LIFE ITS BEST. Text: Matt. 13:45–46. (1) The spirit-filled life. (2) Genuine and real love. (3) The glow of health. (4) Work and a task to perform. (5) An unending process of growth. (6) Enthusiasm and the creative spirit. (7) Realization of our true potential.—Frank A. Court.

GETTING BACK ON THE TRACK. Scripture: Phil. 3:17–21. (1) By remembering our calling (v. 17). (2) By examining our lives (vv. 18–19). (3) By remembering our destiny (vv. 20–21).

Worship Aids

CALL TO WORSHIP. "Having therefore, brethren, boldness to enter into the holiest by the blood of Jesus, by a new and living way, which he hath consecrated for us, let us draw near with a true heart in full assurance of faith." Heb. 10:19–20, 22.

INVOCATION. Most humbly do we thank thee, O Lord, for thy mercies of every kind and thy loving care over all thy creatures. We bless thee for the gift of life, for thy protection round about us, for thy guiding hand upon us and the many tokens of thy love, especially for the saving knowledge of thy dear Son, for friendship and duty, for good hopes and precious memories, and for the joys that cheer us and the trials that teach us to trust in thee. O heavenly Father, make us wise unto a right use of thy benefits, and so direct us that in word and deed we may show gratitude to thee.

OFFERTORY SENTENCE. "Take heed what ye hear: with what measure ye mete, it shall be measured to you: and unto you that hear shall more be given." Mark 4:24.

OFFERTORY PRAYER. Dear Father, may we ever give thee a definite, consistent, and heartfelt service.

PRAYER. We bow before thee, O God, in humble acknowledgment of thy power and in grateful acceptance of thy mercy and grace. We need thy mercy, for we transgress thy laws and fall short of thy glory. We need thy grace, for we cannot offer anything to merit thy favor or gain thy love.

In Jesus Christ our Lord, thou hast shown thyself as the Father of love who welcomes with joy his returning child, as the good shepherd who seeks his lost sheep until he finds it, and as the limitless giver who supplies our every need out of his wealth in glory.

Give us confidence to draw near to thee that we may find grace to help us in time of need, and grant that we may pass our days in the companionship of the everlasting mercy.—Richard E. Gosse.

EVENING SERVICE

Topic: God the Stirrer
Text: Deut. 32:11.

Nothing is more interesting about an eagle than its nesting habits. It chooses a ledge of rock and builds its nest, usually laying two eggs. When the young birds are old enough to learn to fly, the parent eagles stir up the nest, pushing it off the ledge. The eaglets are enticed to jump from the ledge and to try and fly. If the small eagle is in danger of falling onto the rocks below, the older bird will sweep beneath it and catch it on its wings. As Moses looks back over his long life, he likens God to an eagle. Many times God has been a stirrer, breaking up cozy nests and leading his people into new, unknown adventures. God, like the eagle, is a stirrer.

I. God stirs and disturbs but always for reasons of love. As an eagle that stirs up its nest, so is God.

(a) The Bible often presents God as a place of security, for hiding in the day of trouble. He is a shield, a fortress, a rock of salvation. And he is, and we would

be lost without a sheltering God.

(b) There are times when God plays the opposite role. His Spirit pushes us out of our nests of security. He disturbs us with new truth. He throws us into the unknown.

II. When God stirs his people and disturbs his world, all are challenged to take a plunge in faith.

(a) Look again at the eagles. The nest is broken and scattered. Two eaglets are peering fearfully over the ledge as the parent birds entice them to fly. And there is no other way. Only by a plunge into the air will birds ever learn to fly.

(b) God expects of you and me a plunge in faith. The reality of God is not found at the end of a logical argument. Reason may carry us far, but God's presence is only found in the end by an act of faith. "I believe, help thou my unbelief." God becomes real as we plunge toward him in faith.

III. What is the purpose of God stirring the nest, calling for acts of faith? That a greater fulfillment shall be found.

(a) Let us go back to the eagles once more. Twelve months after the stirring of the nest the purpose would be obvious. We would see two young eagles flying high above the mountains, sweeping into the valleys, masters of the air. The broken nest and the plunge in faith have given to the eagles their destiny.

(b) The tragedy of so many lives is that they have become satisfied and stationary. There is no growth any more. Seeing no new visions and attempting no new ventures, life has stagnated. Somehow so many miss their destiny.

(c) God may stir and disturb us, but always he leads us forward and always he seeks to enable us to be the best that we can be.—Alan Walker.

SUNDAY: SEPTEMBER FOURTH

MORNING SERVICE

Topic: God's Good Gift (Labor Sunday)
Text: Ps. 90:17.

Surely labor is a good gift of God. "In the beginning God created." The first verb in the first verse is a working verb.

God created or made the world. The creation account concludes: "And God saw everything that he had made, and, behold, it was very good."

I. *Work is good.* (a) Like a fine craftsman, God stepped back to admire his own work. Surely you have experienced this satisfaction of a job well done. You come home bone tired from an honest day's toil. Or you worked yourself weary in cooking and cleaning. Yet you've been productive and accomplished something. It is a good feeling because work is good.

(b) Where do we get the idea that work is a curse? Not from God. When man sinned, God never pronounced a curse on labor.

(1) Chapter two says, "And the Lord God took the man and put him into the Garden of Eden to dress it and keep it." That was the work assignment before Adam and Eve rebelled. It was a great job. No problem but pure joy.

(2) After sin spoiled everything, God drove them out into a changed world. No longer would they simply keep God's garden. They would have to scratch a living from soil dominated by thorns and thistles. "Cursed is the ground for thy sake" (3:17). Henceforth would the ground be worked "in the sweat of thy face."

(3) The ground was cursed but not work. Labor is not bad; it's a blessing. Not a curse but a comfort. In the Bible work is always mentioned in positive terms.

(c) Hard work is a good gift of God and good for you. There's a blessing waiting in every job. Carlyle said, "Blessed is the man who has found his work; let him ask no other blessing."

II. *Work is good but not for salvation.* (a) Some good things are not good for other purposes.

(1) A ship is great for water but not for land. Cars travel on roads and not in the air. And honest toil is good for man's body and mind but of no help in our ultimate journey through eternity.

(2) What do you consider the most important occupation in the world? The President of our country has a great responsibility. So does the President's physician who monitors his heartbeat. But their jobs cannot save them. Work is not redemptive.

(3) We all stand very equal before God. The most equal factor here on earth is how limited our hands are in this matter of salvation. God's focus of redemption is instead upon our hearts. We are saved not by works but by our faith in God's grace.

(b) Some people let their jobs stand between them and God. That should never happen. Someone else will have your job someday, but no one can occupy your place in heaven. If your vocation hinders you from considering the claims of Christ in your life, quit your job. Nothing is worth more than your salvation.

(c) The same advice applies if your job interferes with the worship of God. It is not God's will for you to work on a regular basis at the expense of worship. Make a covenant and trust him to find you another job with different hours. He will.

(d) A bigger problem for the majority is being so busy in work during the week that they neglect God.

(1) We Americans love to work hard for the better things of life. A new car, furniture, or boat is a goal which pushes us harder. Sometimes we moonlight to get ahead financially.

(2) Isa. 55:2 asks, "Why do you labor for that which satisfies not?" These things trap us on a treadmill of constant labor, yet they don't satisfy. We always want more. Jesus said, "Labor not for the food which perishes but for the food which endures to eternal life" (John 6:27).

(e) Is there any way we can bring together these great values of work and worship? While work is good for us but not good enough for salvation, we can still work for God.

III. *Combine your spiritual and secular work for God.* (a) Enjoy both your earthly vocation and your spiritual vineyard. We need not choose between being spiritual or secular. We live in both worlds. No apologies are necessary for Christians laboring in the world. "Whatsoever you do," St. Paul said, "do all unto the glory of God" (I Cor. 10:31).

(b) The best insurance for a happy vocation is to follow God in the job he wants for you. Then work for the glory of God on your job. "Ye know that your labor is not in vain, in the Lord" (I Cor. 15:58).

(c) Whether in spiritual or secular jobs, we can work for God. Heb. 4:11 encourages us: "Let us labor therefore to enter into that rest." Some people will never know spiritual rest because they've avoided spiritual labor. Rest will not be happy for them in heaven without the memory of good work. They miss that satisfying weariness of work in the spiritual vineyard.—C. W. Bess.

Illustrations

SELECTED BY GOD. However it comes about—whether suddenly or gradually, whether through some vision or by the helpful counsel of Christian friends, by means of an inner persuasion nurtured by many sources or by prayerful assessment of one's consecrated abilities—the sense of being selected by God for full-time Christian service is an essential characteristic of the ministry.—Mack B. Stoke.

TRUE SERVICE. All service which is done from the same motive in the same force is of the same worth in God's eyes. It does not matter whether you have the gospel in a penny testament printed on thin paper with black ink and done up in cloth or in an illuminated missal glowing in gold and color, painted with loving care on fair parchment, and bound in jeweled ivory. And so it matters little about the material or the scale on which we express our devotion and our aspirations; all depends on what we copy, not on the size of the canvas on which, or on the material in which, we copy it. "Small service is true service while it lasts," and the unnoticed insignificant servants may do work every whit as good and noble as the most known to whom have been intrusted by Christ tasks that mold the ages.—Alexander Maclaren.

Sermon Suggestions

WHY WORK? Text: Acts 20:33–35. (1) Work helps us provide for the necessities of life. (2) Work helps us live responsibly. (3) Work helps us to minister to others.—Ernest D. Standerfer.

WHO'S IN CHARGE? Text: Gen. 1:26 (RSV). (1) There is the original God-ordained assignment of having dominion—supervision—over creation. (2) The word and concept of dominion relates to our personal selves. (3) The exercise of dominion brings us into a large and complex realm of social issues.—John H. Townsend.

Worship Aids

CALL TO WORSHIP. "Come unto me, all ye that labor and are heavy laden, and I will give you rest. Take my yoke upon you, and learn of me; for I am meek and lowly in heart; and ye shall find rest unto your souls." Matt. 11:28–29.

INVOCATION. Out of our darkness we are come to thee for light; out of our sorrows we are come to thee for joy; out of our doubts we are come to thee for certainty; out of our anxieties we are come to thee for peace; out of our sinning we are come to thee for thy forgiving love. Open thou thine hand this day and satisfy our every need. This we ask for thy love's sake.

OFFERTORY SENTENCE. "Let the beauty of the Lord our God be upon us: and establish thou the work of our hands upon us; yea, the work of our hands establish thou it." Ps. 90:17.

OFFERTORY PRAYER. God of all good, who hath rewarded our labors, we acknowledge thankfully thy favor and do now dedicate a share of our material gains to the even more satisfying ministries of the Spirit.

LITANY. O thou all-wise Creator of the world, who hast made man in thine image to have dominion over thine other creatures, and hast given him the duty to subdue the earth, that it may yield the riches thou hast hidden therein to supply his need: we thank thee for the blessing of labor whereby we are made workers together with thee:
Bless and guide us, we beseech thee.
By human willfulness and waywardness, ignorance and greed, idleness and oppression, a curse has touched thy blessing, and the joy of man in work has departed from many. For our part in this sin we beg thy forgiveness, our heavenly Father:
Bless and guide us, we beseech thee.
From pride and avarice and tyranny

over the bodies of men, from the hard heart which disregards the need of a fellow servant, and from the dishonest temper which withholds fullness of a promised service, and from laziness, self-indulgence, and inhumanity:

O Lord, deliver us.

From injustice and oppression, from conspiracy and violence, from the choice of force instead of reason, from all denial of our common humanity and our fellowship in Christ, from all contempt of those who toil and suffer, and from all shame of our own work:

O Lord, deliver us.

For all who till the earth and gather the harvest, for all who go down to the sea and do business in great waters, for all who work in offices and in shops, for all who labor in factories and at furnaces, and for those who toil in the mines:

Hear us, we beseech thee.

For all who employ and direct labor, for all who carry responsibility, for all who enrich life through art and science and learning, for pastors and teachers, physicians and surgeons, for nurses and all who minister to the sick, for women in business and in homes, and for statesmen and social workers:

Hear us, we beseech thee.

For all who have lost the reward of their labor, for those who cannot find work, for those who will not work, and for the homeless and the friendless:

Hear us, we beseech thee.

O Lord, our heavenly Father, by whose providence the duties of men are varied and ordered, grant to us all the spirit to labor heartily to do our work in our several stations in serving one Master and looking for one reward. Teach us to put to good account whatever talents thou hast given us, and enable us to redeem our time by patience and zeal.—*Pulpit Digest.*

EVENING SERVICE

Topic: On the Job

Text: Neh. 6:3 (neb).

I. Nehemiah wanted to stay on the job because he saw his work as important. "I have important work."

(a) He was rebuilding the wall around Jerusalem. His work was necessary to the city's security and the people's safety.

(b) Do we see our work as important? If the result of our work is a mere by-product and if our first aim is to make money, the job will never give true satisfaction. Is your task worth doing? If it is you will want to stay on the job and do it carefully, accurately, and completely.

II. Nehemiah wanted to stay on the job because he saw his responsibility as personal. "I have important work on my hands."

(a) He felt that no one else could do his job. If we are just putting in time, we feel no personal responsibility. We must put ourselves into the job.

(b) The account of creation tells us that God saw his work and pronounced it good. As creatures made in the image of the Creator, our satisfaction will come from looking at what we have made and finding it good.

III. Nehemiah wanted to stay on the job because he saw his working time as limited. "I have important work on my hands at the moment."

(a) He had a sense of the fleeting moments, but he was not a clock-watcher. He was not preoccupied with quitting time. He was concerned with having enough time to complete the job at hand.

(b) Every human undertaking must reckon with the passing hours. Nehemiah knew that no one has all the time in the world. Time has limits.—Bramwell Tripp.

SUNDAY: SEPTEMBER ELEVENTH

MORNING SERVICE

Topic: The Joy of Sins Forgiven
SCRIPTURE: Ps. 32:1–5 (NASV).
This psalm projects at least five evangelical themes. While each is more fully developed in the New Testament, these are integral to David's own experience at his moment of most acute spiritual need.

I. *Repentance.* (a) Repentance is derived from the Greek "after knowledge." The basic truths which one must grasp in order for contrition truly to be repentance is that he is a sinner, that he is unable to save himself, and that he must abandon himself to the mercy and grace of God in Christ.

(b) David was awakened to his sin and to God's expectation by Nathan's parable of the poor man's ewe lamb: "I have sinned against the Lord." And the prophet responded, "The Lord also has taken away your sin; you shall not die" (II Sam. 12:13, NASV). David's action was clearly a change of mind, course, and conduct, which is the very essence of repentance.

II. *Forgiveness.* (a) Replete with significance for both time and eternity, forgiveness is the sublimest expression of tongue or pen. The redeemed today identify with David in the joy of sins remitted and the peace of God conferred.

(b) The apostle John comments on the universal application of this theme: "If we confess our sins, he is faithful and righteous to forgive us our sins and to cleanse us from all unrighteousness" (I John 1:9, NASV).

III. *Atonement.* (a) The psalmist rejoiced that his sin was "covered." God does not treat our sins superficially—"sweep them under the rug," as it were—but eradicates them, never again to remember them against us. "As far as the east is from the west," exulted David, "so far has he removed our transgressions from us" (Ps. 103:12, NASV).

(b) David pled that his sins might be blotted out (Ps. 51:1, 9). When his—and ours—are thus "covered" or "atoned," we are justified in God's sight. Acquitted of guilt before a holy God, we can exclaim triumphantly with Paul: "Who will bring a charge against God's elect? God is the one who justifies; who is the one who condemns? Christ Jesus is he who died, yes, rather who was raised, who is at the right hand of God, who also intercedes for us" (Rom. 8:33–34, NASV).

IV. *Imputation of righteousness.* (a) Scripture assures us that in Adam all die both spiritually and physically, but as the sin of Adam was imputed to the race, so the righteousness of Jesus Christ, the Second Adam, is imputed to all who believe. (See I Cor. 15:22, 45–47; Rom. 3:23; 5:12–21.) Forgiveness, atonement, and imputation of righteousness converge in the marvelous declaration, "He [God] made him [Christ] who knew no sin to be sin on our behalf, that we might become the righteousness of God in him" (II Cor. 5:21, NASV).

(b) The apostle Paul cites David in illustration of the believer justified by faith, quoting our text in support of the psalmist's experience of grace. (See Rom. 4:5–8.) Indeed, the teaching here is the universal application of God's gifts, the commonality of grace for his own in every time and place.

V. *Witness.* (a) David has promised in Ps. 51 that he would extol the divine mercy if God would but restore him (vv. 12–15). Ps. 32 is partial realization of that pledge, for his happiness at the Father's gracious dealings with him can scarcely be contained.

(b) Jesus has challenged those who bear his name to be busy in the world while remaining separate from the world system. (See John 17:13–21.) Dietrich Bonhoeffer interpreted Jesus to be commending a "holy-worldliness," a living for Christ in a hostile society that so desperately needs to see a Christian.—Donald N. Bowdle.

Illustrations

HALF HAPPY.   So many stand just outside the greatest joy that can come to any human being this side of the grave—the joy of conscious fellowship with God and with those to whom he is the one great living reality. You are half-way committed to Christ, and you have your reward in a heart which is half happy.—Samuel M. Shoemaker.

BEGINNING AGAIN.   When he created man, God gave him a secret. That secret was not how to begin but how to begin again. It is not given to man to begin; that privilege is God's alone. But it is given to man to begin again.—Elie Wiesel.

Sermon Suggestions

JOYOUS LIVING.   Text: John 15:11. (1) Joy is nurtured on warm, radiant fellowship. (2) Joy is nourished by and thrives on creative, constructive work. (3) Joy increases with a sustaining, triumphant faith.—William E. Hammond.

LEARNING TO FORGIVE.   Scripture: Matt. 18:21–35. (1) How are we to approach the task of forgiving? (a) With a calculator (v. 21). (b) With a balance (v. 28). (c) With grace (v. 22). (2) How God forgives. (a) By grace that is undeserved (vv. 26–27). (b) By grace that flows from his heart (v. 27). (See Luke 1:78.) (c) By grace that empowers the forgiven sinner (v. 35).—Robert W. Schaibley.

Worship Aids

CALL TO WORSHIP.   "The Lord is exalted; for he dwelleth on high: he hath filled Zion with judgment and righteousness. And wisdom and knowledge shall be the stability of thy times, and strength of salvation: the fear of the Lord is his treasure." Isa. 33:5–6.

INVOCATION.   O spirit of the living God, who dwellest in thy church and who art holiness, wisdom, and might: come thou now in this hour, fill the hearts of thy faithful people, and kindle within them the fire of thy love.

OFFERTORY SENTENCE.   "Give unto the Lord the glory due unto his name: bring an offering, and come before him: worship the Lord in the beauty of holiness." I Chron. 16:29.

OFFERTORY PRAYER.   We praise thee, O God, for thy countless blessings and pray that thou wilt accept these gifts in gratitude in Jesus' name.

PRAYER.   O God, we are mindful of the words of thy Son who said, "If I be lifted up, I will draw all men unto me." Lift us above ourselves that we may be the persons thou dost intend.

Lift us above the petty problems of everyday—the office rivalries, the dirty dishes, the nasty little jobs—and help us to see behind it all the growth in personal relations that can supersede rivalry, the fellowship around the table that makes the dishes dirty, and the discipline that comes from doing nasty little jobs.

Lift us above our faults—the quick temper, the thoughtless words, the easy criticism—and help us to temper our tempers, to exchange sluggish minds and hasty words for quick thinking and careful words, and to turn from criticism of others to an appreciation of ourselves and of them.

And lift us above today with its desperate pressures to do this, to be that, and to go there. Help us to remember that we are meant for more than today and that we have eternity in which to do thy will, to become what thou wouldst have us be, and to be lifted up unto our Lord.—Harry W. Adams.

EVENING SERVICE

Topic: Victorious Living

TEXT: John 16:33 (NEB).

I. What does Jesus not mean? (a) Jesus was not telling us that our Christian faith will guarantee the removal of all the obstacles, difficulties, and tragedies that all people, including Christians, encounter in life. His words, "In the world ye shall have tribulation," are hardly the promise of a life or a world without stress and strain. Christianity is not a retreat from life and its hard and bitter experiences. We overcome the world by facing the world as it really is and, in the encounter, finding the secret peace and a power that make us more adequate to meet the challenges both of prosperity and of adversity.

(b) Our faith as Christians does not promise us everything in life that we'd like to have. To follow the way of Jesus involves no lifetime guarantee that everything will work out as we would like it to. Jesus had more than a little to say about cross-bearing, and crosses are seldom something that we ourselves choose or hope to receive. Yet it is often in the midst of frustrations and in the face of the denial of our hopes and aspirations that many of our greatest personal victories can be and are achieved.

(c) In order to live abundantly and victoriously we don't have to become everything that we know we ought to be. When we become followers of the Way, we do not suddenly arrive at a state of perfection. We are still our old, unruly, and often unworthy selves—sinners. But we are forgiven sinners in process of becoming saints and persons who are accepted by God and used by him in spite of very real shortcomings and inadequacies.

II. What does it mean to live abundantly and victoriously? (a) Such living happens when we find ourselves released from the blind alleys of self centeredness into the streets and avenues of service and commitment. Jesus was right when he insisted that the way to find true blessedness and fulfillment is to lose yourself—to get yourself out of the center and to find in some cause or person a point of focus that directs your energies and your attention outward rather than inward.

(b) Victorious living happens when we find release from fear and anxiety through faith in a power not ourselves which is greater than we. It is possible for us to come to the place where we can move forward on the assumption and in the assurance that the reality we call God is surely with us. When we launch out into life, accept it as it comes to us, and enjoy it as God's good gift, then we begin to know what true faith means. We are given everything for living our lives victoriously and abundantly that we need.

(c) Victorious living means release from aloneness and solitariness by moving into the context of a new community. The Christian life has often been referred to as a pilgrimage. As we make our pilgrimages through life, all of us need to be reminded that there have been and now are other pilgrims who travel with us along the same way, the cloud of witnesses of which the letter to the Hebrews speaks. Even in our moments of seeming forsakenness we, like Jesus, can say, "I am not alone, but the Father is with me." The forces that are for us are stronger than those which are against us.—Edward C. Dahl.

SUNDAY: SEPTEMBER EIGHTEENTH

MORNING SERVICE

Topic: The Most Happy Fellow
Text: Matt. 10:39.
Henry Thoreau made the statement that as long as a man stands in his own way everything seems to be in his way. The most happy fellow is the one who has gotten himself out of the way. We face a task of finding ourselves and yet sacrificing ourselves. We must have the courage to be a part of others. The happy fellow is the person who no longer is in his own way.

I. A happy fellow is one who has an increasing ability to forget himself, not to forget in an effort to escape but to relate to causes and to people in such a way as to enter into genuine response.

(a) Some people are so tied up with image projecting that they cannot enter into any relationship that is authentic. Continued self-reference is always getting in the way. We don't want to jump to the conclusion that every word that has self in it is bad, for in a sense we are all self-centered, and self-centeredness does not mean selfishness in particular. The psychologists are continually telling us that we need a centered self and a real self-affirmation. We are not trying to come to a place of selflessness but to a place where extreme or abnormal self-centeredness does not get in our own way. Self-centeredness is a God-given part of the process of growth and development. It is a necessary stage in the growth of the conscious personality.

(b) When Jesus said, "Lose your life and you will find it," was he a King Canute in futile fashion trying to sweep back the ocean of self-interest? "Lose" in Greek may be translated to mean "let loose" or "free" or "release." This does not mean a rejection or a complete denial of self, but it means finding oneself in relationship to others, a self-release toward others. Whoever releases his life finds the kingdom. The true egoist is the one who can never forget himself or get any release from himself.

(c) The happiest times are those in which we do forget ourselves. Haven't we had those moments of self-abdication? It is then that we find our true happiness. This is a crucial thought for us to understand for practically every personality defect has its origin in extreme self-centeredness and egocentricity. The person who is always trying to save himself has a miserable existence. Whittier in one of his poems wrote of the dreary selfishness that becomes the prisoner of a soul. Some never break out of that. They are always in this prison.

(d) This truth not only comes from a psychological viewpoint but also from a theological viewpoint. St. Augustine spoke of a man who was curved inward upon himself. Many people are battling with this inward curvature of their psyches. The psychologist and the theologian join hands in saying that a man cannot constantly turn inward toward himself and have any health of spirit. He cannot operate totally from the reference of what it is that he wants. The egoist, doing only what his own selfish desires proclaim, ends up hating everything he does. He is like the child in the progressive school who wailed, "Do I always have to do what I want?"

II. The happy fellow is not the possessive person. He's able to go from a possessive type of living to a sacrificial type of living.

(a) This is one of the principles of life we have to accept. George Herbert Palmer, who had such a reverent regard for the rights and person of his own wife, Alice Freeman, said, "I never call her mine." A too possessive person soon comes to the truth that his possessiveness loses what he really desires. Everything we see and touch we want to possess. We want to get our corner of the world and call it our own. This attitude is quite prevalent in trying to squeeze all the joys and pleasures out of life as though life itself were our possession.

(b) The happy people are not the possessive people; they are the sacrificial people. We often feel sorry for the person out in some mission station. He works twelve hours a day in unpleasant conditions, but usually when we meet him he has a radiance about him.

(c) Sacrifice is written right into the universe. All the common processes of nature are sacrificial. Nothing lives here on earth except when something dies. We may complain about the process, but we cannot escape it. You would not be here without sacrifice. It is not the possessive person but the sacrificial person who approaches the portals of a happy life.

III. The most happy person is the one who cares passionately. (a) Kierkegaard said that life without passion is no life at all. No child was ever conceived without passion. No great poem was ever produced without passion. No great piece of music was ever composed without passion. Passion is what takes us beyond the superficiality of life to a deep and wonderful glow in which we learn to care. Life demands that we care about something beyond ourselves.

(b) It has been suggested by some scholars that caring should substitute for the word "charity" in I Cor. 13. If we are not people who care, nothing will make up for it. Though I speak with the tongues of men and of angels and I do not care, I am as sounding brass or tinkling cymbal, for caring never ends.

(c) Do we care enough to surrender our lives? Robert Frost in one of his poems had this line: "We found salvation in surrender. Such as we were, we gave ourselves outright." Sometimes it is hard for us to believe this. The man who surrenders himself to a great cause about which he cares passionately finds indirectly that it has led him to his own salvation.

(d) Our weakness and our failures seem subdued when we surrender ourselves to a greater cause. It is here that we lose our poverty. It is here that we are caught up to be part of something that is beyond us and that breaks our self-centeredness and expands our care. In a sense we have to really lose ourselves in something greater.—C. A. McClain, Jr.

Illustrations

UPPER LEVEL KNOW-HOW. A group of men who were having lunch began to talk about an absent friend. They all seemed to have such admiration for him. Everything always seemed to go right for him. "Why is it," one of them asked, "that everything he does seems to turn out all right?" One man who knew the absent gentleman quite well answered: "There is something you fellows are overlooking about him. What he has is upper level know-how." Someone asked what he meant by upper level know-how. The man is literally saturated with the wisdom of God and Jesus Christ and the Bible. And to a very remarkable degree he has eliminated the mistake tendency.—Norman Vincent Peale.

DOUBTING THOMAS. It is unexpected but extraordinarily convincing that the one absolutely unequivocal statement in the whole gospel of the divinity of Jesus should come from Doubting Thomas. It is the only place where the word "god" is used of him without qualification of any kind and in the most unambiguous form of the word. And this must be said not ecstatically or with a cry of astonishment but with flat conviction, as of one acknowledging that two plus two equals four: "You are my Lord and my God!"—Dorothy L. Sayers.

Sermon Suggestions

THE BLESSINGS OF CHEERFULNESS. Text: Prov. 17:22. (1) Cheerfulness beautifies the countenance. (2) Cheerfulness enhances health. (3) Cheerfulness beautifies worship. (4) Cheerfulness makes duty a pleasure. (5) Cheerfulness is a winsome grace.

TO GOD BE THE GLORY. Scripture: Rom. 11:33–36. (1) God is the source: "from him" (v. 36). (2) God is the power: "through him" (v. 36). (3) God is the goal: "to him" (v. 36).—Gerhard Aho.

Worship Aids

CALL TO WORSHIP. "The kingdom of this world has become the kingdom of our Lord, and of his Christ; and he shall reign for ever and ever." Rev. 11:15.

INVOCATION. Most holy and gracious God, who turnest the shadow of night into morning: satisfy us early with thy mercy that we may rejoice and be glad all the day. Lift the light of thy countenance upon us, calm every troubled thought, and guide our feet into the way of peace. Perfect thy strength in our weakness and help us to worship thee in the spirit of Jesus Christ our Lord.

OFFERTORY SENTENCE. "What shall I render unto the Lord for all his benefits toward me? I will pay my vows unto the Lord now in the presence of all his people." Ps. 116:12–14.

OFFERTORY PRAYER. O Lord Jesus Christ, who hast taught us that to whomsoever much is given, of him shall much be required: grant that we, whose lot is cast in this Christian heritage, may strive more earnestly by our prayers and tithes and by sympathy and study to hasten the coming of thy kingdom among all peoples of the earth, that as we have entered into the labors of others, so others may enter into ours, to thy honor and glory.

PRAYER. O God, from whom come all good things in man and nature, we would sensitively open our spirits to thee this hour. Thou art never far from any one of us, and yet in this pavilion of thy worship we would more intimately find thee and be found of thee. Infinity of grace and goodness, lift us up into a new faith in thee and a new vision of thee. For dark hours come when questions rise concerning thee and doubts throng in.

The beauty of nature, its symmetry and order, harmony and color—that we see. The virtues of human life on its noblest altitudes, integrity and honor, courage and good will—that we see. The achievements of man's mind and character, the truth that science seeks, the beauty that art creates, the goodness that high-minded manhood gains—that we see. The victories of righteousness, where light has risen out of darkness and love has proved stronger than hate—that we see.

O God, from whose great reservoir of goodness these streams flow, make us more certain about thee until today we too shall say, "The Lord is the strength of my life; of whom shall I be afraid?"

In this faith lift us up into a new courage. Thou seest our daily need of fortitude and valor. Save us from soft optimism. Let not sentimentality beguile us. Save us from saying, Peace, peace, when there is no peace, and may we never try to heal deep diseases with easy words. Give us honesty to face hard facts and yet, with it all, give us courage, we beseech thee.

Thou seest with what varied needs thy children seek thy face. O thou who dost meet us in the solitariness of our own souls, with thy still, small voice deal with us one by one. If we have sinned, grant us the grace of sincere penitence and renunciation, and cleanse us with thy pardon. If we are in grief, comfort us with the steadfastness of thy strong foundations under us that the storm may not beat us down. If we are in anxiety, clarify our vision and direct our steps. Unsnarl some tangled life in this company, we beseech thee. If we are proud, humble us, and if we have been humiliated, lift us up. So girded, send us out to be soldiers of the common good.—Harry Emerson Fosdick.

EVENING SERVICE

Topic: Do You Want to Give Up?
Text: John 6:68 (rsv).
Our life pilgrimage is far from easy. All sorts of stumbling-blocks and hardships intervene which make our passages troublesome. There are times when our journey seems too difficult to endure. "I give up," we want to say.

I. The word of Christian faith for this circumstance was articulated in a dialogue between Jesus and his followers centering upon the severe demands and difficulty of his teaching.

(a) Some of Jesus' followers began to say aloud: "This teaching is too hard. Who can listen to it?" Their grumbling had to do not only with a particular topic of conversation but also with their frustration in handling life's challenges in general. They had a hard time coping with things as they were, and Jesus seemed to be complicating their struggle. Knowing of their unrest, Jesus addressed these followers by asking simply, "Does this make you want to give up?"

(b) A number of them did give up. "Because of this," explains John's gospel, "many of Jesus' followers turned back and would not go with him any more." Finally the disciples likewise had to answer Jesus' question. To this company Jesus said, "And you—would you also like to leave?"

(c) It was a moment of truth, a time for decision. There was a real pull in the direction of quitting, even among the twelve, just as there had been among that larger following. Who knows how many times these most stalwart of Jesus' companions had to deal with feelings of frustration? They had to handle the problem of personal insufficiency. "Giving up" was an enticing option.

(d) What happened was just the opposite. Here is where we begin to learn the lesson which can be applied to ourselves in similar hours of desperation.

(1) It was not in turning away but in drawing closer to Jesus that the disciples found their footing once again. Peter became spokesman for the twelve, and he answered Jesus' question about quitting by saying: "Lord, to whom would we go? You have the words that give eternal life."

(2) Totally aware that the issues were not solved nor simplified, Peter refused to withdraw, and the others agreed. Those followers persevered in their allegiance,

sensing that "the words of eternal life" were to be found only in Jesus. No other source would satisfy their truest and deepest need.

II. Your problems and mine are not typically the same as those facing the disciples. Our frustrations build around other matters, but the clue to resolving them can be extracted from this incident between Jesus and his friends.

(a) When Peter said, "Lord, to whom would we go?" he was giving us the first part of the solution. There is a person—Jesus himself—who can be depended upon and who can be trusted through a dark and despairing time.

(b) Jesus has yet other vistas to open to his followers, other understandings to reveal. He has more to teach, more to give. He alone has the words of eternal life.

(c) Our urge to give up, our temptation to quit and walk away is resoundingly conquered by drawing closer to the Master.

III. This story admits that while any of us may falter and any of us may want to give up, there is always another possibility.

(a) Just for today we can determine to live not upon our own resources but upon those which Christ provides. St. Paul said, "In him who strengthens me I am able for anything."

(b) Just for today we can persuade ourselves to hang on a little longer. Isaiah testified, "I the Lord thy God will hold thy right hand, saying unto thee, 'Fear not; I will help thee.' "

(c) Just for today we can work to raise our sights higher, recalling Jesus' words, "Seek first the kingdom of God and his righteousness and all these things shall be yours as well."

(d) Just for today we can accept the fact that God has more waiting for us around the next corner than we have known before. Paul declared, "It is God who is at work within you, giving you the will and the power to achieve his purpose."

(e) Just for today we can lay hold of the promise, "The Lord of hosts is with us; the God of Jacob is our refuge."

(f) Give up? Not with these affirmations and not with him who loves us and has the words that give eternal life.—John H. Townsend.

SUNDAY: SEPTEMBER TWENTY-FIFTH

MORNING SERVICE

Topic: Preparing for Christian Mission
TEXT: Rom. 1:14–16.

Four words in Greek are translated "ready" or "prepared."

I. The word *aday* means "readiness of adjustment," "things properly adjusted," and in that sense "ready."

(a) Paul used this word in II Tim. 4:6. He said, "For I am now ready to be offered." Paul had no fear of death. He had made all arrangements necessary for death.

(b) For a Christian this readiness means adjusting one's schedule to include a time of daily communion with Christ. A prepared worker must be a man of prayer and a student of the Word. Prayer is to the soul what breath is to the body. If a person doesn't breathe, he dies. If he doesn't pray, he dies a spiritual death.

(c) Strength for the Christian battle comes from union with Christ. (See Eph. 6:10.) The vigor of a man's arm comes from the strength of his body. If the arm is severed from the body, it will lose its strength. So it is with the child of God; his strength comes from his abiding in Christ. If the branch is cut from the vine, it cannot bear fruit. Union with Christ will determine the results of this spiritual battle.

II. The second word, *paraskeudso*, means "interested and about to begin."

(a) Joshua had this in mind when he said, "Let us now prepare to build us an altar" (Josh. 22:26). Peter used this word when he was on the housetop praying. "And he became very hungry, and would have eaten: but while they made ready, he fell into a trance" (Acts 10:10).

(b) This idea is expressed in a track meet. The runners listen as the judge calls, "Get set, get ready." Then he fires the gun.

(c) This preparation is illustrated when

a convert says: "Christ has saved me. I want to work for him in the church." The new Christian is interested and ready to begin.

III. The third word, *hetoimadso,* means "to be prepared in the sense that everything is finished." This word occurs at least forty times in the New Testament. (See Matt. 25:34; II Tim. 2:21.)

(a) *Hetoimadso* refers to an Oriental custom of sending persons to level the roads and make them passable for the king. John the Baptist was sent in this way to prepare the Jewish nation for Jesus' coming.

(b) The Word of God demands that we make this kind of preparation to meet God. That preparation must be completed when the great day comes. Not only must we be prepared to meet God, but we must also be prepared to help others to meet him. This preparation demands study, sacrifice, and action.

(c) Christ spent thirty years preparing for three years of public life. The doctor, the lawyer, and the professional man spend many years in hard study and application that they may be efficient when the crucial moment arises. Let an unskilled surgeon bungle his work, and a child may become crippled for life. Such a mistake is tragic but not so serious as the blunder of a Christian worker who ministers to an immortal soul.

IV. The fourth word translated "prepared" in the New Testament is the one which Paul used in Rom. 1:14–16, *prothumos.* It means "readiness, eagerness, passion, desire that consumes."

(a) The other words translated prepared or ready lack the peculiar quality of this word. This is a living word. A steam engine can be properly adjusted, completely finished and prepared and ready to begin, but a steam engine has no life, no passion, and no consuming desire.

(b) *Prothumos* means "proper adjustment," "careful preparation," and "interest." It has the meaning of the three Greek words mentioned with an addition. That plus is eagerness and passion.

(1) Paul said, "A debtor I am, and to me there is *prothumos*—readiness, eagerness, passion, desire that consumes me to preach the gospel."

(2) The hound on the leash, ready to pounce—that is *prothumos.*

(c) Mechanics are not enough; know-how is not sufficient; techniques won't do the job. These must be saturated in love and compassion in order to communicate the gospel.

(1) The apostle Paul was consumed with this burning desire. He demonstrated it in Phil. 3:6: "Concerning zeal, persecuting the church." Then in v. 14 he said, "I press toward the mark for the prize of the high calling of God in Christ Jesus."

(2) In the Greek the same verb is used for the translation of "persecute" and "press." Thus these phrases could be translated "persecuting the church" and "I persecute toward the mark." Paul was devoting the same passionate devotion and determination to obeying Christ that he had used when following Satan.

(d) Readiness of adjustment, readiness of interest, and readiness of preparation are important, but they are not sufficient. It is only when this strange, overwhelming, passionate desire to get at men with the gospel fills the church and consumes us all that the work of the church will march triumphantly forward.—Douglas LeRoy.

Illustrations

OFF THE FENCE.   If the basic Christian thesis is true and Jesus is the Son of God, then you can never be the same after your discovery as you were before. You cannot fit Jesus at the end of a microscope or at the end of a telescope and say, "How interesting!" Jesus Christ is not interesting. He is profoundly, morally, and spiritually disturbing and challenging. If there is anybody who forces us to get off the fence and to enter the field of moral commitment, it is Jesus Christ. If he is God, he deserves our worship, not just our patronage. Not just our admiration but our adoration.— John Stott.

DEPOSITS AND WITHDRAWALS.   A lady wrote her church a letter. She had been in Sunday school since age ten, had been married in the church, her sons baptized in the church, and she had worked on church committees and taught Sunday school. "My account seems to be overdrawn. I deposited myself; I withdrew a way of life. I deposited my wedding vows; I withdrew a wonderful and satisfying marriage. I deposited my sons for baptism; I withdrew all the joys and blessings of motherhood. I deposited time; I withdrew the friendship of young and old. I deposited money. Now that seems to be a touchy subject. What did I get for my money?

"A beautiful building, yes, but more than that, an investment in the children and young adults of our church. A place to worship, a place to meet friends, old and new. A place where I feel good deep within and knowing I am doing right.

"A minister—well, who can measure in dollars and cents the value of a person who baptizes our children, marries our young, visits our sick, and comforts the bereaved, in addition to the other formal duties of the church? I am getting a good return on my money.

"I know of no other organization where I am free to decide how little I want to deposit in it and still feel free to withdraw as much as I need. I will try in the future to make greater deposits, but please don't count on my being able to balance my account as I know I'll be overdrawn always."

Sermon Suggestion

MOVING AGAINST THE STREAM. Scripture: Matt. 5:1–12. (1) The Christian moves against the stream in the basic hungers of his life. (2) The Christian moves against the stream in his relationships with other people. (3) The Christian moves against the stream in his inner life. (4) The Christian moves against the stream in the ultimate issue of his life.—Gordon Clinard.

Worship Aids

CALL TO WORSHIP. "He that dwelleth in the secret place of the most High shall abide under the shadow of the Almighty. I will say of the Lord, He is my refuge and my fortress: my God; in him will I trust." Ps. 91:1–2.

INVOCATION. Most holy and gracious God, who turnest the shadow of night into morning: satisfy us early with thy mercy, that we may rejoice and be glad all the day. Lift the light of thy countenance upon us, calm every troubled thought, and guide our feet into the way of peace. Perfect thy strength in our weakness and help us to worship thee in the spirit of Jesus Christ our Lord.

OFFERTORY SENTENCE. "It is God who is at work within you, giving you the will and the power to achieve his purpose." Phil. 2:13 (PHILLIPS).

OFFERTORY PRAYER. Almighty God, whose loving hand hath given us all that we possess: grant us grace that we may honor thee with our substance, and remembering the account which we must one day give, may be faithful stewards of thy bounty.

PRAYER. God our Creator, we thank thee for life, for the privilege of being born and of being permitted to travel for a season through this world of beauty and abundance. We thank thee that thou hast so wondrously made us, giving symmetry to our bodies, faculties to our minds, and an infinite capacity to grow in strength and apprehension. We thank thee for our lot in life, for natural endowments, nurture, education, for work given our minds and hands to do, and for the joys of human relationships. We thank thee for the peculiar fascinations of this period in history, for the fruits of those who labored in other days, for material opportunities undreamed of by past generations, and for the moral challenge presented by revolutions in science and culture. We thank thee that the things of this world cannot satisfy us because thou hast made us citizens of eternity, implanting within us longings which only thou canst fulfil, and praise be to thee, O God, who hast answered our deepest desires in Jesus Christ. —Leonard Griffith.

EVENING SERVICE

Topic: How Shall We Think of God?

TEXT: Ps. 63:1.

I. The psalmist could have said, "Oh God, thou art God." (a) The Jewish people were surrounded by all kinds of pagan influences. Polytheism, the god Baal, the gods of the fertility cults, worship of the sun and the moon—all prevailed. One God is what Judaism gave to the world.

(b) It is important for us to know that there is a benevolent God, who controls this universe and that it all hangs together under the mind and control of one God. We are not insignificant in this universe. He created us, and we are here as his instruments and as his creatures. The psalmist could have said that, and it would have been tremendous. It meant to him and to us that we have a God who is trustworthy and loving.

II. The psalmist could have said, "Oh God, thou art our God." (a) He was the God of the Jewish people. The problem was in their thinking that he was the God of anybody else. Jonah preached to the people of Nineveh and they repented. Jonah argued with God that he was really God of the Hebrews and not of the Ninevites.

(b) The Puritans landed in New England. The minute they set their feet on Plymouth Rock they fell on their knees and thanked God for a safe voyage. They put God into the structure of their new little world. That's the way it's always been in America. We have stamped on our coins, "In God we trust." We open legislatures with prayer. We've said that we are a people who root our lives in faith in God. That means a great deal to us as Americans. But it really isn't enough to have a God of a nation. This submerges God in a greater entity and takes him away from us as persons.

III. The psalmist said, "Oh God, thou art my God!" (a) Isn't this the greatest impulse within us as we cry out to touch reality? Don't we long to relate ourselves to him who made us in the wonderful miracle of birth and who redeemed us in Christ, his Son?

(b) We have found God to be a living, real experience. We know him, we talk to him, we hear him talk to us, we draw near to him in prayer, he forgives us of our sins through Jesus Christ his Son through whom we have access to him, and he fills our life with meaning. This is intensely personal.

(c) The trouble is that many of us choose to stumble through this life believing that there is a God, believing that God is the God of our nation and the God of our families, but never quite coming to the point where we can say, "Oh God, thou art my God."—Thomas A. Smith.

SUNDAY: OCTOBER SECOND

MORNING SERVICE

Topic: They That Worship Him (World Communion Sunday)

TEXT: John 4:23.

I. However differently individuals or groups may appraise traditional forms and places of worship, we are in general agreement on some basic definitions of the purpose of Christian worship.

(a) Christian worship is the attitude and activity designed and employed to give expression to reverent respect for and adoration to the eternal God as revealed in Jesus Christ.

(b) Christian worship is the act of seeking to relate the whole life to God through adoration, confession, affirmation, and dedication.

(c) The Christian worshiper seeks to lay hold upon that which is eternal, permanent, and invisible amid all that is temporal, transient, and visible.

(1) Christians perform acts of worship in the confidence that by this means they can discover and dedicate themselves to the most important things in life which they cannot live without if they are to live on the levels which they believe God wants.

(2) Christians worship that they may quicken their consciences as they behold

the holiness of God, to feed their minds with the truth of God, to experience God's cleansing, redeeming power of love in their hearts, and to dedicate themselves more fully to the will of God.

II. The term "service" as used in the phrase "worship service" springs from the biblical meaning of the term "servants." The worshipers of God were his servants. Worshiping people stood in awe and adoration in the presence of their master—God.

(a) They who worship God in spirit and in truth come before God in the spirit of humility, as a servant approaches his master, seeking to discover God's desire and asking him what he wants them to do to please and help him, and then they go forth to do his bidding. They exalt God and affirm their confidence in him and their responsibility to him.

(b) Because a servant is expected to do something which will acknowledge his servant role to his master, the Christian worshiper discovers that if the worship service is to have any real meaning, he must do more than just attend in the sense that he is simply there physically.

(1) The English word "attend" stems from the Latin *tenders*, meaning "to stretch." We are to exercise our finest faculties. Those who really enter into the worship experience must bring their whole beings—their minds, their hearts, their souls, and their bodies.

(2) They are in the presence of the Almighty to offer him praise and adoration, to ask his forgiveness, to plead for his mercy, to make petitions to him, and to pledge absolute allegiance to him from this time forth and forevermore. This requires more than attendance. It demands participation.

III. For many people the act of worship is largely a mechanical procedure—making monetary contributions, voicing incantations, or simply going through the motions of some liturgical form, so that after spending a short portion of time they feel their obligation discharged and now are free to go their own way according to their own plans, however inconsistent they may be with what they may have learned and said they believed about the plans of God.

(a) When Christians worship, they should enter into the experience with such completeness that they become aware that their ordinary lives have been in the presence of the extraordinary.

(b) When people worship in spirit and in truth, they should seek the inspiration which creates an inner glow brought about by the awareness that they are persons of divine worth whose loftiest nature has the capacity to respond to the highest concepts of spiritual reality. This quality of worship kindles a thirst for ideas and ideals which are beyond the present grasp of the worshiper.

(c) Christian worship should elevate the spirit of the worshiper to such heights that he may catch a vision of the holiness of God to the degree that he is aware of his own unworthiness and of his need of God's cleansing, redeeming, and strengthening power.—Homer J. R. Elford.

Illustrations

SYMBOLIC FELLOWSHIP. German theologian Wolfhart Pannenberg has characterized the church as a symbolic fellowship —symbolic of the way life will be in the kingdom. Every church member plays a symbolic role as well as a literal one. The way we do business, the way we worship, and the way we pursue the mission of the church should inevitably point to a reality yet to come when all God's children shall sit down at God's messianic banquet in peace, equality, and love. That is the image the church must project even while we struggle to actualize it.—Charles F. Golden in *Circuit West.*

COMING TOGETHER. From all directions, from the four corners of the earth, we come to the Christ of the table. We come from different religious backgrounds, and we have been taught differently. Each person has his own view of Christ and the Christian faith. No matter. As we come to Christ of forgiveness, we all meet at the focal point—the loaf of bread in communion, Christ the bread of life. But the point we must see is that the closer we come to Christ the closer we come to each other. It is at communion that we reach the point of solidarity in Christ.—John R. Brokhoff.

Sermon Suggestion

WHERE DO YOU LIVE? Scripture: Rom. 8:1–11. Life at its best is lived in a series of concentric circles with a common center, one circle within another and the most inclusive being the purpose and will of God. (1) The center of the innermost circle is the self or the individual. (2) Next is the circle of family and intimate friends which may add much to the richness of life. (3) Beyond are the groups of which we are a part, primarily groups within one's own community, although some may reach to the ends of the earth, as does the Christian church. (4) Life reaches its highest level of significance when one remembers that "the eternal God is your dwelling place" (Deut. 33:27).—Nenien C. McPherson, Jr.

Worship Aids

CALL TO WORSHIP. "Now in Christ Jesus ye who sometimes were far off are made nigh by the blood of Christ. For he is of our peace, who hath made both one, and hath broken down the middle wall of partition between us. Now therefore ye are no more strangers and foreigners, but fellow citizens with the saints and of the household of God." Eph. 2:13–14, 19.

INVOCATION. Almighty God, fountain of all good, kindle in us insight and aspiration, that this hour of prayer may be a moment of time lived in eternity. Open our ears that we may hear. Soften our hearts that we may receive thy truth. Reveal thyself to us that we may learn to find thee everywhere.

OFFERTORY SENTENCE. "I will freely sacrifice unto thee: I will praise thy name, O Lord; for it is good." Ps. 54:6.

OFFERTORY PRAYER. O thou who art the Father of all, may we live as the children and brothers of all whom thou hast made to dwell upon the face of the earth that thy kindness may be born in our hearts.

PRAYER. Eternal God our Father, who hast taken us from our aloneness and set us in the circle of thy love and concern, we come before thee to acknowledge the manifestations of thy love toward us. Our minds are stretched, our eyes are opened, and our spirits are filled when we come to thee in the wonder of these empowering moments of prayer.

In times of need and anguish our tears have been shed before thy throne of mercy. We have beheld thy provisions each day. We have known how thou art through Jesus our Christ. Before such graciousness we confess our sins. For we see our unworthiness and our dependency upon thee. For every chance to improve ourselves, we are helpless without thee. We look about our world and see the shortness of our vision and our neglected opportunities.

We would be aware of this world in which we live. Before thee we remember the seeking and the searching—our brothers around the earth, the leaders of nations, the sick, the sorrowing, the troubled, and those who are bound by problems. May thy brooding spirit linger over them, and may our own lives be so renewed that we become truly thy servants to minister to them.—Earl W. Scarbeary.

EVENING SERVICE

Topic: The Eucharistic Fellowship
TEXT: I Cor. 10:16.
One of the classic names for Holy Communion is the Eucharist from the Greek for "gratitude." Reasons for claiming to be eucharistic center in the rediscovering of four aspects of the power of Holy Communion.

I. A study of Christian worship reveals that the source of early Christian prayers at the Lord's Supper was primarily thanksgiving. We must be careful to thank God for more than the symbols upon the table. Proper thanksgiving in the gathered church has been for the life and ministry of Jesus Christ, for his suffering and death, and for his work of saving men and women from their sins.

II. A second aspect of a eucharistic fellowship is found in the offering.

(a) For centuries the church has made it a point to include the offering, a gift of ourselves, our lives and labors, for the purposes of God, as a vital part of the Lord's Supper. As early as the third century, prayers were offered to suggest that the gifts brought under the influence of the Eucharist become blessed by an extended action of thanksgiving that has transformed the offering and made it a part of the work of Christ.

(b) In the offering we not only sanctify the money we give for the purposes of God. We also offer thanks for Jesus Christ, make a statement of our faith in his power, and then give the material gifts for the maintenance of the church and the carrying out of God's purposes in this world.

III. A third aspect of the eucharistic fellowship is the presence of Christ in the bread and cup.

(a) Some of us need to get acquainted with the New Testament resurrection stories, such as the meeting of Christ with the men at Emmaus, and rediscover how the young church seemed to see Christ's presence when there was some eating going on. It is striking to see the many instances in the New Testament where the risen Christ appeared to the disciples in the context of a meal.

(b) There is some connection between the Christian celebration of the Lord's Supper and the Lord's appearance at meals. In the twentieth century we need to permit a little bimodal consciousness or imaginative thinking to help us put some of the mystery back into the Lord's Supper. The early church never felt the need to explain that the Lord was present in the breaking of the bread.

IV. The fourth aspect of the eucharistic fellowship might be to remember what communion means.

(a) Communion with the living Lord is the means by which the Christian community has ministered to its wounds and maintained the integrity of its fellowship. Communion may not be separated from consecration, thanksgiving, offering, or presence.

(b) Christians not only recognize the presence of their Lord; they also experience a sharing of communion with him. Nor do they do this in isolation but always in a company of believers. Separately we may offer thanks, individually we may make our oblations, and privately we may sense the presence of Christ, but only together can the community share the power of Holy Communion.—W. F. Terry Reister in *The Disciple.*

SUNDAY: OCTOBER NINTH

MORNING SERVICE

Topic: The Layman's Witness (Laity Sunday)

Text: II Tim. 4:5 (neb).

Questions conscientious Christian laymen often ask are: How can I work to spread the gospel? How can I be what the Bible calls an ambassador for Christ, a witness to him? How can I lead others to him? How can I show them he makes a difference to me? How can I demonstrate my Christianity in the marketplace? Our best witness is ourselves and how we relate to people. If we are unsympathetic, unsmiling, and unloving, nothing we are going to say will make any difference. Four attributes seem to be essential ingredients of a Christian laymen's approach to others.

I. *Laughter.* (a) By this I mean a radiant countenance. Wherever Christ really means something to people, there is a joy and gladness of heart that cannot be masked by a dour disposition or a sour countenance.

(b) We sell Christianity by our appearance. Someone who goes about his daily rounds in a constant scowl, with his brow continuously furrowed, and his lower lip always protruding, as if he's just looking for something to criticize or argue about, just waiting for someone to slip or make a mistake so he can pounce on him, is not a very good recommendation for Christianity.

(c) Christ came to set people free from darkness, from gloomy thoughts, and from a negative approach to life and people. The man who is going to commend Jesus Christ to me is the man in whose face I can see that Jesus Christ has made a difference. "Rejoice in the Lord" (Phil. 4:4).

(d) If you're really in love with Christ, tell your face about it. Remember to smile, to be cheerful and pleasant. Laughter can ease a lot of life's tension. The devil flees from laughter.

(e) Christian laymen can spread the gospel by relating to people cheerfully, by worshiping and going to meetings at church with open faces that show confidence in God's grace rather than fear of human weakness, and by remembering to laugh and be gay because Christ has set us free from the burden of our sins.

II. *Listening.* (a) Listening will inform our witnessing if Christ has really liberated us from self-preoccupation so that we can relate meaningfully to others. Christ spent a lot of his time listening to people. Sometimes we are so eager to propagandize our point of view that we really could care less what the other fellow is thinking or saying. We're interested in talking, not listening.

(b) Some of the most effective Christian work takes place when a Christian practices the art of listening, which means the art of being interested in hearing about the other fellow's problems and needs and ideas instead of telling him about your own.

(c) To listen to someone else is to affirm his worth as a person. It is to communicate to him non-verbally that he counts for something. It is to be patient with him and to bear his burden with him as he unburdens himself to you. And so it is to fulfill the law of Christ.

III. *Loyalty.* (a) Loyalty in the Christian community means believing that we should all be one in Christ, loyalty to our church, to the denomination of which we are a part, to the church-at-large, to the cause of Christ, to our Christian heritage, and to fellow Christians.

(b) I do not mean blind loyalty, not the unthinking kind that blinks at things needing correcting, whitewashes everything, and holds unswervingly to its object whether right or wrong but rather the kind of loyalty that does not indulge in irresponsible talk, that does not pretend that one side of a story is all there is to tell, that does not ridicule unnecessarily, that does not in public give vent to private spleen, that does not sit back in silence when an untrue and unfair statement is made about the church or a fellow church member or a minister or the denomination.

(c) If we are loyal to the people and traditions to whom we belong in this Christian community which is the church, we will help create a freer atmosphere where there is less suspicion and fear. It will make more open communication between conflicting points of view possible. And it will help to build people up, not tear them down. This is part of our Christian duty. It's what Christ was warning us about when he said in the sermon on the mount: "Anyone who nurses anger against his brother must be brought to judgment. If he abuses his brother he must answer for it to the court; if he sneers at him he will have to answer for it in the fires of hell." (Matt. 5:22, NEB.)

IV. *Love.* (a) The loving person is one who can laugh, who can listen, and who is loyal. Love is the sovereign virtue from which all others spring. Anything that attaches the name "Christian" to itself and has not love is not only a noisy gong and a clanging cymbal but also a mockery and a sham.

(b) Christianity is about love, and the person who does not have in his heart the love of God revealed in Jesus Christ nor loves his brother whom he has seen is no Christian layman or clergyman, regardless of his masquerade. "Love one another with brotherly affection" (Rom. 12:10). "Make love your aim" (I Cor. 14:1). He who would spread the gospel of Jesus Christ and lead others to him must be a person who would spread love and in his own life demonstrate it.

(c) Love affirms people. Love is caring. Love is a sense of responsibility about the other person. Love is compassion. Love is standing in someone else's shoes and saying, "I know how you feel." Love is bearing somebody else's burdens with him. Love is serving others, helping others, strengthening others, comforting others, and ministering to others. Love goes beyond just liking the other fellow. Love means building a bridge to him even if you don't like him. Love means patience when it is tempting to fly off the handle, cheerfulness when it is easier to be grouchy, and affirmation when it is possible to be negative.

(d) Anyone who loves will, in the glorious words of scripture, cross the frontier from death to life (I John 3:14, PHILLIPS). Any layman who brings love to others will help them cross that same frontier and acquit himself well of his responsibility as a Christian to spread the gospel of love which is the gospel of Christ.—William H. Hudnut, III.

Illustrations

SCATTERED SEED. In Colchester, England, a young man was drifting into careless ways and his habits were shiftless. While he was waiting for some evil companions, he had an impulse to turn into a church. It was a cold, snowy winter day. Because the preacher did not arrive, a layman conducted the services and undertook to speak. There was something so sincere and earnest in the layman's appeal that this young man that morning accepted Christ. The handful of corn scattered that day produced in Charles Spurgeon a harvest that satisfied a worldwide need.

THREE LESSONS. In the first forty years in Egypt, Moses learned to be a Somebody. In the second forty years in the wilderness, Moses learned to be a Nobody. In the third forty years, he learned what God can do with a Somebody who is willing to be a Nobody.—Dwight L. Moody.

Sermon Suggestions

WHAT CAN LAY PEOPLE DO? Text: I Pet. 4:10. (1) A ministry of listening. (2) A ministry of learning. (3) A ministry of loving. —Craig Biddle III.

SUBPOENAED TO TESTIFY FOR CHRIST. Scripture: I Pet. 3:15–18. (1) Testify for Jesus by your style of speaking (v. 15). (2) Testify for Jesus by your lifestyle (vv. 16–17). (3) Testify for Jesus by telling what he did (v. 18).—Bruce J. Lieske.

Worship Aids

CALL TO WORSHIP. "They that wait upon the Lord shall renew their strength; they shall mount up with wings as eagles; they shall run, and not be weary; and they shall walk, and not faint." Isa. 40:31.

INVOCATION. O God our Father, who dost dwell in the high and holy place, with him also that is of a humble and contrite heart: grant that, through this time of worship in thy presence, we may be made the more sure that our true home is with thee in the realm of spiritual things and that thou art ever with us in the midst of our common walk and daily duties so that the vision of the eternal may ever give meaning and beauty to this earthly and outward life.

OFFERTORY SENTENCE. "Every man according as he purposeth in his heart, so let him give; not grudgingly, or of necessity: for God loveth a cheerful giver." II Cor. 9:7.

OFFERTORY PRAYER. Our Father, forgive our indifference and neglect, and help us to hear thy call to partnership with thee in making a new heaven and new earth.

PRAYER. We bless thee, O Father, for the good earth out of which our sustenance comes—for the fertile fields, the pregnant seed, the sun and rain; for strength for our tasks; for machines which lighten our burden; for the fruit which has crowned our labors.

We thank thee for those who have faithfully planted the seed of thy truth in our lives, who have carefully watered the newly planted seed and cultivated the soil, that thy great purpose might come to fruition in and through us. For the glory of this mountaintop experience of worship, when, through a consciousness of thy livingness, our lives are strangely transformed, we give thee thanks.

Our heavenly Father, may we not leave the glory that we experience in worship in the sanctuary, but may we carry it forth into the valley of human need that all of life's relationships may be transformed by thy loving presence. Help us to see our work as a sacrament, for the Master's hands were calloused from the carpenter's tools. Then the workbench where we ply our trade will be transformed into an altar, and we will see that no shoddy product comes from our hands. Help us to bring to every task the glory that we have experienced in our vision of thee in this place. "Whatever we do in word or in deed, may we do all in the name of the Lord Jesus."

Our Father, may we realize that we are bound together in a common bundle of life and that no one lives unto himself and no one dies unto himself. We make intercession for all those to whom we are indebted for life-giving services that we all too often take for granted—good clothes to wear, wholesome food to eat, tools for our work, cars for transportation, and comfortable houses in which to live.

In behalf of those who man the outposts of thy church in difficult places, for all who are working for the cause of peace and understanding among the nations, and for all who are striving to break down the dividing walls between race and race, nation and nation, class and class, we pray.

O God, grant to each of us such commitment that the good work which thou hast begun in us may be perfected to thy honor and glory.—John Thompson.

EVENING SERVICE

Topic: Portrait of a Christian

TEXT: Acts 11:24.

Barnabas was a good man, and his goodness expressed itself in all his actions.

I. The first thing reported of him is an act of great generosity. "Joseph, who was surnamed Barnabas, a Levite of Cypriot birth, sold a farm belonging to him and brought the money which he placed before the feet of the apostles." Jesus said that one kind of goodness that would get you into the joy of the Lord was to help those who need your help, the hungry, the naked, the prisoners, and the sick. Barnabas had that kind of goodness.

II. He had the insight to discern between the genuine and insincere. When the young church was afraid of Saul, "Barnabas took him, and brought him to the apostles, and declared unto them how he had seen the Lord in the way." Barnabas was not influenced by gossip or public opinion. When he saw that Paul was genuine, he decided to stand by him whether it was popular or not.

III. When the church in Jerusalem wanted to get a thorough report of the work that was being done in Antioch, it was Barnabas they sent. Barnabas, free from jealousy and self-seeking, could give an unbiased report. The work of God was always first with Barnabas.

(a) The good man can never be the yes man, so Barnabas took his stand against Paul and for Mark in their controversy. Barnabas was right and Paul was wrong, for Barnabas saved Mark when Paul might have destroyed him. Barnabas stood for loyalty to the right at any cost.

(b) Barnabas was never glad when others went wrong. He was gladdened by goodness. He was always eager to believe the best about everybody, always patient with everybody. No man is truly good who is not in sympathy with his fellow men, who has not a large-hearted tolerance for their weakness and failures, and a passionate interest in their welfare.

IV. He was a man through whom God loved. That was why the apostles called him the son of encouragement. One could not be near him without being helped, renewed, and restored. If one were in the depths of discouragement and failure and met Barnabas, he would leave with his head high and eyes shining with new hope. Barnabas, the good man, radiated encouragement and life and hope and power and love because God was with him.—Ernest Edward Smith.

SUNDAY: OCTOBER SIXTEENTH

MORNING SERVICE

Topic: How Can We Know God?

Scripture: Exod. 3:1–15.

How can a person know what God is like? God is so vastly different from us that it is not easy to grasp what he is like. We are mortal, but God is immortal. We are visible to each other, but God is invisible to us. Our knowledge is at best fragmentary and limited, but God is all-wise. We are often frustrated in our purposes, but God is almighty. We are morally weak, but God is holy. A great gulf separates us from God. The gulf is so vast that it would seem utterly impossible for us to know what God is like.

I. *God reveals himself to Moses.*

(a) How can we know the inaccessible God? This is the problem with which Moses grappled as he faced the task of leading the children of Israel out of Egypt. Our scripture relates God's call to Moses to go down into Egypt and to announce that the Lord would soon deliver these people from slavery. Sometimes we get so enthralled with the questions about the burning bush that we lose sight of the scripture's real point. At the heart of the story is the question of how a person can know what God is like.

(b) Moses was commanded to go to Egypt and tell the Israelites that the Lord had called him to lead them out from the Pharaoh's bondage. Moses raised the question which he knew would be foremost in his people's minds: "If I come to the people of Israel and say to them, 'The God of your fathers has sent me to you,' and they ask me, 'What is his name?' what shall I say to them?" (Exod. 3:13). Among the Hebrews the name of a person was supposed to reveal the character of that person. Moses was asking, "What shall I tell the people you are really like?" God gave this reply: " 'I AM WHO I AM' . . . Say this to the people of Israel, 'I AM has sent me to you.' " (Exod. 3:14).

(c) This is a strange answer, and yet what other answer could be given? God is not a little clay idol to be weighed and measured and meticulously described. He is too great to be encompassed by man's small mind. Would we have respect for any God whom we could fully grasp? Because God is God he is far beyond our comprehension. A God who is only of our own magnitude would be no God at all.

(d) All that we can say about God's ultimate nature is that he exists. "Say this to the people of Israel, 'I AM has sent me to you.' " God by necessity is enveloped in ineffable mystery.

II. We see God in the lives of others. (a) Something of what God is like can be known. In the very next verse we read, "God also said to Moses, 'Say this to the people of Israel, 'The Lord, the God of your fathers, the God of Abraham, the God of Isaac, and the God of Jacob, has sent me to you' " (Exod. 3:15). God cannot be fully known, but he can be significantly known through those with whom he has had dealings. The people of Israel could know that the great God who would rescue them was the God who dealt with Abraham and Isaac and Jacob. Each God-touched life gives us a fragment of what God is like. The enslaved Israelites, looking back to Abraham, could learn something of God. Looking back upon the lives of Isaac and Jacob, other aspects of what God is like could be found. No one life was adequate in itself to show what God is like, but together they begin to add up to a clearer picture.

(b) What was the God of Abraham like?

(1) Looking at the God-touched life of Abraham, we see that God is one who commands and expects absolute obedience.

(2) When Abraham was seventy-five years old, he heard the Lord say, "Go from your country and your kindred and your father's house to the land that I will show you" (Gen. 12:1). And Abraham, not knowing where the Lord was taking him, yet obediently went forth.

(3) God commands and expects absolute obedience. We of today, who may

pride ourselves on a deeper knowledge of God, usually fall short of grasping this demand of God for absolute obedience.

(c) What was the God of Isaac like? (1) Isaac's experience of God was quite different from that of his father Abraham. Isaac is not what we today would call a particularly religious man. Isaac was a man of wealth. The scriptures say that Isaac sowed and reaped in the same year a hundredfold. He had possessions of flocks and herds and a great household.

(2) The important thing to note about Isaac's God is that he sees God to be the source of his bounty. He saw that all that he had came from God. It is God who blesses with the good things of life.

(d) What was the God of Jacob like? (1) Probably the most familiar incident in Jacob's life is his dream. We recall that Jacob was traveling away from home, and laid down to sleep with a stone for a pillow. While he was sleeping, he dreamed that there was a ladder set up on the earth. The top of it reached to heaven, and angels of God were ascending and descending on it. He saw the Lord stand beside him.

(2) This dream through striking symbolism teaches Jacob that heaven and earth are connected and that God watches over the destinies of men wherever they may be. The God of Jacob is the God of watchful care for men.

III. God at work in persons. (a) Our knowledge of God is not likely to come to us in some sudden flash of inspiration. It comes through observing how God has dealt with others and how he has touched men's lives. If we would know something about God, we must turn to the experiences of men who have had dealings with God.

(b) This is one of the great values of the Bible. It puts us in touch with the lives of men and women who have had dealings with God in vital ways. In their lives we come to see what God is like.

(c) Through the fellowship that we see between Jesus and the heavenly Father we come to know God as Father. When I look at Jesus and see the influence for good that God had upon Jesus' life, then I cannot help but confess that the father of Jesus is truly my father too. It is not some abstract God that I find myself believing in but the God of Jesus Christ.

(d) In our moments of questioning and doubt concerning God and his goodness, our need is not to turn to those persons whose lives have been touched and transformed by the living God. It is through coming to know the God of Abraham, Isaac, and Jacob, the God of all the men and women of the Bible, the God of Jesus Christ that we come to a certain and clearer knowledge of what God is like. It is through the lives of men who have known God that we too come to know the ineffable God, the great I AM.—Colbert S. Cartwright.

Illustrations

EFFORTLESS PRAYER. Centuries ago Tibetan monks mechanized prayer. They built a large hollow drum and in it placed small pieces of paper upon which were written prayers. The drum was equipped with a crank and placed beside a frequently used trail. Each passerby could give the crank a few turns, thus offering up thousands of prayers simultaneously. Then some enterprising monk improved upon the idea. He geared the drum to a waterwheel that automatically turned it day and night. In this way every one who passed got credit for prayers without any extra effort.—John Wade.

WHAT WE SEE. It is by love that God is known. We cannot see God because he is spirit; what we can see is his effect. We cannot see the wind, but we can see what it can do. We cannot see electricity, but we can see the effect it produces. The effect of God is love. It is when God comes into a man that he is clothed with the love of God and the love of men. God is known by his effect on that man.—William Barclay.

Sermon Suggestions

DOING ALL THINGS THROUGH CHRIST'S STRENGTH. Scripture: Phil. 4:10–13, 19–20. (1) I can deal with my personal relationships responsibly through Christ who strengthens me. (2) I can deal with my worldly needs through Christ who strengthens me.—Lloyd Strelow.

WHAT IT MEANS TO HAVE FAITH IN GOD. Text: Mark 11:22. (1) Believing in the power of God. (2) Believing in the goodness of God. (3) Believing in the purpose of God.—Charles H. Buck, Jr.

Worship Aids

CALL TO WORSHIP. "Let us search and try our ways, and turn again to the Lord. Let us lift up our heart with our hands unto God in the heavens." Lam. 3:40–41.

INVOCATION. O thou who art the light of the minds that know thee, the life of the souls that love thee, and the strength of the wills that serve thee, help us so to know thee that we may truly love thee and so to love thee that we may fully serve thee, whom to serve is perfect freedom.

OFFERTORY SENTENCE. "Thy prayers and thine alms are come up for a memorial before God." Acts 10:4.

OFFERTORY PRAYER. Our heavenly Father, may thy kingdom be uppermost in our minds, our hearts, and our lives. Accept our gifts and with them the rededication of all that we are and have to thy greater glory.

PRAYER. Almighty God, our loving heavenly Father and our ever-living friend, we turn to thee with eager, expectant, and grateful hearts. Thou whose thoughts are above our thoughts and whose ways are above our ways, thou who art ever the hope of our days and the strength of our nights, we praise thy name. We gather with happy recollection of our experience of thee and thy saving and redeeming power in times past. We have personally tasted of thy goodness, and we have known the wonderful strength of thy outstretched arms and the deep benevolence of thy holy purposes. We confront life with faith, courage, and fortitude, knowing that thou hast yet more wonderful things to break forth out of the treasury of thy promise whenever we are ready to receive thy goodness.

We thank thee for the privilege of our fellowship together as we come from many homes and from many types of work. Here we are united in heart, mind, and soul, in singleness of purpose as we look to thee in faith, adoration, and happy love. Let thy blessing be upon each member of the congregation, upon each home represented here, and upon all of our loved ones. Teach us so to open our lives to thee in faith that we may be able to receive the wonderful blessings that thou hast for us. We rejoice in the privilege of worship that lifts up our souls and gives a glory to the times of work and the hours of recreation. For all the uplifting wonder of this sacred hour, we praise thee.

We pray for thy church that it may have a deep life of prayer, a strong outreach in service, a fine spirit of expectant faith, and a heart rich in brotherhood. We pray for thy church in every land that all the voices of faith may lift one great anthem of praise and worship to thee with pentecostal power. We pray for those who are outside the fellowship of the faith that thou wilt kindle a hunger and a thirst in their souls for the joy of belonging to thee and thy church. Grant that this world may so receive the refreshing touch of thy Holy Spirit that it may truly become thy world.—Lowell M. Atkinson.

EVENING SERVICE

Topic: A Kingdom Which Cannot Be Shaken

TEXT: Heb. 12:28.

Our scripture lesson, while recognizing the fact that we live in a world which is constantly shaken, reminds us of a kingdom which cannot be shaken and remains even "through the wreck of empires and the crash of worlds." Four elements of this kingdom we can rely on and find our anchorage and eternal security.

I. The king of the kingdom—the fact of God, the eternal, infinite, absolute, supreme being whom Jesus called Father with all the warmth and richness, personality and reality that he gave to the term.

(a) God is like Jesus. He is the Christlike God. If the supreme being, behind, beyond, and within everything, is like Jesus, then we may trust him fully.

(b) The person who believes in God will not be swept by the winds of change, the rains of pessimism, and the floods of despair but will weather turbulence, trouble, shock, and storm.

II. The fact of Jesus Christ, the key to the kingdom. (a) Mighty changes in human thought and custom have taken place since a babe was born in Bethlehem more than 1900 years ago. Kings and rulers have risen and fallen. Teachers and leaders have come and gone. But there remains the changeless, timeless Christ, our eternal contemporary, the same yesterday, today, and forever. His cross towers triumphantly o'er the wrecks of time.

(b) He is the Lord of all life, the light of the world. He said, "Heaven and earth shall pass away but my words shall never pass away."

(c) His sermon on the mount is the manifesto of the kingdom. His loftly principles tower like Mount Everest over our world, still challenging and still waiting to be tried.

III. The fact of loving, sacrificial, and redemptive service. (a) One of Jesus' biographers summarized his matchless life in a single majestic sentence: "He went about doing good." Jesus in the parable of the good Samaritan said to his disciples, "Go thou and do likewise." He said to all men, "If any man will come after me, let him deny himself, take up his cross daily and follow me."

(b) Following Christ in loving, sacrificial, and redemptive service is not a phenomenon confined to the first century and will continue as long as the world lasts.

IV. The fact of everlasting life in an eternal kingdom. (a) All religions teach of the yearning soul for life beyond the grave, but how vastly superior to all others is the Christian's assurance of the future life.

(b) Hear the word of the crucified, resurrected, living Lord: "I am the resurrection and the life. . . . Because I live, you shall live also. . . . My sheep hear my voice and I know them, and they follow me, and I will give them eternal life, and no one shall snatch them out of my hand." What eternal security!—George H. Hall.

SUNDAY: OCTOBER TWENTY-THIRD

MORNING SERVICE

Topic: What's Wrong with Christians?
Text: I Pet. 1:8.

Whether you are a Christian or not, it is worthwhile to look at some of the things about the Christian experience that should make us wonder about Christians and ask whether there might be something wrong with them.

I. Christians seem to have an extremely strong attachment to a single book, the Bible.

(a) It is not uncommon for people to become exceptionally interested in an author and his books, but it is quite another thing to make a single book the absolute center of one's life. I know Christian people who read a section of the Bible at practically every one of their meals, they make sure they read fifteen or thirty minutes in this book each day, sometimes they bury themselves in the study of this book, and then on Sunday they go to church where, of all things, they sit through rather long explanations of this book.

(b) This attachment to the Bible is not just a temporary fascination, but in some cases it can continue from an early age until a person either dies or becomes too feebleminded to read the Bible anymore.

(c) Such prolonged exposure to one book makes a tremendous impact on these people. Finally they arrive at the state in which they just don't think of anything except in the light of what the Bible says. Is it possible that this profound attachment to this book indicates that there is something wrong with these people?

II. Another element of Christian life, which is often noted but perhaps not sufficiently recognized as being absolutely astonishing, is the way Christians view themselves in relation to Jesus Christ of Nazareth.

(a) We would expect that Christians would admire him since they carry his name and all, but the way they talk about him goes far beyond simple admiration.

(b) In one of the letters of the apostle Peter there is a sentence which catches the essence of the relationship Christians have with Jesus Christ, and when Peter describes it, he seems to be somewhat astonished by it. He says, "Without having seen [Jesus] you love him; though you do not now see him you believe in him and rejoice with unutterable and exalted joy" (I Pet. 1:8). Even Peter seemed surprised, for he thought a lot about Jesus, but he had been with him and had a whole book full of things to tell about Jesus, but these other people who had never seen Jesus at all—they loved him too.

(c) This was not just a figure of speech —this use of the word "love." It wasn't then, and it isn't now. Christians love Jesus Christ as if he is still alive and able to receive this love. Christians think about Jesus a good deal of the time. When they make decisions, they are concerned that Jesus approve of their decision. They are concerned that Jesus approve of what they do. Apparently they don't want to displease him. They act as if he is still alive and is still able to observe their lives and have opinions about them.

III. Christians talk to Jesus. (a) When they pray to God, they often mention Jesus' name, and they ask God to listen to their prayer because of what Jesus did on the cross. Often they talk to Jesus directly.

(b) I have found this among young Christians. Small children, going to bed at night, don't drop off to sleep until they have talked to Jesus first. I've found it among the middle-aged and elderly.

(c) Wouldn't you agree that that kind of conduct with relationship to Jesus is enough to make us wonder about Christians?

IV. Christians give the impression that they are in touch with another world.

(a) Not only do they insist that they still have contact with Jesus Christ, but they seem to think that they are actually citizens of heaven, where Jesus supposedly is.

(b) The apostle Paul expressed himself rather frequently in terms of the contact he had with this strange realm. He said, "Our citizenship is in heaven" (Phil. 3:20). At another time he said, "If then you have been raised with Christ, seek the things that are above, where Christ is, seated at the right hand of God. Set your minds on things that are above, not on things that are on earth." (Col. 3:1–2.) He wrote of a special vision which he had and which he claimed to share with other Christians: "We look not to the things that are seen but to the things that are unseen; for the things that are seen are transient, but the things that are unseen are eternal" (II Cor. 4:18).

(c) Many Christians even today have been deeply influenced by language like that. They feel very close to this other realm that the apostle Paul was talking about. They consider their earthly concerns somewhat secondary when they compare them to the realities of their heavenly involvement. Some of them even say that their national citizenship is not as important as their citizenship in the kingdom of heaven. Some of the most faithful Christians allow their vision of the heavenly kingdom to influence the way they act in the present. They are not as interested in material things as other people are. They don't get shook if they don't get rich. They want to obey God rather than man.

V. What's wrong with Christians? (a) Well, what's wrong with them in terms of our mixed-up and confused world is exactly what is needed if our lives are going to be straightened out. After all, there is a God, and Jesus Christ is alive and he is the ruler of this earth, and there is a kingdom of God and we must live obediently to the will of God. This is true, and no amount of denial on the part of those who have rejected God will change the truth.

(b) If there is a God, it is disastrous to ignore him. If Jesus Christ is the only Savior we have—the only one who can take care of our sin problem—it is disastrous to ignore him. Because so many do exactly that, we live in the middle of disaster all the time.—Joel Nederhood.

Illustrations

INSPECTOR. Joseph Hough says his father tried to live by Jesus' teaching that we shouldn't judge other people, but he also knew that Jesus said of Christians, "You will know them by their fruits." He said, "I'm just an old fruit inspector."

WHEN GOD COMMUNICATES. A person imprisoned in a tower tried to get the attention of a passerby so that he might send a message to his family. He had a silver coin and a gold coin and decided to drop them to the street to get attention. He dropped the silver coin. A man hurriedly picked it up and went rejoicing down the street. He tried again with the gold coin and had the same result. In desperation he dropped a small stone that struck a man who was passing by and injured him. He immediately looked up to see who had thrown it. Then the prisoner was able to get his message through to his family. Is there a parable here of God's dealing with us? When his blessings fall upon us daily, we take them for granted and rush on without giving attention to the source of blessing. Then trouble visits. In that instant we look up to God and ask, "Why?" It is then that he communicates best with us.—A. Purnell Bailey.

Sermon Suggestions

ON BEING CONTENTED. Text: Phil. 4:11. (1) Contentment may be achieved independently of outward circumstances. (2) Contentment is primarily a Christian grace. (3) Contentment is something to be learned and practiced.—Tom Madden.

WHEN JESUS FACED TEMPTATION. Scripture: Luke 4:1–13. (1) The temptation to personal preservation. (2) The temptation to political conquest. (3) The temptation to sensationalism.—Bobby Perry.

Worship Aids

CALL TO WORSHIP. "Trust in [God] at all times; ye people, pour out your heart before him: God is a refuge for us." Ps. 62:8.

INVOCATION. O Lord of light, in this hour of worship in thy house make pure our hearts, and we shall see thee. Reveal thyself to us, and we shall love thee. Strengthen our wills, and we shall choose the good from the evil and day by day manifest in the world the glory and power of thy blessed gospel, which thou hast made known to us through thy Son Jesus Christ.

OFFERTORY SENTENCE. "Whatsoever ye would that men should do to you, do ye even so to them: for this is the law and the prophets." Matt. 7:12.

OFFERTORY PRAYER. Cleanse and accept these our gifts, O God, and may they be used according to thy will to redeem, restore, and renew the ministries within thy kingdom.

PRAYER. O God, whose breath blows upon us as a refreshing breeze, whose faith in us revives us as cool, clear water does the parched tongue, whose hand rests upon us as gently and yet as firmly as does a mother's love, and whose very power overcomes our weakness and becomes our strength, we pray for thy forgiveness.

Forgive us for being filled with our own self-importance, our own self-interest, and our own self-sufficiency. Forgive us for having eyes and seeing not, for having ears and hearing not, for having tongues and speaking not, for having hands and serving not, and for having minds and neglecting to use them. Forgive us for being content with that conversation that is but an echo of our own opinions, for hearing only that music that is none other than the blowing of our own horns, for shutting out the cacophonous sound that is the wail of the world, for being concerned only with those who fit into our limited circle, and for drawing into our selfish selves when we should be going out in love and service to mankind.

Our Father, we pray that thou wilt grant us the will and wisdom to use in thy service all the gifts and attributes with which thou hast endowed us. Help us to recognize that we serve thee best when we serve each other without thought of self. As we are forgiven for past follies and failures, may we be guided into fresh and fertile areas of Christian service.—Chester E. Hodgson.

EVENING SERVICE

Topic: The Practice of Praying
TEXT: Jas. 5:16.
Most of the questions about praying are

about the "how" of doing it. These are some suggestions to test.

I. *Plan.* The prayer life of many people is haphazard and occasional. To make it effective develop a simple plan and then pray regularly. Save a special time and place for it. Work out a personal pattern of Bible readings, meditations, and prayers.

II. *Praise.* True prayer begins with a deep sense of gratitude for blessings God has given. Even before asking for anything more, thank God for what he has already provided. In the spirit of genuine thanksgiving, praise God for all the expressions of his divine love toward you.

III. *Penitence.* Before the goodness and holiness of God, you are bound to realize your own unworthiness and sinfulness. Then you will be in the mood to pray for God's pardon.

IV. *Petition.* Jesus encourages us to go before God with practical requests for ourselves and for others. In a lesson on praying, Jesus used three lively verbs— "Ask," "Seek," and "Knock." Bible scholars explain that the form of those words indicates continuing action—"Keep on asking," "Keep on seeking," and "Keep on knocking."

V. *Proof.* It is in order to put our spiritual practices to practical tests. This is not a mark of doubt or disbelief. It is an intelligent way to check and to confirm the validity of our religious habits. Gideon was a successful farmer and leader. God asked him to serve as a general and commander of Israel. Gideon wanted to make certain that this was not merely a symptom of personal ambition but rather a divine summons to national service. So he asked God to join him in an experiment. (See Judg. 6:36–40.)

VI. *Persistence.* Too many people give up too soon when they fail to see the results of their prayers. Jesus anticipated this condition and offered a parable, the lesson of which is not to give up but to keep it up instead (Luke 19:1–18).—Emil Kontz.

SUNDAY: OCTOBER THIRTIETH

MORNING SERVICE

Topic: Entrusted with This Ministry (Reformation Sunday)

Text: II Cor. 5:18–19

I. *"Ministry is . . . God's gift."* Ministry begins with God's initiative: "God was in Christ reconciling the world to himself" (II Cor. 5:19, rsv).

(a) A child's description of Jesus as "the best picture God ever had took" is theologically correct even if grammatically questionable. Jesus Christ made visible God's continuing concern for the world.

(b) The church, the body of Christ in the world, is God's continuing instrument to reunite men and women alienated from their best selves, out of relationship with one another, and separated from him. Obedience to God's purposes leads the church to accept this gift of ministry.

(c) One way the church acknowledges God's gift of ministry is through worship. The community gathers to rehearse its history and to anticipate its future. It assembles to remind itself who it is and whose it is.

(d) At its finest the church gathers to worship and study that it might be equipped to share God's gift of ministry with the whole world. This gift is for men and women consumed by greed, oppressed by injustice, enslaved by illusions, handicapped by negativisms, and disillusioned by false expectations.

II. *"Ministry is . . . man's response."* (a) God's priority in ministry was summed up in H. Richard Niebuhr's description of the four elements in a "call to the ministry." God calls everyone "to be a Christian." Some men and women within the church are inwardly persuaded—"the secret call" —to prepare for special functions within the community of faith. "The providential call" is the awareness that a person has the necessary gifts and the ability to learn ministerial skills. Finally, the church calls the individual—"the ecclesiastical call"—and prepares the person for professional leadership through theological education and ordination.

(b) A sense of God's claim upon a person's life for ministry may develop gradually throughout the years as with Timothy. (See II Tim. 1:5–6; 3:14–15.) Or a sense of calling may happen unexpectedly in a cataclysmic encounter as with Paul. (See Acts 9:1–31.) The method is secondary to the awareness that the man or woman is "under orders."

(c) In contemporary society a person responding to God's call to the ministry normally is required to have seven years of academic training—four years of college and three years of seminary. A man or woman genuinely called to the ordained ministry can be expected to have gifts for ministering, capacity for graduate-professional education, and ability to learn ministerial skills and determination to improve those skills.

III. "Ministry is . . . partnership." "For we are partners working together for God," says Paul (I Cor. 3:9, TEV).

(a) Partnership involves sharing, responsibility, and accountability. Individuals and groups responsible to one another and accountable to God for continuing his ministry get insights about themselves and the world of accelerating changes from the interaction of conflicting ideas.

(b) Partners in a home or business may not agree. Unless they work at understanding, however, the partnership undergoes stress and risks dissolving.

(c) Reuel L. Howe refers to "inclusion" and "exclusion" as two opposing life principles.

(1) An inclusionist is "open" as contrasted with an exclusionist, who is "closed" to learning from the totality of human experience. An inclusionist recognizes every part of life as interdependent. Thus an inclusionist gains new understanding about himself, his environment, and the one who calls him to partnership in ministry.

(2) An inclusionist knows that classifying ministry into "lay" and "ordained" is exclusionist. It represents only a partial understanding of the biblical record.

(c) Within the unity of ministry is a diversity of functions. This understanding brings increasing appreciation of the gifts and roles of all persons in the household of faith.

(d) An ordained minister has different functions, not higher status within the body of Christ. The ministry of the ordained usually is more church-directed than world-oriented. At its best, ministry is working together for God's sake.

IV. "Ministry is . . . responsible involvement." God calls the church to be a community of faith whereby persons are redeemed and life in society is renewed.

(a) A minister is a man or woman qualified by training and certified by the church to help the community of faith live as the people of God. Responsible involvement has two focuses: listening and responding. (See Matt. 7:24.)

(1) Sometimes the church seems to suffer from a hearing deficiency. It is easier to "talk" about listening than it is to listen. Men and women often have to go to extremes to get our undivided attention. We must listen with the third ear before we can respond constructively.

(2) Attentive listening opens the way to responsible action. Effective ministry in the 1980s demands skills for managing conflict, gathering information, setting goals, designing strategies, outlining tactics, and evaluating results. The church needs men and women who can help congregations to become responsibly involved as God's agents to redeem lives and to renew society.

(b) The church needs people who are able to ask the right questions.

(1) In the light of what we have heard, what needs to be done in this situation? What ministries can this congregation provide at this time? Ministries with youth? Ministries with persons in the middle years? Ministries with men and women approaching or already in retirement?

(2) Who can best do what needs to be done? Where shall we begin? How will we know if we achieve our goals?

(c) God needs ministers and congregations willing to listen sympathetically without becoming sentimental toward what people are saying and to act responsibly to meet human needs.

V. "Ministry is . . . commitment to Christ." Jesus Christ demonstrates what ministry is all about. The Galilean is the church's model of caring. He sets the pace.

(a) To encounter Christ and respond to his impact is to be liberated for ministry in his spirit. We have good news to share. The old life is gone, and the new life in Christ has unlimited possibilities. The focus of our attention shifts from what we cannot do or did not do to what we can do. The future is seen as promise.

(b) Jesus Christ is God's great "yes" to the contradictions and ambiguities of life. To say "yes" to him is to discover new alternatives for real living.

(c) An inflexible commitment to Jesus Christ and a flexible expression of that commitment in the world God loves gives new vitality to the church's ministry. When a congregation has an exclusive commitment to the Servant Lord of history then it can be inclusive in its concern for "one of these poorest brothers of mine" (Matt. 25:40, TEV).—William H. Likins.

Illustration

CHOOSING. We don't choose to be born. We don't choose our parents. We don't choose our historical epoch, or the country of our birth, or the circumstances of our upbringing. But within all this realm of choicelessness, we do choose how we shall live—courageously or in cowardice, honorably or dishonorably, with purpose or in drift. We decide what is important and what is trivial in life. We decide by what we do or what we refuse to do.—Joseph Epstein.

Sermon Suggestion

CHRIST'S INCREDIBLE DEATH. Text: John 19:30. (1) His death was real. (2) His death was voluntary. (3) His death was the death of death. (4) His death means life for us.—Gerhard Aho.

Worship Aids

CALL TO WORSHIP. "Blessed is the man that trusteth in the Lord, and whose hope the Lord is." Jer. 17:7.

INVOCATION. Our Father, we thank thee for thy word and for the eternal truths which guide us day by day. We thank thee most of all for the living word. Jesus Christ, and the sureness of his presence. Teach us how to turn unto thee so that thy thoughts may be our thoughts and thy ways our ways.

OFFERTORY SENTENCE. "Offer unto God thanksgiving; and pay thy vows unto the most High." Ps. 50:14.

OFFERTORY PRAYER. Dear Lord and Savior of us all, may be become obedient to thy will both in the dedication of our tithes and of our talents.

PRAYER. O God, whom we could not seek hadst thou not first sought us, we thank thee for the good gift of faith whereby mere men hold converse with thee. We thank thee for those times when our own faith has been strong and we have been sure that thou art indeed our Father. We thank thee more for the faith of others —the constant faith of the praying church, the faith of the saints made real in the movements of history—which buoys us up when our faith flags. We thank thee, Lord, for faith.

O Lord, who hast so made us that we despise chains, we thank thee for the good gift of freedom, for that freedom of the soul which grows in Protestantism, and for that freedom in our social life which is guarded by democracy. We remember with stern self-appraisal that no freedom is true liberty save only the liberty wherewith Christ hath made us free from sin and death. Make our love for righteousness strong and deep that we shall need no ruler save thee.

O Father, who out of thy love didst make man to love and to be loved, we thank thee for the good gift of fellowship, for fellowship with thee that judges and heals us and for fellowship with one another whereby life is made joyful. Let the loneliness of our hearts be ended by the knowledge that thou art with us, and may the hours spent with thee make us worthy of the love and companionship of other men.

Almighty God, who by the grace of faith hast given us to live in freedom and fellowship in this thy good and beautiful world and who dost desire that thy will may be done in the world as it is in heaven, grant us to hear the call whereby thou dost summon the church to be thy people and to go forth from this holy place to make all places holy.—Nathanael M. Guptill.

EVENING SERVICE

Topic: Our Great High Priest
Text: Heb. 4:14.

I. *Christ's priesthood, the purpose* (Heb. 4:14–16). (a) In this Christian age, each obedient believer is a priest in his own right before Jesus (I Pet. 2:5, 9). Christ gives the Christian access to God (Rom. 8:34). As a Christian I do not need a human priest to serve for me. I am my own priest, and Jesus is my high priest.

(b) Because of this priceless relationship, Christians are exhorted to "hold fast" their confession. Jesus is the subject of that confession of faith. (See Matt. 16: 16.) If we do not hold fast our confession, we renounce him whom we once confessed and seal our condemnation (Heb. 6:4–6). Our exhortation is to advance with Jesus because of his priestly greatness and to draw near to him because of his human experience.

II. *Christ's priesthood, the qualifications* (Heb. 5:1–4). The Mosaic high priest was to serve as a mediator between God and man—to offer gifts and sacrifices to God because of sins, to sympathize with the erring, to bear gently with the ignorant.

(b) In comparison, Jesus was appointed of God (vv. 5–6). His response is recorded in Heb. 10:7. Jesus is qualified to sympathize (vv. 7–8; 4:15). By his sacrifice he became the "author of eternal salvation." The gospel message contains the proof offered by the Holy Spirit that Jesus is the divine Son of God. This evidence is capable of renewing the mind and bringing man into the presence of the living God.

III. *Christ's priesthood, the superiority* (Heb. 7:1–10:39). (a) Jesus is a priest of a higher order than Aaron (7:1–19). Melchizedek was above Abraham, for Abraham brought him tithes. Melchizedek's priesthood towered above the Levitical priesthood. Melchizedek was king as well as priest. Christ's priesthood was even more unique, for he is the Son of God and his office is eternal.

(b) Jesus was made priest by the oath of God (7:20–22). God's oath is irreversible (Ps. 110:4).

(c) Jesus is permanent priest (7:23–25). He lives forever.

(d) Jesus is sinless (7:26–28). He is holy, guiltless, undefiled, separated from the evil purposes of men. He is now at the right hand of God (Rom. 8:34). He offered his sacrifice once and for all time. He is perfect.

(e) Jesus is the priest of a better covenant (8:1–13).

(f) He serves in a better tabernacle (9: 1–28).

(g) He is the priest of a better sacrifice (10:1–39).

IV. Because the one sacrifice of Christ was sufficient, "there is no more offering for sin" (Heb. 10:18). Since only by Jesus do we have access to God, we must act or we shall lose the reward of eternal life. Now is the day of salvation. Christ is the only saving high priest.—Ard Hoven.

SUNDAY: NOVEMBER SIXTH

MORNING SERVICE

Topic: His Wonderful Miracles
Scripture: Matt. 11:2–5.

I. What is your best reason for believing Christ was God? (a) John the Baptist wanted a reason for believing. He sent word to Christ asking, "Art thou he that should come, or do we look for another?" What was his reply? "Go and show John again those things which ye do hear and see; the blind receive their sight, and the lame walk, the lepers are cleansed, and the deaf hear, the dead are raised up, and the poor have the gospel preached to them" (Matt. 11:3–5).

(b) The proof I am Christ, he was saying, is seen by the miracles I perform.

(1) Nicodemus said, "No man can do these miracles that thou doest, except God be with him" (John 3:2).

(2) On the day of Pentecost Simon Peter

described Jesus as "a man approved of God among you by miracles and wonders and signs, which God did by him in the midst of you, as ye yourselves also know" (Acts 2:22).

(c) You can best become acquainted with Christ through learning of his miracles, the climax of which was his resurrection from the grave. Some people say, "But miracles don't happen." As long as you believe there is no such things as miracles, you can hold yourself back from Christ. If you do believe in miracles, sooner or later you will feel compelled to be a Christian.

II. Why did Jesus perform miracles? To teach people that he was the Christ? At times it seems he did have that in mind.

(a) There was the occasion when the paralyzed man was let down through the roof of the house where Christ was speaking. Immediately he saw the man's greatest need was spiritual, so he said, "Thy sins be forgiven thee." But certain others were greatly upset. They said: "Why doth this man speak blasphemies? Who can forgive sins but God only?" No doubt these men were sincere in their condemnation. They did not understand that Jesus was God. So Jesus replied, "That ye may know that the Son of man hath power on earth to forgive sins, I say unto thee arise, and take up thy bed, and go thy way" (Mark 1:1–11).

(b) After he had fed the five thousand and demonstrated his marvelous power to multiply the loaves and fishes of one little boy's lunch, he later said, "I am the bread of life: he that cometh to me shall never hunger; and he that believeth on me shall never thirst" (John 6:35). Surely he used his power to let people know who he was. However, that was not the only reason for his miracles, but it wasn't his main reason.

III. Did Jesus work miracles to teach his message? Certainly we see revealed the truth he taught in many of his miracles.

(a) There was the occasion of healing the boy at the foot of the mount of transfiguration. The disciples had tried to heal the boy and had failed. After Jesus had accomplished the miracle, he said, "This kind can come forth by nothing but by prayer and fasting" (Mark 9:29). He wanted to teach them the true source of spiritual power.

(b) Word was sent to Jesus that his friend Lazarus was sick. Jesus said, "The sickness is not unto death, but for the glory of God, that the Son of God might be glorified thereby." Instead of hurrying to his bedside, Jesus waited two days until his friend died. As he was coming, Martha went out to meet him, and to her he spoke those glorious words: "I am the resurrection, and the life: he that believeth in me, tho he were dead, yet shall he live: And whosoever liveth and believeth in me shall never die." Then he added, "Believest thou this?" She replied that she did believe, but she didn't and couldn't. The finality of death was fixed in her mind. Death was the end. Death was hopeless. Then later, as Jesus called Lazarus from the grave, they did believe he was stronger than death and that life does not end with the grave (John 11).

(c) One day a sick woman touched the hem of his garment. Immediately she was healed, and to her Jesus said, "Thy faith hath made thee whole" (Mark 6:34). In that instance and in many others, he was demonstrating that faith is the key to his power. He wanted to teach men there is no limit to the things which prayer and faith can accomplish. His miracles do convince us of that truth.

IV. In the miracles of Christ we see revealed the Son of God and the truth of God. The miracles create belief and faith. But those were not the main reasons for his miracles.

(a) Suppose I were walking along the sidewalk and saw a child lying badly hurt. Would I say, "Here is a chance to demonstrate my strength to pick up this child"? Or would I say, "If I pick up this child, maybe it will be grateful and turn out to be a better person"? If I saw a child hurt on the sidewalk, I would think of none of those things. Any of us would do what we could because we are made that way.

(b) The Bible says, "When he saw the multitudes, he was moved with compassion" (Matt 9:36). Every miracle he performed was to help somebody, and that is why he performed them—not to teach anything but to make it better and easier for someone. His miracles happened because he loved every person he met. And that is the Christ you really want to know.

(c) The old song says, "The great Physician now is here, the sympathizing Jesus." You see his sympathy in every miracle, but nowhere do you see that side of Christ better than on the cross. He was so weakened that he was unable to carry the weight of the cross up Calvary's hill. His muscles cried out with pain. He felt the piercing of the nails in his hands and feet. He suffered the mockery of the crowd as they spit upon him. He felt the agony of deep thirst.

(d) Yet he looks over the crowd and sees his mother. He remembers how she loved and nurtured him and the many happy hours together in the home. He saw the white strands in her hair. He knows she is not as young as she used to be. Now she is a widow, and there will be lonely nights. His concern is not his own pain but for her. He speaks to John: "Woman, behold thy son. Son, behold thy mother" (John 19:25–27). That is, "John, take care of my mother."

(e) By his side is another who is dying, a man who was a thief and admitted he deserved his punishment. Yet Jesus' love went out to that man in such a complete way that the man's eyes were lifted away from his suffering and toward paradise.

(f) Today he is the same Christ—kind, loving, sympathetic, and reaching out to help even me. That is the Christ you want to know.—Charles L. Allen.

Illustration

SAINTLY COMPANY. In the contemporary world, the dedicated Christian often feels lonely. Surrounded by more or less unbelieving neighbors, in a society of low moral standards, in a world apparently bent on its own destruction, Christians have adequate reasons for discouragement. Yet in these circumstances comes the good news of the festival of All Saints. This feast makes us aware of the vast army of which we are a part. It puts before us Christianity not simply as an idea but as a life really lived by a multitude of men, women, and children in every age and in every part of the world. With them at this time we lift our hearts "to the things that

are above, where Christ is, seated at the right hand of God."—*The Living Church.*

Sermon Suggestion

WHAT IS THE FULL LIFE? Scripture: Rom. 5:6–11. (1) The full life requires a mature understanding of God. (2) A full life involves a healthy relationship with God. (3) A full life embraces a healthy relationship with our fellow human beings. —David W. Richardson.

Worship Aids

CALL TO WORSHIP. "Lift up your heads in the sanctuary, and bless the Lord. The Lord that made heaven and earth bless thee out of Zion." Ps. 134:2–3.

INVOCATION. O God, who makest thyself known both in the stillness and in the flurry of life: come to us as we seek to come to thee in this place of prayer. In music, word, and song lift our hearts to thee, and so purify our thoughts and strengthen our resolves that we shall go forth into the world of tomorrow, confident that thou art with us.

OFFERTORY SENTENCE. "Remember the words of the Lord Jesus, how he said, It is more blessed to give than to receive." Acts 20:35.

OFFERTORY PRAYER. Our Father, open our eyes, we pray, to the glorious opportunities of sharing with others our blessed experiences of fellowship with one another and with thee.

PRAYER. O Lord and God, we come to thee seeking to put our priorities in order and to submit our minds and our memories to thee. Help us in this hour to remember all that is pleasing to thee and to forget what is better forgotten.

We remember the great dreams of youth when we were unselfish and chivalrous and wanted to go forth and do great things for the world. May these memories summon us again to the heroic and brave and true.

We remember when love was young and hope was living and faith was strong. We remember the great and hallowed experiences of earlier days which ought to enrich our lives evermore.

We remember the great comrades of the past, princely men and queenly women we have known, strong and radiant spirits whose path crossed ours. We remember the sweet souls which we have known and loved and lost awhile.

We remember the sickness and sorrow which led us nearer to thee. We remember our unanswered prayers and know that had all been answered as we wished it would have brought leanness to our souls. We remember our failures which were steppingstones, by thy grace, to real achievement.

May the greatness of Christ and his gentle soul so captivate our imaginations as to swing us away from our selfish selves and into his way of compassionate love.—William C. Swygert.

EVENING SERVICE

Topic: Thy Kingdom Come
Text: Matt. 6:10.

Christ said in Matt. 6:33, "But seek first his kingdom." In the model prayer we ask for the kingdom of God to come.

I. The words "Thy kingdom come" are related to the second coming of Christ. The Bible teaches the return of Christ which will bring an end of the world as we know it. The closing chapter of the book of Revelation tells of a new heaven and a new earth where there will be no more war or suffering or pain or grief or sin and God will wipe away every tear from our eyes.

II. When we pray "Thy kingdom come," we are speaking of more than a place for the children of God after leaving this world. While we look forward to heaven as the place of eternal happiness with God, wonderful as that is, the kingdom of God is more than that.

(a) Part of the kingdom of God came with the birth of Christ and is sustained by those who follow and do the work of God. When John the Baptist saw Christ, he cried, "Repent for behold the kingdom of God is at hand."

(b) Part of the kingdom of God is already here. You and I are part of that kingdom, which is probably why the words, "Thy kingdom come," follow the words, "Hallowed be thy name." We must put our Father God first, our Savior Jesus Christ first, the kingdom of God first, and God's will first in our personal commitment.

III. We believe in the heavenly kingdom as the place that Christ went to prepare for us in accordance with the words in John 14.

(a) We emphasize that part of the kingdom, but we must also emphasize the earthly part. We must be committed to the entire heavenly and earthly kingdom of God. When we are committed more to one than the other, we are not following the admonition, "Thy kingdom come."

(b) St. John wrote, "Holy, holy, holy, is the Lord God Almighty, who was and is and is to come" (Rev. 4:8).

(c) When we pray the words, "Thy kingdom come," we refer to God who was and is and is to come, whose kingdom has been and is now and will be. We are asking that his kingdom will come today and in the future. We are saying that the Father is first in our lives. His kingdom is first.—Myron W. Arledge.

SUNDAY: NOVEMBER THIRTEENTH

MORNING SERVICE

Topic: The Divine Helper
Text: John 14:26 (RSV).

Our scripture reminds us of a simple truth. God has planned, in his economy of providence, to share a helper, the Holy Spirit, with us to teach the ways of God to us. This verse says something to us about our relationship with God which requires my relating life to the truth as I find it in God's word and in his Son Jesus Christ. It means coming to grips with truth, facing it squarely, and aligning life to its premises.

I. A relationship with the God of truth requires openness: "He will teach you."

(a) It is important to have a teachable mind and a teachable spirit. Our divine helper, the Holy Spirit, has life's greatest news for us—divine truth! But unless our hearts and minds are open, it goes for naught.

(1) Nicodemus came to Jesus at evening time not because he was coward but because he was serious about truth and wanted precious moments with Jesus apart from the crowd and the companions. And there takes placc a deep dialogue.

(2) There is something in that scene that we need to grasp. The future of Nicodemus depended on his openness to Jesus. Was he willing and ready to hear Jesus with his heart? Robert Duke reminds us, "What is required of him is not the sacrifice of his thoughts but their subordination to the words of Jesus."

(b) We can debate a lifetime the technical aspects of truth, but God asks us to journey with the simple, basic answers we have and add to them the more profound as they unfold.

(c) The God of truth with whom we seek relationship is the God of the way, the nitty-gritty. He is the God of the mountains and the valleys. He is the God of the dark nights of the soul and the days of joy. He is the God of the uncertain, anxious moments and the God of hope. He is the God who reveals himself to us in the halls of daily learning and living. Many of his answers he can only give us as we are involved, living, and facing life.

II. A relationship with the God of truth requires obedience. The Counselor, our divine helper, assumes obedience to follow the promise to teach us all things.

(a) Abraham leaves an epithet on the pages of the Old Testament that challenges us: "He journeyed onward, not knowing where he was going." The item to underscore is that "he journeyed onward." He obeyed and everything Abraham learned about God from that moment onward hinged on that simple act of obedience.

(b) Saul's transition to Paul was down the corridor of obedience. And the future of relationship between God and Paul points back to that moment and act of obedience.

(c) General Montgomery was named commander of forces in North Africa for the purpose of rescuing the Allied forces from a dreaded debacle. He met with his subordinates and told them simply, "Orders no longer form the basis for discussion but for action." Obedience was the prelude to victory.

III. A relationship with the God of truth requires love, and love requires others: "He will teach you all things, and bring to your remembrance all that I have said to you."

(a) What did Jesus teach more than anything else? Love! Why do you suppose he said that? Because he knew that life "does the truth" in the arena of living. In that arena are others, and "doing the truth" with others would never work without love. We're in bad enough shape with love. Can you imagine what it would be without love?

(b) Reuben Welch was right: "We really do need each other." But we need Christ more. We need his love, and we need to love, if relationship with God is to be real.

(c) Jesus knew that life would forever be fouled up unless proper lines of relationship were established. That's why he gives us the divine helper, the Holy Spirit, to teach us the holy way of love.

(d) Relationship with the God of truth will for us unfold along the avenues of love—our love for God and our love for others. The holiness message gives no other option.—C. Neil Strait.

Illustrations

SIMPLE TRUTHS. Charlie Brown is visiting Lucy, who is at her famed psychiatrist's stand, and offering her help for a nickel. Charlie says: "I need help! Tell me a great truth. Tell me something about living that will help me." Lucy asks, "Do you ever wake up at night and want a drink of water?" "Sure," responds Charlie Brown, "quite often." Lucy says: "When you're getting a drink of water in the dark, always rinse out the glass because there might be a bug in it! Five cents please!" Charlie walks away, saying, "Great truths are even more simple than I thought they were."

DELIVERED. In the sixteenth century some members of a Christian group in

Scotland, known as Covenanters, were being pursued by their persecutors until their strength was exhausted. Reaching a hill, which separated the Covenanters from their pursuers, the leader said, "Let us pray here, for if the Lord hear not our prayer and save us, we are all dead people." He prayed that the Lord would cover the hill with mist and that the enemy down the hill might not see them. Before he had finished praying, a mist rose up about the hill, wrapping about the pursued like a very thick cloak. In vain their enemies sought to find them. Wearied, they turned and went away.—Carol Wilson.

Sermon Suggestion

STEWARDSHIP ACROSTIC.   Text: I Cor. 4:1–2. (1) Sensible and sensitive. (2) Talented. (3) Energetic. (4) Wise. (5) Accountable. (6) Responsible. (7) Devoted. —Doris Judy.

Worship Aids

CALL TO WORSHIP.   "Oh that men would praise the Lord for his goodness, and for his wonderful works to the children of men! For he satisfieth the longing soul, and filleth the hungry soul with goodness." Ps. 107:8–9.

INVOCATION.   Most gracious Father, who withholdest no good thing from thy children and in thy providence hast brought us to this day of rest and of the renewal of the soul: we give thee humble and hearty thanks for the world which thou hast prepared and furnished for our dwellingplace, for the steadfast righteousness which suffers no evil thing to gain the mastery, for the lives and examples of those who were strangers and pilgrims and found a better inheritance in peace of soul and joy in the Holy Spirit, and above all for the life, teaching, and sacrifice of Jesus Christ.

OFFERTORY SENTENCE.   "As every man hath received the gift, even so minister the same one to another, as good stewards of the manifold grace of God." I Pet. 4:10.

OFFERTORY PRAYER.   Our Father, enable all Christians to know that their lives may be lived with Christ in God and that their gifts are means by which thy love in Christ may reach into the lives of wayward and needy persons everywhere.

PRAYER.   Eternal Spirit, whom we could not seek unless thou hadst first sought us, give us responsive hearts today. Make us receptive to thy presence. Make us sensitive to all that is noblest in our own lives through which thou dost come to us. Make us attentive to the still, small voice by which thou dost speak to us. We have known our godlike hours. Give us for the reward of our worship an hour of communion with thee, from which we shall go forth knowing that we have been in thy presence.

Speak to us through conscience. Let some authoritative word of righteousness come to some heart here that needs it. Startle us out of our complacency. Summon us to ideals that we have forgotten. Refresh within us the memory of knightly hours when we dedicated ourselves to things worth living and dying for.

Speak to us through our ambitions. Shame us from low motives of greed and selfish acquisition. Help us to set our hearts once more on things above where Christ dwells. Lift us up to dream of nobler things for our world, of international brotherhood, of industrial life dedicated to the service of man and not of mammon, and send some young lives, we beseech thee, forth from this place of meditation and prayer to consecrate their strength to the building of the kingdom of God.

Speak to us through our loyalties. We thank thee for our nobler devotions—for friendships, for family fidelity, and for all the dear and sacred ties by which we are woven into the network of humanity. If we have been faithless, forgive us. If we have been inconsiderate and selfish, recover us. Dignify and hallow our nobler loyalties to home, to country, to the kingdom, and to thee.

Speak to us through our sense of gratitude. If we have clouded the sky of our own lives and that of our fellows with our whimperings and complaints, have mercy upon us. Remind us once again of those gracious benedictions through which thou hast shined to make our lives lovely. Bow us down in humility and then lift us up, we beseech thee, with a fresh sense of our unpayable indebtedness.—Harry Emerson Fosdick.

EVENING SERVICE

Topic: Priorities and Paradoxes

TEXT: Matt. 6:33.

Our top priority must be the kingdom of God. We must put first the goal of entering it, the goal of enlarging it. The main desire of our hearts must be that the Lord shall reign in our lives and in every aspect of life around us.

I. Jesus spoke of God's righteousness in the priority he set for us. (a) Righteousness is used in two senses in scripture.

(1) There is imputed righteousness; that is, God considers us right with him by virtue of the saving work of Christ. It is God's will that people of every culture should seek and experience this righteousness.

(2) The Bible uses the term "righteousness" to describe a practical doing of that which is right, as God has revealed what is right. It is God's will that people of every culture should do what is right in his eyes.

(b) There is a paradox connected with the priority Jesus set for us. In the context of setting the priority, he was condemning the anxiety that people have for material things, things to eat, things to wear. Our Father knows we need them, but we are not to worry about them. The paradox is this: if we put first things first, if we share in Jesus' concerns, then the things we are not anxious about but which we need will be abundantly supplied for us by our heavenly Father.

(c) In the materialistic age in which we live, it is easy to share the priorities of the world without even realizing it. We may nod assent to the teachings of Jesus, but the important questions are: What are the actual priorities in our individual lives? What are the actual priorities of our congregations? Let us not just give lip service to the right priorities. Let us make them the measure of our actions. According to the promise of Jesus, if we do this we will not suffer loss.

II. There is another passage of scripture in which Jesus discusses priorities: "For whoever would save his life will lose it; and whoever loses his life for my sake and the gospel's will save it" (Mark 8:35).

(a) Christ says that our highest priority must not be self; it must be Christ and the gospel. Again, lip service will not do. If Christ is our top priority, we will use our time, our talents, and our treasures for him. I we do not do so, we apparently have other priorities, whether we realize it or not.

(b) Here Jesus introduces a paradox. He says that if we are only concerned for ourselves, then we will gain nothing for ourselves. However, if we forget about ourselves, the end result will be our gain.

(c) If you accept the priorities set by Jesus and if you give of yourself, of your time, and of your possessions generously, at first glance it would seem that you will be poorer. In fact, according to the promise of Jesus, only by such sacrifice can you experience the abundant life Jesus came to give. That may seem paradoxical, but it is true.—Harry Buis.

SUNDAY: NOVEMBER TWENTIETH

MORNING SERVICE

Topic: Heart Murmur (Thanksgiving Sunday)

TEXT: Ps. 103:1.

We are all familiar with the medical term "heart murmur," an abnormal sound found by listening to the heartbeat. It is produced by vibrations of the walls of the heart and great vessels.

I. There is a different kind of heart murmur often found in life. It is non-physical and concerns the spirit and attitude of the heart. This kind of murmur is an expression of discontent and displeasure about all of life.

(a) A person can go through life with a low murmur of dissatisfaction. To these suffering with such an ailment there is something wrong with almost everything, and they are all set to complain about it. Their steady string of complaints deprive them of the attitude of enthusiastically endorsing anything. They seem to enjoy this little murmur of dissatisfaction.

(b) This malady is probably the greatest barrier to a spirit of real thanksgiving. One can never feel grateful for anything and complain about it in the same breath. More often than not, this is an internal condition and has no relationship to outward circumstances.

(1) The Hebrew people who had their harvest festival of thanksgiving were poor people who lived in a land of rocky barrenness. With a few goats, a little house, a tiny field of poor grain, limited water supply, and invading armies, these people wrote psalms of thanksgiving and sang hymns of their faith of the goodness and generosity of God.

(2) The American settlers spent a mighty miserable winter after landing at Plymouth. Every school child is familiar with the hardships, exposure, and death which moved among the colonies. But the next fall they set a day for going to church and thanking God.

II. At Thanksgiving time we would do well to bring this heart murmur of grumbling under control so our souls would be joyously free to follow the counsel of the psalmist, "Let everything that hath breath praise the Lord."

(a) Thanksgiving is an attitude of remembering. We are in danger of losing the power of memory. We trust so much on the printed word that remembering might become a lost art. We ought to practice remembering the great things of life, the great deeds of God, and the great heroism of persons. We ought to tell and retell these things worth cherishing and keeping alive in our minds.

(b) We overcome this heart murmur and develop thankful hearts when we accept life as a gift of God. This means that we not only thank God when things are obviously good and suited to our taste, but we also accept life as we receive it—good or bad. It is a superficial religion when one gives thanks to God when all goes well but is inclined to be very critical when they do not go well. Can you accept all that comes your way?

Thanksgiving is a time of accepting.

(c) Another method of overcoming this heart murmur of grumbling is to substitute praise. The Hebrew people lived in desert poverty, but their religion was built around singing. There must always be musical accompaniment to religious life. True Christianity takes the truth of God and makes it glow and become vibrant until it is transfigured and suddenly bursts into song of sheer happiness.

(d) One more part of Thanksgiving is serving. A real investment of self in the needs of others will help greatly to dispel the danger of a heart murmur of grumbling. A person who is busy trying to lift the level of living for others has little time to grumble. Serving is a true expression of thanksgiving. It moves thanksgiving into thanksliving.—Joel A. McDavid.

Illustrations

PROVIDENCE. When George Washington wrote the first Presidential Thanksgiving Proclamation on November 26, 1789, after our country became a free and independent nation, he began his message by acknowledging God's providence. He concluded that message by recognizing the Lord as the giver of national prosperity, and in between were no less than two dozen forceful references to the goodness of God. There was no doubt in Washington's mind that the birth of this nation and its marvelous blessings were cause for deep gratitude to God.

In his diary on that day is found this entry in his own handwriting: "Being the day appointed for Thanksgiving, I went to St. Paul's chapel, though it was inclement and stormy, but few people at church." The father of our country had seen the crimson snow at Valley Forge, had heard boasts he would be defeated, had seen some of his own men deserting and others proving themselves traitors, and could not but be grateful to God. Therefore he went to church on that first Thanksgiving to praise and thank God. Yet most of his neighbors in Virginia let the weather keep them from publicly thanking God for founding our nation.—*The War Cry*.

REMEMBERED EXAMPLE. Certainly there has been quite a change in the American image since that early winter cruise which brought the Pilgrims to these shores in 1620. On the *Mayflower*, which was not regarded by its passengers as an unhappy ship, there were no cocktail lounges, no champagne hours, and no breakfasts in bed. There was, however, as William Bradford makes clear in his *History of Plymouth Plantation*, a plethora of religious service. It was so strong as to be almost mutinous. When the captain wanted to turn back because of the battering by stormy seas, his passengers committed themselves to the will of God and resolved to proceed.

Bradford, who was for thirty years the governor of the colony, has left us an unforgettable account of that first winter when it was touch and go as to whether any would survive. He writes: "In the time of most distress there were but six or seven sound persons who, to their great commendation be it spoken, spared no pains, day or night. But with abundance of toil and hazard of their own health, fetched them (the sick) wood, made their fires, dressed their meat, made their beds, washed their loathesome clothes, clothed and unclothed them; in a word, did all the homely and necessary offices for them which dainty and queasy stomachs cannot endure to have named, and all this willingly and cheerfully without any grudging in the least, showing herein their true love unto their friends and brethren—a rare example and one to be remembered."

Although we ourselves are prone to forget this unromantic image of America, it is indeed one to be remembered and never more so than at a time when the picture we project to others is that of a people who think that luxury is the main road to happiness. Quite the contrary, as Governor Bradford emphasized, it is the will to sacrifice ourselves for others that is the basis of the Christian faith.—Felix Morley.

Sermon Suggestions

O GIVE THANKS! Text: Ps. 106:1 (RSV). (1) Thanksgiving is a time for remembering. (2) Thanksgiving means family sharing. (3) Thanksgiving is an occasion for individual and personal reflection. (4) Thanksgiving is a time for acting out our convictions and beliefs. (5) Thanksgiving is a time for caring. (6) Thanksgiving is a time for loving.—Clarence L. Johnson.

WORD FROM THE LORD. Text: John 1:14. (1) The Lord has a word of judgment for us. (2) The Lord has a word of wisdom for us. (3) The Lord has a word of meaning for us.—J. A. Davidson.

Worship Aids

CALL TO WORSHIP. "Make a joyful noise unto the Lord, all ye lands. Serve the Lord with gladness: come before his presence with singing. Enter into his gates with thanksgiving, and into his courts with praise: be thankful unto him, and bless his name." Ps. 100:1–2, 4.

INVOCATION. O God our Father, giver of all good things, we are grateful for the Thanksgiving season of the year when we come with gratitude for bountiful harvests filling granary and bin. Give us such a spirit of thankfulness that every day and every season and all thy continuing gifts may be occasions for thanksgiving and all the year be blessed with an ever-continuing gratitude. As thy mercies are new every morning, so may our praise rise to thee each day and hour.

OFFERTORY SENTENCE. "Go, and sell that thou hast, and give to the poor, and thou shalt have treasure in heaven: and come and follow me." Matt. 19:21.

OFFERTORY PRAYER. O God, thou giver of all good gifts, in gratitude we bring our gifts on this day of joyous worship. Refine them, we pray thee, in the mint of thy divine purpose and use them to the end that thy kingdom may come and thy will be done on earth as it is in heaven.

PRAYER. Almighty God, whose blessings we enjoy in all times and seasons, at this special season of the year we are made aware of thy constant goodness. We offer thee thanks for provident care and sustaining blessing.

We thank thee for bounteous harvests and for the promise of adequate food. Help us to be sharers.

We bless thee for families and homes, for communities and fellow citizens where we live.

We bless thee for beauty that surrounds us and for this marvelous habitation we call earth.

We are grateful for peace in our land and for the hope of durable peace in the world.

We praise thee for the hope that lies before us and for high expectations that urge us forward.

We thank thee for our country and for thy guiding hand over us in times past. Forgive us our trespasses.

We are grateful for one another and for ties that bind us together.

We bless thee for the church and for our being part of it. Help us to continue to grow and deepen our lives spiritually.—*Forward.*

EVENING SERVICE

Meditation: An Awareness of Purpose
Text: Ps. 146:1–2.

Gratitude is our response to our Creator. If we had no creator, if the universe were just an accidental collection of atoms, if there were no supreme being who had caused us or the world we live in, there would be no one to be grateful to. If no one is in charge, there is no one to be thanked.

There is more to it than this. If existence is nothing but a strange accident, then there is really no basis for gratitude even if there were someone to whom it could be expressed. The gratitude we feel for life is not simply because life is pleasant, for often it isn't. Nor is our gratitude for nature simply based on the abundance of turkeys, cranberries, and pumpkins. In most parts of the world, most people are hungry most of the time. Life can be very painful, and it often is. If life were just a practical joke played by the universe, it would be a cause for more tears than laughter.

Gratitude springs from the awareness that there is purpose or significance in our life and in the world within which our earthly life is lived. Gratitude has to do with a sense of meaning. We feel little gratitude to someone who accidentally helps us without having any desire or intention of doing so. The action, whatever it was, lacked purpose and personal meaning. We do feel grateful to someone who tries to assist or benefit us, even if the effort is unsuccessful, for purpose and personal meaning are there.

The church solemnly affirms that to give thanks is right and fitting at all times and in all places—always and everywhere. Life, and the universe of which it is a part, does have meaning because it conveys the loving purposes and personal intent of a creator whose goodness overflows in all his works. To him we give thanks.—H. Boone Porter in *The Living Church.*

SUNDAY: NOVEMBER TWENTY-SEVENTH

MORNING SERVICE

Topic: Joyous Assurance (Advent)
Text: Luke 2:10.

How can we celebrate the advent of God into human life with joyous assurance? The answer is to be found in the message which God gave the shepherds that first Christmas eve. Christmas is not our reaching out or up to God. Christmas is God reaching down to us. Our response is found in a faith which believes that at the center of the universe is an undefeatable power of love on which we can rely and to which we are called to join our efforts. That is the joyous assurance which comes with Christmas.

I. Happiness does not come as a result of our persistent efforts to capture it. Happiness remains for all of us a gift. And Christians believe it is a gift of God. Why is the joy of happiness so elusive for us?

(a) We look for joy and happiness in the wrong places. Some there are for whom life is a constant straining for happiness. It is never really found this way. What may be found is a counterfeit form of joy which may have gaiety but little long-term satisfaction. It sometimes takes a lifetime to learn the secret that pursuing happiness for happiness' sake is a fruitless effort.

(b) We identify happiness and joy with the cushioned life. A life free from sorrow, pain, and want would seem to promise happiness. One writer asks, "What can a life of untrammeled bliss know about living?" Dr. Fosdick wrote: "A heart of joy is never found in luxuriously coddled lives, but in men and women who achieve and dare, who have tried their powers against antagonisms, who have met even sickness and bereavement and have tempered their souls in fire. Joy is begotten not chiefly from the impression of overcoming power. If we were set upon making a happy world, then we could not leave struggle out or make adversity impossible. The unhappiest world conceivable by man would be a world with nothing hard to do, no conflicts to wage for ends worthwhile, a world where courage was not needed and sacrifice was superfluous."

(c) Happiness is elusive because we are purely selfish in our search for joy. Our goals are self-centered and our search is self-minded. Sometimes we pursue happiness so hard we are not aware when it has been given us.

(d) Among those who look for happiness in the wrong places are the persons who bog down in the sad, melancholy gaiety of the sensualist. Every age, ours included, has its practicing hedonists. *Hedone* is the Greek word for pleasure. How many persons who go down this pathway find that it inevitably leads to boredom! To pursue pleasure alone may fatten the body, but it shrinks the soul. Boredom is really emptiness of soul.

(e) Part of our problem in this pursuit is that we fail to see joy as a miraculous gift which God gives us, not something we can achieve as a possession. The great joy promised in the annunciation to the shepherds in Bethlehem did not call them to pursue this joy on their own but announced it as a gift God is giving to all the people. It is the gift of life and love in Christ.

II. If the problem of experiencing joy in life is found in our efforts to pursue happiness, the answer to the problem comes to us with the joyous assurance which Advent brings. There is good news of great joy. It is God's gift to all who will receive it. God's Christmas gift of joy is found in a way of life that is basically joyous.

(a) Jesus' life was one of continuing joy because of his relationship with God. Do not dismiss lightly the sorrow, the tragedy, the frustration, the disappointment, the failure, the defeat, and the death on the cross. These were real. These were stern. But the scripture says Jesus embraced these with that same basic joy unmarred.

(b) He was criticized often because of this joyous element in his life and faith. People called him a glutton and winebibber because he could enjoy good company and good food. His best-remembered sermon talks about nine ways to be happy. The life of Jesus is a joyous assurance of God's love and care.

III. If the answer to our joyous assurance is in Christ, what does he provide for us out of which joy and happiness come?

(a) The inner stability of a dynamic faith. (1) Jesus offers us no outer security against the storms of life. He was always at the mercy of his enemies, and they finally did him to death. He cannot shut out for us the temptations, the tragedies, and the sorrows that befall us.

(2) Jesus brings us the understanding and confidence that our well-being is not wholly at the mercy of happenstance. There is more to life than the things that happen to us. The inner stability of a confident faith in God's love and power can enable us to withstand whatever the world may fling at us and still maintain that inner glow of joyous assurance.

(b) The wholeness of life-giving hope.

(1) Happiness is always a by-product of holiness. Another word for holiness is wholeness. God in Christ provides for us the fulfillment of total self. In no other way can we be fully alive, totally aware, and completely fulfilled. W. E. Hocking said that wholeness means "the state of going somewhere wholeheartedly and unanimously."

(2) To find such wholeness may well call for a complete conversion of life. We shy away from the term "conversion" because there are so many differing interpretations

of what it means. It certainly means a rebirth into the life made human for us in Jesus Christ, the divine Son of God. It certainly means directing our lives toward wholeness, which alone can bring hope for happiness.

(3) Our response to the joyous assurance of the Christmas good news is one that involves our total person and which promises the wholeness of vital hope that believes God alone can give us happiness.

(c) The redemptive usefulness of vital love. Jesus lived and taught that the highest form of human happiness is found in self-forgetful devotion to something beyond self. Self-seeking is self-defeating and never really leads us to joy.

(1) The real joy in Christmas is in the giving rather than the receiving. What a joy to see stars dance in your child's eyes on Christmas morning! What a thrill to have provided a catch-in-the-voice response of a loved one at her response to the beauty and love of your modest gift! I call that the redemptive usefulness of a vital love. It moves one from the seeker after gifts to the one who becomes a giver of gifts. It saves us from self-seeking and leads us into that happy realm of self-forgetful devotion to someone or something beyond self.

(2) Happiness is redemptive usefulness when we give wholeheartedly our devotion to those ends for which God works in his creation. When we respond to the good news of Christmas, we find ourselves committing our lives and talents to helping to spread that good news through our own loving and our own serving.

(3) Christmas enables us to see that such service is joyous because it links us with the God who came to us as a baby in a manger and because it enables us to open up areas of our lives to joy that heretofore had been tightly shut. Here is the chance to make our faith more vital, our hope more vital, our love more vital—alive and living in Christ.—Hoover Rupert.

Illustrations

NAMELESS HELPERS. No more saints? With LeChambron, Albert Schweitzer, Mother Teresa, and who knows who else? No more suffering for and with the suffering Christ? Outstanding saints and martyrs have always been in short supply. But silent Christian witnesses, those who yearn and pray for others, nameless helpers who in so many ways complete Christ's sufferings—these have always thought of themselves as lent to be spent.—Hugh T. Kerr in *Theology Today.*

FROM LIGHT TO LIGHT. Antoine Saint Exupery became hopelessly lost while flying at sunset over the Sahara. As darkness fell he looked desperately for the light of the airport and finally saw on the horizon a blinking light. With joy and relief he turned his plane toward that light only to discover that he was flying toward a rising star. He turned toward another blinking light on the horizon only to find in minutes that he was again flying toward a star. Time after time he frantically turned toward a far-off light of promise and hope only to be disappointed. "There I was," he wrote, "hopelessly lost in the vastness of the night going from one light to another desperately seeking that one light that could being me safely home."—F. Wellford Hobbie.

Sermon Suggestions

EXPECT GREAT THINGS FROM JESUS. Scripture: Matt. 11:2–11. (1) Expect him to deal understandingly with our problems. (2) Expect him to do for us what needs to be done. (3) Expect him to regard us as great in the kingdom.—Gerhard Aho.

INVITATION TO LIFE. Scripture: John 1:19–28. The church has always held that Advent is more than a preparation for a festival; it is an invitation to life. (1) It calls our spirits to the great experiences which would capture us. (2) It bids us cease from letting minor matters command our major time and urges us to let those spiritual purposes for which we were created find us. (3) It invites us to open our eyes to the glory of the eternal and to find new meaning in life through him.—*Today.*

Worship Aids

CALL TO WORSHIP. "Arise, shine; for thy light is come, and the glory of the Lord is risen upon thee. Lift up thine eyes round about and see." Isa. 60:1, 4.

INVOCATION. Grant, O Lord our God, we beseech thee, that now and every time we come before thee in worship and in prayer we may be vividly aware of thy presence, become conscious of thy power and a sense of thy protection, and finally know in our hearts and minds and souls the wonder and the grace of thy peace.

OFFERTORY SENTENCE. "If thou draw out thy soul to the hungry, and satisfy the afflicted soul; then shall thy light rise in obscurity, and thy darkness be as the noonday." Isa. 58:10.

OFFERTORY PRAYER. Our Father, help us to trust thee more fully and to accept our responsibility toward thy work and thy children who are our brethren in Christ.

AN AFFIRMATION OF FAITH. As members of the Christian church, we confess that Jesus is the Christ, the Son of the living God, and proclaim him Lord and Savior of the world. In Christ's name and by his grace we accept our mission of witness and service to all people. We rejoice in God, maker of heaven and earth, and in the covenant of love which binds us to God and one another. Through baptism into Christ we enter into newness of life and are made one with the whole people of God. In the communion of the Holy Spirit we are joined together in discipleship and in obedience to Christ. At the table of the Lord we celebrate with thanksgiving the saving acts and presence of Christ. Within the universal church we receive the gift of ministry and the light of scripture. In bonds of Christian faith we yield ourselves to God that we may serve the one whose kingdom has no end. Blessing, glory, and honor be to God forever.—Myron J. Taylor.

EVENING SERVICE

Topic: Our Advent Candles: The Prophecy Candle

SCRIPTURE: Mic. 5:1–4; Matt. 2:1–6.

The first candle is known as the prophecy candle because it looks at the promise of the messiah's coming and then looks back to tell us that that promise has been fulfilled in the coming of Jesus Christ as a babe to Bethlehem's manger.

(a) Micah, a younger contemporary of Amos and Hosea, lived near the end of the eighth century. Conscious of the sins of his people, he predicted the downfall of Samaria and the destruction of Jerusalem. At the same time he looked beyond the day of darkness and held up before them the hope of the messiah's coming. "Micah stands among the first," wrote George Adam Smith, "if he is not the very first, who focused the hopes of Israel upon a great redeemer." Micah's word is a word of prophecy, a prediction, a promise for the future that the messiah will come.

(b) Matt. 2 is a proclamation of that prophecy's fulfillment. After centuries of waiting and longing—almost nine hundred years—the evangelist announces that in the person of Jesus Christ the savior has come.

(c) Within the compass of those two passages lies the significance of the prophecy candle. On the one side is the promise of messiah's coming; on the other side the announcement of his arrival. Prophecy and fulfillment. What is the significance of that for us in this twentieth century and in this hour of history in which we stand?

I. A vision of God upon which to stay our souls. What is that vision? (a) We see God as a God of love, a God of great compassion and of wondrous mercy.

(b) We see God as a God of faithfulness. God is faithful to his covenant in spite of their faithlessness. God refuses to cast off his people but rather seeks them in discipline as in blessing and remains undeterred and undiscouraged by the passage of time.

(c) We see God as a God who is able to accomplish that which he desires, who is able to keep that which he has promised, and who is able to finish that which he begins. (See Gal. 4:4–5.)

II. A vision of the blessings of God to assist us on our journey.

(a) The dominant note in the celebration of Advent is expectation. That mood of expectation was valid for the Jews as they looked forward to the coming of the messiah, and there is a sense in which it is still valid for us as we look not for his coming as a babe in Bethlehem's manger but for his coming again at the end of the age to establish his kingdom in all its fullness and glory. For Christians, the dominant note is no longer expectation but fulfillment. Jesus Christ has come. That is the primary message of Advent.

(b) By his coming he has made available to us the blessings of God and made possible for us resources beyond our own. What are they?

(1) The peace of a quiet conscience. (See Rom. 5:10.)

(2) The certainty of God's guidance. (See Gen. 24:27.)

(3) The reinforcement of God's Spirit. (See Phil. 4:13; II Cor. 12:9.)

III. The victory of God to spur us on our way. (a) There have been those down through the centuries of waiting who have questioned the validity of their hope. Some have said, "It is an illusion of the mortal mind, wishful thinking, religious humbug." Others have said: "God has cast us off. He has been turned away by our sins." Still others have added: "God is preoccupied with other things. He has forgotten his promise."

(b) Jesus came and joined battle with Satan and all the hosts of darkness, and when the dust of battle had settled the victory was God's. Paul tells us that "the foolishness of God is wiser than men and that the weakness of God is stronger than men" (I Cor. 1:25). God is not only wiser and stronger than men; he is also stronger and wiser than Satan.

(c) The New Testament makes it clear that Satan has been a defeated enemy since the coming of Christ. He has been bound. He has been disarmed. (See Col. 1:15.) Oscar Cullmann put it this way: "The decisive battle in a war may already have occurred in a relatively early stage of the war and yet the war still continues. The present time of the church is the time between the decisive battle, which has already occurred, and the Victory Day."

(d) That means the victory of God is sure. It means that the eventual triumph of God is certain. In that assurance you and I can face the future with confidence and hope, knowing that Christ can break the fetters of sin in our individual lives, knowing that he can quell the forces of evil in our world and usher in the fullness of his kingdom, and knowing that he can keep that which we have committed unto him against the day of judgment.—S. Robert Weaver.

SUNDAY: DECEMBER FOURTH

MORNING SERVICE

Topic: The Humanity of Jesus (Advent)
SCRIPTURE: Heb. 2:9–18.

Who is this Jesus at whose birth the herald angels sang and whose birthday 2,000 years later is still celebrated by people of all classes and all races all over the world? It has strained the limits of human language to try to answer that question. In the New Testament the writers used an endless succession of titles in their attempt to capture the scope of his greatness. There is another side to Jesus we often lose sight of in the midst of the heralding angels and visiting magi and brilliantly shining star. This forgotten side of Jesus is his humanity.

I. *The reality of Jesus' humanity.* (a) Verse 9 is a reference to Ps. 8 which is a psalm about a man. There the psalmist said that man had been made a little lower than the angels. The writer of Hebrews asserts the same thing about Jesus. What can be said of man can also be said of Jesus.

(b) Verse 11 says that both he who sanctifies (Jesus) and those who are sanctified (man) are from one Father.

(1) The word literally means "out of

one" and refers to the source from which they came.

(2) The word "brethren" in v. 11 means those "from the same womb." The writer is saying in v. 11 that Jesus is from the same source and out of the same womb as man.

(3) In v. 14 he says that Jesus partook of flesh and blood, those aspects of life in which all men share.

(4) V. 17 says that Jesus became like his brethren in all things.

(c) Here was no god masquerading in a human body, no divine being who only seemed to be human but Jesus who really and truly became what we are.

(1) In Mark, Jesus' knowledge appears to be limited at times (13:2), and Jesus disclaims absolute goodness when in response to the reference to him as "good teacher" Jesus answered: "Why do you call me good? No one is good except God alone" (10:18).

(2) In Matthew we have the vivid description of the temptations Jesus faced, temptations to short-circuit God's plans and glorify himself, temptations that he faced not just at the beginning of his ministry but all the way through.

(3) In Luke we have that never-to-be-forgotten summary of his earlier years when Luke said, "And Jesus kept increasing in wisdom and stature, and in favor with God and men" (2:52). This verse declares that Jesus shared with all mankind the experience of growth.

(4) In John, where Jesus' divinity is so clearly proclaimed, we also see his humanity. John shows Jesus fatigued (4:6–7) and thirsting. John tells us that when Jesus' side was pierced with the spear as he hung on the cross, blood and water came out (19:34) to guard against the idea that his sufferings were illusory. John shows the human emotion of Jesus when, standing by the tomb of his friend Lazarus, Jesus wept.

(5) Paul repeatedly emphasized Jesus' origin from a Jewish family. To the Galatians he declared that Jesus was "born of a woman, born under the law" (Gal. 4:4). In the pastoral epistles Jesus is referred to as "the man Christ Jesus" (I Tim. 2:5).

(d) Throughout the New Testament Jesus' humanity is affirmed in the life of his body with its limitations, in his mental growth in wisdom and his physical growth in stature, in the reality of the temptations he endured, in his dependence upon the Holy Spirit, and in his gradual achievement of his life purpose and mission under the earthly conditions of time and space. Jesus was flesh of our flesh and bone of our bones. With the one exception, the fact that Jesus did not sin, the New Testament affirms the full humanity of Jesus.

II. *The result of Jesus' humanity.* What difference does it make? What is so important about affirming the humanity of Jesus? The writer of Hebrews discusses the results in human life that would have been impossible without the full humanity of Jesus.

(a) His humanity was important because it enabled Jesus to reclaim man. In v. 10, the writer of Hebrews says that in the life, sufferings, and death of Jesus, God brought "many sons to glory."

(1) Through the life Jesus lived, God has glorified us. To glorify means "to make, or make seem, better, larger, or more beautiful." That's what Jesus did for man.

(2) We hear so much about the depravity of man, and we see it constantly on television, the movie screen, magazines and newspapers, as well as from the pulpit. We see how low man can sink.

(3) A truth twentieth century man needs to hear, a truth rooted in the humanity of Jesus, is the dignity of man. We see how high man can soar. When Jesus became man, took on flesh, and lived life on this earth, he exalted manhood to a level of dignity, value, and worth, and he reclaimed man as the crown of creation, the one creature who was made in God's own image. His humanity enabled God to bring many sons to glory.

(b) His humanity was important because it enabled Jesus to redeem man.

(1) Man who was created in God's image came under bondage to Satan because of sin. Death was the penalty, that abyss of darkness into which every life eventually plunged. Man needed a savior, one of his

own ranks who had not succumbed to temptation.

(2) In vv. 14–15 the writer of Hebrews tells us that because Jesus became a man, lived our life, experienced our death, and then won victory over it, he broke the hold Satan had on man. He opened a new highway for man that would lead not to death but to eternal life. He became what we are, one of the early church fathers said, so that we might become as he is. He redeemed us.

(c) His humanity was important because it enabled Jesus to relieve man.

(1) The most glorious result of the humanity of Jesus is that he is able to understand what we are going through. Verse 18 says, "For since he himself has passed through the test of suffering, he is able to help those who are meeting their test now" (NEB).

(2) When you get tired and don't think you can go on, he understands. When you are treated unfairly by others, he understands. When those that you love most dearly let you down, he understands. When you are confronted by a temptation so powerful that it almost sweeps you off your feet, he understands. When your parents don't understand you and your brothers make fun of you, he understands. When you are left out of the crowd, he understands. When your best laid plans are sabotaged by the jealousy and envy of others, he understands. When you stand at the tomb of one that you loved with all your heart and cry, "Why did it have to happen?" he understands.

(3) Because of his humanity, he can sympathize with us. Because of his sympathy with us, he is able to help us. He can truly say about us, "I know what you're going through." He will redeem us from this bondage and restore us to our rightful place before God.—Brian L. Harbour.

Illustration

WHEN CHRIST ENTERS.   A group of noblemen had gathered for a royal conference, when the sovereign entered. They all knew him as a personal friend, yet they honored him as their king. So when he came into the conference room they all stood. "Take your seats, gentlemen," said the king. "I count you my personal friends." Then jokingly he added, "I am not the Lord, you know!" One of the nobles responded: "Your Majesty, if you were our Lord, we would not stand. We would fall on our knees."

Sermon Suggestions

TO LIGHT A CANDLE.   Text: Gen. 1:3. (1) The candle of friendship. (2) The candle of faith. (3) The candle of knowledge. (4) The candle of understanding.—Nell Farrell Stevenson.

GOD'S GLORY AND OURS.   Text: John 17:22 (NEB). (1) When God becomes flesh, God chooses to be accessible. (2) When God becomes flesh, it is as if the human is the proper setting for God. (3) When God becomes flesh in the life of Jesus, he also takes flesh in your life and mine. (4) God's Word made flesh at last conquers death.—John L. Kater, Jr.

Worship Aids

CALL TO WORSHIP.   "Lo, the star, which they saw in the east, went before them, till it came and stood over where the young child was. When they saw the star, they rejoiced with exceeding great joy." Matt. 2:9–10.

INVOCATION.   O Father of infinite love, whom even the heavens could not contain, our hearts beat quickly with joy as we behold thee coming into the world incarnate at Bethlehem. Reveal thyself to us in all thy glorious majesty and holiness as we kneel at the manger of thy Son.

OFFERTORY SENTENCE.   "Offer the sacrifices of righteousness, and put your trust in the Lord. Ps. 4:5.

OFFERTORY PRAYER.   O God, who didst give to us the gift of thy Son, stir us with such love toward thee that we may gladly share whatever thou hast entrusted to us for the relief of the world's sorrow and the coming of thy kingdom.

PRAYER.   Our Father, we thank you that no circumstances of life can shut out your presence and that no situation that befalls us can cut us off from your love and grace. Health and sickness, joy and sadness, life and death, and every easy time and every time of adversity can become the means of your grace, for always you are with us and always you care.

Make us to know that you are with us not only in this time of worship but in every moment of our existence. Help us so to trust you and to obey you that you become to us the faith that arms us and the grace that sees us through, whether we face temptation or sickness or assume the responsibilities that become ours as we seek your will and way.

What a friend we have in Jesus! He loves us when we are unlovely. He offers forgiveness when we wander from the right path. He comes to us in whatever hell we have managed to create for ourselves. He comes with the gift of redemption. Help us, O God, more and more to become to Jesus the friend that he has been to us always. Grant us vision to see his purpose for us as a purpose of ministry and service. Give us strength to fulfill our decisions to be with him where he is at work in the midst of a needy world.—Edward W. Norman.

EVENING SERVICE

Topic: Our Advent Candles: The Bethlehem Candle

SCRIPTURE: Luke 2:1–7.

The Bethlehem candle speaks to us of the preparation that was made for Christ's coming.

(a) In any consideration of that preparation we naturally think of the human preparations that were made. There were certainly preparations which Mary and Joseph made. How much love and forethought and provision is hidden in the simple statement, "She gave birth to her firstborn son and wrapped him in swaddling bands" (Luke 2:7). There were preparations which Zechariah and Elizabeth made. Simeon and Anna also made preparations for his coming.

(b) Those preparations were all significant and necessary, but they are nothing more than 'the fine dust of the balance' compared to the preparations God made. God prepared a place for Christ's coming in accordance with prophecy and in line with his ancestry as a Son of David. God ordered events so that Caesar Augustus, the ruler of the world, issued a decree which took Mary and Joseph to Bethlehem where Mary gave birth to a son. God prepared a time when conditions were favorable politically, economically, socially, and spiritually. Jesus came into a world that was ready and prepared for his coming. God prepared a soul. He prepared Mary to be "the handmaid of the Lord," to be the instrument of the incarnation, to be the mother of Jesus. For every coming of Christ into a human heart there are preparations which must be made.

I. There are preparations which God always makes. (a) God always prepares the cradle of our souls. He awakens in our souls a sense of need. John Vincent said, "To receive a savior, you must have a need for one."

(b) Saul of Tarsus had little or no sense of his spiritual need. But God began, gently and gradually, to create in him a recognition of that need. He brought him into contact with Christian men and women whom Paul discovered had a peace and a joy which he lacked. Then God caused him to be present at the stoning of Stephen where Paul discovered that that first Christian martyr had an assurance and a hope of which he knew nothing. And finally in the person of Jesus Christ, God confronted Paul on the road to Damascus where he came to see the evil which he was doing in persecuting the church and the rebellion of which he was guilty in resisting the Holy Spirit.

(c) God provides a mother. Mary was the medium, the instrument God used to bring Jesus Christ into the world. Since that day God has raised up many mothers. Timothy's physical mother was Lois, but his spiritual mother was the apostle Paul. Augustine's earthly mother was Monica, but his Christian mother was Ambrose, the bishop of Milan. For each and everyone of us the story is the same for when God would send Christ into a human soul, he provides a mother. That mother may be a faithful pastor, a concerned teacher, a devout relative, or a good friend.

(d) He sends the Holy Spirit to serve as a midwife to bring the birth of Jesus Christ to reality within our hearts. Conversion is ultimately the work of God and not the work of man. It is a birth from above made possible by Christ's death for us. God sends his Holy Spirit to make salvation—reconciliation—a living reality within our hearts. He sends him to bring us the assurance of his pardon, to awaken within our souls new desires and aspirations, and to reinforce our wills and strengthen our resolve.

II. There are preparations which we can make. What are they? (a) We can make sure that we are hospitable to the truth. Harry Emerson Fosdick said, "The major enemy of Christianity is not atheism but secularism, not the theoretical denial of Christ but the practical crowding out of Christ and everything that he stands for." How important that we be hospitable to the truth, that we sit down before the scriptures and ponder its message, that we put ourselves in the way of the church and see if there is not something there which we lack.

(b) We can be obedient to the Word. We can take those simple and yet decisive steps which the scriptures demand of those who would enter into discipleship and would grow in their Christian experience. Being convinced that Jesus is indeed the Christ, we can acknowledge him as savior. And having acknowledged him as savior, we witness for him in baptism and take our place within the fellowship of his church. And having taken our place within the fellowship of his church, we can strive to live to his glory and for the extension of his kingdom.

(c) We can wait in expectation of his Spirit. (See John 3:8.) The Spirit of God is under the control of no man. In view of that the proper attitude before him is that of patient expectancy. It is to wait upon him in prayer and to look for him in faith. (See Heb. 2:3.)—S. Robert Weaver.

SUNDAY: DECEMBER ELEVENTH

MORNING SERVICE

Topic: What We Miss at Christmas (Advent)

Scripture: John 14:6–10.

The Christmas story has become too familiar. That's a pity. When the incarnation of God as the baby Jesus becomes as repetitious as turkey leftovers, we lose sight of the significance of God's incredible act.

I. In the comfortable warmth of the manger scene, we forget why God chose to become human. A man woke up to find that two birds had somehow flown into his house. He opened doors and windows for them, but they couldn't find their way out. He tried to shoo them out, but they only became more panic-stricken. In his frustration, he thought: "They can't understand that I'm trying to help them. But if I could become one of them, I could show them the way out—" And he stopped, suddenly realizing that was what God had done. All through the Old Testament, God tried to tell humans how to free themselves from sin. Because we wouldn't or couldn't, God decided to show us. So the Word became flesh and dwelt among us.

II. The glory of the heavenly host and the glamor of the kings distract us from the risks that God took.

(a) There's a difference between becoming human—which is what happened in Jesus—and merely assuming a human disguise. God could have taken the form of an instant adult, bypassing thirty years of growing pains. But then God would not really have been one of us.

(b) God's choice was to share the full human experience from birth to death. Gasping for that first breath. Falling down stairs. Surviving the childhood illnesses and epidemics. Avoiding poisonous snakes. In Jesus, God even took the extra risks of being born far from home, fleeing as a refugee, and growing up under the tyranny of an occupying army.

(c) We forget how precarious a child's

existence can be. We have doctors, hospitals, immunization, and child-abuse regulations. But in the rest of the world, children are not so fortunate. In many cultures children are seen as the property of parents, to be used, neglected, beaten, exploited, and abandoned. The appalling child labor conditions described by Charles Dickens were an extreme example but not an exception to the rule that children have few rights and little security.

(d) To be a human, to show us the way, God voluntarily took those risks.

III. The halo of light surrounding the baby in the manger blinds us to the fact that he was not an ideal but a person.

(a) There's a temptation to think of Jesus as an amalgam of everyone. Yet he had his own face, his own hair, and his own habits. People recognized him by his way of walking, of talking, of waving his hand or scratching his head, just as each of us has our own recognizable characteristics.

(b) Often when we run into opposition, we are consoled by the words, "Don't take it personally." In becoming a person, God closes that too-convenient escape hatch. People took Jesus personally. No doubt some never heard his message because they were turned off by his Galilean accent or by the odor of his body after a long, hot day.

(c) At the other end of the Christmas story stands the cross, which was anything but a philosophical response to an abstract principle. Jesus knew that when he agonized in Gethsemane. So did those who nailed him to the cross. I can't imagine them saying, as they pounded the nails through his wrists, "Don't take this personally."

(d) Christmas reminds us that we can't separate the politician from the policy, the executive from the business practices, the writer from the words written. As followers of Christ, we can't make a distinction between what we believe and what we are.

IV. Because the Christmas story has an ending—when the wise men go home by another route—we forget that it was really a beginning.

(a) Jesus wasn't crucified for his own sins. He died for the sins of humanity. When God entered history at that time and place, it was both as a specific person and as a representative of other people.

(b) The incarnation says we cannot claim immunity from the acts of our profession, class, or race. All of us have an obligation that goes beyond merely ensuring that our own acts are right and just in the eyes of the Lord. God also expects us to take responsibility for the acts of our society.—James Taylor in *United Church Observer*.

Illustration

ANALOGY.   C. S. Lewis used the example of toy soldiers to explain Christmas. He asked if a boy does not often think what fun it would be if a tin soldier were turned into flesh and blood. In the incarnation we have one human being out of all humanity who did become completely divinized, but, as Lewis pointed out, the illustration breaks down here. If one tin soldier came to life, it would make no difference to the rest of the tin soldiers. They are all separate. But human beings are not. "If you could see humanity spread out in time as God sees it, it would not look like a lot of separate things dotted about. It would look like one single growing thing—rather like a very complicated tree. Every individual would appear connected with every other individual. Consequently when Christ becomes man, it is not really as if you could become one particular tin soldier. It is as if something which is always affecting the human mass begins at one point to affect the whole human mass in a new way. From that point on the effect spreads through all mankind."

Sermon Suggestions

THE LIGHT OF LIFE.   Scripture: I John 1:1–7. (1) Light is a universal gift. (2) Light is a free gift. (3) Light is a useful gift. (4) Light is a welcome gift.—Jerry Hayner.

THE GOOD NEWS OF CHRISTMAS.   Text: Luke 2:10. (1) The good news of Christmas is the fact that human decency still prevails. (2) The good news of Christmas is the good news of a world-wide Christian fellowship. (3) The good news of Christmas is the good news of man's self-forgetfulness during this season of the year.—Ben F. Lehmberg.

Worship Aids

CALL TO WORSHIP. "O Zion, that bringeth good tidings, get thee up into the high mountain; O Jerusalem, that bringeth good tidings, lift up thy voice with strength; lift it up, be not afraid; say unto the cities of Judah, Behold your God!" Isa. 40:9.

INVOCATION. Dear Christ, who art the light of the world, shine, we pray thee, so that all who walk in darkness and dwell in the land of the shadow of death may have the light of life. May thy word at this season be for us a lamp unto our feet and a light unto our path.

OFFERTORY SENTENCE. "Lay up for yourselves treasures in heaven, for where your treasure is, there will your heart be also." Matt. 6:20–21.

OFFERTORY PRAYER. May we find it to be a joyful experience, O Lord, to offer these gifts in the name of Jesus. Grant unto us the wisdom of the men of old who found a token in a star, worshiped the child as a newborn king, and made offerings at his feet.

PRAYER. Eternal God, thy majesty exceeds anything that we know on earth, and yet thou hast made our rude hearts thy dwelling place. Let the honor which thou hast bestowed upon us awaken us to our debt to thee.

We praise thee for the joys that are ours —the joy of believing, the joy of singing, the joys of the Christmas season, the joy of loving thee and one another, the joy of sacrifice, the joy of prayer, the joy of hope, and the joy of heaven.

As we make ready for Christmas, grant that we shall not be so blinded by the artificial glitter of tinsel, the red and green, gold and blue of decorations and gift wrappings that we are unable to behold thee. Teach us to look for thee in the most unlikely places—in the face of a child, in the warmth and coziness of the home, in humble places and in the simple things— lest even this Christmas we shall miss the choicest gift of all, the gift of thy savior Son.

Grant unto each of us some measure of the gentleness, patience, and fragrance of the Christ of Christmas so that the peace we long for on earth may be established now in our hearts and homes.—Harry D. Hawthorne.

EVENING SERVICE

Topic: Our Advent Candles: The Angels' Candle

SCRIPTURE: Luke 2:8–14.

The angels' candle raises the question of angelic beings. Who are they?

(a) They are God's creatures. Angels are not gods and not divine beings that either compete or cooperate with God but creatures that God has made. They do not accept worship nor do they encourage adoration for themselves. They exist only to glorify God and to magnify his holy name. In the story of the nativity the angels praise God, saying, "Glory to God in the highest and on earth peace for men whom he favors" (Luke 2:14).

(b) They are God's messengers who are sent forth to do his will and to further his purposes. While Zechariah the priest was burning incense before God in the temple, an angel of the Lord appeared to tell him that his wife Elizabeth would have a son who would turn many of the sons of Israel to the Lord and who would prepare the way of the Lord. The angel Gabriel brought the news to Mary that she had found favor with God and would bear a son who would save his people from their sin. An angel came to Joseph telling him to proceed with his plans to marry Mary because that which was conceived in her was of the Holy Spirit. An angel appeared to the shepherds as they kept watch over their flocks by night and proclaimed the savior's birth.

(c) They are God's ambassadors, God's envoys, God's representatives who do not stand on their own but who are fully backed by him. Karl Barth wrote, "An angel is not merely an emissary; he is a plenipotentiary." He is one who has at his disposal all the authority and all the power of God. (See I Kings 19:7–8; Dan. 6:22; Acts 5:19; Acts 12:23.)

(d) What meaning does the angels' candle have for us today?

I. We are not alone with our sin. (a) Have you noticed in the nativity stories how afraid of God those who made up the original cast were? How terrified they were of any manifestation of the supernatural? Zechariah "was troubled when he saw the angel and fear fell upon him" (Luke 1:12). Mary was "greatly troubled" when she received Gabriel's salutation (Luke 1:29). And when the angel of the Lord appeared to the shepherds, "they were sore afraid" (Luke 2:9). They were all afraid because they assumed that they were alone with their sin and they knew that God was "of purer eyes than to behold evil and that he could not look upon iniquity." Multitudes today are afraid of God because they are conscious of their moral failure and they know that God is "a consuming fire to destroy that which is evil" (Heb. 12:29).

(b) The angels' candle points to the activity of God, to the irruption of God into our world, to the breaking in of the supernatural, and thus to the proclamation that there is "peace on earth for those who find his favor" in Jesus Christ. God has come to grips with our sin, he has carried it away, and by his grace there is forgiveness for our sin not because we are worthy but because in Christ we have a savior who died for us.

II. We are not alone with our struggles. (a) An Old Testament story makes that clear. The setting is a conflict between Israel and Syria. At the time Elisha was in the city of Dothan. In the morning when the servant of the man of God arose he saw horses and chariots round about the city. Rushing to his master he said: "Alas, my master! What shall we do?" To which Elisha replied, "Fear not, for those who are with us are more than those who are with

them!" (II Kings 6:16). Then Elisha prayed, "O Lord, I pray thee, open his eyes that he may see" (v. 17). Whereupon the Lord opened the eyes of the young man and behold the mountain was full of horses and chariots round about Elisha. When the Syrians came down against the people of God, the Lord struck them with blindness so that the people of God were delivered out of their hands.

(b) There is one who stands with us in our struggle against evil and can break the power of cancelled sin and set the prisoner free. God is here and his grace is sufficient for all our need.

(c) Speaking to a group of young people in a German refugee center on Christmas Eve, Helmut Gollwitzer said: "We are no longer alone and dependent on ourselves. Even in the worst loneliness there is one who takes his place beside us and is there with possibilities quite beyond description."

III. We are not alone with our sorrow. (a) Death came quietly to Caesar Augustus at Nola in his seventy-sixth year. To the friends at his bedside he uttered words often used to conclude Roman comedy: "Since well I've played my part, clap now your hands, and with applause dismiss me from the stage." That is not the way most of us view death. We see it not as comedy but as tragedy. We are saddened at the thought of leaving loved ones here, and we are filled with sorrow when our loved ones leave us to cross the river.

(b) The Christian faith recognizes the genuineness of our grief and the poignancy of our separation. But it offers us the assurance that in that sorrow we are not alone. God is there with us. And when God is there, even death is transformed and transfigured.

(c) Christ brings the comfort of knowing that our beloved dead are in his care and that nothing can separate them from his love. He brings us the confidence that in him death is not the end but only the gateway to a larger, fuller, and richer life.—S. Robert Weaver.

SUNDAY: DECEMBER EIGHTEENTH

MORNING SERVICE

Topic: Christmas Reconciliation (Advent)

TEXT: II Cor. 5:19.

The coming of Jesus to Bethlehem was the giving of a new spirit of reconciliation to the world. This was the conviction of those who, like Paul, stood near to the great event. "It pleased the Father by Christ Jesus to reconcile all things unto himself." "God was in Christ reconciling the world unto himself." From this crossing of the chasm which separates man from God comes a new power by which man can be reconciled to man.

I. The Christmas message supplies healing for injured human relationships because of the peculiar spirit of reconciliation which seems to rise from the plains of Bethlehem.

(a) The spirit of Christmas is of tremendous importance to a world crying out for reconciliation. It is characteristic of human quarrels, be they between nations or individuals, that with time a spirit of bitterness and distrust and fear develops which makes normal human relations virtually impossible.

(b) The only way to soften hardened attitudes is for some new spirit of good will, forgiveness, trust, and selflessness to come in. If only some power can be introduced which will lift the whole issues on to a new level of thought and feeling, previously insoluble problems disappear.

(c) Part of the secret of the power of Christmas is that it offers this new spirit. Christianity rarely presents to mankind precise, ready-made solutions to social, international, or even personal problems, but it does provide general principles for guidance and a mood of faith and good will in which success can be achieved. It is this spirit which comes near at Christmas time.

II. The reconciling spirit of Christmas arises out of a reconciling faith.

(a) The true Christmas spirit is the expression of tremendous convictions about God and about man. Unless that faith is present the spirit about which we have spoken will soon evaporate and life will fall back to its former level.

(b) There is great peril in the way we celebrate Christmas. We make so much of the spirit of warmth and friendly generosity of this season that there is little time left for the thought which gives life to the spirit. Yet surely it is obvious that if Christmas has no other foundation save in sentimentality, pleasant carols, and poetic imagery it has no word for a lost world.

(c) Christmas comes to us in terms of a compelling challenge. It demands that we accept the convictions by which Jesus came and with which he lived and died if we are to know the power of reconciliation. God is the fundamental reality. Peace, not war, is the truth about this universe. History moves not toward Caesar but toward Christ. Every man—yes, that insufferable person whom you regard as your enemy—is a child of God. Human nature responds quicker and more consistently to love than to force or fear. There is only one way of getting rid of enemies —by forgiving them. Love, creative, active good will which flows out to the ends of the earth is the only binding, constructive principle in society. These make up the Christmas faith.

III. If the Christmas spirit rises from the Christmas faith, the Christmas faith arises from what God has done for all mankind. It is because "God was in Christ reconciling the world unto himself" that a power is at work today drawing men back into fellowship one with another.

(a) The fundamental need of the whole world and of every life is right relationships with God. Probably more than we ever realize our troubles rise from this deep level of reality. "No man can be at war with God without being at war with everything in his environment," says James Stewart. "When there is disharmony at the center, there cannot be peace at the circumference. There is only perpetual maladjustment and strain." If God is the ultimate fact of the universe, it seems hard to escape that judgment. And then reconciliation, the restoring of right relations with God, becomes the most urgent thing in the world.

(b) How can that relationship be restored? Reconciliation always involves two people, which means in this case God and us. Whatever be our attitude, he must speak before fellowship can be regained. But will he speak the word of forgiveness, the word of reconciliation? We could not be sure, we dare not even assume that it could happen but for the coming of Jesus. The good news of the gospel of Jesus is that that word has been spoken.

(c) On Christmas we celebrate more than the birth of just "one of the children of the year," to quote Alice Maynell. Bethlehem was more than the birth of another child to another mother. It was God breaking into history. It was the action of God setting out on his long journey of seeking a lost world. Christmas is God taking the initiative, for our sakes. He in Christ is making every other reconciliation possible.

(d) Once again we hear the familiar story of Bethlehem. For most of us it does not fall upon our ears with any strangeness. In a sense we seem to belong. We seem to know that Bethlehem is the true home of the human spirit. In fellowship with God and fellowship with each other is the way in which we were meant to live. We come to ourselves after the wanderings and the distortions of the year. We touch again the peace and the power of God's reconciliation through his Son Jesus Christ.—Alan Walker.

Illustrations

WHY HE CAME.   A minister visited a family whose child had died a few weeks before Christmas. He noted that a bare tree was standing before the front window and a box of decorations lay on the floor. When he commented that they were in the process of decorating, the mother said: "Oh, I have lost all interest. It is too sad to think of Christmas." "But," the minister explained, "it is because of such events as you are experiencing that Jesus came into the world." God sent the Son to live among us so we through him would be able to cope with situations of life and death, sorrow and pain, loss and estrangement.—Harold A. Schulz.

GIFTS HE GAVE.   When we give one another our Christmas presents in his name, let us remember that he has given us the sun, the moon and the stars, the earth with its forests, and mountains, and oceans and all that lives and moves upon them. He has given us all green things and everything that blossoms and bears fruit—and all that we quarrel about and all that we have refused. And to save us from our own foolishness and from all our sins he came down to earth and gave himself.—Sigrid Undset.

Sermon Suggestions

CHRIST'S BIRTH AND OUR ADOPTION. Scripture: Eph. 1:3–6, 15–18. (1) Christ's birth and our adoption have their roots in the past. (a) The Father in eternity chose his Son to be the savior. (b) The Father in eternity chose us to be his children. (2) Christ's birth and our adoption became realities in time. (a) At God's appointed time the Word became flesh. (b) In God's appointed time we became flesh so that we might receive adoption as sons. (3) Christ's birth and our adoption should be celebrated now and through eternity. (a) We celebrate the birth of Christ with praise and thanksgiving. (b) We celebrate our adoption through confession and service. (c) We wait for the ultimate celebration in eternity when we will know "what are the riches of his glorious inheritance in the saints."—Ronald Irsch.

LED BY A STAR.   Text: Num. 24:17. (1) A call to directed worship. (See Matt. 2:1–2.) (2) A call to determined worship. (See Matt. 2:2.) (3) A call to devoted worship. (See Matt. 2:11.)—Stephen F. Olford.

Worship Aids

CALL TO WORSHIP.   "Behold, I bring you good tidings of great joy, which shall be to all people. For unto you is born this day in the city of David a Savior, which is Christ the Lord. Glory to God in the highest, and on earth peace, good will toward men." Luke 2:10–11, 14.

INVOCATION. Our Father, help us during this special season to remember the many ways thou hast pointed out to us the coming of our Lord Jesus Christ. May we be ever mindful that thou wilt not let us sit in darkness, but if we are receptive we will see the light of thy many signs in the prophets, in the lives of our neighbors, and in the eyes of our family.

OFFERTORY SENTENCE. "And they came everyone whose heart stirred him up, and everyone whom his spirit made willing, and they brought the Lord's offering to the work of the tabernacle of the congregation, and for all his service." Exod. 35:21.

OFFERTORY PRAYER. Our Lord Jesus Christ, whose birthday has become a season of benevolence and giving, bless these our gifts which we offer in thankfulness for thyself, God's unspeakably precious gift.

A CANTICLE OF PRAISE. For the magic and mystery of this season that quickens our spirits with anticipation and brings to remembrance angel voices and a star shining,
We give thee thanks, O God.
For the warm pleasures of hearth and home, for candlelight and holly berry, for loving hands that prepare food and drink, for the eager joy of children's faces looking up, holding wonder like a cup,
We give thee thanks, O God.
For music-making and holy merriment, for legends told by the old and wise to the young in verse and song, that echo here the angelic choir, as when the morning stars sang together and all the people of God shouted for joy,
We give thee thanks, O God.
For our daily tasks to which we return from the manger with heart renewed to weave the fabric of community and keep it strong, to ease the suffering of neighbors far and near, to nurture the young, to welcome the stranger, to turn the despair of loved ones into hope, to fill lonely spaces with friendship, and to give of ourselves in myriad, menial ways and find thy glory shining in them all,
We give thee thanks, O God.—Waldo Beach.

EVENING SERVICE

Topic: Our Advent Candles: The Shepherds' Candle
TEXT: Luke 2:17.
The biblical basis for the shepherds' candle is the adoration of the shepherds. Joachim Jeremias points out three things about that story which help to bring it into proper focus.

(a) He reminds us that, setting aside the parables and figurative sayings, these are the only shepherds mentioned in the New Testament. This is quite surprising when you realize that, throughout the biblical period, tending flocks along with agriculture, was in Palestine the basis of the economy.

(b) He tells us, on the strength of archeological findings, that in Palestine caves regularly served as stalls for animals and that in Bethlehem the local tradition points to a cave as the place of Christ's birth.

(c) He suggests that the shepherds, not the innkeeper, were the owners of the stall. That is quite probable, and it is further corroborated by the lack of any specific directions from the angelic messenger to the shepherds as to the location of the manger where Christ was born.

(d) It is against that background that we should read the account of the angel's appearance to the shepherds and their subsequent visit to the manger to offer adoration to the Christ Child. What is the message of the shepherds' candle to us in our celebration of Christ's birth?

I. It underlines the importance of our being sensitive to the needs of others.

(a) When Caesar Augustus issued his decree that a census be taken of all those living within the confines of the Roman Empire, Mary and Joseph found themselves in a very difficult position. Their place of enrollment was Bethlehem, for they were of the house and lineage of David. Bethlehem was some seventy miles from Nazareth which was a long way for a woman to travel whose time was at hand. Nevertheless, compelled to go, they made the long, wearisome journey only to find when they arrived that the inn was full.

(1) It has been customary to picture the innkeeper as a greedy soul who reserved his rooms for the highest bidder—a portrait of him which is without any biblical support—and who at the last moment relented and offered Mary in her extremity a place in the manger. If Jeremias is correct, that is not what happened at all. The innkeeper, inundated with guests, turned them away. Then chancing upon the shepherds, they informed them of their plight. Whereupon the shepherds responded by offering them shelter in one of the caves where they were wont to house their cattle.

(2) That tells us something about the shepherds. They may have been rough, uneducated men, but they were sensitive to human need and to Mary's plight.

(b) The shepherds provided help to a woman in need and were privileged to play a part in the coming of the Savior and to share, even in a humble way, in the salvation of the world.

(c) By responding to human need, they not only played a part in the redemption of the world but also gained a great reward. They were rewarded with the angelic proclamation and were granted an audience with the King.

(d) We have become so impersonal, so machine-oriented, and so computerized that we no longer see people as persons with human faces. We see them as numbers that are cold, remote, and impersonal. In the face of such anonymity we need to warm our hearts at the shepherds' candle until once again we are sensitive and responsive to the needs of those around us.

II. It emphasizes the necessity of our being open to the truth. (a) The shepherds were open to the truth. When they were told who it was who was born in the manger, they accepted the message, saying, "Let us go over to Bethlehem and see this thing which has come to pass which the Lord has made known to us" (Luke 2:15).

(b) Many of us face life with preconceived ideas. (1) We have minds which are fixed and unyielding. We set limits to what God can do, lacking completely the childlike spirit of trust and humility. Many, imbued with the spirit of this scientific age, arbitrarily dismiss "the answers of religion as the lies we tell to make ourselves comfortable."

(2) That is anything but the truth, for the answers of religion often make us very uncomfortable. Take the biblical description of man as a sinner who stands under the wrath and judgment of God. Or take Christ's call to discipleship. "If any man will come after me let him deny himself and let him take up his cross and let him follow me" (Matt. 16:24). That is not an invitation to ease and comfort. It is a summons to a cross. That cross has meant suffering, sacrifice, and service. Take the doctrine of the incarnation which has been the heart and center of historic Christianity from the very beginning. To ask men to believe that the Word became flesh and that God became man is a challenge to our credulity, but how else do you explain the fact of Christ? His virgin birth? His perfect life? His incredible miracles? His amazing influence? His undeniable resurrection?

(c) God's thoughts are not our thoughts nor his ways our ways, for as the heavens are high above the earth so are his ways higher than our ways and his thoughts than our thoughts (Isa. 55:8–9). We don't know a millionth part about anything. In the light of that it behoves us to sit down before the facts as they are revealed to us and to open our minds to their truth and significance.

III. It stresses the significance of our being responsive to the heavenly vision. The shepherds, having found the Christ, "made known the saying which was told them concerning the child" (Luke 2:17).

(a) Is that not the imperative need of the church today? Are we not in danger of becoming introverted, ingrown, and preoccupied with our own life and comfort rather than being concerned about the needs of those outside? And does our very existence as a fellowship not depend upon the rediscovery of our calling, upon our recapturing a sense of mission, and upon our bearing witness for Jesus Christ both at home and abroad?

(b) Before we can be witnesses, we must be Christians. Before we can tell others of Christ, we must have firsthand experience of Christ. And that means that each of us must accept God's gift of Christ as Savior and our Lord.

(c) Think what God's offer could mean in your life! And realizing that, open your heart to him, and after you have found him and "have tasted and seen that the Lord is good," go out and tell others what you have found. Then the shepherds' candle will glow not only at the Christmas season but throughout the whole year.—S. Robert Weaver.

SUNDAY: DECEMBER TWENTY-FIFTH

MORNING SERVICE

Topic: The Glory of Christmas
TEXT: John 1:14.

I. So much about the first Christmas was ordinary, even commonplace. Yet a strange aura surrounding it is reflected in that majestic and mystical word "glory," which the ancient authors used in narrating the blessed event.

(a) Phillips Brooks incorporated this truth fittingly in "O Little Town of Bethlehem." For many features of the first Christmas were common indeed. It involved plain places—a hillside field and a country barn. It involved plain people—some rural shepherds and a town carpenter. It involved a plain event—a tiny baby in a hay manger.

(b) The word "glory" signifies the light of divine presence. This apparently human drama was glorified with the aura and mystery of divinity. All the plain features of the first Christmas were blessed and beautified with a cosmic and eternal significance of abiding value and vitality. The glory of Christmas can touch and transform our experience of it now as it did then.

II. Christmas can glorify our work. (a) The first news of Christmas came to some workers while they were on the job. When the proclamation from God was made to the shepherds out in the fields, the record relates, "And the glory of the Lord shone round them" (Luke 2:9).

(b) The revelation of God's love can put meaning and dignity into our life and work. Whatever our task may be in the home, in the store, in the factory, in the street, or wherever, Christmas reminds us

that we can be aware of and blessed by the sense of God's presence. Divine purpose can be reflected in our character and service. We need to be receptive to the divine presence, even as the shepherds were.

III. Christmas can glorify our faith. (a) Among the first to share in the original Christmas experience were wise men, men of intelligence, thinkers who were in a sense the scientists of their day. Their knowledge was glorified by a faith in God's revelation of his guidance which led them to Christ. Obediently they followed the light of God's glory reflected in a star.

(b) We moderns with our knowledgeable outlook and our vaunted sophistication need the humility which glorifies our faith and prompts us to recognize and worship Christ as Lord and Savior.

IV. Christmas can glorify our homes. (a) The first Christmas did not occur in some bright and pretentious place. It happened in the humble home of those whom we call the holy family. Artists have pictured the scene of Mary and Joseph and the babe in a wide variety of ways but always depicting them with "the glory of the Lord which shone about them."

(b) Here was God's love made real and personal in live people. How much our modern homes with all their pressures from the outside and the tensions on the inside need the stabilizing and strengthening power of divine love! How many modern homes are fractured by unloving divisions and weakened by contentious strife!

(c) We need a renewed sense of the hallowed purposes of God for people living in families. With a vivid awareness of the divine presence, every family ought to be in a sense a holy family, blessed and beautified by God's love. Then it could be said of our families that the "glory of the Lord shone round about them."

V. Christmas can glorify our society. (a) Following Jesus' presentation in the temple when he was only eight days old, he was seen and blessed by a veteran patriarch of the temple, Simeon. His famous pronouncement over the baby is commonly known as the "Nunc Dimittis." Here is a part of it: "Lord, now lettest thy servant depart in peace . . . for mine eyes have seen thy salvation which thou has prepared in the presence of all peoples; a light for revelation to the Gentiles, and for glory to thy people Israel" (Luke 2: 29–32).

(b) Christmas is intended as God's revelation for all mankind. Its purpose is to bring divine salvation to all humanity and to redeem mankind from the judgment of sin and from the domination of death.

(c) Christmas comes while mankind lives under the dark shadow of fear and apprehension. How much we need the glory of love and hope in the Christmas promise of "peace on earth and good will to men."—Emil Kontz.

Illustrations

TRANSFORMATION.   An ancient king, to show his concern for his subjects, announced that he was going to visit in the homes of some of the peasants who lived in the lowliest cottages in his realm. But instead of rejoicing at the king's announcement, the peasants were quite upset. "It would not be proper for the king to visit in our rude huts, to sit on our crude furniture, and to eat our humble food. Please do not come!"

But the king went anyway, taking with him his servants, his own furniture, and his own food. As a result each cottage he visited was transformed into a little royal palace. Thus even the most humble peasant who received him into his home could rejoice.

Is this not what happened when our Savior came to earth? The most humble person who receives him is transformed. —John Wade.

HE GAVE HIMSELF.   Shah Abbas, a Persian monarch, disguised himself in clothes of squalid poverty and went into the public baths. There he descended into a tiny cellar and sat by a fireman who tended the furnace. When mealtime came he shared the man's coarse food and talked with him as a friend. He did this until the poor man cast aside his reserve and became attached to him. One day the shah revealed his true identity to his friend. When the truth sank in, the poor man spoke: "You left your palace and your glory to sit with me in this dark place. You became my friend in the midst of my loneliness. You have given me the greatest gift of all. You have given me yourself."—Sundar Singh.

REIGN OR RESIGN?   An error appeared in the printed program of a performance of Handel's *Messiah*. The Hallelujah Chorus was listed as: "The Lord God omnipotent resigneth." Was it just an error, or was the printer a real cynic, deducing from the condition of the world that the Lord God had, in fact, resigned and had given up the world as a hopeless mess?—Halford E. Luccock.

Sermon Suggestions

FOLLOW THIS SIGN.   Text: Luke 2:12 (RSV). (1) Follow the sign to the manger, and it shall lead you to a revolutionary concept of humanity's true status. (2) Follow the sign, for it signifies that the mighty God has come to us in our need and longing. (3) Follow the sign, and you shall discover that God's concept of power is our idea of weakness. (4) Follow the sign to Bethlehem, Galilee, Calvary, and Olivet if you would know that life which is ultimately victorious.—David A. MacLennan.

ANOTHER WAY.   Text: Matt. 2:12. The wise men returned along the way (1) of faith fulfilled, (2) of hope more surely founded, and (3) of love rekindled.—Reginald E. O. White.

THE FIRST CHRISTMAS SERVICE: A MODEL FOR CHRISTIAN WORSHIP.   Scripture: Luke 2:8–20. (1) In its message. (a) Declared by a unique messenger (v. 9). (b)

Directed to the hearers: "to all people" and "to you" (vv. 10–11). (2) In its praise. (a) Praise to God for what he is (v. 14). (b) Praise to God for what he has done (v. 14). (3) In its worshipers. (a) They were attentive. (b) They believed (vv. 15–16).—Gerhard Aho.

Worship Aids

CALL TO WORSHIP. "Make a joyful noise unto the Lord, all the earth: make a loud noise, and rejoice, and sing praise. Sing unto the Lord with the harp; with the harp, and the voice of a psalm. With trumpets and sound of cornet make a joyful noise before the Lord, the King." Ps. 98:4–6.

INVOCATION. Hushed be our hearts, O God, by the mystery and the wonder of the birth of the Christ Child. Make us truly wise with the wisdom of a little child that once again the highest truth may be born afresh in our hearts. Let not our souls be busy inns that have no room for thy Son, but this day throw wide the doors of our lives to welcome our holy guest.

OFFERTORY SENTENCE. "When they were come into the house, they saw the young child with Mary his mother, and fell down, and worshiped him. And they presented unto him gifts; gold, and frankincense, and myrrh." Matt. 2:11.

OFFERTORY PRAYER. Enlarge our hearts this day, O Christ, that with a world vision we may offer these gifts in the assurance that by thy grace they may proclaim the message of Christmas to those who yet await the coming of thy redeeming light.

PRAYER. O thou giver of every good and perfect gift of Christmas—for the wonder of it, for the love of it, for the peace of it, and for the hope of it.

We are grateful for the bread of Christian fellowship broken in the life of this congregation as we worship, study, and serve together and for the families that thou hast given us and with whom we have the privilege of sharing this glad season. We give thee thanks for friends who double all our joys. For children's voices that make glad our hearts in song, for the mature voices of men and women who witness to the triumph of faith in thee, for health enjoyed, and for adversities that challenge us to live more deeply, we give thee our hearty thanks.

O Father, in that thou hast first given to us Christmas, may we capture the rapture of it, the wonder of it, the glory of it, and the saving grace of it that life will never be the drab, colorless existence of past days but that it will be transfigured by the many splendored love that comes to us in Jesus the Christ. Lead us to understand how thou dost use the weak things of the world to confound the mighty lest we should seek power over men to use them rather than to love them into fulfillment. May we live in the blessed assurance that thou hast come, art here, and art coming. May the meaning of thy incarnate love become real through us as we become as broken bread given for the life of the world.

O thou who dost so love the world that thou hast given thy only begotten Son, help us to share the good news that Christmas brings with all peoples. May we not be so rigid that we fail to bring to international tensions the imagination born of thy love. Bless those who have the opportunity to be leaders in the community of nations that they may have that disposition of mind to seek thy will that all people may echo back the angels' song: "Glory to God in the highest, and on earth peace among men of good will."

Be with those who are lonely because they are bereft of loved ones or friends or because they are far away from families and friends.—John Thompson.

EVENING SERVICE

Topic: Our Advent Candles: The Christ Candle

TEXT: Luke 2:10.

We have gathered around the Christ candle to celebrate the birth of Jesus Christ as a babe in Bethlehem's manger. That celebration has become an annual event of gigantic proportions, but it is surprising when you remember that the birth of Christ was largely ignored by the world into which he came. To the world of that day it was a quite insignificant event. Thousands of babies were born every day, and to them this was simply another birth. That world, preoccupied with other things, neither knew nor cared that Jesus Christ had come. In view of that ignoble beginning, how do you explain our modern observance of Christmas and particularly the note of joy which it evokes?

I. The birth of Jesus Christ is a fact of history, and through the years we have come to appreciate the significance of that fact.

(a) That Jesus is a fact of history simply cannot be denied. To be sure there have been those who have denied his historicity and have argued that he never lived but was only a myth developed for religious purposes. No historian of any repute has ever committed himself to such a theory.

(b) Since the first days of the Christian era we have come increasingly to appreciate the significance of his coming. A. T. Olmstead wrote of him as "the central figure of world history, and P. T. Simpson said, "Jesus Christ is, beyond all reasonable question, the greatest man who ever lived." Jesus divides our calendar. His influence is not so much written as plowed into history, and increasingly we see him as the sole hope, the whole hope, and the sure and certain hope of the world.

(c) There has to be an explanation for influence like that, and the only explanation that fits the facts is that Jesus is, what the New Testament claims he is, God incarnate in the flesh, God taking upon himself the form of a man, and God dying upon the cross for our redemption. This man is God. This God is the savior. That is why we celebrate Christmas as we do and why we offer him our adoration and our worship.

II. He is a fact of experience who does for us what no one else can do.

(a) What is it that he does? He brings peace to our hearts, the peace of God's forgiveness. (See Rom. 5:1.) He brings reinforcement to our wills, the inward strengthening of his divine spirit. (See Phil. 4:14.) He brings meaning to our lives. (See Phil. 3:13–14.)

(b) Karl Barth said, "The nativity of Christ is the nativity of the Christian man; Christmas day is the birthday of every Christian." Jesus Christ is not only the savior of the world; he is my savior. He has lifted the burden of sin from my soul, he has brought strength to my will, and he has given direction to my life. Christmas is no mere observance of the historic birth of Christ. It is more personal. It is the expression of my thanksgiving and praise unto God for the coming of Jesus Christ into my life.

III. He is also a prophetic fact. (See Acts 1:11.) (a) Jesus is coming again, he is coming to take us home, he is coming to establish his kingdom, and he is coming to judge the living and the dead.

(b) That expectation, that assurance, that certainty, and that confidence sustained the apostles and early disciples as they met opposition and persecution, Confronted by evil, they did not give way to despair but cried: "Christ is Lord! He shall reign King of kings and Lord of lords!"

(c) We still need an assurance like that. Bishop Berggrav of Norway, speaking to a Christian Youth Conference at Oslo, drew attention to the ceiling of the cathedral in which they worshiped and said: "Have you observed the ceiling of this church? It is low and heavy. The atmosphere is made oppressive. I wish I could take it away. Then you would see the most lovely and mighty scenery, prepared through these eleven years by one of our Norwegian painters. He needed this temporary low ceiling as the floor of his workroom. In one year we hope to have the view of what is above. Then you will have the most convincing sermon which painting can give of Christ the Lord. But you cannot see it today, just as it is not given to us today to see Christ as the actual lord of the world. But he is! When the low ceiling of life in time is taken away, you will get to know that he was there all the time and that the low ceiling of today was his working floor."—S. Robert Weaver.

SECTION XII. *Ideas and Suggestions for Pulpit and Parish*

BISHOP ASBURY PREACHING.   From time to time Bishop Francis Asbury steps out of the past to speak to the Main Street United Methodist Church in Columbia, South Carolina, on his conversion and early preaching in England, his assignment to America as a missionary, and his preaching and organizing of churches throughout the American frontier during the late 1700s and early 1800s and to remind 20th century Christians of their heritage and witness. Asbury is portrayed by W. Robert Borom, who is appropriately costumed for the role.

CHURCH SURVEY.   The Colonial Heights Church of Christ in Norfolk, Virginia, conducted a short answer and essay-type survey—"Church Analysis and Need Assessment"—to help church leaders to determine the needs of members, to bring about growth and a more effective ministry, and to get views and opinions regarding the church and hopes for the future.

PAYCHECK SUNDAY.   The members of the Olivet Christian Church in Newport News, Virginia, were challenged on Paycheck Sunday to give the equivalent of one week's pay to a special church offering.

PLANNED FAMINE.   Young people in the Trinity Reformed Church in Rochester, New York, gained a better understanding of what it means to be hungry through a thirty-hour planned famine that included Bible studies and discussion of the problem of world hunger. Church sponsors of the young people made contributions to World Vision to aid the hungry.

THE CHURCH AND THE TRACTOR.   Lyle E. Schaller in *The Pastor and the People* tells of a church that decided to give a tractor for a mission project in Africa. To be reminded of their commitment a comparable tractor was borrowed from a local firm and parked on the grass near the church door. This infuriated an absentee member who, not having heard of the project, complained that the janitor by leaving the machine there had obstructed the view of the beautiful edifice. When told why, the erstwhile member wrote a check covering the purchase of the mission project.

GIVING GAME.   At a meeting of young people at the St. Matthew Cumberland Presbyterian Church in Burleson, Texas, a churchmanship game was played involving a fictitious gift of $5000 from a fictitious person who stipulated that the donation be used in only one specific area of church work. Each of six committees attempted to persuade the session that its needs were most crucial. The result was a tie vote between world missions and building and grounds.

MEMORY VERSE QUILT.   Fifth and sixth graders in a thirty-week catechism class at the Nooksack Valley Reformed Church in Nooksack, Washington, completed a memory verse quilt in which each square inch represented a Bible verse that had been memorized.

MINISTRY TO THE DEAF.   A special ministry to deaf members and other deaf persons at the Englewood Christian Church in Indianapolis, Indiana, includes the interpretation in sign language of the first worship service, a separate service for the deaf during the second worship hour, and Bible school classes for the hearing handicapped.

NEVER ALONE.   In a program called Never Alone, volunteers in the Eastview Christian Church in Bloomington, Illinois, are paired with elderly persons who live alone. By telephoning at least once a day, the volunteer not only shares Christian fellowship but also assures the older person that he won't be incapacitated by accident or illness without someone knowing.

DARE.   To keep track of members and to meet their needs by *dare*-ing to shepherd them, the Bridgetown Church of Christ in Cincinnati, Ohio, introduced a project called DARE, an acrostic for divide, action, report, and encourage. The congregation was *divided* into forty flocks, each shepherded by an elder, deacon, or other member. Each flock leader *actively* kept in touch with his families by quarterly home visits. Then leaders *reported* on their visits, and all members were *encouraged* in Christian living.

WEIGHT DAY.   On Weight Day at the Faith United Methodist Church in Smyrna, Georgia, every person was weighed during the Sunday school hour and asked to contribute a penny a pound to world hunger.

HUNGER PICNIC.   Members of the First Baptist Church in Phoenix, Arizona, held a salad and sandwich picnic where before food was served each person was given a birth certificate designating where he had come from. Each individual then gave statistics relating to his country's resources and per capita income, and the food was distributed proportionately.

FURLOUGH HOME.   The First Christian Church in St. Ann, Missouri, maintains a three-bedroom home where missionaries on furlough may live on a rent-free basis for periods not exceeding twelve months.

DYFO VOLUNTEERS.   Knowledgeable volunteers, many of them retirees, comprise a ministry called DYFO (Do It Yourself for Others) in the Evergreen Presbyterian Church in Memphis, Tennessee, which is on call to assist without compensation in such routine residential maintenance and repair problems as malfunctioning faucets, broken windows, jammed doors, and troublesome small appliances in the residences of elderly church members and those in financial difficulty.

INTERNATIONAL DINNER.   The United Methodist Church in Ravenna, Michigan, held an international dinner featuring foods representing countries embraced by Christian missions. Exchange students were guests. Proceeds went to world hunger.

MINISTRY TO MENTALLY HANDICAPPED. Believing that the church has always been the place where the Good Shepherd seeks out the lost, the lonely, and the forgotten, members of the Gloria Dei and Messiah Lutheran churches in Knoxville, Tennessee, offer a special ministry to former patients in mental hospitals that includes financial and emotional support and transportation to worship services.

BREAD BAKERS.   Volunteers in the Jesse Lee Memorial United Methodist Church in Ridgefield, Connecticut, bake bread for the worship services on communion Sundays, the bread being standard-sized white bread, French twists, or Israeli flat bread, the type chosen to fit the service.

DIAL-A-STORY.   Members of the First Assembly of God in Walla Walla, Washington, tape Bible stories that may be listened to by persons of all ages who call on a special Dial-a-Story phone number.

MISSION FAIR.   Following a month-long study of missions in the church school classes, a mission fair was held at the Mount Olivet United Methodist Church in Arlington, Virginia, that included displays describing more than forty local, conference, national, and international missions in which the Mount Olivet members participate.

GOOD-BYE RITUAL. This ritual of departure may be incorporated into the worship service prior to the benediction: "In God's plan for life we come to give thanks this day for *name or names* who have been part of our church family and who leave us and our location for a new home, a new work, a new church, and a new life in *place*. In order that their going not be a gradual fading from our lives and our minds but a joyous sending forth of those who have been loved by us in worship and fellowship, we give thanks for their time with us and ask God's blessings on their travels and future lives." Following prayer these words may be said: "Go now with our blessing and our love, and go with God."

A DIME AN INCH. At the beginning of Lent children in the Sunday school classes at St. Thomas Lutheran Church in Sterling Heights, Michigan, measured their heights with a sticky tape to which they daily attached dimes, accumulated through self-denial. The tapes, covered with dimes, were returned on Easter and the monies contributed to Lutheran social service projects.

SEASONAL BANNERS. Junior-age members of the church school of the Reformed Church in Closter, New Jersey, made banners depicting the five seasons of the Christian year. More than 100 church members decorated small butterflies which were arranged into a large butterfly banner symbolizing Christ's victory over sin and death.

DAILY REFLECTIONS. Holy Week services, scheduled from 12 to 12:30 P.M. at the Glen Haven United Methodist Church in Decatur, Georgia, were called Daily Reflections and centered successively on the seven words from the cross.

GIFT OF BREAD. As an expression of hope that they might always work together proclaiming the gospel of peace to the poor, the Perpetual Help Catholic Church gave fresh-baked bread to the Eden Lutheran Church in Riverside, California, for a midnight Easter vigil.

CHRISMONS. More than 100 Chrismons, white and gold symbols of faith, were created by members of St. Paul's United Church in Milton, Ontario, for a Christmas tree and then were used to decorate a cross during Lent and at Easter were converted by the use of lilies and ivy into an Easter cross.

THE TEACHER CORPS. The First Christian Church in Hereford, Texas, has devised a teacher corps plan in which each class has a master teacher and several teacher corps members who agree to serve as substitutes and take over during the summer months, attend teacher training events, and be a participant-observer in class for a month.

APPRECIATION BANQUET. The congregation of the First Christian Church in Bentonville, Arkansas, held a banquet honoring members of the city police department. Guests included the governor, mayor, the county judge, and members of the city council. An award was presented for outstanding Christian character as a working policeman.

DEGREE CLASSES. The Broadway Christian Church in Lexington, Kentucky, scheduled two degree classes for new members. The B.D. degree (basic discipleship) was for those who had been baptized during the preceding twelve months, and the D.D. degree (deeper discipleship) for those who had during the preceding year transferred from other congregations.

BODY AND SOUL. More than 200 women combined physical and spiritual fitness in classes sponsored by the First United Methodist Church in LaGrange, Georgia, where courses include one emphasizing interpretive movement and another for older women is known as Prime Time 50.

JOASH CHEST.   Recalling the time in 820 B.C. during the reign of King Joash of Israel when a chest was prepared in which the people, priests, and the king placed their offerings for the renovation of the temple, and convinced that an individual's pledge is a commitment between himself and God, the United Methodist Church in Culver-Palms, California, asks members to put their written pledges in sealed, self-addressed envelopes and deposit them in the Joash Chest on Pledge Sunday. The following month the unopened envelopes are returned to the members who quarterly receive statements on how much they have given and not on how much they owe.

A JOYFUL NOISE.   Recognizing the arts as a gift from God, the Kenwood United Methodist Church of Milwaukee, Wisconsin, has created an atmosphere where religion and the arts flourish in recitals, poetry readings, art exhibits in the parlor and sanctuary, drama, dance, the Dixieland mass, weekday worship services, and Sunday worship which may include bluegrass, folk, jazz, and classical musicians, dance or drama interpretations of scriptural themes, and congregational singing of the words of praise, confession and forgiveness, scriptures, and commitment to God and man.

TOURISTS ACCOMMODATED.   Baptists including youth groups on mission and study tours visiting the nation's capital are given accommodations—cots, showers, and meals—at the National Baptist Memorial Baptist Church in Washington, D.C., and church staff personnel are available to help groups make arrangements for visits to places of interest.

UNIVERSAL MESSAGE.   The Pentecost banner of the Mt. Hope United Methodist Church in Detroit, Michigan, depicts the descending dove and the proclamation "Praise the Lord" in English, Polish, Latin, Greek, French, Italian, and German.

WHAT'S HAPPENING?   A portion of the outdoor bulletin board of the Trinity United Methodist Church in Lynchburg, Virginia, is designated as a community bulletin board where notices of community programs and services may be placed.

INSPIRATION WALK.   The Second Reformed Church in Kalamazoo, Michigan, has created a quarter-mile Inspiration Walk along the historic Arcadia Creek on church property for church members and others who wish to glorify the Creator and acknowledge that creation is to be glorified, appreciated, and protected by both God and man.

CHURCH IN THE PARK.   During the summer months the Central United Methodist Church in Traverse City, Michigan, holds an informal thirty-minute worship service at 9 A.M. on Sundays in Sunset Park next to Grand Traverse Bay. Following hymn singing and a meditation is an informal fellowship with coffee and punch.

VACATION GUIDE.   The Lyttleton Street United Methodist Church in Camden, South Carolina, produced a "Family Vacation Guide" containing games for travel, family devotionals, Bible study worksheets, and songs.

LOCAL HUNGER.   Frustrated by not knowing how one congregation could help to alleviate world hunger, members of the Peace Presbyterian Church in Eugene, Oregon, decided they could do something about local hunger. They transformed a weed plot on church property into a garden divided into forty-six plots each measuring 20 x 30 feet. Gardeners paid initially a modest fee for soil preparation and the operation of an irrigation pump. Participants provide not only for their own households but also generously share their produce with those local persons who need food through their church, the FISH program, a rescue mission, among others.

A SON-FILLED VACATION.   To meet the spiritual and physical needs of six to twelve-year-old inner city children, members of the Grace United Methodist Church in Atlanta, Georgia, organized a

"Have a Son-Filled Vacation" program at the Community Children's Center where activities included a variety show, craft instruction, recreation, field trips, and devotions.

SHARE OUR SURPLUS.   Members of the Mt. Olivet United Methodist Church in Dearborn, Michigan, placed surpluses from their summer gardens on a Share Our Surplus table in the narthex so that non-gardeners could share the products and contribute thereby to the world hunger fund.

CORN FOR THE NEEDY.   Members of the rural Bayle City Baptist Church near Ramsey, Illinois, planted donated corn seed on two acres of donated land, and at harvest time members of the Uptown Baptist Church in Chicago harvested a trailer load of corn for distribution to people in need in the city.

CHRISTMAS IN JULY.   As part of a Christmas-in-July celebration, members of the First United Methodist Church in Kalamazoo, Michigan, were asked to place canned goods, wrapped in white paper, on the altar to replenish the food pantry, a community service project.

REST FOR THE WEARY.   Members of the Bethany United Methodist Church in Virginia's Isle of Wight Circuit set up a highway rest stop and provided free coffee, colas, and cookies for weary Labor Day travelers.

WORLD SERIES.   The Church of Christ in Barryton, Michigan, held a five-week World Series contest in which the Sunday school was divided into red and blue teams. Each Sunday a person attended, he advanced his team one base. If he brought a visitor, he advanced his team another base. Visitors were assigned to a minor league until a major team signed them to a bonus contract and they began playing for that team.

DIVERSITY.   Sunday school classes are taught in English, Spanish, and Korean and morning worship services are heard in three languages with the use of earphones for simultaneous translation in the international and interracial ministry of the First Baptist Church in Los Angeles, California.

HOMEBOUND COMMUNION.   Homebound members and friends of the First United Methodist Church in Houston, Texas, are invited to prepare bread and juice in advance and participate in Holy Communion with the congregation during the radio and TV broadcasts. A complete order of worship that includes the words of the hymns and prayers is printed in the church paper.

COMMON WORSHIP.   On the first Sunday of each month the Spanish and English departments of the Chevy Chase Baptist Church in Glendale, California, join for a bilingual service of worship and communion. The bulletin is printed in both languages, and the messages are translated so that all persons can understand.

DIVORCE RECOVERY.   A ministry called Divorce Recovery of the St. Mark Lutheran Church in Woonsocket, Rhode Island, provides separated and divorced persons a place to meet and discuss mutual problems.

HOMECOMING GARB.   Members and guests dressed in turn-of-the-century costumes for Homecoming Sunday at the First Baptist Church in Aberdeen, Mississippi, which included morning worship, a covered dish dinner, skits depicting events in the church's history, and visits to historic homes in the area.

VIVID PORTRAYAL.   John S. Carter occasionally appears in his pulpit in the Trinity United Methodist Church in Lebanon, Pennsylvania, in make-up and costume of a biblical character to read the scripture lesson and claims: "When you come as a monologue, you can say things in the portrayal that would be difficult to get across emphatically otherwise. The character steps out of scripture into the 20th century, and the listener becomes a participant in the events as they unfold."

CHILDREN'S BULLETIN. Faith Cumberland Presbyterian Church in Memphis, Tennessee, distributes each Sunday a special children's bulletin based on the lectionary and including a page to color that fits the theme of the pastor's sermon, a gospel crossword puzzle, and various children's activities.

FOOD STAMPS. Members of the First Cumberland Presbyterian Church in Louisville, Kentucky, collected more than 28,000 postage stamps for the Salvation Army. A hungry child can be fed for one year by the money that 2,500 stamps provide.

DOWNTOWNER CLUB. The suburban Mount Lebanon Baptist Church in Pittsburgh, Pennsylvania, organized the Downtowner Club where business people meet from noon to 1 P.M. one day each week to discuss the problems, frustrations, and challenges of Christian witness in the midst of the business world.

GREETINGS BEFORE WORSHIP. William Skudlarek, author of *The Word in Worship*, suggests that ministers greet people as they arrive for worship and not just as they leave the service. "Having revealed themselves to their sisters and brothers as one with them in the community of faith," he writes, "they will be able to assume the role of leader with the sense that they have been called forth by the community rather than imposed on it from above."

GET THE SIGNAL. When a flag bearing a large blue X on a white field flies from a ship at sea, it may mean "Stop carrying out your intentions and watch for my signals." A similar flag, when displayed in the sanctuary of the Arlington Forest United Methodist Church in Arlington, Virginia, was a new symbol for becoming a part of the body of Christ during the church's Proclaim the Word events.

ART GALLERY. An art gallery in the educational building of the Rocky Ridge Cumberland Presbyterian Church in Birmingham, Alabama, gives members who are artists an opportunity to display their paintings.

A NEW DAY. Dissatisfied with the results of routine confirmation classes, the parish of St. Francis of Assisi Episcopal Church in Simi Valley, California, have introduced a new method called "A New Day," an annual weekend retreat that includes peer group leadership, a careful selection of content goals, the use of various teaching media, and ample breaks for rest and relaxation.

MOTHERS MORNING OUT. A program called "Mothers Morning Out" at the Holy Trinity Lutheran Church in Littleton, Colorado, gives mothers a break for shopping and other activities by providing for a modest fee child care on Mondays and Fridays from 9 A.M. to noon.

BLESSING ON THE ANIMALS. At a special service each year at the First Moravian Church in Greensboro, North Carolina, children bring their pets to receive a blessing of the animals. The tradition makes it possible for children to take to church that about which they most care and to acknowledge their pets as a part of God's creation.

DIAL-A-MISSIONARY. Those attending the Foreign Missions Week at the Ridgecrest Baptist Assembly in North Carolina listened to the voices of ninety-four missionaries tell their stories from all parts of the world on telephones linked with individual tapes arranged in a global walk around.

ORGANIZATIONAL DEVELOPMENT. The application of effective business organization to the church was the purpose of seminars held at the Trinity United Methodist Church in West Columbia, South Carolina. To make the church a more efficient organization, the Trinity Training Center emphasizes communicative skills to achieve a greater degree of openness in the way people relate to each other and tries to balance organizational management with sensitivity training.

CHURCH CLASS DISPLAYS.　　A feature of the Christian Education Sunday program at the First United Methodist Church in Calhoun, Georgia, was displays in the fellowship hall by each of the seventeen church school classes depicting class goals, purposes, and activities and including posters, pictures, curriculum resources, and photographs of members.

A SERVICE FAIR.　　Many churches have found that a service fair is a good transition from bazaars to a more Christian approach toward service and stewardship. The service fair gives an opportunity for talented persons to work together toward one big day of sharing.

Those who knit, crochet, and sew apply their skills to the needs of Church World Service, homes for children, the aged, and the handicapped, and for nursing homes, hospitals, and social agencies.

Baked goods are shared with persons living alone and newcomers in the community, and a gourmet luncheon is served without charge to those attending the fair.

Persons who feel they can participate only by purchasing what others create are called co-sponsors and their contributions assist world hunger and mission projects.—Marilyn L. Trefzger in *The Disciple.*

FEED MY SHEEP.　　Heeding the Master's command, members of the Pace Memorial United Methodist Church in Richmond, Virginia, provide nourishing meals to all who come to the church's bright red door. From 50 to 80 down-and-outers are fed following Sunday worship, and others are served at such times as the drop-in lunches on Fridays. Members of this "feeding church" volunteer as cooks, contribute food at Holy Communion each month, engage in spiritual talk at the tables, and participate in counseling and job and social services referrals.

SEED MONEY.　　Laymen in the United Methodist Church in Sterling, Virginia, distributed one dollar to church members who were given a year to invest the monies in ways individuals choose. At the end of the year the profit on the original investment showed a 2300 percent increase. The seed money was given to the church building fund.

HOBBY SUNDAY.　　More than 160 members of the Church of God in Diamond Oaks, Texas, participated in a Hobby Sunday display that included a variety of handicrafts, knitting and yarn work, paintings, and other creations.

USHERS.　　The usher committee of the Good Shepherd Cumberland Presbyterian Church in Huntsville, Alabama, has involved such combinations of ushers at worship services as brothers, fathers and sons, husbands and wives, mothers and daughters, and sisters.

CHECK YOUR MAILBOX.　　Lyle E. Schaller in *The Parish Paper* wrote of a church where the entrance hall is banked with 432 small cubicles, one for each member and each child, in which name tags are kept and in which the church paper and such things as meeting notices, birthday greetings, invitations, and messages of appreciation are placed.

OUTREACH TREE.　　Wishing to visualize the outreach mission represented by the Christmas offering, members of the Mountair Christian Church in Lakewood, Colorado, during Advent decorated an outreach tree with more than sixty ornaments, each displaying a particular ministry on one side and a brief description on the other.

CARDS FOR MISSIONS.　　Some churches in which members customarily send Christmas cards to one another are inviting the people to contribute the money usually spent on cards and postage to a Christmas mission fund. Those doing so receive a card from the church listing names of all participants.

RED AND WHITE TREES.　　The South Bend United Methodist Church in Rome, Georgia, had two unusual Christmas trees. A red tree, called "The Tree of the Fall," was decorated with thirty-three apples suggesting man's temptation in Eden and the coming of sin and death into the world. The trunk was wrapped with red ribbon as a reminder of our bondage to sin, and the absence of lights symbolized the dark night of sin. A white tree, called "The Tree of Salvation," represented Christ's death on the tree of the cross for our sins, white lights typified Christ as the light of the world, thirty-three white roses spoke of Christ's holy and perfect life, a five-pointed star symbolized the head, arms, and legs of the incarnate Christ, and three white streamers from the star symbolized Christ's three-fold office as prophet, priest, and king.

STEWARDSHIP TREE.   At the beginning of Advent the stewardship tree in the Centenary United Methodist Church in Portsmouth, Virginia, was decorated in white, but by Christmas most of the decorations were red. The ornaments were cut from reversible red and white paper. Printed on the white side were stewardship commitments such as the following: visit four shut-ins, attend worship every Sunday during Advent, visit four persons you have not seen in church recently, and increase your commitment of time for spiritual growth. Members making one or more commitments reversed ornaments from white to red.

NATIVITY SCENE.   The Christmas Eve service of the Reformed Church in North Indianapolis, Indiana, was held in a barn where the pastor, choir, and Sunday school juniors presented a simulation of the shepherds' journey to Bethlehem to find Jesus in a manger.

EPIPHANY FESTIVAL.   Recreating a 17th century ceremony celebrating Epiphany, members of St. Peter Lutheran Church in Lafayette, Pennsylvania, each year present a pageant that includes a procession of more than a 100 parishioners dressed in medieval-like clothing or as participants in the story of Jesus' birth and including a brass ensemble, two choirs, and a bagpipe band and featuring plum pudding, mince pie, a yule log, and a realistic-looking boar's head. The festival is repeated three times daily for two days during the Epiphany season.

SNOW SCULPTURING.   Members of the Sunday school classes of the United Methodist Church in Bear Lake, Michigan, participated in biblical snow sculpturing on the church property and created representations of a lamb, a whale, an open Bible, the cross, the houses of the wise and foolish builders, the empty tomb, a mustard seed, and the pearl of great price.

SECTION XIII. *A Little Treasury of Illustrations*

SEEING GOD. The supreme truth of Christianity is that in Jesus I see God. When I see Jesus feeding the hungry, comforting the sorrowing, befriending men and women with whom no one else would have had anything to do, I can say, "This is God."—William Barclay.

WHAT CHRISTIANS DO. Christianity does not consist in abstaining from doing things no gentleman would think of doing but in doing things that are unlikely to occur to anyone who is not in touch with the Spirit of Christ.—Dick Sheppard.

DUTY. O to be able to say in that day, "Lord, I am no hero, but a traitor or a deserter I have never been. I have tried to do the duty which lay nearest me and to leave whatever thou didst commit to my charge a little better than I found it."—Charles Kingsley.

ONLY A MAN! Marianne Adlard, a bedridden girl in London, read of the work of D. L. Moody among the ragged children of Chicago. She began to pray, "Lord, send this man to our church." In 1872 Moody took his second trip to London, not intending to do any work. But the pastor of Marianne's church met him and asked him to preach for him. At the close of the service Moody asked if there were those who desired to accept Christ. Hundreds rose to their feet. During the next ten days four hundred people were received into the church. Moody wanted to know the cause of all this, and he began to make inquiries. He told G. Campbell Morgan: "I found a bedridden girl praying that God would bring me to that church. He had heard her and brought me over four thousand miles of land and sea at her request."—Phillips Brooks.

AFTER THE STORM. A little girl asked her father, "What was God doing last night during the storm?" Then, answering her own question, she put God's love and care in perfect perspective. "I know, God was making the morning."—C. Neil Strait.

IN A HUDDLE. Going to church is like a team huddle in the midst of a football game. Going to church is like time-out to organize ourselves for the next play. We go into a huddle around the cross. Don't think the only teammates we have are the ones we see. St. Peter is there cheering on the cowards. David and Moses are there cheering on the politicians. St. Francis is there straining to help us find God in simple things like birds and water and flowers and sun and moon. Martin Luther is there, yelling at us in his gruff German voice and telling us not to be afraid to take a stand, regardless of who is against us.—Reid Isaac.

RESPONSE. While contending with the manifold problems of geography and climate in the building of the Panama Canal, Colonel George Washington Goethals had to endure the carping criticism of countless busybodies back home who freely predicted that he would never complete his great task. But the resolute builder pressed steadily forward in his work and said nothing. "Aren't you going to answer your critics?" a subordinate inquired. "In time," Goethals replied. "How?" The great engineer smiled. "With the canal."—George McGlothin.

NEARBY WONDER. People travel to wonder at the height of mountains, at the huge waves of the sea, at the long course of rivers, at the vast compass of the ocean, at the circular motion of the stars, and they pass by themselves without wondering.—St. Augustine.

COME UNTO ME. Alan Walker, after preaching in a big city one night, went to an all-night cafe. While he was drinking coffee, a woman at a nearby table pushed a note onto his table. It read, "Dr. Walker, I went to church tonight and felt like an intruder." He went to where she was sitting and introduced himself. She told him it was the first time in many years that she had been in a church. She was feeling low. Her marriage was on the rocks. She had been walking past the church, heard the singing, and on an impulse went in. She said the choir looked so respectable in their robes. When the ushers stood together, she was almost afraid that they would ask her to leave. She was half afraid that someone who knew her shady past and all of her weaknesses would tell someone who she was. She had been uncomfortable throughout the service. Walker reassured her. He told her that the members of the choir were not nearly as respectable as they looked and that the ushers had never yet put anyone out of a service. Furthermore, he said that no one was an intruder in the presence of God, least of all someone who came in humility and penitence.

CONTINUAL PRAISE. In some of the old monasteries there was a law that the chanting of praise to God should never cease. When one brother ceased to sing, another took up the chant. Thus praise continued day and night.

LEGEND. A Greek athlete desperately wanted to win at the public games. Although he was extremely competitive, he lost in his attempt at fame and fortune. In honor of the winner, a statue was created and placed in the center of the local town. The athlete who had so desperately wanted to win was outraged by the honor. Every night under the cover of darkness he made his way to the statue and chiseled at its base. Finally he accomplished his purpose and the statue fell. The only problem was that it fell on him, and he was killed instantly.—Larry Kennedy

WIND BENT. A North Carolina mountaineer says that the finest violins are fashioned from the spruce trees that grow high in the Blue Ridge Mountains. Here they must endure the snows, merciless storms, and be bent and tossed by the hard winds to develop the resonance necessary for the best violins.—James E. McReynolds.

DEDICATION. I used to ask God to help me. Then I asked if I might help him. I ended up by asking him to do his work through me.—Hudson Taylor.

BEAUTY. Where there is beauty apparent, we are to enjoy it; where there is beauty hidden, we are to unveil it; where there is beauty defaced, we are to restore it; where there is no beauty at all, we are to create it.—Robert M. Brown.

CAPSULED FRIEND. Young people have been asked by psychiatrists and sociologists, "If you had the choice of giving up your television or your daddy, which one would you choose?" And they chose overwhelmingly to give up daddy because this is their friend, their teacher, the companion, the one who guides them into the obvious conclusion that the answers to all of life's problems must be contained in thirty to sixty minute capsules.—Pat Robinson.

REMEMBERING. In Don Robertson's novel, *Praise the Human Season,* the main character approaches the time of his death with these words: "This is not to say I value all the dying. I do not. Rather, I value all the living that preceded the dying. All the living and all the love. Now and then, when I am unable to sleep, when I lie musing and remembering, I try to sort out the separate varieties of love that I have known. The love of son for father and mother. The love of brother for brother. The love of brother for sister. The love of father for child. The love of husband for wife. And I say to myself: The older you become, the more persons who are included and—the more who are taken away. Entrances and exits abound. It may not reflect well on me to admit such a thing, but I find the remembering all very delicious."

GREAT LIVING.   No steam or gas ever drives anything until it is confined. No Niagara is ever turned into light and power until it is tunneled. No life ever grows great until it is focused, dedicated, and disciplined.—Harry Emerson Fosdick.

GOD AND WALLET.   Tell me what you think about money, and I can tell you what you think about God, for these two are closely related. A man's heart is closer to his wallet than almost anything else.—Billy Graham.

INVITATION.   It is the aim of this church to present a religion as considerate of persons as the teachings of Jesus, as devoted to justice as the Old Testament prophets, as responsive to truth as science, as beautiful as art, as intimate as the home, and as indispensable as the air we breathe. For the achievement of this goal we bid you welcome, and invite your attendance, your prayers, your gifts, and your service.

RELIGION AND RICHES.   Wherever riches have increased, the essence of religion has decreased in the same proportion. Therefore, I do not see how it is possible in the nature of things for any revival of religion to continue long. For religion must necessarily produce both industry and frugality, and these cannot but produce riches. But as riches increase so will pride, anger, and love of the world in all its branches. How then is it possible that Methodism, as a green bay tree, should continue in this state? For the Methodists in every place grow diligent and frugal; consequently they increase in pride, in anger, in the desire of the flesh, the desire of the eyes and the pride of life. So, although the form of religion remains, the spirit is swiftly vanishing away.—John Wesley.

CRYSTAL CLEAR.   Kierkegaard tells a parable about how we at times react to the clear words of the Bible. He imagines a man finding an official document that promises him a large sum of money. He takes it to the officials and claims the funds. They say: "Let's get some experts to examine this paper. Let's get some learned commentators to tell us what it really means." And he says: "Away with your experts and away with your commentators. It's crystal clear. Give me my money!" And so, Kierkegaard says, we receive a message of scripture that is likewise crystal clear and we say, "I don't want to hear that word; I need some biblical experts, some commentaries, to explain it."—Arthur Field.

TWO DOORS.   Søren Kierkegaard told of an immense room with two doors. Over one door is a sign that reads "Heaven," while over the other the sign is engraved "Lecture on Heaven." People are flocking through the door to hear the lecture. Behind the other door stands Jesus, saying, "If you want to live a life so fresh and new that it would be as if you had a real chance to live life over again, then enter here. I stand at the door and knock in order to give you a second chance."

RISING SUN.   When Marcus Aurelius was dying, many of his friends and counselors came to offer comfort and support. The sick emperor thanked them but pointed to the tent of Commodus, his son and successor. He said: "Turn away from the dying sun. Look eastward to the rising sun. Go and greet your new emperor."—William R. Cannon.

WHEN GOD WATCHES.   A woman lived alone at the edge of town. One night a tremendous storm hit, knocking out the electricity, blowing roofs away—all accompanied by crashing thunder and flashes of lightning. A friend called the next morning and was astonished to learn that the woman had slept through it all. "You see," she explained, "I knew God would watch over me, and I didn't see any sense in the both of us staying up."—Carroll R. Richards.

LOOSE LION.   Somebody asked Charles H. Spurgeon to give a course of sermons defending the Bible. "Defend the Bible? I would as soon defend a lion. Loose him and let him go!"

SPIRIT AND FAITH.   That surrender, that "Amen," is faith. And it is the work of the Holy Spirit. We cannot separate these two. From God's side, it is the work of the Spirit; from my side, it is faith. Yet that faith itself is not my independent work; it is the work of the Holy Spirit in my heart. Only God himself has the power to bring my stubborn and rebellious will to the point of surrender. It is when the cross of Christ has shattered our self-sufficiency, humbled our pride, and raised us again from the dust by the power of his love that the Spirit of God can flow into our soul and take control of us.—Lesslie Newbigin.

FORGIVING AND FORGETTING.   A friend of Clara Barton, founder of the American Red Cross, reminded her of an especially cruel thing that had been done to her years before. But Miss Barton seemed not to recall it. "Don't you remember it?" her friend asked. "No," came the reply, "I distinctly remember forgetting it."—Alan Loy McGinnis.

BROKEN THINGS.   God uses broken things. It takes broken soil to produce a crop, broken clouds to give rain, broken grain to give bread, broken bread to give strength. It is the broken alabaster box that gives forth perfume. It is Peter, weeping bitterly, who returns to greater power than ever.—Vance Havner.

CONTRADICTION.   We are a generation of technological contradictions. We can send men and machines to the moon; we can blow the world to bits in a matter of minutes; but we cannot feed one-third of the world's people who are malnourished.—Harry Haines.

ORDINARY PEOPLE.   After World War I there was a parade in London unique in that everyone taking part had been awarded the Victoria Cross. As this somewhat mixed company marched down Whitehall, an observer was heard to remark, "They look a very ordinary crowd." To which answer was made: "But ordinary people are capable of great valor."—Frederick Coutts.

FLYING THE COLORS.   Men and women are much like flagstaffs. Some flagstaffs are very tall and prominent and some are small, but the glory of a flagstaff is not its size but the colors that it flies. A very small flagstaff flying the right colors is far more valuable than a very tall one with the wrong flag. When a man is altogether done with life, I suppose that the most satisfying thing would be the ability to say, I am ashamed that I was not a better, taller, straighter flagstaff, but I am not ashamed of the colors that I flew.—Harry Emerson Fosdick.

REALITY.   Jesus Christ does not confront reality as one who is alien to it, but it is he who alone has borne and experienced the essence of the real in his own body, who has spoken from the standpoint of reality as no man on earth can do, who alone has fallen victim to no ideology but who is the truly real one.—Dietrich Bonhoeffer.

ONE BOY.   Horace Mann stumped his home state of Massachusetts pleading for the establishment of a welfare home for children. At one point in the campaign he became so enthusiastic for the project that he was moved to exclaim, "This home would be worth all the money in the treasury of the state of Massachusetts if it should save only one boy!" Whereupon one opponent to the project cracked back, "Aren't you making that a little too strong?" "No," Mann exclaimed in reply, "not if it were my boy!"—Melvin E. Wheatley, Jr.

RENDITION.   We argue religion too much. Vital religion, like good music, needs not defense but rendition. A wrangling controversy over religion is precisely as if the members of an orchestra should beat the folks over the head with their violins to prove that music is beautiful. But such procedure is no way to prove that music is beautiful. Play it!—Harry Emerson Fosdick.

LOOK OF LOVE.   It has the hands to help others. It has the feet to hasten to the poor and needy. It has the eyes to see misery and want. It has the ears to hear the sighs and sorrows of men. That is what love looks like.—St. Augustine.

ON BEING UNCOMMON.   I do not choose to be a common man. It is my right to be uncommon. I seek opportunity to develop whatever talents God gave me. I want to take the calculated risks, to dream and to build, to fail and to succeed. I prefer the challenges of life to the guaranteed existence, the thrill of fulfillment to the stale calm of utopia. I will not trade freedom for beneficence nor my dignity for a handout. It is my heritage to stand erect, proud, and unafraid; to think and act myself, enjoy the benefit of my creations and to face the world boldly and say, "This, with God's help, I have done."—Dean Alfange.

THE REAL PERSON.   A woman went to her pastor and complained bitterly about her brutal husband. She frankly said that she hated him and could never bring herself to love him again. But the pastor, who was a wise counselor, told her to try to think of her husband as he was in the days when he was courting her and when the best side of him had appeared. Because, the pastor explained, that was his true side. The gradual appearance of brutality and lack of understanding and tenderness was something alien which had crept into him and turned him away from his real nature. And to the degree that this woman was able, lovingly, to get past this alien thing and see again the real person in her disturbed and distorted husband, she was able to love him once again and thus to bring a creatively new and constructive impulse into their relationship.—Adapted from Helmut Thielicke.

BALCONY SEAT.   Harry Emerson Fosdick wrote this about John D. Rockefeller, who more than any other was responsible for building the Riverside Church in New York City: "One Sunday morning a member of the congregation, waiting to be shown to her seat, found Mr. Rockefeller, who had arrived later than usual, standing beside her. She overheard him say to the usher, as he looked at the already crowded nave: "I'll not disturb the congregation by going to my usual pew. I'll find a seat in the balcony." Whereupon an aggressive, pompous stranger, not recognizing Mr. Rockefeller, said to the usher: "Show me a seat downstairs. I am not the balcony type."

THE VIOLINIST'S STORY.   Theodore P. Ferris, while spending a summer at the conservatory in Fontainebleau, noticed a young man in his early twenties who was easily the outstanding musician in the school. He played the violin with consummate artistry and skill. One day he asked the manager of the school, "What about this young fellow?" And she said: "When he was a little boy, the ss troops came and gathered him up with all the other little Jewish children of the community, and they put him in a truck. They were taking them to a concentration camp in Venice. But the driver of the truck, an ss trooper, stopped and got out to light a cigarette. While he was standing beside his truck, a French farmer, the father of eleven children, was scything weeds along the side of the road. He saw this little Jewish boy sitting on the back of the truck, dangling his feet, and his heart was overcome with compassion. He dropped the scythe and, quick as a cat, leaped up onto the road, grabbed the little boy, and ran into the woods. If the ss trooper saw him, he made no indication of having seen what happened, and when he had finished his cigarette, he got back into the cab and drove away. The French farmer, with eleven children of his own to raise, saw to it that this little boy was raised as a Jew. He and his family sacrificed in order to give him violin lessons, and now he has become one of the great musicians of Europe."

THE DOCTOR'S PRAYER.　　Some time after the Communists were in control in China, a Christian doctor was preparing to operate on a party official. As the nurse prepared to administer the anaesthetic, the patient saw the doctor turn aside for a moment. He asked him, "What are you doing?" The doctor replied quietly, "I always pray before an operation, asking God's help." The party official in a whisper said, "Doctor, pray for me!"—Tracey Jones.

EXPECTANT EYES.　　Life is always opening new and unexpected things to us. There is no monotony in living to him who walks even the quietest and most humdrum, unexciting path with open, expectant eyes. The monotony of life, if life is monotonous to you, is in you and not in the world.—Phillips Brooks.

COUNSEL.　　Dwight L. Morrow was invited to address a student conference. In the discussion that followed, one of the students asked him what course of study he would recommend for someone who wanted to be a banker. He had a strange answer for that student. He said: "I don't know that I can prescribe any special subjects that could fit you for that particular job, but I can tell you this. If you pick out from the curriculum the hardest subjects you can find, and I don't care much what they are, and on top of these you add the hardest courses on the elective list and give to that program all the time and effort you can muster, I won't promise that you will become a banker, but I am sure when you are through, there won't be a bank in the country that will not be glad to employ you, and you may end up being its president."

TRIUMPHANTLY.　　Edwin Markham stepped off the train one night at midnight in a small midwestern town. A greeter asked him how he was. Markham threw his hat high in the air and startled everyone by shouting, "I am living triumphantly."

HOLY MIRTH.　　There is an enduring mirth of the Christian that no event can destroy. A missionary lady in China was being taken out to be beheaded by bandits. On the way she thought how ridiculous it would be to see her head rolling down the hill and she in spirit watching it. She burst out laughing. When her captors asked her what she was laughing about, she told them and then laughed. "Well," they said, "if it's going to make you happy, we are not going to do it." So they freed her. She laughed her way out of her own beheading.

THE MASTER'S TOUCH.　　One Saturday morning in Germany the old cathedral organist was practicing in preparation for Sunday. A younger man came in, listened for a while, and then asked permission to play the organ. The old man was jealous of his instrument and refused. But the younger man persisted, and at last, most reluctantly, the old organist gave his consent. In a matter of moments the entire cathedral was filled with magnificent music, its walls echoing and re-echoing with the organ's rich and mighty chords. The local organist listened enraptured, and when the brief concert was over, he said to his guest, "Excuse me, sir, what is your name?" The stranger replied, "My name is Felix Mendelssohn."

FAMILY.　　A few days after his coronation, Pope John XXIII gave a special audience for the members of his family. This is traditional with each newly elected pope. The members of John's family entered the apartments of the pope's palace with shyness and timidity. Never before had these humble farm folk stood in such splendor. They were unnerved. Finally, bashful and confused, they stood before their relative, the pope, who was dressed in white. There was an awkward confusion, but then they lowered their presents of ham, wine, and peasant bread, which were wrapped in brightly colored handkerchiefs, to the floor. Pope John looked at them standing there, staring at him with open mouths. It was a humorous scene to be sure, but John did not laugh. In a fatherly way, he said to them: "Don't be afraid. It's only me."—Thomas C. Short.

GREAT DESIRE. Bad will be the day for every man when he becomes so absolutely contented with the life that he is living, with the thoughts that he is thinking, with the deeds that he is doing, and when there is not forever beating at the doors of his soul some great desire to do something larger.—Phillips Brooks.

ENCOURAGEMENT. To the perplexed seeker whose most diligent seeking for truth has seemed to lead away from God and Christ it must be said: "Do not stop seeking but look still deeper. Do not stop thinking but think harder. Do not be less honest with yourself but more honest." Certain it is that the quest itself, no matter how frustrated it seem, and the concern itself, no matter how little satisfied, are evidence of God's spirit at work in our hearts.—John Baillie.

CONVICTION. When William Penn was imprisoned in the Tower of London, he was told either to recant of his writings or die a prisoner. The Quakers were then both hated and misunderstood, particularly on account of their pacifism, their refusal to honor worldly rank or to swear on oath. Penn's reply was typical: "My prison shall be my grave before I will budge a jot, for I owe my conscience to no mortal man."—*Forward.*

DEEPENING FAITH. You have to experience the darkness that descends when the flickering candles of personal merit have gone out before you can discern, rising out of the gloom to meet you, the light that never was on sea or land. You have to feel the foundations shake beneath your feet before you can sing "Rock of Ages" as it should be sung.—James S. Stewart.

WRAPPED IN THE DIVINE. Archbishop Anthony Bloom tells of one of the first people to seek his advice after his ordination. She was an elderly woman who claimed, "I have been praying almost unceasingly for fourteen years, and I have never had any sense of God's presence."

Bloom discovered that her prayer time mostly consisted of her talking to God, so he advised her to set aside fifteen minutes a day to "sit and just knit before the face of God." Later the woman reported that when she tried to converse with God she felt nothing but when she sat quietly, placing herself deliberately before God, she felt wrapped in the divine presence.

DOWRY. "My life is spiritually very poor," said a friend of Nicolai Berdyaev who was questioning whether to enter the Orthodox Church. "I feel that we should come to the church with a dowry." "No," replied Berdyaev firmly, "you should come into the church naked."

ALL THAT IS NEEDED. The touch of Christ, the voice of Christ, the look of Christ, but above all the prayer of Christ! "I have prayed for thee." What else shall we need if only we realize this?—J. B. Lightfoot.

MOVING THE EARTH. Archimedes, the ancient mathematician and inventor who used levers to raise heavy objects in his experiments, declared that he could move the earth if only he were given a place outside the world upon which to rest his lever. "The Archimedian point outside the world," claimed Søren Kirkegaard, "is an oratory where a man really prays in all sincerity, and he shall move the earth."

FINDING GOD. In finding God you must have as much patience as a man who sits by the seaside and undertakes to empty the ocean, lifting up one drop of water with a straw.—Mahatma Gandhi.

PURIFYING FIRE. In certain parts of Africa, fire renews the plains as the grasses grow to such a density and height that it is impossible to be cut or plowed under. Large areas will be burned to prepare for the planting of the gardens. With the land cleared, it is much easier to cultivate and grow the crops. The Holy Spirit works in much the same way. It comes as a consuming presence to clear away the debris of our lives so new growth may take place.—Burt G. Kreps.

SANCTUARY.   A Scottish widow was known and respected for her great piety. Though she worked long, hard hours to keep her family together, she was never known to complain, and she had a word of encouragement for everyone who came her way. One day her minister stopped by to call upon her. "How is it, my good woman, that with all your work you have so little opportunity to pray and meditate and yet you have a deep spiritual life? You never have time during the week to come to the sanctuary to pray, and yet you give great evidence of a rich prayer life." "Oh, but it's not that hard to visit his sanctuary," she replied. "In the midst of a busy day, I just pull my apron up over my head, shut the world out, and visit with him in his holy sanctuary."—John Wade.

REMEMBERED KINDNESS.   It was a stormy night. The wind blew in all directions; the rain came down in torrents. An elderly man and his wife sloshed up to the desk of a small hotel in Philadelphia. Half in apology he asked: "Can you possibly give us a room? All the big hotels are filled." "Every room is taken, sir," replied the clerk, "but I can't send a nice couple like you out in the rain at one o'clock in the morning. Tell you what: you can sleep in my room." "But where will you sleep?" asked the guest. "Oh, I'll make out," replied the young clerk. "Don't worry about me."

Next morning as the guest paid his bill he told the young man who had given up his room: "You are the kind of manager who should be the boss of the best hotel in the United States. Maybe some day I'll build one for you."

Two years later the young clerk received a letter with a round-trip ticket to New York and a note from the guest of that stormy night asking the clerk to meet him in the big city. The old man led the young man to the corner of 5th Avenue and 34th Street. Pointing to a towering new building, the old gentleman declared, "There is the hotel I have built for you to manage."

Almost speechless, the young man,

George C. Boldt, stammered his thanks. His benefactor was William Waldorf Astoria. The hotel was the most elaborate of that day, the original Waldorf Astoria.—Arthur Tonne.

EXPLANATION.   James T. Cleland's minister father and austere mother disapproved of all Sunday amusements. One Sunday afternoon James, a lad in Glasgow, Scotland, gathered his toy soldiers around him for a mock battle. Suddenly he saw his mother standing in the doorway with a frown spreading across her face. In a flash James responded, "Look, Mother, the Salvation Army!"—Robert D. Dale.

MIDDLE WAY.   The knowledge of God without that of our wretchedness creates pride. The knowledge of our wretchedness without that of God creates despair. The knowledge of Jesus Christ is the middle way because in him we find both God and our wretchedness.—Blaise Pascal.

STARGAZER.   In *The Republic* Plato told about the crew of a ship who decided that their pilot was mad because they noticed that he took observations from the stars. They argued that a ship sails on the sea and is influenced by the winds and tides and currents and that stargazing was a foolish and impractical procedure. They shut up the pilot in the hold and sailed on —to shipwreck.

IDENTITY.   After World War I some French soldiers who suffered from amnesia did not know their names, their backgrounds, or anything about their past. Some were shell-shocked, some had been gassed, and others were psychologically responding to the horrors of war. While being transported to the mountains for rest, their train was forced to stop in a small town to allow another train to pass. During the rest stop, the men were allowed to leave the train and walk around. The attendant noticed a strange expression on the face of one man and decided to follow him. The soldier left the station and walked down the street as if he knew where he was going. He walked until he reached a certain cottage. There he knocked on the door, and momentarily he was greeted by an old man, who looked at first in disbelief and then he threw his arms around the neck of the soldier and began weeping. "I'm glad you've come home," the old man said. And the soldier said, "Dad, I'm glad I found you. Now I know who I am."—Jerry Hayner.

END PRODUCT.   Lawrence of Arabia was taking a photograph of Wells Cathedral from a distance. In the background, so far off that she looked like a tiny white daisy, was a little girl. The thought came to him that she was the most important thing. To save her life, if need be, one would tear down that magnificent structure, stone by stone. For her life the world was created. The end product of the universe is not a factory or an office building or a machine or a church building. The end product is a person to be loved and respected and listened to and nurtured and for whom no sacrifice is too much.—Craig Biddle III.

INNER BRACES.   A congressman was having a hard time explaining his vote on a measure objectionable to members of his constituency. At last he said, "But, gentlemen, you simply don't understand the outside pressure brought to bear on a man in my position." "Outside pressure!" roared an old sea captain in the audience. "Where are your inside braces?"—*Sunday School Times.*

MISERABLE SINNER.   A woman poured out her troubles to a minister. "Reverend," she sobbed, "something has to be done about my husband. He doesn't come home at night. He mistreats the children. He doesn't give us enough money to live on. Instead he's always gambling, drinking, running after pretty girls." "You have my deepest sympathy," responded the other. "Your husband is a miserable sinner." "A sinner he is, reverend," she said, "but miserable he isn't. He's having the time of his life!"—Raymond E. Balcomb.

NEW AND OLD.   A man was watching a farmer chop some wood with an axe. He noticed that it was a particularly fine axe. The farmer said: "Indeed, it is. This axe was the axe my grandfather used to clear this land." The visitor said: "Surely this can't be the same axe. That's such a long time ago." The farmer said: "Yes, it's the same axe. It's had three new heads and six new handles, but it's the same axe."—Mark Trotter.

PERIPHERY AND CORE.   The tempo of modern civilization has a centrifugal force that carries us outward from the core of life toward ever-expanding peripheries. One should return frequently to the core and to the basic values of the individual in natural surroundings, to simplicity and contemplation. Long ago I resolved to so arrange my life that I could move back and forth between periphery and core.—Charles A. Lindbergh.

CHOICE.   More than any other time in history, humankind faces a crossroad. One path leads to despair and utter hopelessness. The other, to total extinction. Let us pray we have the wisdom to choose correctly.—Woody Allen.

POINTS OF VIEW.   Destiny came down to an island centuries ago, summoned three of its inhabitants and put this question to them: "What would you do if you were told that tomorrow this island would be completely inundated by an immense tidal wave?" The first inhabitant was a cynic. He responded, "I would eat, drink and carouse all night long." Another inhabitant, a mystic, replied, "I would go to the sacred grove with my loved ones, make sacrifices to the gods, and pray without ceasing." The third resident was a realist. Said he, "I would assemble our wisest persons and begin at once to study how to live under water."—Bevel Jones.

NEVER GIVE UP.   A father was trying to encourage his dejected son by saying, "Don't ever give up!" The boy replied, "But I cannot solve my problems." The father said: "People who are remembered never give up. Think of Robert Fulton, Thomas Edison, and Eli Whitney. They didn't give up. And look at Isador McPringle." The boy said, "Who is Isador McPringle?" "See," said the father, "you never heard of him. He gave up!"—C. Neil Strait.

BELONGING.   A little old lady walked into the office of the city editor of a large newspaper. She said she'd come to register a gentle complaint. The census takers of the United States had forgotten her. Like most of us, she needed to be noticed. The lady had read in the newspaper that the census takers would be coming around, so she had gotten all the required information down on paper and waited day after day for the census takers to come. But they never did. The United States of America had forgotten her. So she went to the newspaper editor's office to find out if it would be possible to somehow call the matter to the attention of the President. To her it made a difference if the population was 200 million or 200 million and one. She had a deep need to belong, and if we're honest, so do the rest of us.—Arthur McPhee.

REST.   Two artists each painted a picture illustrating his conception of rest. The first chose for his scene a still, secluded lake behind far-off mountains. The second threw upon his canvas a thundering waterfall with a fragile birch tree bending over the foam. At the fork of the branch, almost wet with the cataract's spray, a robin sat on its nest. The first artist pictured not rest but stagnation. The second had the truer conception. It is not cessation from life's activities, not freedom from life's burdens, not idleness, nor slackness of either hands or spirit, not exemption from toil or any honorable demand but rest, refreshment in the midst of life's activities and in spite of life's burdens.—Ernest Trice Thompson.

ONLY THE BEST.   Man finds it hard to get what he wants because he does not want the best. God finds it hard to give because he would give the best, and man will not take it.—George Macdonald.

THE ENCHANTED FOREST.   The old forester was said to be the only person who knew the way to the Enchanted Forest. In the forest, according to legend, beauty was in every rock and tree and stream; the deer approached humans without fear; sun and shadow, earth and sky, the sounds and stillness of the forest all combined to give the visitor a sense of exaltation and clear vision.

Every year people visited the old man to ask the way to the forest, but he answered in what seemed to be irrelevancies. To some he said, "I'll teach you the ways of the birds and wild animals," but that didn't satisfy them. Or he would say, "I'll teach you how to live off the land, to find water where no one else can find it, to find shelter from the cold, to find food," but that didn't interest them either. Sometimes he said, "I'll teach you the ways of the nature person—patience, endurance, seeing, listening, being a part of nature." His offers satisfied no one.

When the old man died, his daughter married a young man who knew that part of the country well, and one day he asked her if it wasn't true that there was no Enchanted Forest. "Not a place on the map," she replied. "Then why didn't your father tell his visitors that?" "Because he was stubborn. If they had let him teach them the ways of God, they would have discovered the only enchanted forest there is. It has many locations but few discoverers."—Bevel Jones in *Wesleyan Christian Advocate*.

WATCHING EYE.   A one-eyed lumberman from Europe lived at Port Gentil in Africa. He decided to go away for awhile, yet he had no one to place in charge of the natives who worked for him. So he removed his glass eye and put it on his office desk. Then he called his laborers and told them that he was to be gone a few days but that he was leaving his glass eye to look after everything and to watch over them in his absence. Later, when he returned, he was delighted to discover that all had kept very busy at their usual tasks! Now satisfied that he had the answer to the problem of absentee supervision, he embarked on a longer trip. Again he left his glass eye in a conspicuous position on his desk. When he returned after two weeks, he was dismayed to find that almost no work had been done by anybody. Rushing into his office to seek an explanation, he discovered that a large hat had been placed over his glass eye!—Adapted from Albert Schweitzer.

THREE WISHES.   An old story called "The Monkey's Paw" tells how an Englishman of modest circumstances came into possession of a magical monkey's paw. Assured that it had the power to grant him three wishes, he immediately wished he might come into a "pile 'o money."

Shortly thereafter a messenger arrived announcing the Englishman's son had been horribly mangled in an auto accident and did not survive. When insurance claims had been settled, the father was awarded a fabulous sum of money only to realize that the source of the newly acquired wealth was his son's tragic death.

Grieving over that chain of circumstances, the Englishman utilized the second wish for his son's return to life. Upon hearing a slow, arduous clomping sound nearing his door, he realized that his son was only a living, mutilated monstrosity. Aware that such was worse than death, the father wished his son dead again and thus used up the power of the monkey's paw.—*Proclaim.*

BELL'S PROBLEM.   Alexander Graham Bell did not invent the telephone by dreaming of some distant time when the world would be interconnected by a communications system of his making. He had an immediate problem, which in being done well led him on toward designing the instrument that made him famous. It wasn't fame he sought, nor wealth, nor the telephone—at least not at first. Mr. Bell had been a teacher in a school for the deaf, and while there he married one of his pupils. Later he began a series of experiments with electrical apparatus hoping he could devise an instrument that would help his young wife to hear. It was in that effort that Bell invented the telephone.—Harold E. Kohn.

HEADLINE.   Orville and Wilbur Wright in 1903 sent this telegram from Kitty Hawk, North Carolina, where they had gone to carry on their experiments, to their sister in Dayton, Ohio: FIRST SUSTAINED FLIGHT TODAY FIFTY-NINE SECONDS. HOME FOR CHRISTMAS. The sister took the message to a Dayton newspaper office, and the next morning a brief news item appeared under the headline, POPULAR LOCAL BICYCLE MERCHANTS WILL BE HOME FOR THE HOLIDAYS.

A LITTLE KNOWLEDGE.   A high school girl was seated next to a famous astronomer at a dinner party. During the course of the dinner she struck up a conversation by asking, "What do you do for a living?" He replied, "I study astronomy." The teenager, very wide-eyed, said: "Really? Why, I finished astronomy last year!"—Daniel Evan.

PAIN AND BEAUTY.   The French artist Renoir was so pain-wracked with rheumatism that every stroke of his brush brought perspiration to his anguished face. Being unable to stand, he sat in a chair. Despite his suffering, Renoir painted enduring masterpieces of great beauty. A friend asked, "Why do you continue to torture yourself?" Renoir replied, "The pain passes, but the beauty remains."—Nina M. Sandel.

ENCOURAGEMENT.   A woman, traveling in the West and enjoying the unsurpassed beauty of the mountain scenery, rounded a curve and was surprised to see that the road ahead seemed to end in the impenetrable face of the mountain. The road narrowed to one lane, and as she drove closer she saw a sliver of an opening into a tunnel. It was so narrow that it looked impossible to drive through without scraping the craggy rock walls. Then she saw a hand-lettered sign to the right of the tunnel entrance, left by someone who had passed that way before. It proclaimed, "YES YOU CAN."—Joan Unger.

AAA—O.   A regiment in World War II was sluggish and lacking in morale. A new colonel was assigned to the outfit. Before long it was one of the finest regiments in the Army. They were enthusiastic, eager, and ready to move at the first command. One day a general came to visit. During his inspection he saw that the colonel had the letters AAA—O written on his helmet. The same letters were on much of the regiment's equipment. "What do the letters AAA—O mean?" asked the general. "They stand," answered the colonel, "for Anywhere, Anytime, Anything bar Nothing."—Charles E. Ferrell.

TOO SOON TO QUIT.   A man organized a company to make prefabricated wall systems for mobile homes, but he began to run into one difficulty after the other. Some of those who worked with him suggested that he give up the whole thing. But he was a man of prayer, and he kept asking God to show him the best way to make his product. He kept praying until one day he got the idea that he should make a prefabricated floor to go with his prefabricated walls. It turned out to be a winning idea. A big manufacturer of mobile homes bought his system, and he didn't have to worry anymore. This man coined a phrase which I like very much. "It is always too soon to quit," he said.—Norman Vincent Peale.

MISSING JEWEL.   The purpose of God in sending his Son to die and live and be at the right hand of God the Father was that he might restore to us the missing jewel, the jewel of worship; that we might come back and learn to do again that which we were created to do in the first place—worship the Lord in the beauty of holiness, to spend our time in awesome wonder and adoration of God, feeling and expressing it, and letting it get into our labors and doing nothing except as an act of worship to almighty God through his Son Jesus Christ.—A. W. Tozer.

COMMON MASTER.   Would to God that all party names and unscriptural phrases and forms which have divided the Christian world were forgot and that we might all agree to sit down together, as humble, loving disciples, at the feet of our common Master, to hear his word, to imbibe his Spirit, and to transcribe his life on our own.—John Wesley.

ACUTE AWARENESS.   Prayer is simply a form of waking up out of the dull sleep in which our life has been spent in half-intentions, half-resolutions, self-creations, half-loyalties, and a becoming acutely aware of the real character of that which we are and of that which we are over against. It is an opening of drowsy lids. It is a shaking off of graveclothes. It is a dip into acid. It is a daring to read the text of the universe in the original.—Douglas V. Steere.

DESTINATION.   Justice Oliver Wendell Holmes when he was in his eighties was riding on a train, deeply engrossed in what he was reading. The conductor asked him for his ticket. Frantically Holmes searched but could not find it. The conductor said, "Never mind, Mr. Justice, when you find it, just mail it to the company." "But I must find it now," Mr. Holmes said. "Unless I do, how in the world will I know where I'm supposed to be going?"—Bernard Brunsting in *The Church Herald*.

AN AFFIRMATION FROM ZIMBABWE.   I believe in a colorblind God, maker of technicolor people, who created the universe and provided abundant resources for equitable distribution among all his people.

I believe in Jesus Christ, born of a common woman, who was ridiculed, disfigured, and executed and who on the third day rose and fought back. He storms the highest councils where he overturns the iron rule of injustice. From henceforth he shall continue to judge hatred and arrogance.

I believe in the spirit of reconciliation, the united body of the dispossessed, the communion of the suffering masses, the power that overcomes the dehumanizing forces of humanity, the resurrection of personhood, justice, and equality, and in the final triumph of the community of believers.—Canaan Banana.

PRAYER.   I confess to you, Lord, that I still do not know what time is. Yet I confess too that I do know that I am saying this in time, that I have been talking about time for a long time, and that this long time would not be a long time if it were not for the fact that time has been passing all the while. How can I know this when I do not know what time is? Is it that I do know what time is but do not know how to put what I know into words? I am in a sorry state, for I do not even know what I do not know.—St. Augustine.

MYSTERY.   I am not so much a farmer as some people claim, but I have observed the watermelon seed. It has the power of drawing from the ground and through itself 200,000 times its weight. When you can tell me how it takes this material and out of it colors an outside surface beyond the imitation of art, and then forms inside of it a white rind and within again, a red heart, thickly inlaid with black seeds, each of which in turn is capable of drawing through itself 200,000 times its weight—when you can explain to me the mystery of the watermelon, you can ask me to explain the mystery of God.—William Jennings Bryan.

RESPONSE.   Christian stewardship is man's recognition of God's sovereignity through creation and is a grateful response to God's manifold gifts. Man's response is expressed by his dedicated and creative use of all these gifts toward fulfillment of Christ's mission in the world. Christian stewardship is a response to the love of God as revealed in Christ and is expressed in terms of a worthy administration of all resources available for the sustenance and enrichment of life.—The United Methodist Church.

WORLDS BEYOND.   The Bible is like a telescope. If a man looks through his telescope, he sees worlds beyond, but if he looks at his telescope, he does not see anything but that. The Bible is a thing to be looked through to see that which is beyond, but most people only look at it, and so they see only dead letters.—Phillips Brooks.

WORK AND WILL.   Believing that this is our Father's world motivates us to search God's works as well as God's Word. Whatever God has found worth creating we find worth studying, both for its own sake and for what it may teach us concerning the works and will of God.—David G. Myers.

NO ROOM AT THE INN.   In the fall of 1775 the manager of Baltimore's largest hotel refused lodging to a man dressed like a farmer, who in actuality was Thomas Jefferson, vice-president of the United States. After Jefferson had registered at a smaller hotel and the other manager had discovered the identity of the guest he had turned away, he invited Jefferson to return as his personal guest. The patriot's reply was, "If he has no place for a dirty American farmer, he has none for the vice-president of the United States."—John N. Vaughan.

INDEX OF CONTRIBUTORS

SERMON TITLE INDEX

(Children's stories and sermons are identified cs; sermon suggestions ss)

SCRIPTURAL INDEX

INDEX OF PRAYERS

INDEX OF MATERIALS USEFUL AS CHILDREN'S STORIES AND SERMONS NOT INCLUDED IN SECTION X

INDEX OF MATERIALS USEFUL FOR SMALL GROUPS

INDEX OF SPECIAL DAYS AND SEASONS

TOPICAL INDEX